William
Tecumseh
Sherman

William Tecumseh Sherman 1820–1891

William Tecumseh Sherman

by JAMES M. MERRILL

illustrated with photographs

RAND McNALLY & COMPANY

Chicago   New York   San Francisco

Other books by James M. Merrill

*The Rebel Shore: The Story of Union Sea Power
in the Civil War*

Quarter-Deck & Fo'c's'le

Uncommon Valor

Target Tokyo: The Halsey-Doolittle Raid

Spurs to Glory: The Story of the United States Cavalry

*Battle Flags South: The Story of the Civil War Navies
on Western Waters*

Photo Credits—Notre Dame University Archives: 23, 24, 25, 143, 144, 261, 262, 396, 397, 398; West Point Museum Collections: 37, 39, 395; Department of Earth, Space & Graphic Sciences, USMA: 38; National Archives: 263.

First printing, September, 1971

For Ann

CONTENTS

William Tecumseh Sherman

Introduction

SOME YEARS AGO I stumbled upon a cache of William Tecumseh Sherman papers at Notre Dame University and the Ohio Historical Society. I discovered literally thousands of letters: intimate letters between husband and wife; letters from Sherman to his children; scores of letters from devoted brothers and in-laws; from neighbors and close friends; from comrades-in-arms; from statesmen; from admiring strangers. I was amazed to find that so many of these personal and private papers had been preserved and that none had been used in previous full-scale biographies.

As I eagerly read the correspondence, Sherman's image as the fiercest of all battle captains, an image so prevalent in textbooks, faded; and Sherman for the first time became a versatile, real, and vital personality, a warm man who was, above all, deeply devoted to his family. Sherman's restless energy made him a prolific letter writer, permitting us to examine his ambitions and frustrations, his innermost thoughts and emotions. He mourned the heavy loss of life on the battlefields; he bared his grief on the day his firstborn son died; he stormed in temper when his second son entered the Roman Catholic priesthood. The defeated and prostrate South admired this Union general, who had fought so successfully against its armies, but who, at the end of hostilities, had tried to secure a generous peace which would have reintegrated the beaten states into the Union and restored them as equals. The South honored him at the New Orleans Mardi Gras and urged him to run for the presidency of the United States in the 1870s.

When I finally finished reading this host of new material, I was convinced that another biography of General Sherman was needed. If Sherman's earlier biographers had had access to this correspon-

13

dence and to the wealth of excellent secondary materials which have appeared since their books were published, their picture of the general would have had a much keener focus.

The Sherman story mirrors an era, eventful and stormy, one of growth and ferment, of frustration and fulfillment. Army lieutenant in the South; ambitious banker in California; adventurer in Kansas; Civil War general; and, later, General of the Army, Sherman touched history at many points.

Today there is a need for an understanding of Sherman's sense of human values, his devotion to law and order, his ability to rise above partisanship, his concept of the soldier's task in its relation to society and to peace in the world.

This book is more than a Civil War biography. While it deals with this conflict, battle sequences and tactical maneuvers are held to a minimum. In essence this popular biography attempts to analyze how one great man, who typified so much of what was American in the nineteenth century, met and solved complex problems. I have tried to see the nineteenth century through the eyes of William T. Sherman. I have been less concerned with justifying than with understanding my subject's particular angle of vision. I also have attempted to present Sherman with all his eccentricities, his blemishes as well as his virtues, so that he may be seen in his full humanity.

My sincere thanks go to the University of Delaware for its grants-in-aid and to the following individuals without whose help this book could not have been written: Lawrence Bradley and the late Father Thomas McAvoy, the Archives, Notre Dame University; Elizabeth Martin, Ohio Historical Society; John Dawson and his staff, Morris Library, University of Delaware, especially Nathaniel Puffer, Charles Mason, Rachel Elliott, and Elizabeth Russell; Cynthia Vartan, my editor, Rand McNally & Company; and Carol Morris, research assistant, University of Delaware. A final word of thanks goes to my wife, Ann, whose constant help and encouragement speeded the work along and made the whole enterprise more enjoyable.

JAMES M. MERRILL
University of Delaware

"...take Cump. He's the brightest."

In the 1820s Lancaster, Ohio, was an energetic town, cultured and progressive, set on a level plain on the post road in the upper Hockhocking Valley. There was a hilly rise at the center of town which gave an excellent view of the surrounding countryside. To the north rose Mount Pleasant, or as the Indians had named it, Standing Stone, while to the south lay the Kettle Hills. Near Lancaster was Niebling's Pond, where in days gone by, 500 Wyandot Indians had camped.

Since 1800, immigrants from the east had traveled through southern Ohio on their way west. Many liked the upper Hockhocking Valley and decided to settle there. By the mid-1820s Lancaster had 200 houses, half of them brick, half frame. The seat of Fairfield County, the town had a sickle factory, four gristmills, and near the rapids of the Hockhocking River, a powder mill and a factory for scutching flax. Citizens also pointed with pride to their courthouse, market house, jail, and 12 general stores. The town's social and business energy was concentrated on Main Street, Lancaster's chief thoroughfare. In winter it was a series of frozen ruts and hummocks; in the fall and spring it was a river of mud; and in the summer it was hidden beneath a deep layer of dust.

Charles Robert Sherman had been a hustling young lawyer in Connecticut but soon found his native state too confining and provincial. With his wife, Mary, he went west to Ohio in 1811. Settling in Lancaster, he practiced law, prospered, and began touring the state in a far-flung circuit. Frequently, Thomas Ewing, a rising attorney who had migrated to Lancaster in 1815, traveled with Sherman. They became as intimate as brothers, sharing beds, meals, and lawbooks.

It was while Sherman and Ewing were on the circuit that the former's sixth child, Tecumseh Sherman, was born on February 8, 1820. He was named in honor of the Indian chieftain who played an important part in the frontier history of Ohio. Later Charles and Mary affectionately nicknamed him Cump, as Tecumseh proved too long and cumbersome a word for his sisters and brothers to pronounce.

On learning of the new arrival Maria Ewing had hurried over to the Shermans to care for the older children and to see the baby. "What are you going to name him?" she asked Mary.

"Charles says I promised that if this was a boy he would be named Tecumseh."

"Tecumseh! After an Indian?" cried Maria.

Charles Sherman, coming into the house, heard the conversation. "My dear girl," he said to Mrs. Ewing, "he was much more than an Indian. He was a very wonderful man and I'm glad Mary is going to let me name this little redhead after him."

In November of that same year, Mary Sherman went up the street to help in the Ewing household after Maria gave birth to Philemon Beecher Ewing. For several years after this babies arrived rapidly in both the Ewing and Sherman homes. At the Ewings' came Eleanor (Ellen), Hugh Boyle, Thomas, Charles, and Maria Theresa. After Cump's arrival in 1820, Mary Sherman gave birth to Lampson, John, Susan, Hoyt, and Fanny. Considering the intimacy of the Shermans and the Ewings, it was natural that the two sets of children were almost interchangeable. Cump's best playmate was Phil Ewing, with Lamp Sherman and Ellen Ewing tagging along behind.

Charles and Mary Sherman and their children had moved into a new two-story frame house on the corner of an alley and Main Street. Old Mr. Wright, the Presbyterian clergyman, lived in the brick house across the alley. Next to him was the Work and Reed Shoe Shop, and on the corner, the Widow Stimpson's home. Across the street from the Shermans' were the tobacco shop of Mr. Young and a saddle-and-harness establishment.

Half a block away, on the summit of a hill, stood the Ewing house, a solid, substantial edifice, "a prominent residence," with commodious yard, well shaded by trees—elm, walnut, and birch, with here and there a tall sycamore. A high wall with a gate separated the house from the street, screening it from passersby. A brick walk curved up to the huge front steps. Built of white brick, the house had a welcoming hall with a winding stairway. There were deeply recessed windows with folding shutters, and white woodwork, paneled doors, carved cornices, and handsome marble mantels.

The Ewing mansion was the pride of Lancaster. It was the preferred stopping place for political notables; there they were assured of a cordial welcome, an attentive audience, and good meals. Henry Clay of Kentucky often passed through on his way to Washington. Governor DeWitt Clinton of New York and Daniel Webster, senator from Massachusetts, always stopped at the Ewings' on their way through Ohio.

Thomas Ewing was a man of stature, physically and intellectually. "He looks," said a friend, "as if he could chop more wood than any other man, as well as chop more logic than the great mass of men."

Ewing was a native of Virginia, whose family had brought him to Ohio as a small boy. On the frontier in what is now Athens County he had shown an avid interest in books, and before he was eight, according to his autobiography, he had read the entire Bible. Labor in the Kanawha saltworks enabled him to study at Ohio University, where he received an A.B. degree in 1815. He studied in a Lancaster law office and became prosecutor of Fairfield County. In the 1820s he was not yet a rich man, but he was gaining national recognition as a lawyer and statesman.

In spite of some financial difficulties, Charles Sherman was at the same time winning a reputation within the state. He was appointed judge of the Ohio Supreme Court, a position which forced him to be away from home much of the time during Cump's early childhood. A large man with restless energy, Judge Sherman liked to work in his garden when at home during the spring and summer months. He set out most of the asparagus beds for the entire town of Lancaster and introduced grapes to the upper Hockhocking Valley. The judge was also "a kind of Doctor," and when the regular physicians were not on hand, people called him in emergencies, and he seemed always able to help.

When Judge Sherman arrived back in Lancaster after a tedious circuit ride, it was the custom of the Sherman boys to run and meet their father. Whoever reached his horse, Dick, first was privileged to ride him back into the stable on the rear of the lot.

Cump was six when he first won the race, and Jim, his older brother, hoisted him onto Dick. Cump proudly patted the horse and headed for the stable, while Jim ran through the house and across the lot to open the door. Cump and Dick arrived at the stable first, and the horse, becoming impatient, started for the Kings' stable, where he normally was kept. Suddenly, the horse went plunging down the steep alley at Weavers' and threw his rider off into a pile of rubbish. Cump's brothers, seeing the accident, rushed to pick him up and gently carried him into the house. His face had been cut open on the right cheek, and after the cut healed it left a permanent scar.

On a bright June morning in 1829, the children walked toward their school, the Academy, on Wheeling Street. First up the steps of the Academy were Bill Irvin and Bill King, trailed by Cump Sherman, his brothers, and the Ewing boys. Once the boys were in their seats, the schoolmaster, Thomas Parsons, began the day's recitations.

Abruptly, Tom Green, a close family friend of the Shermans, opened the door, and walking up to Parsons's desk, conversed with the teacher in whispers. The Sherman boys suddenly heard their names called. They were instructed to return home immediately. Picking up their books, they followed Green to their white frame house.

When they opened the big door, they discovered their grandmother in the parlor, crying quietly. In hushed tones, Green told them the tragic news. Their father, who had left that week for Lebanon, Ohio, had died. Their mother was upstairs in the bedroom, ill.

Too stunned to grasp the entire meaning of Green's words, they accepted their grandmother's warning to be quiet and her urging that they go outside. Out under the elms, the Sherman boys resolved to care for their mother and sisters.

At the Ewing mansion, Mrs. Maria Ewing saw Elizabeth, the oldest Sherman daughter, running across the lawn. Elizabeth rushed into the house crying, "Oh, Mrs. Ewing, my father is dead! My father is dead!" Mrs. Ewing stared at the girl in disbelief. "Oh, Elizabeth, it can't be true," she responded.

"But it is, Mrs. Ewing," sobbed Elizabeth. "It is!"

Several days later, Thomas and Maria Ewing walked down Main Street to the Shermans'. Thomas Ewing suspected, but did not know exactly, the financial crisis faced by the widow and her 11 children.

When they arrived at the house, they found Mary Sherman away, but Elizabeth invited them into the parlor. Sitting there in the evening gloom, she began to cry and told them the whole tale of the family's finances. Mary Sherman had a small pension and her mother-in-law, then living with her, had some income, but this would not be enough to feed, clothe, and educate 11 children. Fortunately, Charles Ewing Sherman, the oldest boy, was studying law in Mansfield, Ohio, and Elizabeth was engaged to William Reese, a young attorney. But the problem of the other nine children remained.

For several days Thomas Ewing considered the fate of the grief-stricken Shermans. He confided to Mary Sherman that he and his family would like to rear one of her sons, to cancel a debt he felt he owed her husband for helping when he was starting out as a lawyer.

Again talking with Elizabeth while her mother was out, Thomas Ewing asked, "Well, Elizabeth, which of the boys is going to be mine?"

Without hesitating, the girl blurted out, "Oh, Mr. Ewing, take Cump. He's the brightest. Wait a minute and I'll call him."

Leaving the parlor, Elizabeth soon returned with Cump, mud caked on his face and hands. He and Phil Ewing had been making mud pies. Smiling, getting up from the overstuffed chair, Thomas Ewing extended his hand to the child and said, "Well, Cump, you're going to be my boy now. Want to come along?"

Cump nodded. He had realized that the family would be broken up. Without going upstairs for his belongings, he and the Ewings walked out of the house into the June evening and up the hill to Cump's new home.

From the moment Cump Sherman came to live with the Ewings, Maria treated him as her own. As Cump was to remember, he was "on a par" with the rest of the children, although he never called Mrs. Ewing "Mother" or Mr. Ewing "Father." The Ewing children took Cump's presence for granted.

The young Sherman was tall and lean and commonplace in appearance. He was always careless about his dress, and it was only through Mrs. Ewing's efforts that he escaped being unkempt. He was restless and imaginative, with an urge to get on in the world. Already he was acquiring nervous habits, and Mr. Ewing would often chide him about drumming his fingers on the library table.

He came and went from the house on the hill down to the Sherman house, where he often had his meals with his brothers and sisters. Yet Cump was fast identifying with the Ewings, a family with strong loyalties.

Although Mary Sherman secured the family homestead and garden, she still had too large a family for her income, and further separation was imperative. James, the second oldest son, accepted a clerkship in a Cincinnati store; Lampson was adopted by Charles Hammond of Cincinnati, a distinguished lawyer; John Sherman, a cousin who was a prosperous merchant in Mount Vernon, Ohio, adopted John.

Every month a Roman Catholic priest traveled over from Somerset to say mass in the little church in Lancaster. Frequently, he remained in town to instruct the children. When Maria Ewing learned to her surprise that her foster son had never been baptized, she asked Mary Sherman, a Presbyterian, if she minded having a Roman Catholic priest baptize Cump. Mary consented.

In the front parlor of the Ewing house, Father Young, Cump, and Mrs. Ewing, who was to be godmother, stood at one side of the fireplace while the Ewing children looked on. The service of baptism went well until it came time to name the child. Father Young was astonished when he heard, "Tecumseh." He repeated the name in disbelief: "Tecumseh?"

"His father named him so, Father," replied Maria Ewing.

"I'll name him that too, but he must have a Christian name besides," said the priest. "This is Saint William's Day, so perhaps that would be a good name for him." So the boy, who had fidgeted through the entire service, was christened William Tecumseh Sherman.

Although he was baptized a Roman Catholic and was to grow to manhood in the home of a devout Roman Catholic foster mother, it was Thomas Ewing's sense of honor and his tolerant religious views which influenced Cump's early attitudes toward religion. Mr. Ewing, who always remained aloof from the Roman Catholic faith, insisted that the boy should not have to take any religious affiliation. In the years that followed Cump observed but did not participate in the Roman Catholic rites of the Ewing home. He came to view tolerantly the dedicated religious convictions of Maria and her children, but he resisted the pressure of any religious orthodoxy.

Cump went to school with the rest of the Ewing children, and Maria insisted that he join her two oldest in their private French lessons. At the Academy, Cump recalled, "We made progress in mischief if not in learning."

Along with Phil Ewing, Bill King, and Bill Irvin, Cump played endless games of baseball on the Academy lot. The yard and garden of a Mr. Wolster, a carpenter, bordered the back of the school, and many times the ball sailed over the fence. Some of the braver boys would leap the fence, fetch the ball, and race back across Wolster's freshly spaded garden beds before he could intercede. To prevent such depredations, Wolster stationed his own children to watch the game. Once when the ball landed in their yard, they picked it up and ran with it to their father, who promptly burned it.

When Cump and his cohorts learned what had happened to their ball, they prepared one with a powder core. The game started, the ball bounced into the garden, and the Wolster children quickly carried it to their father. There was a terrible explosion. Wolster was burned and his house was nearly set ablaze. The carpenter stormed out of his shop, climbed the fence, caught and whipped severely the slowest runner in the group.

After Cump Sherman's first teacher, Mr. Parsons, retired from the school, a young man, Charles Brown, became head of the Academy. "He took it easy and we thought it glorious," recalled Cump. He gave the children all the holidays on the calendar and refused to mete out punishment, but under his leadership the Academy declined in academic stature.

Brown was succeeded by Matthew Howe, a first-rate teacher

and disciplinarian, and the Academy soon began to acquire the reputation of being the best school in southern Ohio. Howe taught grammar, arithmetic, and languages; and he had the great faculty of interesting the boys in these subjects. But he was a supreme autocrat from whom there was no appeal. The boys respected him but hated his domineering ways. Cump confessed later: "I know that what I learned there was of great use to me at West Point and all I know of Latin and Greek which is not much was acquired there."

In the afternoons and on holidays and Sundays, Cump and the Ewing children fished, hunted, collected nuts and berries, and frequently visited the farm of Aunt Sarah Clark out in the country. But during Cump's early schooling, he was never farther away from Lancaster than Columbus.

In 1831, two years after Cump had gone to live with the Ewings, Thomas Ewing, then 41, was elected United States senator on the Whig ticket. The Whig party, which included such stalwarts as Daniel Webster and Henry Clay, was not in sympathy with the popular, democratically oriented movement which supported President Andrew Jackson. Jackson attracted the mass of voters to him but polarized the others into a pattern of opposition.

One of the major issues that arose during the 1830s was the nullification threat from South Carolina. Since the late 1820s South Carolina had been threatening to nullify the tariff laws of the United States, which, the state's representatives in Congress claimed, favored Northern manufacturers to the detriment of Southern cotton and tobacco growers.

Senator Robert Y. Hayne of South Carolina suggested an alliance of the South and West for low tariffs and cheap land. Daniel Webster of Massachusetts defended the Northeast's interest, accusing South Carolina of advocating disunionist policies. He argued that the Constitution was a compact of the American people, not merely of the states. The Union was perpetual and indissoluble. Webster's defense of nationalism made the states' rights position seem close to treason and effectively halted the formation of a South-West alliance in Congress.

Thomas Ewing supported Webster's policies and struck back at South Carolina's theories of state supremacy in a speech that Hayne's biographer would later describe as an even stronger

The Ewing home in Lancaster, Ohio

Thomas Ewing

Ellen Ewing Sherman

argument than that of Daniel Webster. To Ewing, nullification amounted to a declaration of war. "The allegiance which a citizen owes to his State," he declared, "[must] yield to that paramount allegiance which he owes to the Union."

Cump Sherman began to understand, faintly, these national issues from the conversations of politicians visiting the house on the hill. In Lancaster in December, 1832, Cump and the other boys listened to Whig orators praising their enemy Democrat, President Jackson, because he had warned South Carolina that if she nullified the tariffs and defied the United States government, he would call out the army and the navy to enforce the law.

Sherman was to grow to manhood accepting many of his foster father's political principles—the Union, the Constitution, the Law. Senator Ewing had petitioned Congress to abolish slavery in the District of Columbia, but then he realized that the issue threatened to disrupt the nation, and he considered the preservation of the Union far more important than the abolition of Negro slavery.

It was impossible for Maria Ewing to join her husband in Washington; the family was too large, and even with a horde of servants, there was much to do. At Christmas Thomas Ewing sent gifts for all the children. Among the books was a nine-volume set of Peter Parley. Thomas Ewing wrote his wife that the books would furnish material for the children's amusement and recreation during the winter evenings and would, in addition, keep the boys from "falling into vicious practices in my absence.

"After the work is done, set out the lamp on the table and gather them all around it and the fire," continued Mr. Ewing. "Phil and Cump and Ellen and Hugh and let Tom have a place too. The *Geography* would be the best to start on." Thomas Ewing fully realized that listening to the children read aloud would be irksome to his wife, "but perseverance in it for a short time will make it much less so, and the object my dear Maria is one of most vital importance. There is nothing I assure you that causes me more intense anxiety than the formation of minds and habits of those lads at this important crisis, when I am compelled . . . to leave the heavy charge to your unaided emotions."

In the evenings, soon after Christmas, the family gathered

around the library table as Mr. Ewing had requested, and Phil and Cump took turns reading aloud for an hour. The Peter Parley maps were small, but Phil and Cump took their school atlases and pointed out to the younger ones the places that the books described.

After one of the evening sessions in the library, Maria wrote her husband: "I assure you, I keep pretty steady watch over them; they do not show that disposition to run abroad that they did last winter. They have not spent any evening from home since you left but one."

Soon after the first of that year, 1832, Cump sent a letter of thanks to his foster father: "I am well, I received your letter and book with much pleasure and one more of Peter Parleys tables, of Africa. I had a spell of sickness it only lasted but four days since I wrote to you before, but not bad and all the people in town are getting well of a bad cold.... We are nearly through the first book in Caesar, I think it is better for us than *Viri Romae* and we write at school.... We have had fine skating and sleighing but it is all gone now."

In the spring of 1832 Ellen Ewing entered Somerset Convent School, an excellent boarding school in the charge of Dominican sisters. Maria Ewing, with Phil, Tommy, and her niece, Abby Clark, went by stagecoach to Washington for a reunion with her husband. Rachel Clark, coming down from the family farm, stayed in the big house on the hill, supervising Cump and Hugh Boyle.

In the years that followed Maria's first visit, Thomas Ewing stayed in Washington a good deal of the time. When he did return to Lancaster, he was forced to ride the various circuits. But Thomas Ewing was a family man first, and a lawyer and politician second. Each year, when in Washington, he insisted that one of the children live with him, and when on the circuit in Ohio, he often traveled 50 miles on Saturdays and Sundays to reach home in time to take his wife and children to church.

When her husband was away, Maria wrote often of the family and urged her children to do likewise. In January, 1833, Cump wrote a note with a boyish disregard for grammar and spelling:

Dear Sir. I am going to a grammar school to Mr How he says a good grammarian will learn as fast again and understand a thing better than one that was not by a great deal....I am studying latin and arithmetic....our weather is like spring but it is very muddy....Mr How has about twenty scholars no[w] but only about half a dozen studys latin. The Chicken pox is in town now my mothers family is all well all of us are well except Mrs Ewing she is a little better.

In the summer of 1835 Cump's younger brother John, aged 12, returned to Lancaster from Mount Vernon. His cousin had a growing family now, and John felt in the way. Also, Mary Sherman was anxious for him to come home.

Cump, three years his senior, took John in tow and guided him through his initial days back in Lancaster. John fired his first gun over Cump's shoulder, and Phil took him on their hunting expeditions for squirrels and pigeons. But townspeople came to consider John Sherman a troublemaker, wild and reckless, eager to argue and to fight; and his marks in school were poor.

Unlike his brother, Cump Sherman was doing extremely well in school, and Thomas Ewing was giving serious thought to his future education. As United States senator from Ohio, Ewing had at his discretion certain appointments to the United States Military Academy at West Point. Already, in 1835, the senator had appointed a relative of Maria's, William Irvin, to the academy; the following year, either Cump or Phil Ewing would be eligible. As early as 1833, writing Maria from Washington, Thomas Ewing had said: "I want Phil to come down and stay with me the rest of the winter. He will be company for me and besides he will be really useful. Perhaps Cumpy would think himself slighted if he had not the offer coming, but Phil is so much more of a business lad in the capacity in which I want him that I would greatly prefer to have him here and you may tell Cumpy that I want him to learn fast that he may be ready to go to West Point or to college soon—and that I don't think Phil will be stout enough to go to West Point. Say nothing in a way that will mortify him—but try and prevent Cumpy getting the idea that he is less beloved by me.

"Kiss the little fellows for me."

Word came from Washington in the spring of 1836 that Cump had been accepted as a cadet at West Point. That same day he began gathering the required documents, including his mother's consent, and then he sent his acceptance to the secretary of war:

Lancaster, Ohio
May 5, 1836

Sir

Your notice of the 5th of March informing me that the President of the United States had conditionally appointed me a cadet in the service of the United States, has been duly received.

I hereby respectfully notify you that I accept the appointment and will strictly comply with the requisitions of the War Department annexed to said appointment.

I am very respectfully
Your obedient servant
Wm. T. Sherman

West Point

WHEN CUMP DISEMBARKED on the wharf at West Point, a soldier in dress uniform with a slate in his hand was recording the name of every person who landed. After being given the necessary details, Cump and the others picked up their bags and toiled up the winding road to the plain where the barracks and the "professors' buildings" were located.

They mounted the steps of an imposing stone building, knocked, and entered the adjutant's office, where each registered his name, signed official papers, and left his money. From the adjutant's office they were directed to the barracks and were duly installed as new cadets. Cump lost no time in looking up his friend from Lancaster, Bill Irvin, who had been at the Point for a year and who quickly appropriated the plebe as "his."

That first afternoon the newcomers were interviewed by the superintendent and at the Store were issued one arithmetic book, one lamp, one bucket, one broom, and a pair of blankets. These, they were told, formed the sum total of a plebe's estate upon which he was to build his fortune.

Weary from the day's efforts, Cump returned to the barracks, where, after poring over *Regulations*, he fell asleep. Suddenly he was awakened by the roll of the drum and the command: "Turn out, *new* cadets!" Along with the others, Cump tumbled out of his room and down the stairs and met for the first time "his comrades for life." There was no time for introductions as someone yelled: "Fall in!" Once in formation, the plebes were marched around the corner to the South Barracks to view evening parade.

"I felt," Cump said later, "the beauty of Military parade and show—the fine music—the old cadets marching by companies,

30

stepping as one man, all forming in line, heard the roar of the evening gun and saw the flag fall and the parade dismissed, then my highest ambition was to be an old cadet."

In the days that followed the new cadets were drilled three times a day—once soon after daylight, then again at ten and four. Each plebe recited daily in an arithmetic section. Under strict discipline, they were confined to their rooms except for a few minutes after each meal.

During the last week in June a board of army officers examined the plebes, and Sherman was startled at how easily he was admitted to the academy. After the examination was passed, the plebes were marched to the tailors and issued a full suit of grays with short tails and buttons.

Two days later the corps went into summer camp. Sherman was assigned to Company B, and his first tentmates included Bill Irvin and Edward Otho Cresap Ord. He was warned "to study arithmetic *hard*, learn to write correctly, and read aloud with proper pauses and accent."

The days were taken up with infantry drill, artillery drill, and dress parades. The upperclassmen considered Sherman "smart but careless in conduct," and from the first the plebe started amassing demerits. In the first week he had collected four, which fortunately were not counted until after July 1. In the week following the Fourth of July, Sherman was given his first official demerit, for not carrying the butt of his musket far enough back at parade. By mid-August he had "a few more demerits than I desired."

Although Sherman took pride in West Point and in being a part of the army, he was restless and independent, full of energy, often impatient with regulations and bumbling superiors, and occasionally inclined toward pranks to dispel irksome details.

There was an enormous gulf between the tranquil, easygoing life of Lancaster and this world of discipline, regulations, strict obedience, and correct etiquette. The Point was neither a boys' school nor a university. Its basic function was to turn out soldiers. It was a professional institution for professionals. Its product was an officer who could fight, who could submerge his individuality in prompt, implicit obedience. Cadets who might excel in the classroom and on the drill field would be summarily expelled if their demerits in one year reached the 200 mark. In his first letter to

Thomas Ewing, Sherman jotted down a partial list of offenses for which demerits were given: one for soiled clothing, three for absence from roll call, eight for absence from drill or parade.

"I wish to God," he once wrote Phil Ewing at Oxford College, "we could be as independent as you, that is recite when we please, and study when we please, and do whatever we please, but no, drill & recite all day . . . which means study all night or take the consequences."

From the time Sherman entered West Point until the beginning of the Civil War in 1861, the academy experienced its greatest era. In academic affairs its influence spread as it improved its other courses, while remaining eminent in science. Under the guidance of a series of energetic and farsighted professors and superintendents, the cadets studied harder than their counterparts in colleges. The course work was so strenuous that only those men with outstanding ability stayed in school. Those plebes who had been to other colleges and universities before entering the academy were surprised at how much the professors expected them to know. Mathematics was by far the most important subject, being the basis for later studies and counting most in making up the honor roll.

There were 115 members in Sherman's class. While several of his classmates were graduates of other colleges, some of the plebes had studied mathematics but little, and a few had "seen nothing in the math line except arithmetic." Others might have been better prepared than Sherman, but he became convinced that "close study and application" were worth as much as previous knowledge in a subject.

After returning from summer camp, the plebes were arranged alphabetically into eight sections and began studying Bourdon's *Algebra* and French grammar. Soon transfers were made from one section to another, according to ability. Professors switched Sherman into the first mathematics section and into the second in French.

Sherman and his comrades feared the January examinations; the upperclassmen had spread the rumor that upwards of 40 plebes were always dismissed. But Sherman sailed through those first finals and had a good position in his class in all his studies.

In one of the first letters he wrote from the academy, he asked

Maria Ewing to send some money to help supply his equipment needs—especially gloves, which were not issued plebes: "You may think it strange that I should ask for money but in reality I would be the last person that would ask for it unless it were absolutely necessary, but you yourself know that it would be no means comfortable to walk post in the open air with a cold gun and thin gloves."

During that first winter and for the next four years, Sherman discovered that young Ellen was to be his best Lancaster correspondent. She wrote lengthy letters about the family and her activities at Somerset Convent and occasionally sent along pencils, erasers, and candy. "God knows," Cump confessed to Phil Ewing, "I shall always feel myself under obligation to her for the kindness and good will she has ever shown me."

From Ellen, Cump learned that his younger brother John had taken a job as junior rodman in an engineering concern engaged in improving the Muskingum River in Ohio. Once, in a letter written from West Point, Cump counseled his brother: "In my opinion a man's success in his profession depends upon the impressions he receives at the beginning; for if these are favorable, most undoubtedly he will endeavor to succeed, and success will be the necessary consequence. You have now been engaged at that employment about a year and must be by this time an expert engineer. I would not be much astonished if when I came home I would find you superintendent of some public work."

Sherman went into summer camp with the other cadets and remained there throughout August, 1837. When classes resumed Sherman wrote with pride: "I flourish as usual with regards to my studies, especially in drawing which is an entirely new thing. I have succeeded far beyond my expectations, and think that by taking pains and patience I will be able to draw tolerably well."

That November a cadet was court-martialed and sentenced to perform six extra Sunday tours of guard for going to Benny Havens', an off-limits grocery store two miles from the Point. But this did not stop other cadets from doing the same thing or from further defying academy regulations by cooking in their quarters. Soon after the court-martial, Sherman himself sneaked off to Benny's to buy a bushel of oysters, and often he and his friends roasted potatoes in the log fires in their rooms. A fellow cadet,

William S. Rosecrans, recalled: "He was always ready for a lark and usually he had a grease spot on his pants from clandestine night feasts. He was the best hash-maker at West Point. Food at the table was cheap and poor and we stole boiled potatoes in handkerchiefs and thrust them under our vests; we poked butter into our gloves and fastened them with forks to the under side of the table until we could smuggle them out of the dining room as we departed.

"We stole bread and when we got together at night 'Old Cump' would mix everything into hash, and cook it on a stew pan over the fire. We ate it hot on toasted bread. We told stories and at this, too, Sherman was the best. We would all risk expulsion by going down to Benny's Haven [*sic.*] at night to eat oysters."

In January, 1838, Sherman again had no trouble passing his examinations. Early in the spring he earned a host of demerits for going to the hospital without permission to have a tooth extracted. By April he was preparing for his first summer furlough, and in July he was back in Lancaster for the first time in two years.

To the Ewings he looked strange and different in his cadet uniform. He had developed the posture to wear it correctly. A regard for personal appearance had already been beaten into him at the Point, and he looked an integral part of the corps. Fourteen-year-old Ellen Ewing, awestricken at her former playmate's appearance, soon discovered that he was the same old Cump, still adept at teasing girls. Relatives came to Lancaster from all parts of Ohio to see him, and with his brother Lamp, he visited Phil Ewing in college at Oxford.

Before returning to West Point, Sherman did some sight-seeing in New York State, including a stop at Niagara Falls, which he said "far surpassed anything my imagination had pictured from its description." Perhaps because he had spent his childhood so closely tied to Lancaster, Sherman throughout his life seized every opportunity to travel and visit new places.

When classes began again, Sherman and his friends suspected that the instructors had chosen the most difficult textbooks they could find. "Our mechanics contains 400 and odd pages," Sherman told Phil, "which we will be examined on next January, every little law is deduced mathematically. I've been cursing all philosophers & chemists but I ought not to have included all chemists, for one professor is a gentleman and renders chemistry as interesting as possible."

In October and November the congressional elections were a topic of much debate, and many bets were placed on the outcome of those in Pennsylvania, New Jersey, and Ohio. Cump was so sure that Thomas Ewing would be reelected to the Senate that he wagered a fatigue jacket that the Whigs would win a majority in the Ohio legislature, which would send Ewing back to Washington. But Thomas Ewing's term was at an end when the Democratic legislature chose another for his seat. The abolitionists in the Old Northwest, who were multiplying rapidly, were not Ewing men. They found him too conservative.

Cump Sherman too was becoming a marked conservative on national issues and displayed an intense interest in the politics of his foster father and in those of Ohio. Despite what some biographers have said about the politics and attitudes of Sherman, there is no indication that he fell under the influence of Southern cadets while at West Point, nor is there anything in his considerable correspondence to show that he was receptive to their beliefs.

One of the most notable superintendents of West Point, Maj. Robert Delafield, took command of the academy that fall. At first the cadets termed him "a plain good-hearted old man," but they soon came to regard him as "a Tartar." Discipline became harsher. Bill Irvin complained to a friend, "We have caught hell at last sure enough." He bitterly denounced the host of new regulations, "which came near putting the corps in a state of mutiny.... If they had not been so well disciplined and so long accustomed to obeying all orders without questioning them, it is difficult to say what they would not have done."

One of Cump's classmates was expelled for mimicking an officer, but fortunately for Sherman, Irvin, and 12 others, the arresting officer failed to notice the beakers of whiskey punch about the room. "I am beginning to get frightened," Cump wrote Phil Ewing. "Beside the one mentioned above two others have been dismissed for very trivial offenses, one for going off limits merely, a violation of the regulation I commit, almost every day certainly Saturdays."

In less than three years Sherman's class had been reduced from 115 to 43. Sherman explained to Phil, "The only way is to trust to luck and thank fortune when we are presented with diplomas."

Bill Irvin, a year ahead of Sherman, was already looking forward to graduating and being free of West Point. On many occasions he announced that he did not intend to stay in the army more than one year. He would resign to study law. "No doubt you admire his choice," Sherman wrote Phil, "but to speak plainly and candidly I would rather be a blacksmith. Indeed the nearer we come to . . . . graduation day the higher opinion I conceive of the duties and life of an officer of the U. S. Army, and the more confidence in the wish of spending my life in the service of my country."

In the barracks during the winter evenings, Bill Irvin and Sherman discussed their futures in detail. Once Irvin wrote to Phil Ewing that the life of a soldier compared to that of a civilian "is an easy one, he is not distracted by those cares which constantly attack the citizen, his pay is sure, his promotion is sure, and the scenes of ambition and glory . . . are . . . frequent. . . . Instead of factories and noisy clamor of a legislature, instead of the high political station, held only by the breath of the fickle and changing public, he dreams of the tented camp, the hard stricken field, and the gratitude of his country for services in her time of need."

Sherman's and Irvin's attitudes about the army differed radically. Irvin's belief in democracy, his belief that liberty was the highest pride of man and ought always to be cherished, prevented him from choosing the army as his career. Sherman, on the other hand, was and would remain more autocratic than democratic, more a believer in law and order than in the will of the people. He had a low regard for most politicians and was antagonistic toward those who meddled in the affairs of the army.

Sherman's third year at West Point was coming to a close. "Thank God for that," he rejoiced. "It was the hardest time I have ever experienced." He and his classmates could look forward to the fourth and last year, supposedly the easiest, a year in which they would bear the dignity and importance of being first classmen.

Sherman was eager for some of the Ewings to visit him at the academy. But Ellen went with her father to Georgetown near Washington, D.C., to enroll at the Visitation Convent School, and neither she nor any other member of the family found it possible to visit the Point.

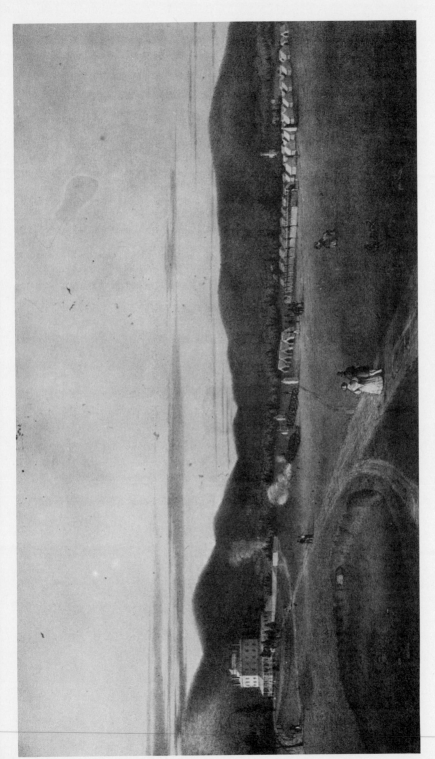

Cadets Encampment, West Point, 1835

Sherman's own drawing as a cadet

West Point from Garrison's Landing, 1840

The last encampment was over on August 30. The final year's curriculum, although indeed easier, was the most important, as it embraced both civil and military engineering, the construction of fortifications, and the tactics involved in attacking and defending them. The course of study also included geology, rhetoric, and law, as well as "many other minor studies which the scientific officer requires."

In October cavalry practice was introduced into the curriculum for the first time, and by December the cadets were galloping and charging about the plain. When the weather became severe, they moved into the exercise hall, learned the use of the broadsword, and practiced with pistols.

Despite the frequency of cavalry drills, upperclassmen fell into idle habits. Their courses and military duties were too easy. They let their studies slide throughout the fall and early winter and were forced to spend most of December boning for the January examinations. In engineering Sherman stood fourth in his class; in geology, rhetoric, and moral philosophy, sixth. But although Sherman made a fine showing in the examinations, he had a host of demerits, about a hundred. Yet he was not concerned, as he was looking forward to the remainder of the year, to graduation, and to service in the field.

"You may well suppose that we are all anxious for the arrival of June," Sherman wrote John. "The thoughts of graduation, the freedom from academic labors and restraints, already engross our minds and form the subjects of all our conversations and talks."

Already the class had selected its class ring, and members had ordered their swords, epaulets, and hats and were waiting for measurements to be taken for their uniforms. In the barracks Sherman and his friends endlessly discussed their futures in the army. Sherman favored the Fifth Infantry Regiment, then garrisoned along the Northwest frontier, a section of country he had always wanted to see and where he believed a major Indian war would break out.

To Ellen Ewing he wrote: "If I think so much of home and friends and consequently venerate old Lancaster—why do I not, you ask, conclude to live there hereafter. You forget this, I have adopted the Army as my profession and must be posted somewhere on the frontier. I am so convinced that even you would prefer the

Far West to the East that I would almost be willing for you to choose for me."

War at that moment did seem imminent with Great Britain, but for years disputes had plagued Anglo-American relations. The still unsettled boundary between Maine and New Brunswick provided an ugly source of trouble, and the issue became critical in 1838 when Canadians began cutting timber in the Aroostook Valley, which was claimed by the United States. When Maine sent an agent to remonstrate with the lumberjacks, he was arrested. Maine and New Brunswick each called up militia and the Aroostook "War" followed. No one was killed, but the danger of a real war with England was great.

If this were to happen, then Sherman preferred duty with the artillery, as this corps was stationed east of the Alleghenies and would surely be at the scene of action. Service in the artillery was desirable in a war "against civilized people." Fortunately, President Martin Van Buren acted with admirable restraint and sent to the area Gen. Winfield Scott, who was able to arrange a truce.

With his high standing in the class, Sherman could have had a choice of corps—artillery, infantry, or cavalry. But he delayed making the necessary applications and was finally assigned to Florida, where the Third Artillery was fighting a savage guerrilla war with the Seminole Indians. Hunting down those "cursed devils" was an almost impossible task, and the army was bogged down in the Florida swamps.

As graduation neared, Sherman thought often about Lancaster, the Ewings, and his own mother, sisters, and brothers. He had a deep sense of loyalty to the Ewings, but he fully realized, much to his embarrassment, that he would never be able to repay their many kindnesses. He hated being dependent and once wrote to his mother, asking her for a five-dollar loan to satisfy some debts, as "I do not wish ever to ask Mr. Ewing again for assistance."

His absence from the house on the hill had increased Cump's affection and love for Thomas and Maria Ewing. "Although I have rarely spoken of it," he wrote Ellen, "still I assure you that I have always felt sincerely and deeply grateful, and hope that some event may occur to test it." When Cump was an old man, he came to believe that these two, Thomas and Maria, who had hospitably welcomed him into their family, had been the most important influence in molding his character. "Of all the great men amongst whom my early days were cast," he said, "the noblest Roman of them all was Thomas Ewing. A better, nobler, more intellectual man never lived."

Just before graduation day Sherman, with examinations behind him and "having nothing better to do," visited cadet Richard S. Ewell and his roommates in South Barracks. Lounging about, talking over their careers, they heard an officer coming along the hall on his tour of inspection. Quickly, Sherman darted for the chimney and hid behind the jamb. After the inspector left the room, Sherman stayed on for over an hour, chatting with his friends. Suddenly Sherman's roommate burst in, exclaiming, "Where have you been? The Officer of the Day has been in our room three times!"

On the following day Sherman was reported absent from quarters for an hour and a half. Later his punishment was posted—three Saturday afternoons of guard duty, which meant that he would be detained after his class had graduated and gone on furlough.

Sherman had never imagined his punishment would be so severe, and he felt his only hope was in going to Superintendent Delafield and telling the truth. Delafield suggested that he write out an excuse to which he would give his personal attention. This was done, the report was changed, and the punishment given Sherman was only five demerits without extra duty hours.

On the first day of July, 1840, William Tecumseh Sherman graduated from West Point, sixth in a class of forty-three. His standing would have been third, but his demerits, which averaged 150 a year for four years, carried him down three notches.

Forts Pierce and Morgan

THE UNITED STATES in the 1840s was experiencing unprecedented growth and expansion. Population was doubling in every decade. By 1860 this hardy generation of Americans would have broken a hundred thousand acres to the plow with only the crudest of tools and would have produced 10 million bales of cotton, one billion bushels of wheat, and nearly 2 million bushels of corn. They would raise a dozen cities to metropolitan proportions, seal the fate of the Indian on the continent, and occupy the Oregon Territory and the vast empire in the Southwest yielded up by Mexico.

That American life was buoyant, self-confident, and aggressive should hardly elicit wonder. Planters, miners, ranchers, lumbermen, and whalers; Irish Catholics, Mormons, Quakers, and Campbellites; old stock Carolinians and New Englanders mingling with Germans, Norwegians, and others of the immigrant flood; men and women molded by the narrow conventions of the eastern towns two centuries old or by the chaotic ferment of the frontier beyond the Mississippi River—all went to make up America in the 1840s. Above all, the whole nation from eastern seaboard to western frontier was a land, observers agreed, which offered greater prosperity, more social equality, and ruddier hopes than any other country in the world.

A writer for the London *Economist*, traveling throughout the country, was impressed with the genius of the American people. "The Americans," he wrote, "seem to be an eminently practical race. Their numerous inventions all tend to the common and general advantage, to bring about equally beneficial results for all by less labour. Their intellect is exerted for the benefit of all. It is not warped to consult the gratification of a few. They open their

eyes and their senses to the present wants, and set all their faculties
to work to gratify them. They look Nature in the face, attend to
her minutest signs, learn to read quickly her directions, and they
are inventive, skillful, and prosperous. . . ."

All visitors to the United States discovered that two Americas
existed—the North and the South. Much of the nation's vitality
and nearly all of its industry were concentrated in the Northern
states; most of the leisure, chivalry, and pride resided in the
Southern states. Disliking Negro slavery, heat, and inferior travel
facilities, most travelers from Europe avoided at least the lower tier
in the Southern states, but those who did brave the cotton states
usually felt well rewarded. If there was poverty, there was also
picturesqueness. If the Negroes were pitiful to look upon, the
whites seemed more English, more Old World in outlook than
their counterparts in the North.

The American West was a world in itself, a region of rapid
change. The musket, ax, and saddlebag were giving way to
civilization brought by the flood of settlers moving westward. The
conquering of the continent, the exploitation of its forests and
mineral wealth, the stringing of railroad lines, the founding of raw
villages—which, in numerous instances, sprang into unruly cities—
were occurring at a faster pace than ever before. This vitality of
growth and expansion gave life in the 1840s an unparalleled
excitement.

Second Lieutenant Sherman, after visiting Ellen at her school
in Georgetown, journeyed to Lancaster, which he found dull that
summer—a terribly provincial place compared with Washington
and New York. He was happy when the orders arrived assigning
him to the Third Artillery, Company A, in Florida. He was
directed to report for duty with recruits at Fort Columbus, New
York Harbor, on September 20.

With relief Sherman left Ohio and traveled to Buffalo, N.Y.,
again went sight-seeing at Niagara Falls, and then went back to
West Point to have a last look around and say good-bye to under-
classmen friends. Sherman always took deep pride in being a
graduate of West Point, and throughout his life he made many
trips back.

Along with some others of his class, who had also returned,
Sherman spent the night in the hotel and went up to the barracks

the next morning for a visit with his friends. There he relaxed in one of the rooms for a half hour after morning call to quarters. Sherman realized that his actions were counter to regulations, but as a second lieutenant he thought himself immune to academic rules.

Later, as he left the barracks, Sherman saw Lt. George G. Waggaman, then adjutant of the academy, hurrying toward him. Sherman was astonished when Waggaman told him to consider himself under arrest for visiting cadets during study hours. Limits for lieutenants, he said, were the hotel and its grounds, not the barracks. Sherman argued briefly, then turned abruptly and strode off to the hotel.

Ordered to New York City "in arrest," Sherman arrived at Fort Columbus on September 20, called on the commanding officer, Major Dimick, and handed him a package of papers from the academy.

Dimick rustled through them, then glanced at Sherman.

"So you are in arrest?"

"Yes."

"Well, it looks like a small matter."

Sherman thought so too.

"But as the arrest comes from Major Delafield," continued Dimick, "it must be respected."

Sherman was ordered to report for duty the next morning at ten. By that time all of Sherman's friends who were assigned to the Third Artillery had reported in and were assigned to companies of recruits. But Sherman, being under arrest, could exercise no command; so, with the major's permission, he was free to go into New York.

Before leaving, Sherman wrote to Major Delafield, apologizing for his actions: "I can only say that I had no intention of openly setting the regulations at defiance, in fact, I do not think I thought of regulations at all, but acted in accordance with my feelings, which prompted me to do a common & friendly act, bid my friends a farewell upon parting with them some perhaps forever."

Upon receiving his letter, Major Delafield recommended to Washington that Lieutenant Sherman be restored to duty.

By mid-October, 1840, Sherman had arrived in Saint Augustine, Fla., and was soon heading southward for Fort Pierce and Company A. Built on a sandbank, only 20 feet from a lagoon, Fort Pierce was a complex of log huts forming three sides of a rectangle, open on the water. The companies garrisoned there, A and F, were relatively small, and orders had not yet arrived to begin active operations against the Seminole.

Sherman was greeted by Lt. Edward J. Steptoe and led off to headquarters. The officers' mess was laid on a table of loose boards spread over sawhorses. Over whiskey toddies Sherman met Lt. George Taylor and Dr. Simmons, the surgeon. As the officers talked, they made no attempt to hide their interest in the new lieutenant. Where had he been? How was his trip? What was going on in Washington? Was Washington ignorant of conditions in Florida? He was flattered by the attention. It was pleasant to sit among veterans of the war.

During his first months in Florida, Sherman had no cause to regret his assignment. The dreaded climate proved delightful; the sun was hot, but there was always a breeze. There were no Indians about, scouts reporting that they had all gone to Tampa Bay. He enjoyed living in primitive style. The log cabins were thatched with palmetto and furnished with rough bedsteads, tables, and chairs. For decorations the officers hung up feathers and wings of birds, rattlesnake skins, and the heads and teeth of sharks.

Nine horses were attached to the post for hauling wood and doing manual work, but the officers often rode them on hunting expeditions as well. Deer, turkey, fish, and oysters were the main fare of the men. When the fishing and hunting failed, the command reverted to sea biscuit, pork, and beans.

Around the campfires at night Steptoe, Taylor, and Simmons filled Sherman in on the particulars of Florida and the Seminole War. A good portion of the territory was cut up by innumerable rivers, streams, and rivulets. Weeds, grass, palmettos, and oaks abounded. The strongholds of the Indians were hummocks, tracts of wooded land higher than the nearby swamps, on which the Indians built their huts and raised their corn and pumpkins, the thick growth concealing their fires and securing their escape.

The Seminole pillaged and burned, fighting when they pleased, where they pleased. A strong army had marched in to seek out and destroy them, but the astute Indians retreated, hid, and fought again. Detachments of infantry and artillery were impotent against an enemy that would not stand and permit himself to be engaged. The war against the Seminole had dragged on since 1835, a war of countless skirmishes, of wading through morasses, of fighting mosquitoes as deadly as the Indians. Soldiers marched and counter-marched and battled fatigue, exposure, and privation.

It was obvious to Sherman that any war between Indians and whites could not be conducted by the maneuvers taught in the field manuals. "There is no use on earth talking with them [the Indians]," he wrote Phil Ewing. "They'll break their word when it is to their interest—they will not acknowledge the authority of any self constituted chief to treat for the whole." The only solution to this war, in fact the only way to win wars with Indians, was to "send a sufficient number of troops to literally fill the territory, declare martial law and then begin the war of extermina-tion, this would be the most certain and economical method. The present method will not do—experience has shown it—persons who have not seen the country should not blame the army for they have no idea of the wild and dangers they have undergone un-rewarded by success or considerations."

Sherman never abandoned this ruthless strategy to end resistance. To him it was the most effective method of subduing an enemy.

In letters from home, those at Fort Pierce learned that Gen. William Henry Harrison had been elected president of the United States. Of particular interest to Sherman was Thomas Ewing's appointment to the cabinet as secretary of the treasury. One prominent Bostonian, Abbott Lawrence, had written a friend that Thomas Ewing, taking "him all in all," was the best man for the Treasury Department in the country, for he enjoyed the con-fidence of the great rank and file as well as of the moneyed interests.

Early in December, 1840, Maj. Thomas Childs and Stewart Van Vliet, Sherman's friends from West Point, arrived at Fort Pierce bringing 70 recruits to bolster the strength of the companies. Immediately the officers prepared for active operations. On the first expedition against the Seminole, Sherman, to his disappoint-ment, was left behind to guard the fort. His comrades returned, triumphant, having routed an enemy camp and captured 34 men, women, and children. Sherman was fascinated with this first glimpse of the Indians and was impressed with their stoic demeanor. To his sister Susan, he wrote: "I wish you could see the group in its savage state, although many have lost their husbands and wives still they show no grief. Several wounded, one little girl with a ball through the back and coming out in the cheek, but scarce utters a murmur. I regretted not having been along, but consoled myself with the idea that I'll have a chance yet."

In March, 1841, Sherman accompanied a scouting expedition into the interior. For eight days they probed streams and creeks but failed to make contact with the enemy. Despite the absence of action, Sherman found his first scouting expedition to be an exhilarating experience. But the more he saw of the war, the more he became convinced there was no end to it. The Indians robbed and killed and hid in the brush. The army hoped it could persuade them to come into the army posts voluntarily and be assigned to reservations.

Therefore, when Coacoochee ("Wild Cat"), one of the Seminole chiefs, rode over to Tampa Bay and told the general-in-chief of the Florida army, Walker K. Armistead, that the Indians were weary of the war and anxious to emigrate if they were given assistance and time, the army command was gratified. Armistead issued a safe-conduct pass which permitted Wild Cat to enter any military post on the Florida coast. It ordered all commanding officers to help the chief collect his people.

One steaming day in the spring of 1841, Major Childs, learning that Wild Cat was near Fort Pierce and "very tired from his long march and his people, too," ordered Lieutenant Sherman to take 12 mounted men, find the Indian chief, and bring him in. Five miles into the interior, they came upon the Indians in a clearing. Wild Cat was a handsome man and considerably younger than Sherman had supposed—"certainly not over twenty-four. At first he had on buckskin shirt and leggings but when I told him I'd a horse for him, he began his dressing, putting on highly ornamented leggings, head dress, shirts. He put on all his wardrobe embracing half a dozen common vests and then four highly ornamented hunting shirts."

Wild Cat and the detachment rode back to Fort Pierce, trailed by the other Indians. All that day and the next, Major Childs talked with the chief, until finally Wild Cat promised that in one moon his people would be ready to migrate to the reservation. Toward evening the Indian caravan rumbled out of the fort, loaded with flour, sugar, coffee, and whiskey in fawn skins.

During the next few weeks small parties of Seminole trickled in, but the local command mistrusted them and feared that they would suddenly go on a rampage. Childs beseeched Col. William Jenkins Worth, who had succeeded to the command of the Florida army, for authority to disregard the safe-conduct pass. The order came back—seize Wild Cat.

The next time the chief and his warriors arrived at Fort Pierce for more provisions, they were captured and clamped into irons. On the following day Lt. Col. William Gates, commanding the Third Artillery, marched into Fort Pierce with an additional company. Gates ordered that the captured Seminole be shipped at once to New Orleans and Indian territory beyond. Colonel Worth, who planned to use Wild Cat to bring in other Seminole, chastised Gates for issuing such orders without permission and had the chief brought back to Tampa. Worth arrested Gates, but when that officer explained the reasons for his actions, he was released and sent north on furlough.

"The Florida war is not at an end," Sherman wrote Phil Ewing, "and thus no troops can be removed. Yet there are enough men here if companies be kept full to end this war if we be directed as we now have hopes of by a man of energy and talents. . . . If [Colonel] Worth will keep us in columns of from 50-100 moving where we know the Indians to be, there will be less discontent and more success.

"Some old fogies . . . have demanded to be relieved from duty in Florida. . . . A soldier to demand to be relieved from the very spot where his duty calls him is an absurdity and I assure you that however anxious officers of this regiment are to go north after six years service here, yet not one except the colonel [Gates] would think of such a thing as demanding it. . . . We've all made up our minds to stay here until the end of the war, when that will be God only knows."

While Ellen Ewing was attending school at Georgetown, Phil Ewing became Sherman's best Ohio correspondent. But Mrs. Ewing had not forgotten her foster son, although she seldom wrote him. In a letter to Ellen, Maria noted: "I was happy to hear

Cumpy had written you, and that you had time for answering his letters, do not neglect him. . . . When you write, give my best love to the dear fellow, tell him he must not regard my apparent neglect or forgetfulness of him in not writing, tell him, whenever he receives a letter from Philemon he must regard it as coming from *all at home*, and that we think just *as much, and love him as much as* if we had all written."

During the stifling summer months, military operations ceased, and Sherman and his comrades whiled away the time collecting shells, rattlesnake skins, and sharks' heads. "I have a pony, not a pretty one, but one I purchased from the Indians for Hugh," Cump wrote home, "but how can it be gotten to him, I don't know. . . . I've got more pets now than anyone—I've got innumerable chickens, tame pigeons, white rabbits beside a full blooded Indian pony rather small matters for a man to deal with you doubtless think but it is far better to spend time in such trifles than in drinking or gambling."

In November Sherman was promoted to first lieutenant. Although it usually required five years to attain that rank, Sherman secured it in only 17 months. He was pleased, but it meant separation from Company A and from officers to whom he had become attached. He was transferred from the war district and the "land of curiosities and wonders" to Picolata, Fla., where he took command of a detachment of Company G.

Located along the banks of the Saint Johns River, Picolata was an old settlement consisting of a large frameboard house, barracks, outhouses, guardhouses, and stables. It was a beautiful spot, a decided improvement over Fort Pierce. Sherman moved into spacious quarters, where he had regular communication with the outside world.

There was little society in Picolata, but the officers could ride the 18 miles into Saint Augustine, the oldest town in the United States, originally established by the Spanish in 1565. Not until 1819 was Saint Augustine and all of Florida ceded to the United States.

Sherman was impressed with Saint Augustine's plaza, Spanish houses, and orange groves, so thick as to exclude the sunlight. "The town's appearance," he wrote John, "does not belie its age, —narrow, winding streets, close-built houses with the balconies meeting overhead, denoting its Spanish population. There are some few old English families . . . and together with the few Americans whom the delightful climate has enticed, constitute the best society. . . . There is an old fort, built at enormous cost by the Spanish Government; but for want of appropriation, it is fast falling to decay. . . . [T]he inhabitants still preserve the old ceremonies and festivities of old Spain."

The tempo of the old town was slow and leisurely and the long, sun-washed days and perfumed nights lent themselves to idle pastimes. In the late afternoons the men sat in the public houses to drink, gossip, or play cards and dice. An occasional horse race or a cockfight satisfied their competitive spirits. Soldiers in the streets, carefully turned-out ladies and gentlemen in their carriages, and the banks of brilliant flowers and rustling palms gave an air of carnival to Saint Augustine.

With a few exceptions, Sherman found the Spanish ladies "ignorant but pretty," with particularly beautiful hair and eyes. But already 12 of the prettiest had married army officers, so for Sherman and other bachelor lieutenants there was "not much to choose from." He was, however, attracted by Saint Augustine's masquerades and parties. "Indeed, I never saw anything like it," he told John, "dancing, dancing, and nothing but dancing, but not such as you see at the north. Such ease and grace I never before beheld. A lady will waltz all the evening without fatigue, because it is done slowly, with grace; but it is in the Spanish dance they more especially excel, enchanting all who behold or participate. This, together with the easy and cordial hospitality all extend to officers, is what has captivated so many within the past years."

Sherman's stay in Picolata was short-lived. Soon after the first of the year, the entire Third Artillery was ordered to garrison the Gulf posts, and Company G, Sherman's outfit, was sent to Fort Morgan at the mouth of Mobile Bay, Ala.

On March 8, 1842, the steamer *Cincinnati* pulled alongside a small dock. Once the men of Company G had disembarked, the steamboat got under way for her return; Sherman, turning, watching her maneuver out of the channel, realized that "the last link with Florida was gone." Two weeks later, Company H, Capt. James Ketcham commanding, arrived, and Sherman warmly welcomed three friends, Lts. James Rankin, Sewall L. Fish, and George W. Ayers.

Fort Morgan was a series of heavy casemates and arches arranged in bastions, surmounted by a heavy barbette battery. The monotony of post routine was broken only when the officers went into Mobile. The business of the city, though prosperous, lacked the vitality and variety of the North. Yet Mobile society was more homogeneous than Northern society, more settled and more conservative in its ways. The city had fine streets, hotels, and stores and shops, decorated much like those in New York and Philadelphia. The homes of merchants, who had spared no expense in furnishing and ornamenting their residences and grounds, were white, with piazzas all around and with roses and other flowers creeping up the latticed porticoes.

The officers' uniforms were their passports to the best homes in Mobile. They were invited everywhere, to balls, theaters, art exhibits, balloon ascensions, and even temperance parades. Sherman looked up a cousin, Mrs. Bull, the former Cornelia Pyle, who with her husband and three children resided in a magnificent house, undoubtedly one of the most delightful spots in Mobile. Mr. Bull—"a Yankee southernized," said Sherman—was a cotton commission merchant and one of the most prosperous men in the city. After months of roughing it, Sherman luxuriated at the Bulls'. "There was," he wrote Ellen, "an air of quiet and home spread over all, that tendered it a perfect paradise for me."

Sherman had a standing invitation at the Bulls', but so extravagant were the Mobilians and so prohibitive were the prices, that his visits were limited to about one a month. Hotel bills were exorbitant, from three dollars a day, and a horse and buggy for an afternoon cost six dollars. But the invitations, the attentions, the flirtations, the hospitality, and the warmth of the receptions made it difficult for him to keep away.

During those months at Fort Morgan, Cump wrote to Ellen Ewing describing the parties, the good times, the moonlight rides into the Alabama countryside. From his correspondence it is evident that at that time he considered Ellen nothing more than a good friend. Letters from Ellen related the Lancaster news, and in one, she asked him why he remained in the army.

"Why don't I leave the Army? you ask," he wrote her in reply. "Why should I? It is the profession for which my education alone fits me, and as all appearances indicate the rapid approach of a time when the soldier will be required to do his proper labor, when a splendid field will be spread before him, every reason exists why I should remain. Moreover, I am content and happy, and it would be foolish to spring into the world bare-handed and unprepared to meet its coldness and trials."

And to John, Cump wrote: "The Army is far better than diving into the world empty handed or falling back into a state of dependency still more objectionable, but there are advantages which an officer of the Army enjoys that are very great as I myself have experienced, in having this early in life seen so much of our own country and its people as well as seen that world of people whose principles can not be taught in books but must be learned from experience and by mingling freely with it."

Yet, despite these advantages, Cump doubted that the army was the place for a married man, unless his wife were willing to forsake home and the comforts of civilized life. He could not bring himself to believe that a family could submit to the frequent changes that officers were required to make without destroying that "indoor comfort" that families should possess.

Cump tried to satisfy Ellen's curiosity about his personal religion. After leaving the Ewing home in 1836, he practiced no set creed, "believing firmly in the main doctrines of the Christian Religion, the purity of its morals, the almost absolute necessity for its existence and practice among all well regulated communities to assure peace and good will amongst us. Yet I cannot," he continued, "with due reflection attribute to minor points of doctrine or form the importance usually attached to them. I believe in good works rather than faith, and believe them to constitute the basis of true religion, both as revealed in Scripture and taught by the experience of all ages and common sense. You see that my ideas are very general and subject to be moulded to a definite shape by time, circumstances and experience. . . . Although matters of religion is a source of much discussion amongst us, I think I have written more on this page upon the subject than I ever did before."

In June, 1842, authorities in Washington transferred the Third Artillery from Gulf posts to those along the Atlantic seaboard from North Carolina to Florida. "Hurray! Hurray! for old Fort Moultrie!" cried an old soldier. All men of Company G rejoiced at the thought of going to Fort Moultrie, on Sullivans Island, over-looking the sea and the entrance to Charleston Harbor. Fort Moultrie was then the toast of all who had ever served there. Although he was happy to shake the dust of Fort Morgan, Sherman was not one of those joining in the enthusiasm. He would miss the Bulls and his other good friends in Mobile.

Charleston

MOULTRIEVILLE, the village near the fort, was a summer resort where Charleston families fled to escape the dust and heat of the city. During that first summer Sherman was struck by how lazy the Southerners were, never stirring out of their houses until the sun had descended. Then the old and young, the rich and poor, some in handsome carriages or buggies and others on horseback or on foot, promenaded along the beach.

The officers soon made the acquaintance of the Charleston families vacationing on the island. Bachelor officers were in demand, and they were invited to teas, picnics, and parties. Occasionally the lieutenants engaged the regimental band to play for dancing on the village green. Summer evenings were long and pleasant. There were mild flirtations with the well-bred young ladies, as it was universally accepted that they could flirt as much as they pleased, but no one had the right to expect anything more serious.

By August more and more planters had swarmed to the island, and Sherman became intrigued with studying the various strata of South Carolinian society. Sullivans Island received its full share of men of the highest standing and also "the worthless sons of broken down proud Carolina families," whose boasts about their state, their aristocracy, and their chivalry were "nothing but rubbish." To Sherman, no people in America were so poor in reality, so meagerly provided with the comforts of life, as the Carolinians. But a change was moving across the land. The importance of name and ancestry was giving way to industry and intelligence. Under the control of energetic owners employing new methods of cultivation, many plantations which for years had been deteriorating were beginning to look prosperous again.

At the fort the military routine was not taxing. Every morning, officers and men rolled out at reveille and drilled at sunrise. Breakfast was at 7:00, the usual dress parade at 8:00, and the changing of the guard at 8:30. After that, Sherman told John, "Each one kills time to suit himself till reveille of next morning commences the new routine." While some of the officers simply loafed, Sherman took up painting. In Charleston he purchased artist's equipment and prepared a tiny studio in the fort. Without any instruction he began painting landscapes and portraits, which one of his fellow officers described as "good." During these months he developed a deep love for painting and confessed that he sometimes became so fascinated it pained him to lay down the brush. He also learned to his pleasure that Ellen Ewing shared his interest. It appeared in a Washington paper that she had won second prize in drawing at school.

Charleston was only five miles away from Fort Moultrie. A steamboat made four trips daily from the city to Sullivans Island. Sherman was enchanted with Charleston, a beautiful, fairylike city. The mighty fortunes that built the clusters of its handsome houses, unequaled anywhere in America, were founded upon one thing: the back of the Negro slave. Not only was labor, the source of all wealth, tied up in slaves, but the slaves themselves were capital— the most important capital the South owned, underpinning the Southern economy.

Born and bred in southern Ohio, early influenced by Thomas Ewing, who held rather conservative views on the Negro, and serving his first years in the army in Southern states, Sherman felt no abhorrence toward Negro slavery. "The Negroes are well dressed and behaved," he told Phil Ewing, "never impudent or presuming and so far as I can judge feeling very light indeed the chains of bondage. Servants are treated with remarkable kindness and in no instance would I see a difference in them and ours of the North were it not for the market place where they are exposed for sale."

Sherman became an apologist for the institution. When abolitionists in the North began talking about the sin of slavery, he regarded them as dangerous troublemakers. "I am no advocate for slavery as a means of wealth or national advancement," he wrote, "yet at the same time I know that the idea of oppression and tyranny that some people consider as the necessary accompaniment of slavery is a delusion of their own brain."

Even in Florida, when he watched runaway Negroes being captured in the swamps and led back into bondage, Sherman thought of the institution as one he had sworn to defend. Early in the 1840s he strongly believed that slavery would eventually die of its own accord. "If the abolitionists suggest the removal of slaves from Maryland and Virginia, Kentucky and Missouri, just so surely will it not be done," he told John Sherman. "But if they lie low common interest, the sole motive power that can remove slavery, will cause the sending of slaves from those states to states further south, where white labor cannot be had. There is no doubt that in Maryland and Missouri labor is absolutely cheaper than slave, and so will it be in the southern states in succession as a poor white class enters, then negroes will go.

"Texas will serve as a good receptacle for them, and afterwards, other unoccupied lands in that latitude may in turn draw from nearly all the present states, a negro population that cannot be got rid of by any other scheme. Their condition needs no amelioration, but I have said enough."

On other key issues of the day as well, Sherman was decidedly conservative, pro-Southern in his view. On the question of the United States annexing Texas, he defended the South against Northern charges of duplicity. "As to Texas having been annexed for the sole purpose of extending slavery," he wrote, "I do not believe it. Some politicians may do so, and abolitionists may act upon that [belief] and affect it."

During the winter of 1842-43, invitations from Charleston flooded Fort Moultrie, invitations for balls and masquerades, for the theater and the opera, for picnics, horse races, boating, fishing, and "God knows what"—so many, in fact, that the officers became almost surfeited. The formal balls were frightful bores: the overeager greetings of the ladies, the reserved behavior of the gentlemen, the same old sets of French quadrilles or too-rapid waltzes. The dancing of Charleston girls could never compare with the gracefulness of the Spanish girls in Saint Augustine.

Despite their dislike of Charleston society, the officers continued to go to the functions because they believed it a duty to foster warm feelings between the army and Charlestonians. To conserve their energies, they agreed that only two officers need attend each party and ball. "I'd like to have a little peace or rest," Cump confided to Ellen. "I'm tired of playing a hypocritical part, for I feel no more interest in the people by whom we are surrounded." He longed for Washington "to invent a new Florida war" and, in fact, was seriously thinking of transferring to another company.

Cump did, however, enjoy the company of Mary Lamb, generally considered the prettiest girl around, and he frequently escorted her to the opera or theater. As some Southerners interpreted riding side by side with a lady in a carriage as displaying an intimacy reserved only for an engaged pair, Charleston society began gossiping. "They are damned wrong!" Cump replied. "I had no idea that people here were so foolish as to raise and circulate rumors of that kind." And he swore to Phil Ewing as an army officer, "I'll *never marry....* If I ever do, be sure to knock out my brains." To Ellen, Cump wrote: "A good old bachelor's career is before me and as yet all augurs well for its continuance."

In the summer and fall of 1843, Sherman took a five-month leave and traveled home to Lancaster. Thomas Ewing, who had resigned his post as secretary of the treasury as a result of the president's veto of a bank bill, was again practicing law in Lancaster and Washington. The Ewing children were growing up. Ellen was now 19, and Cump began to show her more real attention than ever before. Until now, their relationship had been that of a brother and sister, of good friends and confidants. Throughout their correspondence over the years, there had never been words of endearment.

But that summer Cump saw Ellen anew, her soft black hair drawn tight over her ears; a delicate, straight nose; blue eyes; the determined thrust of her chin (too bold a chin, it was sometimes said, too assertive for real beauty). She had become more mature, more poised, and far more at ease.

To Ellen, Cump also seemed different, eager to please her slightest whim. She was awed by his apparent knowledge of the world, but he had a way of speaking to her as if she fully understood what he was saying, as if he were taking her into his confidence.

Ellen took it for granted that one day she would be married. This was a matter of course; everyone got married. It gave every girl a special social dignity, a house of her own, with silver and furniture and servants, and a husband who would be gallant to her. That summer, Cump and Ellen were pulled together more and more, and they fell in love. But they masked their feelings well, and nothing was said to Thomas or Maria Ewing.

On his return to Fort Moultrie, Cump stopped off in New Orleans, a city he had always wanted to see. He lingered there for six days, spending as much money as he dared, attending the theaters, cafés, music halls, and restaurants, sampling shrimps, crabs, and gumbos at the market stalls.

On December 27, he was once more in his quarters at Fort Moultrie. The weather was highly preferable to the cold winter blasts of Ohio, and Sherman liked to sit out on the piazza with a screen over his head to shade the rays of the sun. He wished Ellen were near so she could be with him to enjoy the climate, the scenery, and the activities in and about Charleston.

"I would give years of my life if you could have been here this evening," he told Ellen, "to hear Mrs. Keyes sing, have a sociable chat with Mrs. Hawkins, eat some of her mince pies, drink whiskey punch, play eucre.... Afterwards at 11 to stand on the ramparts and see the moon rise slowly from her watery bed."

In February, 1844, Col. Sylvester Churchill, inspector general of the United States, was engaged in taking testimony in relation to the horses, saddles, and bridles lost by volunteers from Georgia and Alabama during the Seminole War, who had petitioned Congress for relief. Their horses, they alleged, had been killed or abandoned during the campaign. Although Congress did pass a law, the auditor termed the soldiers' claims exorbitant and refused to authorize the accounts until they had been investigated. Colonel Churchill was then at Marietta, Ga., working with two assistants. He asked that Lieutenant Sherman be sent to help speed up the investigation.

Sherman was surprised that he had been chosen, but he felt complimented that Churchill, one of the best and hardest working officers in the service, had singled him out.

After six weeks in Marietta interviewing the ex-militiamen, Churchill and his party rode across the mountains to Bellefont,

Ala. Wherever Sherman traveled, he was a close and accurate observer of the topography through which he passed. "The service," Sherman was to recall after the Civil War, "proved to me of infinite advantage for my route carried me over the very ground where my best campaigns were fought, and after an absence of twenty years the ground seemed as familiar as possible. I had a perfect conception of the character of the water, ground, soil, ranges of mountains, etc., that determine the character of roads on which an Army is so dependent."

On this trip Sherman's job was to cross-examine and record the testimony of the ex-soldiers to make sure that the old horse reported killed in Florida was not the same one then working in the cornfield across the way. Under close questioning, Sherman uncovered glaring frauds.

By June, 1844, he was back at Fort Moultrie, and the mail brought news that the report and the testimony had been turned in and the authorities at the War Department were extremely well satisfied.

Soon after Cump's departure from Lancaster, Ellen had confided her feelings about him to her parents. Maria approved the match at once, but Thomas Ewing had deep misgivings. He loved his daughter too much to see her leading the nomadic life of an army wife. Sherman's salary as a first lieutenant was small. He urged Sherman to resign from the army, settle down, and enter a lucrative business in Ohio.

Sherman had a high regard for Thomas Ewing and had always sought his advice, but he realized now that to resign his commission and return to civilian life was out of the question. He would be dependent upon someone until he could establish himself in another profession. Proud and independent, Sherman refused to take handouts, especially from his foster father, to whom he was already indebted for past kindnesses. He asked Ewing: "Isn't it better for me to labor hard and build upon the pretty fair reputation I have already begun to establish as a zealous and active officer rather than neglect it and direct my attention to a new and civil profession?"

"Beside, I have now studied for the military profession and hold a place envied by thousands and for which hundreds of the best young men of this country toil every year," he wrote Ellen.

"It would be madness itself at this late day to commence something new."

In his spare moments at Fort Moultrie, he tried studying law, reading Blackstone with the aid of a dictionary. "But I have no idea of making the Law a profession," he confessed to Phil, "but as an officer it is my duty and interest to be prepared for any direction that Fortune or luck may offer. It is for this alone that I prepare and not for professional practice."

To Ellen he wrote: "I stand well in my present profession, and have done all I can to be respected and esteemed in order that should you join me you would not have cause to regret it.

"You have often advised me to leave the army, probably without thinking that I am perfectly dependent upon it for a living, that I have no profession that would [provide] employment in civil life and that if I should leave the army I would have to begin where I was ten years ago.

"Also my mother depends on me and my purse is pretty lean. I'm at this moment pretty poor though in receipt of a pretty handsome salary."

In this same letter, undoubtedly reacting to pressures from Thomas Ewing and Ellen, Cump wrote something which indicated that regardless of what he had said before, he was actually unsettled about his future: "I . . . propose next spring about May to get a long leave of absence, go to the northern part of Alabama, select some pretty place and then see what may be done as a Surveyor & draughtsman in each of which I am fully competent. Should I meet with partial success then I can complete what I have begun at the Law which I can master sufficiently by one winter's study in a Law office.

"With these I think I could get along slowly and possibly establish myself and you permanently and comfortably—even better than to follow the camp, subject to all the annoyances that are really felt by married persons in the army."

His own preference, he said, was to remain in the army. Even at West Point he had recognized that he was unsuited for the legal profession. Nevertheless, in closing his letter to Ellen, he stated: "This is a risk but I am willing to attempt it for your sake."

Apparently, however, he then rejected the idea of abandoning his military career, for he does not mention Alabama again in his correspondence. "Supposing all things remain for the year as at the present," he told Ellen, "would you if I came home in October, for a few days, return to keep me company through the long and dreary winter nights of next winter? and ever after. I want you above all things to spend one year at Fort Moultrie for various reasons, that you might see the southern people, and become familiar with garrison life. We have here an excellent garrison, with music and company, everything that so attaches us to Army Life, and in the uncertainty of affairs there is no saying how long this state of things may last and how soon I might be sent to some post possessing less opportunity for you to see the Army."

Cump had watched many women adjust to the nomadic life and form an attachment to the army, and he wanted Ellen to have enough experience to make her own decision. He wrote that he knew of no other profession where one is "thrown into contact with only *ladies* and gentlemen" and continued: "[W]e will be as well off as most young men of equal ages, and not possessed of property."

In the realm of religion, Cump promised to bow to her "more pure and holy heart and faith" to intercede for their divine protection in the years ahead. "It would be vain," he said, "for me now to deal in assertions, as you know me and my history well enough to say whether heretofore I have performed my duties to my mother and family in a manner to give you an assurance of continuance of such good conduct toward those with whom I may be destined to spend the rest of my life."

Once he decided definitely on marriage, he wrote Thomas Ewing to ask officially for Ellen's hand, declaring that "My habits are peculiarly temperate and economical" and emphasizing that, while in Georgia, Colonel Churchill had inculcated "habits of business, order and system, which are utterly at variance with my natural inclination and practice of such young subalterns in garrison."

Differences of opinion between Thomas Ewing and Sherman temporarily widened when Cump prompted Hugh Boyle Ewing to apply to West Point. Against his father's wishes, he did so and was accepted. Sherman had never put his thoughts about West Point in any order until he wrote Thomas Ewing on Hugh's appointment: "You have of course given the matter a full consideration and in all probability have resolved that in case he graduates, that moment he resign and make preparation for some civil pursuit or profession.... [But] judging from experience and exposure of hundreds of others, I would not err much in saying that then he would not be so well fitted for civil life as he is at this moment.

"Cadets from the moment they enter the military academy," he emphasized, "are thrown together day after day and year after year, side by side, many in the same room and each depending upon the other for the small social comfort and in consequence form personal attachments, much stronger than are met with at any other college. They are also almost entirely excluded from the world during the four most important years of their life and consequently are easily convinced of the superiority of themselves over everybody else, acquire a sort of contempt for civil pursuits, and live in the hope of one day acquiring the glorious fame of a military hero. These feelings leave an impress upon the mind, long after their better reason and judgment have convinced them of their fallacy."

Rumors of war in Texas and Mexico shadowed Cump's plan for going to Lancaster on furlough in the winter of 1845. Texas had won its independence from Mexico in 1836 and nine years later had become a state of the Union. The Mexican government had then broken off diplomatic relations with the United States. To embitter the situation further, a dispute over Texas's boundary line with Mexico had developed.

Newly elected President James K. Polk's dreams of territorial expansion went far beyond the Democratic platform. He took office determined to acquire for the United States the provinces of New Mexico and California and possibly other parts of northern Mexico as well. He hoped to acquire them by peaceful methods, through the use of diplomacy and money. But if he could not gain them peaceably he was ready to resort to war.

Sherman did not believe there was "a chance for so fortunate a war." He wrote Ellen: "War as such is to be deprecated, but if it is necessary for the interests or honor of the country of course I may with perfect propriety rejoice at the opportunity of being able to practice what in peace we can only profess...."

The tensions eased, and in February, 1845, Sherman went on

furlough. He and Ellen spent a happy fortnight together, but marriage plans, they decided, would have to wait.

War rumors persisted. President Polk sent a small army force under Gen. Zachary Taylor to the border in March, 1846. Braxton Bragg's company at Fort Moultrie was under orders for New Orleans, where it would be converted into a mounted outfit. Sherman sought orders for Texas, but instead, the War Department ordered him to recruiting duty in Pittsburgh, Pa.

Just as he was establishing himself in his new post, news came that a Mexican force had crossed the Rio Grande and had attacked an American patrol. Congress at once declared war on Mexico and authorized the raising and supplying of 50,000 troops. At Palo Alto, north of the Rio Grande, Taylor's army scattered the Mexican forces, and hotly pursuing, the Americans routed the enemy at Reseca de la Palma.

"The news of these victories were spread throughout the land," Sherman wrote, "and there was a universal excitement. For me to stay on recruiting service while a war was going on was so terrible to contemplate that I wrote a strong letter to the Adjutant General, begging him to relieve me and send me to the field." But there was no reply and Sherman became increasingly discouraged. "The recruiting service is progressing slow all over the country," he told John, "and one half the companies are broken up so that officers may be sent out to reinlist new companies. Thus I feel that my efforts to get to Mexico must prove a failure for sometime to come."

Accumulating 30 recruits, Sherman decided to transport them in person to Newport, Ky., in the hope that the superintendent of recruiting for the Western Department would order him west. When he arrived in Newport, he turned the volunteers over to a captain and went on to Cincinnati. Instead of being complimented for his zeal, he "got a regular Army cursing out" by the superintendent and was rerouted back to Pittsburgh.

At his quarters a new set of orders was waiting. He was to go to New York at the earliest possible date and report to Capt. Christopher Q. Tompkins, Company F, for duty. There was also a letter from an old West Point classmate, Edward Ord, telling him that F Company was going to sail at once for California in the naval ship *Lexington*. Sherman was overjoyed. "Ordered to California by sea around Cape Horn!" he wrote Ellen. "Is not this enough to rouse the most placid? Indeed it is so great an event that I cannot realize it in its full force." It was not a fighting front, but California was a part of Mexico and "we shall be pioneers at least in a far off world."

Leaving Ellen so far behind was the hardest part of going west. "But such is the glory of war," he told Phil. "... I would not forego the pleasure of my anticipated voyage round the Cape for any consideration."

"I feel ten years older...."

ON JANUARY 27, 1847, 198 days out of New York Harbor, the *Lexington* made landfall on the California coast and dropped anchor in Monterey Bay. From the quarterdeck Sherman gazed at fresh green grass and at the whitewashed adobe houses of the town, lying in a grove of live oaks with dark pines behind. Monterey swept crescentlike around the blue, sparkling bay. There was a central street from which the other streets radiated irregularly, and toward the center was a plaza around which were a small church and the mansions of the governor and the well-to-do.

Soon after the *Lexington* anchored, Lt. Henry Wise, of the United States Navy, attached to the *Independence*, came on board and reported the news. Months before, while American forces were whipping the enemy in Mexico, units of the United States Army were completing the stranglehold on New Mexico and California. General Stephen W. Kearny had marched into New Mexico Territory without opposition, thus acquiring for the United States what is now Utah and Nevada, most of New Mexico and Arizona, and parts of Colorado and Wyoming. Then Kearny with a force of dragoons departed for California, where he had been appointed governor-designate.

In June the Americans living in the San Francisco Bay region had seized the town of Sonoma and raised a rudely sewn "Bear Flag" as the emblem of an independent republic. In July, Commo. John Drake Sloat had occupied Monterey and proclaimed the annexation of California to the United States. Two weeks later Sloat turned over his command to Robert F. Stockton.

Captain John C. Frémont, an army explorer known as "The

Pathfinder," joined Stockton, and together they received the surrender of the Mexican garrisons in southern California. But the Mexicans renewed their struggle against the Americans, and General Kearny, newly arrived on the scene, was barely able to suppress them. At this junction, Frémont moved in again, was able to make peace, and with Commodore Stockton's approval calmly assumed the governorship of California.

These events were taking place far to the south, and to their disappointment, the officers and enlisted men of Company F realized that they would do no fighting in California. Disembarking from the *Lexington*, they marched to the hill on the outskirts of town and relieved the United States Marine guard. Sherman, however, as quartermaster and commissary, occupied rooms in the Custom House at the wharf.

Not long after Company F had settled in, General Kearny arrived on the *Cyane*. He went on board the *Independence*, where Sherman was dining in the wardroom. Sherman had met Kearny only once previously, but he had always thought him one of the army's best generals.

Sherman thought the general looked haggard and rough, dressed as he was in coarse army cloth with an overcoat slung over his shoulders. Kearny related in detail his march from Santa Fe, New Mexico, to California and his fight with the Mexicans at San Pasqual, where he had lost 3 officers and 20 men. He himself had received lance wounds in the battle.

At the Custom House Sherman issued new uniforms to two of General Kearny's travel-weary officers, Henry S. Turner and W. H. Warner, for which he refused payment. He was so thoughtful and cheerful that Major Turner was deeply impressed by the young lieutenant. By the time he left Monterey, he and Sherman had begun a lifetime friendship.

By April Captain Frémont was in Los Angeles with his battalion of rangers and had assumed such power as to create confusion of authority in California. After the arrival in Monterey of Col. Richard Barnes Mason of the First Dragoons, General Kearny, taking Sherman along as an aide, sailed for San Pedro, the harbor for Los Angeles. Disembarking and hiring horses, the two officers rode up to Los Angeles, 26 miles away, where they conversed with the command of Company C, First Dragoons, and with Capt.

Philip St. George Cooke of the First Dragoons, then in charge of a battalion of Mormon volunteers.

Sherman decided after meeting Frémont and listening to stories about him that he was a "mutinous upstart," eager only to claim the governorship of California. With the arrival of Cooke's battalion and Company C, Frémont could no longer allege his superiority of force. He gave way to Kearny, who ordered the captain to disband his volunteers and to accompany him back to the United States.

Kearny's replacement, Colonel Mason, was a blunt, hard man— a soldier who was a first-rate fighter, but an officer who lacked the pleasant smile and grace of personality that Kearny possessed. On May 1, 1847, Mason assumed command of the Department of California and announced that Lieutenant Sherman would be his assistant adjutant.

By this time Sherman had abandoned his rooms at the wharf for a house in downtown Monterey, staffed by a Spanish woman, a widow, as housekeeper; an Indian cook; and a Negro servant. Three officers joined him at mess daily. The newness and excitement of California, which had at first captivated Sherman, were fast wearing off. "I wouldn't give two counties of Ohio, Kentucky, or Tennessee for the whole of California." And he told Ellen: "The country such as it is, you will, I hope, never see or care about."

The probability of his promotion, while serving in California, seemed remote. He was missing an opportunity for military distinction in Mexico, an opportunity all too rare for a young soldier. "I fear that I leaped the mark in search of glory by coming to California," he noted to Ellen, "but such is the cast of fortune and all must abide by its decrees."

Once he was even tempted to hand in his resignation, for he was chagrined to spend the war in a backwater without ever smelling gunpowder. News of American successes in Mexico depressed him: "These brilliant scenes nearly kill us who are far off, and deprived of such previous pieces of military glory." He became increasingly discouraged. To Ellen, he wrote: "I am so completely banished that I feel I am losing all hope, all elasticity of spirits. I feel ten years older than I did when I sailed, and though my health is good I do not feel that desire for exercise I formerly did. To hear of war in Mexico and the brilliant deeds of the army, of my regiment and my old associates, everyone of whom has gained honors, and I out here in California, banished from fame, from everything that is dear and no more prospect of ever getting back than one of the old adobe houses that mark a California ranche!"

"I cannot reason myself into the belief that it is better that I should be clear of this war," he told Phil Ewing, "for whether it is just or unjust it is the interest of every officer to gain experience in his profession and this can only be done in action, and whilst I have been upon the ocean and here where all is peace others are gaining their experience that will make them our future generals."

Early in the spring of 1848 rumors filtered into Monterey of huge gold and silver discoveries along the western slopes of the Sierra Nevada, east of Sutter's Fort. The military in Monterey soon realized that the report of gold was not just a prospector's delusion. The discovery brought an army of gold seekers streaming into California. San Francisco almost became a ghost town, and it was estimated that two-thirds of the adult population of Oregon had hastened south. Quickly the rough limits of the gold country were marked out. Along the great expanse of the mother lode, any stream or canyon, any ancient gravel bed might conceal a treasure in nuggets, flakes, or dust. Armed with pickaxes and shovels, washing pans and knives, men hacked and dug and sifted the earth and gravel.

Since it was impossible to credit all the stories of rich strikes, Colonel Mason, now the governor of California, decided to visit the goldfields himself. On June 17, 1848, Mason and Sherman, who had been appointed his aide, rode north out of Monterey. They traveled through deserted San Francisco, Bodega, and Sonoma, arriving at Sutter's Fort on the morning of July 2. All along the route mills were idle, houses sat vacant, and farms lay fallow, abandoned for the goldfields.

Sutter's Fort stood three miles back from the Sacramento River and a mile from the American River. Around it large fields appeared to have been cultivated, but they had been trampled under hooves and plodding feet. Where grain had once ripened in the summer sun, there were camps of miners; tethered horses, mules, and burros; entrails and bones of butchered cattle; and tents, shacks, saloons, and stores, the last besieged by frantic buyers who had to have supplies for a try at the diggings. Boatloads of produce were brought from the farms to be sold to transients, lumber arrived from the mill, and flour came by the wagonload.

The overlord of this region was John A. Sutter, once of Germany and Switzerland, who had moved to California in 1839 and had become a Mexican citizen. He early founded and ruled the settlement of New Helvetia in the Sacramento Valley, a semimilitary, semifeudal establishment. The pretentious fort, a quadrangular structure built of adobe brick, became the center of Sutter's domain, where he ranched thousands of cattle and horses and maintained a network of small manufacturing shops to supply his armed retainers. His fort occupied the most strategic position in northern California, so far as the overland trails were concerned, and it became the natural objective for parties crossing the Sierras by the central and northern routes or coming down from Oregon.

Captain Sutter warmly greeted Mason and Sherman. He was "strongly foreign in his manner and appearance," with his sweeping mustache, broadcloth coat, wide-brimmed hat, and Spanish boots. Business was thriving at the fort. Rooms rented for $100 a month and "one indifferent house" for $500; horses that a few months before had sold for $10 now commanded $100. Money was pouring in from rents and sales of land.

At Sutter's urging Mason and Sherman decided to delay their trip for a day to join the Fourth of July celebration. At dinner on that day Sutter presided at the head table, Colonel Mason on his right and Sherman on his left. About 50 sat down to eat, most of them Americans. After the usual patriotic toasts, songs, and orations, the diners helped themselves to liberal quantities of whiskey, champagne, Madeira, and sherry. It was a dinner that would have done credit to any frontier town, and Sherman estimated it had easily cost Sutter $2,000.

Early on the morning of July 5, the two officers resumed their journey. At the sawmill on the north bank of the South Fork, they met James W. Marshall, the mechanic who had first discovered gold. Marshall guided them up the mountain, where, in the beds of small streams, miners were panning more coarse gold. On July 7 the officers left the mill, crossed to Weber's Creek, and worked their way up that stream for eight miles. They saw the heaps of stone and sand dug from holes and heard the sound of shovels grating in the gravel, of picks thumping, of sluice buckets splashing and rattling. They were shown a small gutter where two miners had just reaped $17,000 worth of gold in seven days. Another small ravine had yielded $12,000. Every day new and richer deposits were being discovered.

By mid-July the officers had returned to Monterey. Assessing the trip, Sherman estimated that there were about 4,000 gold seekers and that the value of gold mined was about $40,000 a day. Many men were already rich.

The discovery of gold was fast changing the character of Upper California. "All minds are intent on gold," Cump wrote John. "The citizens of all colors and motives have gone and we are left in the towns almost alone to get our grub the best way we can. Many a one has pulled potatoes, and roasted a piece of meat that in other times would not have touched a dirty handkerchief. A servant cannot be hired in San Francisco, or Monterey for less than $10 a day. Prices of all articles of dress are very high. The Indians who never knew what a breech cloth was now wear a big sombrero. . . .

"I probably can't illustrate the mania or gold fever better than by saying the lazy Californians are actually working, and that the padres of this church and neighboring missions have left their flocks and gone to work for the filthy stuff, none remain behind but we poor damned officers.

"All have their pockets full of gold, and everybody gets more than ten dollars daily for his personal labor, save those in the employ of the government—we are the sufferers."

With rampant inflation, the officers could not subsist in California on army pay. Colonel Mason authorized them to draw rations, and as prices rose their rations became worth more than their pay. To economize, Sherman gave up his quarters and with three others, Capt. Henry Wager Halleck, Dr. Murray Warner, and his close friend Lieutenant Ord, boarded with a prominent Monterey family in exchange for their rations and some money. The head of the house, Don Manuel Jimeno, was frequently off on his ranch 40 miles away, and his wife, Doña Augustina, managed the household in Monterey. Gradually Sherman became a kind of family guardian and was, he said, "very intimate" with the Doña.

Almost simultaneously with the discovery of gold, news of peace with Mexico reached Monterey. Mexico accepted the Rio Grande as the boundary of Texas and ceded the provinces of New Mexico and Upper California to the United States. In return the victors agreed to pay Mexico $15 million and assume the claims of American citizens against the Mexican government. "Great Jehovah!" Sherman shouted. "What a treaty!"

Sherman now urged Colonel Mason to report officially on their journey to the goldfields. Mason assented, and as his adjutant, Sherman wrote the report. Along with specimens of gold dust, it was given to a lieutenant who was under orders to return to the States. He reached New Orleans too late for its incorporation in President Polk's Annual Report to Congress in December, 1848. However, the subject of gold was soon embraced in a special report, and Sherman came to believe that his assessment, fortified by the gold dust itself, was the evidence which dispelled the rumors and counterrumors racing across the country. The arrival of this official intelligence from California "set the whole world crazy."

There was no containing the gold seekers now. During the year 1849, 25,000 of them made their way to California from the East by ship; more than 55,000 others crossed the continent by overland routes.

Bored by his duties, Sherman considered cashing in on the gold rush. He had heard Colonel Mason remark that a Hudson Bay Company's invoice of $10,000 worth of goods would sell in Monterey for $100,000. And he had seen blankets worth $2 in New York palmed off in California for $50.

He was short of capital, but he was convinced that his brother John could make a fortune dealing in merchandise. If John could ship to San Francisco a cargo of highly colored blankets, ready-made clothing, shoes, tobacco, beads, powder, ammunition, wagons with harnesses, and buggies, he could set his own prices. All the gold could not possibly be extracted in a century's time, even though millions of dollars' worth had already been dug, and some men were now earning $5,000 a month. "This is not fiction," he stressed to John. "It is the truth."

Impatient, Sherman decided not to wait for John to make up his mind. He joined forces with Dr. Warner and with Colonel Mason and his clerk. Each scraped together $500, with which they bought a stock of goods and opened a store at the sawmill in Coloma. Such transactions were not prohibited by army regulations. With Mason's clerk as manager, the store operated that fall and winter, and when the partners sold out, each cleared $2,000. Sherman also began speculating in California real estate and occasionally loaning money at high rates of interest.

Making these profits failed to buoy Sherman's spirits. He was still a first lieutenant, and with the war over he had little chance for promotion. To add to his depression, there had been no mail for nearly a year. All the officers felt themselves completely isolated. "I wanted to resign," Sherman recalled, "and so did most of the officers, but Colonel Mason decided that it would be very wrong for us to do so under the circumstances so we kept on."

The arrival of the steamer *California* in mid-February, 1849, "turned us all crazy." Cump received a bundle of letters from home. He read that Hugh Boyle, whose short sojourn at West Point had been an unhappy one, and his cousin Hampton Denman had decided to try their luck in the California diggings. Ellen wrote that she was sending with them a pair of embroidered slippers she had made, cakes of soap, a toothbrush, a black silk cravat, needles and pins, and a watch guard with a gold catch. "I send these which you must consider as so many evidences of my affection for you, Cumpy. The most trifling gift I send bears with it my love, prayers and hopes for you." Ellen had had a picture taken of herself, but at the last minute refused to send it "as I am not so young and pretty as I might be." She missed Cump terribly, she said, and she had doubts more than once whether she would ever be a good wife. In one letter she wrote that she was in poor health and not improving and "I do not hope ever to be able to make a wife—therefore my dear Cumpy if you think that any of the girls of that country compatible of making a companion for you do not let a thought of me prevent your marrying. I have always thought you ought to have a woman much my superior—

handsome, of sprightly mind and character and withal of fine principle and strong affections. If the ladies of California are naturally fine women, and you tell me they are and if they are handsome, you might marry a *young* girl and cultivate her mind and mould her character to suit you after marriage." Health worries, real or imagined, were to play a major part in Ellen's life. She constantly fretted about aches and pains, tried new medicines, and visited physicians' offices.

Thomas Ewing, Sherman learned, had entered political life again. At the Whig national convention in 1848 he had been considered seriously as the vice-presidential candidate, to run with Gen. Zachary Taylor, although the nomination eventually went to Millard Fillmore. But one of Ewing's friends, Samuel F. Vinton, was responsible for piloting a bill through Congress creating a Department of the Interior, and when Taylor was inaugurated, he appointed Ewing its first chief.

Letters from John indicated that after years of drifting and roistering, a new John Sherman was emerging. The year Cump graduated from West Point, John had begun studying law. Now in 1849, in addition to his practice in Mansfield, John had launched into business, proving competent as a partner in a lumber concern and in real estate investments. Prominent in local affairs, John had married Margaret Sarah Cecilia Stewart, the only daughter of a distinguished Mansfield lawyer. He was keenly interested in politics but had not yet run for public office.

Arriving on board the *California* was Gen. Persifor F. Smith, who had come to assume command of the new military division of the Pacific, to be composed of the departments of California and Oregon. Colonel Mason was to be relieved of responsibility when Col. Bennet Riley of the Second Infantry, en route to California, arrived in Monterey.

At breakfast one morning Sherman asked General Smith if he could return to the United States on a furlough and for reassignment. Furloughs, retorted the general, were out of the question. Every man was needed in California.

Somewhat angered, Sherman blurted out his woes. He felt entitled to a furlough. After all, he had been in California for over two years and had been Mason's acting adjutant without any increase in pay or rank. If he returned to Company F for duty, he would become at once the third and lowest officer in the outfit, "a position so mortifying and degrading to my ever humble rank, that I trust you will spare me from it."

Later that day Sherman considered whether it was not a good time to resign from the army and to accept an offer to manage John Sutter's vast California properties. But he rejected the idea, as he knew it took two years of official correspondence and red tape to resign.

The next day General Smith called him to headquarters and asked him to be his acting adjutant, as he needed someone with a familiarity of California and its problems. Sherman assented and began preparations to go to San Francisco. He regretted somewhat leaving Monterey, for his life with Doña Augustina's family had been comfortable, but he especially regretted the end of his association with Colonel Mason, whom he had come to admire.

General Smith set up temporary headquarters at the Custom House in San Francisco. The town had changed dramatically. With the American occupation of California, its population had rapidly increased, and by the spring of 1848, there were nearly 900 inhabitants. Telegraph, Rincon, and Russian hills marked the town's western boundary; the narrow plain on which the adobe and frame buildings stood merged into the waterfront where Battery and First streets now touch Market. San Francisco had established a number of newspapers, had opened a public school, and had begun to be a commercial rival of Monterey.

The first rush to the mining regions had brought this promising growth to a sudden halt; for like all other towns of California, it was virtually deserted by its inhabitants during the first few months of the gold hysteria. But before the year's close, immigrant ships began unloading hundreds of passengers on shore; tons of merchandise were piled in the streets; men were clamoring for places to sleep and eat; and there were eager, hurrying, insistent crowds filling previously empty streets.

In this sudden growth, beauty and comfort found little place. The dwellings were chiefly of canvas or rough lumber, affording only the flimsiest shelter. They straggled from waterfront to hillside, with little attention to the street lines marked out by official survey. Goods were sold at auction in the streets. Gambling and bawdy houses sprouted, and Sherman remembered that it "was impossible to conceive a worse state of morals."

After several weeks in San Francisco, General Smith went north to Sonoma, where he established his permanent headquarters. It was here that he received orders from Washington to grant Sherman a 60-day furlough. For months Thomas Ewing, at Sherman's urging, had been hounding the War Department to take such action.

On their furloughs Sherman and Lieutenant Ord took a surveying job and worked the area near Stockton. This completed, they traveled to Sacramento, then a mere village of canvas and shingle huts, and surveyed for Captain Sutter. After two months they returned to Sonoma with $7,000, enough money to help meet the soaring cost of living in California.

But despite the furlough and the money earned, Sherman remained restless and depressed, as did many of the other officers serving in California. The arrival of Maj. Joseph Hooker, who relieved Sherman as adjutant, left the young lieutenant at liberty to leave the service. "I have had my share," he wrote Mr. Ewing, "and now want to look after my private interests." He became convinced that the army held no future for him, especially after reading the roster of brevet promotions in the newspaper. His name was not on the list, and he felt disgraced.

"I cannot conceal from myself in not receiving some mark of approval, or favor, at the same time," he wrote General Smith, who was then in Oregon, "self respect compels me therefore to quit the profession, which in time of war and trouble I have failed to merit, and accordingly through you I must respectfully tender my resignation of the commission as 1st Lieutenant I hold in the Army of the United States."

General Smith refused to forward it to Washington and pressed him to reconsider. Reluctantly Sherman withdrew his resignation and the general appointed him his aide.

That spring and fall, emigrants continued to pour into the region. Hugh Boyle Ewing and Hampton Denman arrived almost penniless and hastily looked up Cump in Sonoma. It was a warm reunion, the first personal contact he had had with Lancaster in years. After several days of searching, the two men found employment with the army quartermaster.

In December, due to an accident, General Smith was still in Oregon. Sherman, therefore, was ordered to deliver for him a package of confidential dispatches to Washington, D.C., and to see Gens. Winfield Scott and Zachary Taylor to give them his views on the civil government in California. No duty was more welcome.

Before he left, Cump visited old friends in Monterey and arranged with Doña Augustina to escort her two sons to the States for further education. On January 2, 1850, they boarded the steamer *Oregon* for the East.

"You shall be my Adjutant
& Chief Counsellor...."

As THE NEW secretary of the interior, Thomas Ewing had brought his family to Washington and had moved them into Blair House, a roomy, four-story mansion on Pennsylvania Avenue near the White House. The Ewings were soon engulfed by Washington society and had little time to lament leaving Ohio and their home in Lancaster. Ellen, now 26, was particularly drawn into the social whirl of the capital.

Mail service from California was poor. Often months passed before she received a letter from Cump. Her engagement was lasting so long that her hopes for future happiness were growing dim. "I have almost despaired of hearing from you again," she wrote, "and I am now induced to reproach you, who heretofore have been so kind, so prompt, so generous in thought and action, with some neglect or harsh conduct."

On a day in mid-February, 1850, Ellen was in the conservatory of Blair House, giving her canary a bath. Suddenly she heard footsteps, and turning, she saw Cump for the first time in four years. He was startled to see how much lovelier she was than he had remembered. Closing the cage door quickly, she ran into his arms.

He had a six-month leave. "Let's get married on May first," Cump said, "and then we can write our day of joy with all nature." The time was set, the honeymoon trip planned. "The present is ours, let's make the most of it."

The following day Cump took Doña Augustina's two sons to Georgetown College, and several days later he left for Ohio to see his mother and brothers.

In one of his rare tender letters to Ellen, he wrote from Mansfield: "I publically assume the high trust of your Guardian & Master. I will not promise to be the kindest-hearted, loving man in the world, nor will I profess myself a Bluebeard, as there is a wide medium in which the contented happy world moves on, and so will profess contentment and joy. All I believe is that if health be given us, and that love and mutual confidence which I trust we both deeply feel continue, we stand as fair a chance for a slight share of worldly contentment and happiness."

Cump refused to adopt set plans for their future together: "I do not know but that in the uncertainty of our destiny, there be not more true happiness than to be bound down to a certainty. Our hands are not tied and we are at liberty to choose one of a variety of starts on the journey of life, and though our vision extend not far along the avenue, we can form some idea of its character and make a good guess." Touchingly he added: "You shall be my Adjutant & Chief Counsellor, and I'll show you how to steer clear of the real and imaginary troubles of this world. Only be contented, happy and repose proper trust in me, and I think when the time comes for us to part, which I hope will be many a year hence, we will look back upon a fair and goodly prospect. At all events let us live in that hope."

To the adjutant general in Washington, Sherman wrote a lengthy letter requesting that his pay for the period he had acted as adjutant to Colonel Mason and General Smith be adjusted from that of a first lieutenant. He reviewed his experiences and explained that he had written out his resignation, which had not been accepted. "These are all matters foreign to my present subject," he concluded, "but I mention them to show that I fully felt the slight upon my military name and was disposed to take the only step in my power."

His pride was vulnerable and his sense of failure at not being promoted to captain rankled. "The sting is now too deep ever to be effaced," Sherman said, "and I seek it not. I have failed to fill the post assigned to me to the satisfaction of my Government, and my only consolation must be that it was not for want of zeal or effort. This subject is one too painful and delicate to be alluded to by me, except as a collateral reason that at the same time with such loss of military standing I should not lose what might enable me to obtain employment in some more humble sphere."

Ten days later Sherman again communicated with the adjutant general. A bill was before Congress to increase the Commissary Corps by four captains, and he wanted to be considered for one of these commissions if the measure passed. He apologized for proposing himself but cited his bad luck in being posted for the four previous years in distant California, where he had sacrificed his private interests and chance of professional advancement to serve his government.

In Washington plans for the wedding were progressing rapidly. Thomas Ewing decided upon an evening ceremony so that his political friends could attend. In mid-April Washington society received small, lace-edged, engraved cards: "Mr. and Mrs. Thomas Ewing request the pleasure of your company on Wednesday evening May 1st 8½ o'clock." Enclosed were the cards of Miss Eleanor Ewing and Lt. William Tecumseh Sherman, United States Army. Ellen and her mother asked Father James Ryder, president of Georgetown College, to perform the ceremony in Blair House.

Ellen was mildly disappointed that she could not have the "real Catholic" wedding she would have had if she were to have married a man of her faith. But, she rationalized, "well-educated Catholic young gentlemen were scarce and Catholic girls cannot all have an opportunity of marrying suitably in the church." She told herself that to marry a man such as Cump, who belonged to no church, was an intelligent compromise. She cherished the hope that at some future time he might come to believe as she believed.

Belatedly, Ellen began to realize that becoming a wife necessitated a rupture with her past. She was attached to her mother and father and her home. The thought of leaving her family gave her a feeling of insecurity.

As for Cump, like many men who have become accustomed to the state of bachelorhood, he now found it difficult to surrender his freedom. But he had made up his mind that marrying Ellen was the right thing to do.

On his way back east, he stopped off at Philadelphia to visit his sister Elizabeth Reese. He was shocked to learn that her husband's business failure had rendered them almost destitute. Although he had sent her $250 from California, he now advanced a $1,500 loan to keep her family from starving.

The first of May, 1850, was warm and sunny in Washington. Early in the morning Ellen and her mother drove to Saint Matthew's Church for mass. After their return, Cump, alone in the parlor with Maria Ewing, gave her his assurances for Ellen's future happiness. But these promises were unnecessary, Mrs. Ewing told Cump, for her confidence in him was unlimited.

That evening, carriages clattered up to the entrance of Blair House. By 8:15 the guests had arrived; among them were President Zachary Taylor and his cabinet; Sir Henry Bulwer, the English envoy, in court costume; and the distinguished senators Daniel Webster of Massachusetts and Henry Clay of Kentucky (whose gift, a large silver filigree bouquet holder, the bride carried).

In the receiving line after the ceremony, Ellen was so excited that when President Taylor shook her hand, she leaned over and kissed him. "I did not know what I was doing, until I had kissed him," she whispered to Cump. The dinner that followed was stately and lengthy.

After a brief honeymoon in New York City and an excursion to West Point so that Cump could show his bride his old haunts, they visited family in Mansfield and then in Lancaster. As usual on his stays in Lancaster, Cump was restless doing little but visiting acquaintances and making small talk. He was not sorry to return to Washington.

Ellen and Cump arrived at Blair House just in time for a tumultuous Fourth of July celebration. It was an intensely hot day and the crowd, including the president and his official family, stood sweltering, listening to long and tedious orations.

Returning to the White House, President Taylor became ill, and several days later he died. Vice-President Millard Fillmore became the new president. Sherman was ordered by the adjutant general to assist in the state funeral.

During that summer of 1850 the smooth facade of national unity almost buckled from the intensity of the North-South struggle. Two years earlier the nation had won from Mexico a vast empire in the Southwest. Prosperity had come, but not harmony, for the expansion brought the country face to face with the divisive question of Negro slavery. The question, in one sense, seemed hardly worth the national crisis it provoked. Slavery had little future in the territory of New Mexico and less in California. As the Southern extremists fought for the right to bring Negroes into those regions, Northern abolitionists evangelized against this extension of slavery. Most Americans sought to avoid confronting the truth. As patriots, they assumed that sectional conflict could be resolved by compromise. However, not many could look upon the ownership of one man by another simply as an alternative form of economic organization. Slavery was either right or it was wrong; men could not, having faced these dead-end alternatives, stand by unconcerned while it was debated.

By December, 1849, the people of California had overwhelmingly ratified a constitution, organized a government, and were urging Congress to admit the territory as a free state. The South was aghast. To admit California would destroy the balance between free and slave states in the Senate; the idea of allowing new land to become free filled the South with the fear of being surrounded by hostile states.

Through the spring and summer of 1850, debates raged on the Senate floor. Every possible viewpoint was presented, argued, rebutted, rehashed. Southerners reiterated that the South would have to choose between secession and surrender.

Sherman listened intently to the debates, studied the newspaper editorials, and discussed the pros and cons with friends. "Throughout the entire country, peace, plenty, and prosperity are manifest," he wrote his friend Gen. Persifor Smith, "and yet from the debates on the floor of the Senate of which I am a constant (lobby) member, the Country stands upon the brink of a precipice, and scarce a day passes in the Senate, without the rights of nullification, secession and dissolution are discussed, and what amount of oppression will justify secession—I hope and believe it will all come out straight. . . .

"It is the universal clamor for Congress to pass some law, it dont matter what—any law not absolutely disgraceful will be welcomed by all good men—this cry of civil war, secession &c. is becoming too common, and the common even may soon become habituated to it, and think it less be deplored than we have been accustomed to regard it."

The majority in Congress clearly favored some sort of compromise. The Senate and then the House pushed through separate compromise measures. In September California became the 31st state. The rest of the Mexican Cession was divided into two territories, New Mexico and Utah; any states later formed from the territories were to be admitted to the Union when qualified, with or without slavery as their constitutions prescribed. The slave trade in the District of Columbia was abolished, and Congress put muscle into the Fugitive Slave Act of 1793.

The Compromise of 1850 temporarily eased North-South tensions, but no one was completely satisfied with all the provisions of the bill, and extremists in both sections remained unreconciled. Still, hundreds of newspapers gave it editorial approval, and mass meetings all over the country "ratified" the result.

In Washington, Daniel Webster, now secretary of state, expressed the national sense of relief when he wrote: "I can now sleep of nights. We have now gone through the most important crisis that has occurred since the foundation of this government, and whatever party may prevail hereafter, the Union stands firm. Disunion, and the love of mischief, are put under at least for the present, and I hope for a long time."

As the debate subsided it became clear that, because of a division in the Whig party, President Fillmore was intent upon changing the entire cabinet. Thomas Ewing was one of the first to hand in his resignation. Immediately he was appointed by the governor of Ohio to fill the unexpired term of Sen. Thomas Corwin, who in turn had become a cabinet member. Turning Blair House over to the Corwins, the Ewings and the Shermans returned to Lancaster. Young Tom Ewing remained in Washington as President Fillmore's private secretary.

After a few days in Lancaster, Cump drove up to Mansfield to see his mother and brothers. He was pleased with John Sherman's progress as a lawyer and businessman. John, on the other hand, had little patience with his brother, who was "roving about the world fixed in nothing but changeability" and who, after ten years in the army, had little to show for it. He wanted him to resign.

At the same time, Gen. Persifor Smith was writing from California to urge his former aide not to abandon his military career: "On no account resign unless to take advantage of some certainty—to resign, to make experiments on the future is indeed to give up the substance for the shadow and service now in the army does by no means unfit one for other employment when a certainty does present itself."

When his six-month leave expired in September, Sherman was ordered to join Company C, Third Artillery, Capt. Braxton Bragg commanding, at Jefferson Barracks in Saint Louis. Meanwhile, in Washington, Sen. Thomas Ewing was getting assurances from Gen. Winfield Scott that Lieutenant Sherman would receive a captaincy in the Commissary Corps, if and when the bill to increase the army passed Congress.

Cump had fully expected Ellen to accompany him to Saint Louis, but he was finally persuaded by the Ewings to leave his bride with them in Lancaster, as she was expecting their first baby early the following year.

A month later his commission as captain in the Commissary Corps came through, and he was posted in Saint Louis. This appointment was exactly what he had hoped for. With Ellen in Lancaster, he boarded at a house on Washington Street. At his headquarters he gradually mastered the complexities of his new work, and he was again content with his career. There was the chance, however, that by spring he might be ordered away from civilized life to Fort Vancouver in the wilds of Oregon. This possibility upset Ellen.

"Now my Dearest Ellen," Cump consoled, "we must not act like children and be frightened at the first troubles we encounter, but must stand up manfully, make the best of the present, and depend more upon the future.

"For the sake of argument," he continued, "let us admit . . . I am ordered to Oregon. What would I do? Would I resign? No, because I have no other profession than the one I have thus far filled and which has now become one of responsibility—and a good maintenance. To relinquish it for the chances of failure in another beginning would be a risk too great to expose you and yours too—then I am to obey orders, to go to Oregon. Alone?

"No I would take you to New York, where we would despatch to Oregon everything necessary to our comfort there, after which embarking in a fine steamer we would proceed. . . . I tell you, not to convince you, but because you have always been a home body, that there is a good many places in every part of the world, and that it depends more upon ourselves than upon locality, and I would rather have you cheerful and happy on the summit of the Rocky Mountains than dependent and discontented in New York City."

Several of Sherman's speculative ventures in California failed that year. But these reverses did not dissuade him from further speculation.

In late January 1851, Cump was overjoyed with the news of the arrival of a daughter, baptized Maria Ewing Sherman, whom Ellen immediately nicknamed "Minnie." Cump decided that the time had come to establish his family in Saint Louis. "I'm coming for the two of you right away," he advised Ellen.

Senator Ewing in Washington had other thoughts. "Tell Ellen," he wrote Maria, "that she must try and stay until I get home and that I will be responsible for Ellen and the Babe's safe delivery at St. Louis."

But Cump, hurrying to Ohio, insisted that Ellen and Minnie return with him. Ellen hated to leave Lancaster and the security of the house on the hill.

"I had become so perfectly fixed here this winter that I quite felt as if I were never to leave again and should remain always in Lancaster," she wrote her brother Hugh. "I fear I shall be terribly homesick, but Father and Mother are going down, to St. Louis in April & that will help to reconcile me for they will stay some time. Before I knew there was any danger of Cump's being ordered to Oregon I thought St. Louis a great ways off and could scarcely bear the thought of living there but now that I have been well frightened about a worse station I look upon that with very different feelings—But go where we may I am resolved to make the best of our home."

Ellen, Cump, and the baby took rooms at Planter's House, then the most famous hotel in Saint Louis and the largest hotel in the West. It was a focal point where local people congregated to talk business and politics or to while away a few pleasant hours. It was spacious and luxurious with carpets and paintings, china and cutlery made to order in England, and hospitable clerks who remembered guests 20 years after their first visit.

Saint Louis in 1851 was in the process of rebuilding from the devastating fire of 1849, which had wiped out 15 blocks of business and residential property. Each day brought new immigrants from the east, seeking homes, employment, and business opportunities. Others paused only briefly before pushing toward California and the goldfields. If the city's heart remained French and Southern, its robust health was Irish and German.

Saint Louis was the "River Queen," the greatest inland port in the nation, and the levee was still its center. This area was being enlarged after the fire, and still it was crowded—as many as 170 gingerbread-trimmed boats docked at a time along its six-mile wharf. Untidy stacks of freight and produce barricaded the adjacent cobblestones. Mingling with the bells and whistles of the steamers were the sounds of fiddlers, tambourine girls, organ-grinders, and bagpipes and the raucous cries of the apple and orange girls, the shirt women, the cigar and book vendors, the little Negro boiler cleaners, and the bootblacks.

Westward over the hill lay the growing business district, now spilling out beyond Sixth and Seventh streets, obliterating the flowering black locust trees, the old French homes and gardens, and the Indian mounds and sinkholes. Here too all was noise and activity. Old buildings were being destroyed and new ones built; streets were being paved and sewers dug.

The days in Saint Louis passed pleasantly for the Shermans, and by April they were settled in a house on Choteau Street. It was set in a grove of oak trees, a quiet, sunshiny place, and Ellen was delighted to be so independent. She "commenced operations" with a cook, Julia; a boy, Peter; and Catherine, the nurse she had brought from Lancaster. She was in high spirits when she wrote her mother: "We have actually 'gone to housekeeping!' Our house is not very grand and the little furniture we have is not stylish, but we are pleasantly situated and have everything requisite for comfort.... I am begging hard for a wardrobe, but Cump says the money is all gone and I must wait the next payday. Tell Father he must be sure to stop here, for it will not be so inconvenient as he may imagine."

In April Thomas and Maria Ewing did visit the Shermans, and it was an especially happy occasion for Ellen, who had missed them terribly. Thomas Ewing had extensive real estate holdings in Saint Louis, and Cump agreed, in addition to his regular army duties, to oversee the properties and to buy and sell land at his father-in-law's bidding.

Thomas Ewing had finished out his term as United States senator and was now retired from public life, although he never completely lost interest in politics. Even now, in 1851, he had great physical strength and a keen, logical mind. In public and private life he was a man of strong convictions and inflexible will, powerful as a friend or as an antagonist, dignified yet sociable in his relations with men, and a staunch believer in the "good old days."

That spring the Sherman house became a favorite gathering place, and their parlor was the scene of lively dances and card games. Ellen and Cump began to see a great deal of Maj. and Mrs. Henry S. Turner. It had been Henry Turner to whom Sherman had issued a new uniform several years before in Monterey. Now out of the army, the major was a banking partner in the firm of Lucas and Symonds in downtown Saint Louis. He and his wife attended the Roman Catholic church, and Mrs. Turner and Ellen Sherman became warm friends.

Thomas Ewing and Phil stopped off to see the Shermans in June. Mr. Ewing was doing the legal work in closing a lucrative deal for the vast Stoddard property, which overlooked the city. Real estate men assured Cump that in ten years this land would become the fashionable residential section of the city. So with his own savings of $4,000 and help from Mr. Ewing, Cump bought 19 of these lots.

With this investment and other speculative ventures, Cump was experiencing financial strain, and he wrote John: "I had such bad luck in my financial operations [in California] that I will have to settle down to my pay, which in this city is inadequate to my necessities." Cump too was discovering that expense was no consideration with Ellen. Her wants seemed endless. "My household expenses are beyond my means," Cump confided to John. "I thought that gradually I might economize but its impossible."

Pressure was being put on Cump by the Ewings to resign from the army to enter business. "I hope you have not given up the idea of persuading Cump to resign his Post," Maria wrote her daughter. "If you defer much longer you may cease to think of it for it is an established fact that the longer an officer remains in the Army the more reluctance he has to leave it, that he becomes more attached to his profession every day."

There were other pressures. Ellen kept after her husband to embrace the Roman Catholic faith for her sake, for the sake of Minnie and Maria, for his own sake. Occasionally, she called attention to friends who had become converts. At times, she censured him as a nonbeliever.

Sherman's letters to his brother John give every indication that he had no intention of being confirmed a Roman Catholic, although he always displayed a tolerant friendliness toward the church and, through Ellen, supported it generously.

The Shermans took the Stewart Van Vliets into their home. The captain was a West Point classmate of Cump's and a good friend. Realizing the Van Vliets' inability to find proper quarters, Cump offered them a room with full use of the house. At the end of each month, Cump made out the bill of current expenses, including the rent and wages for the cook and houseboy, and Captain Van Vliet paid half the amount. Mrs. Van Vliet and Ellen divided the household chores and the cost of the ironing woman who came twice a week. Fortunately the Van Vliets proved amiable, and everything went smoothly. Ellen described Mrs. Van Vliet as "a nice, trim little Yankee protestant."

Despite this arrangement, expenses mounted for the Shermans. Cump was $800 in debt. In January, 1852, he had asked and received financial assistance from Mr. Ewing, and later, from John. As winter ended, he was beginning to look to the future and to reconsider the possibility of resigning from the army. Not once in his letters during this period did he speak of his military career or of the daily routine of his army post. His correspondence is instead filled with news of speculative ventures in and around Saint Louis.

Often Cump thought of Monterey, the hills of Carmel, and the wild scenes in the "Gold mountains." But the more he studied Saint Louis and the vast Mississippi Valley and compared their possibilities with those of California, the more he was convinced that the former were much richer and better suited to him.

He was pleased to learn that Tom Ewing had decided to settle in Missouri, finally cutting the cord with Lancaster, for he himself was becoming increasingly jealous of Lancaster's hold upon Ellen. "I cannot help feeling sometimes," he confided to Tom, "a degree of dislike . . . to the name Lancaster." Since their marriage,

Ellen had been there too much and "it was full time," he wrote Thomas Ewing, "for her to be weaned."

Ellen, however, made plans to spend the summer with her parents. So with his own future uncertain, and the Van Vliets heading east on furlough, Cump thought the best course of action was to give up the house.

After Ellen's departure, he took a room in a house on Market Street just opposite the Court House. That August orders came. To his surprise and great pleasure, they were not for the Oregon country or Saint Louis again, but for New Orleans. Several days later he received additional information from Washington. He was to relieve Maj. George G. Waggaman in New Orleans, who was in trouble with Gen. David E. Twiggs.

Quickly, Cump disposed of his business affairs in Saint Louis. Ellen, pregnant for the second time, refused to leave Lancaster. Just before departing alone for New Orleans, Cump received news of his mother's death. He was deeply grieved that he could not attend her funeral. "Poor mother!" he wrote Ellen. "She has had hard times and nothing but the kindest, most affectionate and simplest heart could have borne her up under her varied fortune."

New Orleans

IN NEW ORLEANS the rain showers were usually too brief to clean the gutters. After a day of excessive heat, the stagnant water and the garbage slopped in the streets spread fetid odors throughout the city. Yet, for all her squalor, she was indeed the Queen City of the South. Canal Street, reported one sightseer, was the prettiest in America. The shade trees and the enclosed iron fences formed a series of parks for the entire length of the street. On Sunday afternoons the elegant carriages of New Orleans's wealthy went driving out Shell and Gentily roads, and crowds thronged the city park on pleasant evenings. In the cafés, billiard rooms, oyster bars, and saloons, visitors noticed the "French air" of the people. Dwellings in the suburbs were surrounded with spacious yards, landscaped with orange, lemon, magnolia, and other ornamental trees.

Mississippi River steamboating was at its zenith. At the New Orleans levee lay a mile-long expanse of boats; motley passengers —immigrants, soldiers, gamblers, tourists, planters, farmers—and bales of cotton crammed every deck. When the steamboats chugged out on the river, there was a line of twin stacks pouring smoke into the sky. Calliopes thundered, flags waved, and slaves sang "De Las' Sack."

The mightiest river system in the world—the Ohio, Mississippi, and Missouri waterways—flowing southwest, south, and southeast, draining every section of the great central valley, emptied into the Gulf of Mexico at New Orleans. It rolled through the heart of 7 of the 15 slave states and made Minnesota, Iowa, and Illinois the natural neighbors of Arkansas and Louisiana. For Sherman the Mississippi River and its tributaries always held a certain mystique, a power and romance. This, to him, was America. "The Valley of the Mississippi contains by all odds the largest amount of fertile land of any river on the whole globe," he once said. "Its importance cannot be overstated. . . . Whatever power holds it can dictate to the continent. Though railroads and artificial channels of commerce have changed somewhat natural laws, yet the lower Mississippi from Cairo to the gulf is the best channel I know of for the uses of man."

Sherman registered at the Saint Louis Hotel and hunted up General Twiggs and his adjutant. After long conversations with these two officers and a private investigation of his own, Sherman began to piece together the story of Major Waggaman's financial operations.

In purchasing stores for the commissary the major had dealt largely, if not exclusively, with the firm of Perry and Seawell, which had a stranglehold on the army business in New Orleans. Seawell was a nephew of a major who had once served in the Commissary Corps; through this connection Seawell had risen from a coffee and cotton broker on the levee to a rich merchant.

Seawell reaped huge profits from dealings with the Commissary Corps, because prices were not scrutinized. It was not difficult for Major Waggaman to secure a job for his brother with the firm at a good salary. The young Waggaman was too ambitious to remain a clerk and was soon promoted to a full partner. When General Twiggs learned of Waggaman's machinations, he asked the War Department to relieve the major.

As Sherman searched the records, he uncovered other indications of corruption. He was convinced, however, that Waggaman himself had not received a cent of the profit. In a matter of days after the major's departure, Seawell called at Sherman's office. Sherman gave him no assurances of continuing the custom Waggaman had established; instead he rented a storehouse and hired a man to repack all the stores purchased. The Commissary Corps in New Orleans began buying competitively at wholesale like any other New Orleans merchant.

Sherman now moved out of the Saint Louis Hotel and leased a house on Magazine Street for $600 a year. He hoped that Ellen and the children would be joining him before long. Since he was handling huge sums of money, he soon became an important figure in the New Orleans financial circles and was invited to dinners, banquets, and clubs; but when it became evident that he was granting no favors, such invitations slacked off.

That November Cump learned of the birth of his second daughter, who was named for her grandmother, Mary Elizabeth Sherman. Six weeks later Ellen, with the baby, two-year-old Minnie, and Catherine, her faithful maid, left Lancaster for New Orleans.

Cump met the steamboat *Golden Gate* as she docked and with joy ushered his family to the house on Magazine Street. He was delighted with his new daughter, "Lizzie," still a tiny baby with thick dark hair like her mother's.

Ellen found the house terribly small, but livable, and a decided improvement over the Saint Louis home. One of a row, it had two rooms and a hall on the first floor and followed the same plan on the second. There was a back building with kitchen, servant's room, bathroom, hydrant, and cistern. Paved streets and sidewalks extended far beyond the house, and omnibuses running to the city limits passed every few minutes.

New Orleans's cosmopolitan charm captivated Ellen as it had Cump. It was so different from the provincial towns and cities of the Midwest; it had a variety and subtle distinction lacking even in Washington and Saint Louis. "We all like New Orleans very much," Ellen wrote her mother. "We have a pleasant house and I have good girls and so get along, finely."

Sherman's work gave him considerable leisure time, and he often took the family on sight-seeing trips. On Minnie's birthday they went by train to Lake Pontchartrain for a special celebration dinner. It was a pleasant routine, and Ellen would have felt settled if she could have put the uncertainty of their future life in the army out of her mind.

Sherman too was concerned about the future. He could foresee that duty in New Orleans might ruin him financially. His pay, which would have been ample in an ordinary town, was utterly inadequate here. For several years his objective had been to earn a comfortable living and to save enough to insure security for himself and his family. He was beginning to feel he could not do this if he remained in the army.

He continued to be engrossed in various financial possibilities, such as acquiring and improving real estate and investing in speculative ventures. In line with these activities, he wrote a long letter to his friend in Saint Louis, Major Turner, a successful partner in the firm of Lucas and Symonds. Confessing that he was restless and discontented with his low army pay, he inquired about the possibility of joining the company's New Orleans branch. Although in earlier days Sherman had had a low opinion of bankers—perhaps because of contacts with them in his Saint Louis business ventures—he had now changed his mind. Bankers' pay was more lucrative than the army's, and the speculative possibilities seemed endless.

Turner, who for some time had admired Sherman's capabilities, replied: "Take my word for it, the duties of a subaltern, in times of peace, are wholly incompatible with your intellect and energy. By which I only mean, that I don't think such a situation presents a field for the exercise of either."

Although there was no vacancy in New Orleans, Lucas and Symonds were planning to open a branch in San Francisco, to be named Lucas and Turner. The major was to head its operations. He suggested that Sherman arrange a transfer to the Commissary in San Francisco. "I know that you possess an extraordinary business capacity," Turner wrote. "Your situation as Commissary at San Francisco would throw you continually in contact with business men; you would, sooner than any man of my acquaintance, find out & become familiar with the avenues of trade and speculation. You would thus be on hand to avail yourself of the thousand and one opportunities which, as we learn from every quarter, are there presented for making a fortune."

In mid-January, Turner met Sherman in New Orleans and repeated his suggestion. Sherman underscored the point that as an officer in the army, he could not work both for the government and for Lucas and Symonds. He pressed Turner to try through mutual friends in Washington to get him a six-month leave of absence. This would allow him ample opportunity to test the business world of San Francisco before cutting the cord with the army. Before he left New Orleans, Turner made Sherman a definite offer of $4,000 per year plus a share in the profits.

Ellen and Cump discussed the situation at length. James H. Lucas was the richest property holder in Saint Louis, with unlimited credit. Turner was a close friend. Who could be better business associates? This was the time, Cump argued, to leave the army and to establish himself on a firm financial footing. During prosperity, salaried men like army officers were squeezed as prices soared.

On the other hand Ellen hated to go so far from Lancaster. And despite the low pay and past feelings of uncertainty, the army did offer a kind of security. They finally resolved that if Turner could obtain for Cump a six-month leave of absence, he would go to California. At the end of that time, they would reach a decision. "You may depend upon it," Cump wrote John, "that I will not throw away my present position without a strong probability of decided advantage."

John Sherman was enthusiastic.

"In your new undertaking, you encounter some risks, but I think from the statement of your letter, I should have had no hesitation in adopting your course. The spirit of the age is progressive and commercial, and soldiers have not that opportunity for distinction which is the strongest inducement in favor of that profession.

"From your business habits and experience, you ought in a few years to acquire a fortune which will amply compensate you for the loss of the title of colonel. Besides, officers of the Army must either be in large cities, where their pay is insufficient to meet current expenses, or on the borders of civilization, where their families must either be separated from them or share their banishment."

However, Maria Ewing, learning of the proposed venture, wrote her daughter: "Do not Ellen think of ever going there! I shall never consent to it, nor do I think your father ever would."

From New York word came from Turner. He had arranged a six-month leave and had raised the ante to $5,000 per year and a one-eighth share of the profits. Sherman estimated that this would return $7,000 per year, which appeared handsome against his meager $130-per-month army pay.

He decided to go to California immediately. Lucas came from Saint Louis to help expedite his departure and to advise him on financial procedures. The branch was to loan money on proper security, receive deposits, and secure a large part of the western exchange business then monopolized by a branch of Page and Bacon, also of Saint Louis. Sherman and Turner were to have $100,000 working capital, backed by ample credit. As soon as Sherman arrived in California, Turner would return to Saint Louis, leaving him in full command. Sherman signed an agreement promising to stay in the West until January 1, 1860.

The Shermans sold their furniture at public auction for $293.05. Ellen and the children returned to Ohio, where they would stay until Sherman could send for them. "I regret this breaking up," he confessed to John, "but I have counted all the chances and must now await the result."

"...we are not dead by a damned sight."

SAN FRANCISCO had grown tremendously since Sherman was there years before. Sewers, sidewalks, paved streets, commodious and fireproof business houses, and substantial homes had replaced many of the crude dwellings and primitive shacks. Wharves extended a mile out into the bay. Ships and steamers discharged in a day as much freight as scows had taken a month to handle in 1848. "This is the most extraordinary place on earth," Sherman remarked.

The activity and feverish energy which characterized the material development of the city were also evident in its forms of amusement. The saloons and gambling houses, which stood open day and night, were the recognized centers of San Francisco's social life.

"Yet times are changing," Cump wrote Ellen. "Ladies are thronging here by each steamer, churches are springing up in every quarter. Lectures on temperance are nightly listened to by crowded audiences. The city council has already prohibited street gambling and the tendency of things is to root out the gamblers. Their race is run, and their days are numbered."

Henry Turner gave Sherman a hearty welcome to California and prepped his friend on the financial situation. Business still continued to rely upon the mines for much of its prosperity; but a more widely diversified interest in shipping, lumber, agriculture, and other lines of productive activity promised a broader and more secure foundation for San Francisco's future.

The firm of Lucas and Turner was already doing business in a rented room in a good section of town, on Montgomery Street. Gold dust had ceased to be the chief circulating medium and had given place to $10 and $20 gold pieces privately coined and to the

96

$50 "slugs" issued by the assay office. A motley array of silver coins, drawn from almost every country on the globe, served for small change and passed from hand to hand with only a rough attempt to fix values.

San Francisco, reported Turner, was "in its very acme of prosperity." The best and most lucrative business was in discounting paper and loans, with 3 percent a year the lowest rate of interest and some institutions charging as high as 5 percent.

Competition was severe in the banking business. To survive, Lucas and Turner could not rely solely on exchange to make profits. They had to discount paper and loan money on bonds and mortgages. In a letter to the home office, Sherman insisted that for Lucas and Turner to operate successfully in San Francisco, he needed $300,000 working capital instead of the $100,000 originally agreed upon. With this amount, he predicted, they could easily earn $100,000 a year, and after the first 12 months, restore a portion to the bank.

The mails were slow and it was months before Sherman learned that Lucas had acceded to his demands. Satisfied now, he decided to resign from the army. A letter from Ellen indicated that she had serious doubts about leaving Ohio for California. "My hope ... is now," she said, "that you will leave that Country entirely never again to be lured thither by promises of wealth or even by a certain prospect of gaining it. You do me justice in believing that I will cheerfully submit to any course you may determine upon, provided we are not to be separated for years, yet you will not forget to take into account the trial it would be for me to leave my parents, now growing old, with a certainty for not seeing them again for years and a probability of never meeting them again in this world. So if there need anything to incline the balance to either side let this bring you home."

But by now, Sherman had no intentions of leaving San Francisco. "In going to California," he explained to Thomas Ewing, "I knew it was experimental and it has resulted even better than was anticipated. I ... now stand in the position as Chief of a Banking House in the Great City on the Pacific.

"There is no doubt," he continued, "that between going to New Orleans as a Captain and to California as a Banker there is no comparison. Were I to go to the former place I should take my whole family and why not to the latter? There is no doubt of my ability to provide for them handsomely."

Late that summer Sherman went to Saint Louis to consult with his business associates and then to Lancaster where Ellen was already packing for the trip to San Francisco. Her father was opposed to her making the long journey, but when it became obvious that his son-in-law intended to have Ellen with him, Ewing shifted to another tack. He urged Cump not to return to San Francisco, but to remain in Lancaster and become involved with the Ewing business interests. Cump would not hear of it. He said he would much rather be the head of a San Francisco bank than work anywhere in the state of Ohio. Ellen and the children could make periodic trips back to Lancaster.

Ewing then tried to play on Cump's sympathy. He and Maria would be too lonely without Ellen. They would never see the babies again. Ellen might die in California! Perhaps the Shermans could leave little Minnie with them for awhile. At first such a proposal seemed preposterous, but after much thought and discussion, Ellen and Cump decided that it would soften the blow of separation for the Ewings. After all, Minnie could be sent to them before long. They consented.

In September Cump, Ellen, Lizzie, and the new nurse, Mary Lynch, left Lancaster for New York and California. As the carriage rolled down Main Street, Ellen suddenly realized what it meant to leave Minnie. She looked back in tears and saw her father holding the child high in his arms.

From the very outset Ellen detested San Francisco. She was appalled by the dirty streets, the ramshackle huddle of buildings, the vast stretches of sand, and the rowdiness of the people. Speculators, adventurers, merchants, and seamen roistered, gambled, and wenched. "Fancy girls" paraded their wares openly in the streets or from doorways. Fights and murders were commonplace.

The Shermans moved into a rented house on Stockton Street. Ellen complained that there was no backyard, that the street was narrow and full of sand, and that winds whistled through the thin, unplastered walls. Fleas and flies were everywhere, and the neighborhood was overrun with tramps.

There was little of her own furniture to arrange, yet she

worked with the few possessions she had insisted upon bringing, trying desperately to put something of home into the barren place. Cump's surprise gift to her of a piano helped. In the evenings, Ellen would play gay melodies from memory or from the sheet music he found for her. Occasionally, he would dance about the room with Lizzie. His close friend, Gen. Ethan A. Hitchcock, frequently stopped by with his flute, and Ellen played accompaniments.

But for Ellen, housekeeping became increasingly difficult. Good servants were next to impossible to find. Before the first month was out, the Shermans had gone through three cooks. The cost of living was exorbitant. Every Monday morning Cump handed Ellen $75 for the week's expenses—food, coal, and the servants' pay. Yet by Friday it was all gone. Lamb was 50 cents a pound, butter $1.25. Apples sold for $1 apiece.

Cump was troubled with asthma, and it was getting worse. Ellen suffered from her old complaint, headaches. Lizzie caught cold. The house was damp, and there was no fireplace to dry it out and cheer their spirits.

That first Thanksgiving in an excess of self-pity, Ellen confessed to her mother: "I am afraid I will never have that happy art that some Mothers' have of forgetting themselves entirely in their fullness of their regard for husband and children."

She complained, "This is 'El Dorado,' the promised land. I would rather live in Granny Walters' cabin than live here in any kind of style." The wind, the rain, and the sand depressed her, and she claimed that she was not alone in her feelings. "There are *hundreds* here who would go home had they the money to take them." Already she was looking forward to the day she could return to Lancaster for a visit.

January 28, 1854, was Minnie's third birthday, and the Shermans celebrated at home with friends. Ellen well remembered Minnie's last birthday, when Cump had taken the family to Lake Pontchartrain. "How I have changed about of late years for one so fond of home and so inclined to local attachment," she told her mother. "Four years ago in Washington, this day three years ago, at home, two years ago in St. Louis, last year on this day in New Orleans and now in California. It is not improbable that this day, next year, will smile upon me in your midst."

In February Cump bought one side of a brick duplex on

Green Street. It had a parlor, dining room, and kitchen on the first floor and four bedrooms on the second floor, commanding a view of the bay. It had cost $3,500 but it had a backyard where Lizzie could play, and Ellen was overjoyed. She immediately bought a new rug, chairs, and table for the living room.

Once the Shermans were established in their new surroundings, Cump began entertaining important San Francisco businessmen and old army friends at intimate supper parties. There were endless rounds of whiskey punch and games of cards. When the guests were business associates exclusively, Ellen acted as a sort of steward, supervising the cook in the kitchen and directing the activities of the servants. Friends returning to Lancaster reported to the Ewings that the Shermans were living in "splendid style" and that Cump was not only "getting rich as fast as any man could," but that he was "the most popular and influential man in San Francisco."

Ellen was proud of her new home, and it brought her out of her doldrums, but only temporarily. "I am feeling better reconciled to my fate," she wrote Hugh Boyle, "and do not dream quite so often of home." Yet despite the house and her outward contentment, Cump knew Ellen still detested California and was pining for Lancaster.

"If you prefer this outlandish place, because of the business advantages," she told him, "that is no reason why I should be willing to give up home, parents, and friends for life.

"I am content to stay here a reasonable length of time but, Cump, I must be allowed my own opinions. We are making a poor exchange of friends for money. I will not give up my parents and friends in Lancaster entirely. And yet, to see them, I must undergo the fatigue and the exposure and the fear of a sea voyage. I would rather live in Lancaster poor than to be a millionaire away from it. What I wouldn't give to stand one hour in the dear old home with all about me well and happy!"

Cump was discouraged with Ellen's attitude. "I don't know what I'll do," he wrote Turner, "but if she is no better pleased next spring, I may break up, let her go home to Lancaster, there to remain until the expiration of my enlistment."

To Phil Ewing, he wrote a lengthy letter explaining why it was impossible for him to return to Ohio with the family. "I have no profession," he said, "or even a trade, no physical health to undertake a new life, whereas here, I can occupy a place of honor and profit, and by prudence and economy leave something for the children. If I break up every year as I have done the past three or four, it would be folly to expect to benefit my financial affairs."

Major Turner had long since departed from San Francisco for Saint Louis, leaving Sherman completely in charge. With the office lease drawing to its close, Sherman canvassed all possible building sites in the city. He purchased for approximately $30,000 the northeast corner of Montgomery and Jackson, not far from the Plaza, the official center of San Francisco. Montgomery Street was newly graded and planked, and Jackson was now the great thoroughfare to the clipper ship wharves.

Sherman then began planning a two-story bank building, the extra space to be rented to insurance brokers or lawyers. The whole would cost $550,000, but he was convinced that "we will have one of the handsomest buildings in the city." By the last of March he was superintending the driving of the piles and the preparation of the foundation.

Cump had no doubts that the bank's first year's earnings would be $100,000, of which his share would be $8,000. "My expenses are heavy," he explained to John, "but still I can and I hope to lay away from $5–10,000 a year." To Turner he wrote: "We are prospering and I hope another year will make our figures above a million. Neither Lucas nor you desire to be small bankers, and I assure you that I am ambitious of making our name famous among the nations of the earth."

His letters to Turner were full of news about the construction of the new building but at the same time conveyed his nagging doubts about San Francisco's business future. "California has singular ups and downs, not always to be explained from natural causes," he wrote, "but it seems to me that we may assume that San Francisco is beyond question the Great Seaport of Western America, that here must center the commerce of the North West Coast, as well as that of Mexico, the Sandwich Islands &c. Already the Coasting trade is a very considerable item. . . .

"The Miners are this Season doing famously. . . . Notwithstanding this fact, this city is not so prosperous as when you were here. The Merchants complain of high rents & small sales, competition has forced holders of goods to sell at any price so that one cannot but wonder at the heavy sacrifices. . . . The truth is I suppose there are too many merchants for the business, and many of these merchants have inadequate Capital. Real Estate is not Saleable, unless for actual use and then the seller asks old prices."

In mid-July, with much fanfare, Sherman opened the doors of the new building, hung up the sign, "Lucas, Turner, & Co.," and watched the painter letter the word "Bank" on the window.

Although San Francisco was flush with money, business continued dull throughout the summer. The banks were diminishing rather than increasing their loans. The mining industry, though still yielding millions of dollars annually, was unable to support the thousands of persons who had made it their livelihood in previous years. Men came streaming back from the mountains to seek employment in other occupations, especially agriculture.

This transition could not be accomplished without considerable strain upon the machinery of business. Merchants were finding their sales decreasing and ready money far more difficult to obtain. Goods had to be sold in the interior largely on credit, and gold continued to flow out of the state to meet bills already contracted with eastern merchants. Financial difficulties led to nearly 300 business failures in one year.

"California is a perfect paradox, a Mystery," Sherman told Turner. "All large farmers . . . whose names were synonymous with thousands of acres of wheat at a hundred bushels to the acre, turnips as big as a bushel, cabbages as large as our oak tree, are all actually failed or failing, the fact is fences are costly, daily labor from $8 per day, freight to market enormous, commissions, storage, etc. as high as in 1850 and yet wheat is hardly saleable at 90¢ a bushel in the city in good sacks, potatoes 2¢ a lb., barley 2¢ and all produce in proportion."

In addition to these signs of financial trouble, Henry Meiggs, ex-councilman, public benefactor, and leading citizen of San Francisco, absconded, leaving debts of well over $800,000. One city official was arrested and sent to prison for complicity, and another committed suicide. Meiggs himself had fled the state. A banking firm went bankrupt, and other failures were rumored. "The atmosphere is so filled with suspicion that the worst is feared," Cump wrote Turner. He was deeply concerned by the ease with which Meiggs had carried on the fraud, and he began curtailing his loans, especially those he had made for some of his army friends.

Tensions subsided, but almost every banking house had sustained losses, although Lucas and Turner had come out comparatively unharmed. The bank's reputation was increasing steadily.

Sherman's letters from San Francisco at this time showed his eager imagination and a restlessness which had been growing since his Lancaster days. His judgments on various matters were numerous and positive, but he sometimes had difficulty expressing himself correctly, which occasionally led him to make wild statements. He announced plans which he failed to carry out, said things that he did not really believe.

"In giving his instructions," said an observer, "he will take a person by the shoulder and push him off as he talks, follow him to the door all the time talking and urging him away. His quick, restless manner almost invariably results in the confusion of the person whom he is thus instructing, but Sherman himself never gets confused. At the same time he never gets composed."

Throughout these years Sherman was still searching for a road to security, financial stability, and a position in life of which not only he but the Ewings would be proud. He had a great desire to succeed, and to succeed quickly, and he firmly believed this possible.

His belief in a man's duty to his family and associates, to his community, and to his nation was strong. He assigned great importance to facing all situations with honesty and truth, meeting the demands of life head-on, no matter how unpleasant the consequences.

Despite his West Point training, he had as great a disregard for his personal appearance as he had for what others said of him. He was manly but not handsome. Standing nearly six feet in height, he was thin and muscular and there were slight traces of wrinkles now on his face, even though he was only in his thirties. He had thick, sand-red hair, closely trimmed. His dark brown eyes were restless, sharp, and expressive. "With the exception of his eyes," said a friend, "none of the features of Sherman's countenance are indicative of his character."

Sherman could be irritable and sharp-tempered, and he was

susceptible to fits of deep depression. His asthma attacks came frequently now. He suffered so severely that he once wrote, "I care little how soon it terminates fatally." For seven straight months he never enjoyed uninterrupted sleep, and during the nights, was forced to sit breathing the smoke of niter paper. "I am not well now," he confided to Turner. "My head throbs and I have a bad cough. I can see that all here are alarmed. . . . I am weak and pale and much thinner than when you were here." He urged Turner to come west in case he died. He came to believe that sooner or later the climate of San Francisco would kill him, yet he never diverted his energies from the bank and had no thoughts of leaving the city, as he was convinced his presence there added to the stability of the banking house.

Ellen was constantly complaining, and her discontent further depressed him. "We have every substantial comfort that any family could reasonably ask for, and Ellen ought to be content," Cump wrote Phil, "but she is not and probably never will be at so great a distance from Lancaster. I know now how it will result. I *must* stay here. It would be folly, madness almost for me now to give up this position of trust and profit or even to waver in my determination."

Ellen continued to think "California an unfit place for a Christian," he told Hugh. ". . . [F]ate seems to fix me here, and I cannot help myself. Were Ellen to be more satisfied I should be also, but as it is I see it plain that she must go home next spring, and I doubt much if I ever again attempt to bring my family out again. I seem to be cursed to live a vagabond life and might as well submit."

Ellen was convinced that they would have been better off financially if they had stayed in Ohio. Expenses were mounting, yet she was deaf to ideas of economy. "Were we to live any more economically," she wrote her mother, "we would be considered mean. But I drop the subject in deep disgust."

"I occupy an awkward position," Cump wrote. "I cannot confide to Mrs. Sherman the fact that I am not saving money. . . . I can't say a word about economy & the propriety of things but what I am answered [is] that she would rather that I were on a farm barely subsisting my family, than here . . . to which she will not grow accustomed."

The Shermans' first son was born that spring. In the parlor of their home, amongst their friends, Archbishop José Alemany baptized the baby William Ewing Sherman. "Dear Willy" was red-headed, "a Sherman through and through." Cump loved the boy with a tenderness he did not think was possible.

Cump's brother John was elected to Congress from Ohio in the fall of 1854. Not content with county-town law and business, John Sherman had entered politics in the late 1840s and faithfully attended the state Whig conventions. He ran for no elective office until 1854, when the wave of antislavery sentiment carried him into the House of Representatives in Washington along with many other comparative unknowns. During those early years his views were strong in opposition to the extension of Negro slavery into the western territories, and he had wholeheartedly supported the compromise measures of 1850. He became a hard and effective worker for the newly formed Republican party and was elected chairman of the first state Republican convention held in Ohio.

John Sherman stepped into a violently disturbed national arena. The political settlement between North and South in 1850 lasted but four years, until 1854, when Congress passed the fateful Kansas-Nebraska Act. This act organized into federal territories the land west of Missouri and Iowa which lay north of latitude 36° 30″ in a district from which slavery had been excluded since 1820 by the Missouri Compromise. Whether the new lands should become slave or free was left to the decision of the settlers. With the passage of the Kansas-Nebraska Act, the nation took its greatest single step toward civil war.

When Northerners learned that the western territories were now opened to Negro slavery, they responded almost with one voice—businessmen, ministers, lawyers, and newspaper editors taking the van. Such unanimity and force of reaction in the free states had not been seen in America since the Stamp Act. Abolitionists stepped up their campaign. Extremists in the South vociferously defended their "peculiar institution" and their right to transport their slave property into Kansas and Nebraska.

John Sherman had run on an antislavery ticket, but Cump hoped his brother would not be too outspoken during his first term, especially on the Negro question. "Having lived a good deal in the South," he wrote John, "I think I know practically more of slavery than you do. If it were a new question, no one now would contend for introducing it; but it is an old and historical fact that you must take as you find it. There are certain lands in the South that cannot be inhabited in the summer by the whites, and yet the negro thrives in it—this I know.

"Negroes free won't work tasks of course, and rice, sugar, and certain kinds of cotton cannot be produced except by forced negro labor. Slavery being a fact is chargeable on the past; it cannot by our system, be abolished except by force and consequent breaking up of our present government."

On the Kansas-Nebraska Act, Cump advised, "The bill . . . was a mistake on the part of the South, a vital mistake that will do them more harm than all the violent abolitionists in the country. Let slavery extend along the shores of the Gulf of Mexico, but not in the high salubrious prairies of the West.

"It was a mistake to make Missouri a slave State; but it was done long ago, and now there is no remedy except in the State itself. Slavery can never exist here nor north of us, so the North now has the power and can exercise it in prudence and moderation."

Cump persuaded Ellen to leave the children in San Francisco while she returned to Ohio in the spring to visit her parents. Needing more space for the children to play, he sold his duplex for a small profit, purchased a cottage on a large lot on the corner of First and Harrison, and contracted to enlarge it.

Ellen was pleased by the view and the huge yard for the children to run in. "The house will be a first rate one as good as I want," Cump told Turner. He realized that $9,000 was more money than he could spare, but with Ellen so insistent, he decided to borrow $7,000. Meanwhile he invested $500 in the Sacramento Valley Railroad and was elected its vice-president. He was sure that the road would eventually pay heavy dividends.

On February 14, 1855, the cash balance of Lucas and Turner went over a million dollars for the first time, yet Sherman was still deeply concerned over the financial condition of San Francisco. In a letter to Turner, he explained: "[H]ard times continue. . . . Hard is not the exact phrase but dull flat & stupid—No rain, & no gold, and no business—Such a period of Stagnation in all the interests of the Country has not been since the discovery of gold. . . .

"A great deal of attention has been drawn recently to the fact that Emigration to this Country has almost ceased, and the overland Emigrations yearly diminish so that we need population— Our cities and towns are far in advance of the Country and this is the principal reason of Stagnation in business.

"One thing is certain," he added, "that unless we receive greatly increased Emigrations this Country must settle back into a condition of business that will not justify the rates or rent & interest that has produced so much profit to Merchants & Bankers. ... It is as dull along Montgomery Street as in a village on Sunday."

Letters from the home office confirmed that a Saint Louis banking house, Page and Bacon, was "financially embarrassed" and that there was disaffection in its San Francisco branch, then the leading bank of California. Sherman began calling in some of his loans, and following Turner's advice, discontinued banking privileges to banks in other parts of the state.

On February 17 the regular mail steamer *Oregon* neared the wharf on North Beach. Some of the passengers called out to a man on the dock that the home office of Page and Bacon had failed. News of the collapse raced through the financial district. Officers of Page and Bacon quickly informed their customers that the San Francisco branch was solvent and that it was controlled by a different partnership than the home office. Refusing to listen to such explanations, small depositors presented their checks and certificates for payment. On that first day Page and Bacon was able to meet all the demands, and there was no run on the other banks.

On Monday at 9:00 A.M., Page and Bacon opened as usual. The bank seemed to have everything under control. Deposits were made, checks drawn, but more money was going out than coming in. Tuesday and Wednesday were the same.

On the following day, Washington's Birthday, there was a huge parade down the streets of San Francisco. Page and Bacon failed to open, but many citizens believed that it was because of the holiday. By noon, however, it was being whispered that Page and Bacon was bankrupt. Sherman had learned this earlier in the day, when a friend told him that a receiver had been appointed.

While many people lined the streets watching the parade, others were drawing their money from their banks, Lucas and

Turner included. After a close check of each depositor's account, Sherman was confident that his bank was sound and could weather a panic. The books showed that he had on hand $480,000 in cash; $60,000 in gold bullion, ready for shipment to the East; $700,000 in notes, with large additional securities in state, county, and city funds and scrip; and about $100,000 in mortgages. The bank owed its city depositors, those who could call the next day, about $650,000. If there were an actual run on the bank, all he would have to raise would be $65,000. And he was sure that his friends would take his word that Lucas and Turner was solvent and not demand their money.

On the morning that he was to fight "The Battle of the 23rd of February," Sherman arose early and walked to the bank. Crowds milled about Montgomery Street. It seemed as if everyone in San Francisco were demanding his money.

At the entrance of Lucas and Turner, Sherman pushed through the crowd, hurried inside, and gave orders to his employees on how to meet the pressure. At 9:00 A.M., when the doors swung open, the mob surged in, pushing and jostling. Remaining cool under the press of people, the tellers carefully examined the checks and certificates. If good, they paid them calmly and without confusion. Sherman paced the floor behind the counters. Suddenly, a group of friends poured into the bank to ask, "For God's sake, Cump, what are things coming to?"

Slowly, he explained that he did not know what other banks were doing, but that Lucas and Turner would never break. In a loud voice, so that most of the customers could hear, he suggested that anybody feeling nervous about his deposits could step up to one of the tellers and draw all his money. Many of Sherman's personal friends took his word that Lucas and Turner was solvent and left the premises without drawing a cent.

Assured that the machinery of the bank was running smoothly, Sherman went out and called on all important depositors. He pledged the bank's ability to stand the run, and to a few, confided that Lucas and Turner would be pushed, unless it could come up with an additional $65,000.

He returned to the bank. By 1:00 P.M. the crowd had died away; yet, depositors kept coming in one by one to cash checks and certificates. By 3:00 the bank trays looked slim, about $40,000 in small gold and silver, and the situation began to look desperate. Rumors circulated that there were serious runs on other banks and that Adams and Company and several smaller banks had closed their doors, while Wells Fargo had not opened at all.

Palmer, Cook, and Company, however, a bank which received all city, county, and state taxes and was therefore not liable to sudden calls, had experienced no panic. That afternoon Sherman had a short conversation with its officers and came away with $10,000. A friend brought in $5,000 from his assay office and others Sherman contacted deposited small sums. Word went around the city that the run on Lucas and Turner had ceased and that deposits were coming in. The clock was provokingly slow, but at last it was closing time. A hurried check disclosed that $45,000 remained and not one dollar of the bank's securities had been pledged.

"The Battle is over," Sherman wrote Turner enthusiastically, "and we are not dead by a damned sight.

"A magnificent future opens before us," he added, "and you may be easy that whilst aiming to deserve and avail ourselves of any and every opportunity, I shall not lose sight of the lesson taught by this awful calamity."

Although certain individuals had been ruined financially in the panic, the general economy of San Francisco did not collapse. The crisis destroyed only two of the great banking houses, Adams and Company and Page and Bacon, and two smaller institutions. Wells Fargo resumed operations quickly, but Sherman never forgot that it had let Lucas and Turner bear the brunt of the panic.

Upon reflection, Sherman wrote several days later: "I am beginning to take a different view of the effects of this Run—it was a tornado required to purify the elements, and I feel assured that it has not been as disastrous as it at first sight appeared. The aggregate amount of money lost to individuals is not great and is widely distributed."

Sherman was proud of what he had done and believed that his judgment on the day of the panic had been superior to that of many individuals who knew more about ledgers and daybooks and bills receivable. "I find mathematics as applicable to banking as to artillery," he said. He was indebted to his old army friends, who had sustained him and inspired public confidence in Lucas and

Turner. But he was angered at most of the businessmen and merchants who, instead of hurrying to the rescue, had sat in their offices, "scared and paralyzed," leaving Lucas and Turner to stem the current unaided. "War is fool's play compared to this," he told Turner. "I thought when leaving the Army, that wars and rumors of war could be forgotten, but it is one continuous strife."

He was deeply pleased when he received a congratulatory letter from Major Turner, sounding him out about going east to head up the bank in Saint Louis. "I do believe you . . . really are deceived into the belief that I am of some importance," he answered, "but don't let that belief carry you beyond my load of responsibility. You must know by this time that I don't love money but that ambition is mixed up with my plans."

To Thomas Ewing's still-frequent suggestions of returning to Ohio, Cump wrote: "As Mr. Lucas and Major Turner have done everything I could expect, I am determined if I live to stick out my full term of six years, and then will be prepared to act for the future. . . . I am better known here than anywhere else. I have been so long identified with California that it would be foolish to change, so I look upon this as my home, and whether I ever change is a question I leave to be solved by the future." At times, Cump told Ewing, he felt that he would like to be free from the anxiety of credit transactions, "but I am in for it, and must take the chances."

"...it is a lesson I will never forget...."

THE EVENTS of February had drained Sherman physically and mentally. He suffered a severe attack of asthma aggravated by a cold and inflammation of the lungs, and in the days that followed, he became depressed, convinced that his asthma was incurable, and in time, would be fatal.

In one of his black moods he wrote Turner that the banking business was becoming a "terrible drudge." "All day," he said, "questions of thousands of dollars must be despatched without hesitation and here is night with piles of money to be arranged, counted, &c., boxes of bullion to be packed, Notes & drafts to be arranged and classified, letters & lists to be written. Our Clerks have hard work, there is no doubt of it. Midnight will not let us off this time, and instead of getting lighter, it is getting harder."

Sherman regretted that he had bought the new property on Harrison. He could not afford it, and he began to wonder if he were following a false path. Yet Ellen was pleased with the new house "as indeed we all are," he explained to Turner, and "this will serve to make her contented & of course ease my situation materially—Building is a dangerous thing at all times but I hope I am now done with it, and will never be called on to do it again. I certainly shall not as long as I am in California & hope what I have done will not seriously embarrass me."

In April the Shermans moved into their spacious house. Ellen, who was to visit Ohio without the children, refused to make the trip unless there was some responsible woman to care for them. She made an arrangement with friends, the Bowmans, and Mr. Nesbitt, Cump's assistant at the bank, to live at the house in her absence. This was not to Sherman's liking, but it was preferable to shouldering the expense of hiring some woman who would have "to be fed on sugar plums." That spring while she prepared to depart, Ellen could not mask her sadness at leaving Willy and Lizzie, but in her letters to her mother, she never once indicated her feelings at parting from Cump.

On May 13 Ellen arrived in New York and met her brother Charlie, who was to escort her to Ohio. That evening in her hotel room, she wrote a lengthy letter to Cump: "I find I have got to nerve myself daily to bear up, or I shall be grieving for the children as I grieved for Minnie when I first went to San Francisco. And yet I do not regret having left them." She then told Cump that, according to Charlie, Mr. Ewing could not live without Minnie, so they would have to give her up for his lifetime. "The probability is we will have a large family and it would seem the more selfish to refuse one to Father. Do not ask me to take her away from him—I know you are too kind to insist upon it."

Back in the familiar surroundings of Lancaster, Ellen began missing Cump, and her letters indicate that she was genuinely concerned about the recurrence of his asthma attacks. "The apprehension of your suffering," she wrote, "distresses me more and the possibility of my absence from you, driving you to seek pleasures you would otherwise not think of would put an end to all my happiness could I admit it to myself. If you feel the loss of company and want me to come home I hope you will say so. It is of course my duty to be near you unless you can freely consent to my absence as you did when I left."

Once at midnight, Ellen sat writing: "Minnie is sleeping sweetly near me but my heart is yearning for those who are so distant from me. What I would not give to be with you now— to know that you are well and happy and to enjoy your amiable and entertaining society. How much more closely our married life binds our hearts and interests? You are now so necessary to my happiness that I feel as if life would lose all its charms and I would be desolate indeed without you."

Ellen was pleased when she received word from Cump to let Minnie stay with the Ewings. "We fully appreciate your kindness in consenting to give her to them," she wrote. "I feel it to be far more generous act on your part than on mine—for it is to *my* parents she is given. Be assured that you are kept alive in her recollections and that all her powers of love and respect are awaked in your regard."

In early December Ellen returned to San Francisco. She thought Cump seemed weighted with business worries. He was doing double duty at the bank while his assistant was away, and often sat up all night finishing official reports for Saint Louis. At the same time, he was becoming more involved in civic affairs.

His reputation in San Francisco was mounting rapidly. He was appointed chairman of the Committee to Memorialize Congress for the Building of an Overland Wagon Road to California. He rejected candidacy on the regular Democratic ticket for city treasurer. When the officials came to Sherman to offer him the nomination, he told them frankly that he was not a politician and not a Democrat; he was a Whig.

That fall and winter the merchants in the city were buying and selling on credit. They had considerable capital, but on their speculations they leaned heavily on the bankers. Sherman began watching their operations and was worried to see them writing checks without regard to their balances. Usually after banking hours they would come to the office with sufficient cash to cover their checks for that day, but the practice was unsound. Sherman, determined to stop it, instructed his tellers that when someone had no money to his credit, they were to answer, "No funds. Call after 4:00 P. M." It was soon known throughout San Francisco that Lucas and Turner had refused the checks of several influential merchants. Sherman, when queried, simply explained that the checks would be covered but that he would not pay them in advance of deposits.

High-ranking San Franciscans continued to contend they had the right to write checks all day provided they made the account good by nightfall. "It may be that I am not sufficiently courageous for success," Sherman wrote Turner, "but it is one thing to venture one's own neck and head and another to venture the wealth and name of others who have trusted to me and who ought to expect rather excessive caution than excessive boldness."

Letters from Turner were encouraging, congratulating Sherman on his prudence and on his growing reputation throughout the city. As a token of appreciation for his fine record, the firm offered to buy the now completed house on Harrison Street and let the Shermans live there rent free.

Sherman was pleased with Turner's confidence, but he refused the offer. "I am perfectly satisfied with my position and prospects," he told the major, "and would rather be associated with you and Mr. Lucas than any two men on earth, and yet I would not go through the keen cares and anxieties of last year's experience for an absolute fortune."

As one of San Francisco's most prominent bankers, he continued to avoid political factions and social movements. However, on a day in May, 1856, the governor of the state, J. Neely Johnson, called at the bank and offered Sherman a commission as major general of the Second Division, California State Militia. Sherman was averse to accepting, as it would distract him from the banking business, but Johnson argued that the appointment was simply for the purpose of organization and that little time would be necessary to perform the duties. The governor persisted, and reluctantly Sherman agreed.

Throughout San Francisco the crime rate was increasing rapidly. Corrupt officials were making a mockery of the law. James King, the owner and editor of the *Daily Evening Bulletin*, crusaded against those whom he considered guilty of corrupting the city's morals or of defrauding the people through political power. He dealt in personalities rather than in generalities and did not hesitate to publish the names of offenders.

King was waging a newspaper war with the owner of the *Sunday Times*, a politician named James Casey. Sherman regarded Casey as "a scamp," who was deeply involved in the political machinations of San Francisco.

On May 14 at 5:00 P.M., Casey, enraged at what he had read about himself in the *Bulletin*, shot King on the street and then surrendered to the sheriff. The city was aroused. There were threats of lynching, and a call went out for the members of the old Vigilance Committee of 1851 to meet. The mayor, in turn, called out the volunteer companies, but that night passed without incident.

On the following day, Sherman, determined to support the

forces of law and order, visited the jail, where he found the sheriff uneasy, anticipating an attack. After a hasty reconnaissance, Sherman informed the mayor that the city jail could not be defended; a mob could easily occupy the few surrounding buildings and drive out any posse that the sheriff might command.

That evening the volunteer companies called up by the mayor failed to muster. The Vigilance Committee was in session. San Francisco was taking sides. Those representing law and order were vehemently opposed to the Vigilance Committee and its methods. "These events have shaken my confidence in this city," Sherman wrote Thomas Ewing, "and once or twice I have wished that [my family] were in a safe place, and regretted that I ever incurred the expense of my dwelling house, which must tie me down here.

"Of course I myself cannot leave here, but if matters do not improve, I may at some future time accept your kind offer to take them home till such time as I can properly return. . . . Understand, I fear no molestation of person, but I fear the effect of this on property, on money and credit."

Late afternoon on the following day, Sherman met with a 60-man posse, which the sheriff had gathered. He explained that as major general of the California Militia he had no authority to lead them; by law the sheriff was the legal peace officer. He pointed out the jail's vulnerability to attack unless the surrounding buildings were occupied, but it was too late for that. Vigilance Committee members had already taken them over.

Throughout the day the Vigilance Committee had been strengthening its position and now totaled 5,000 members. Sherman and Governor Johnson met with William T. Coleman, the committee's president, who reiterated that his purpose was not to subvert the law, but to aid the community, purging it of ne'er-do-wells. Courts and juries were useless. The conference broke up with the understanding that no mob violence was contemplated.

King died the next day. The funeral was scheduled for Sunday, and Sherman felt sure that the leaders of the committee could not control their men and would be forced to take extreme measures. Casey and Charles Cora, a prisoner who had killed a United States Marshal, were doomed. "All the elements of the Paris Committee of Safety are here," he said, "and once put in motion they cannot be stopped. I regret having been placed in this position, but I am bound in honor to serve the governor of the state to the best of my means and ability."

On the day of King's funeral, the mob broke into the jail and hanged Casey and Cora in the street in front of the committee rooms.

"San Francisco is now governed by an irresponsible organization claiming to be armed with absolute power by the people," Sherman wrote Turner. "The government is powerless and at an end. I don't care if they take the jail, the courts, and what they please." The hanging of Casey and Cora was a trifle in comparison to what might follow. "The Vigilance Committee are now in full possession of San Francisco, and in a free American country, where we pay taxes and four percent on full valuation, we are now at the mercy of irresponsible masses."

Sherman went to Benicia to meet the governor and Gen. John E. Wool, who commanded the forces of the United States Army in California. It might be necessary, Johnson said, to call out the militia to enforce the law in San Francisco. He had no arms or ammunition, but the army had an abundance.

"Now General," Johnson said, "all our plans turn on you; in case I am compelled to call out the militia can we depend on you for arms?"

General Wool promised that they could rely on him.

On the first of June, 1856, the judge of the state supreme court in San Francisco issued a writ of habeas corpus commanding the sheriff to bring before him one William Mulligan, known to be held in one of the Vigilance Committee's jails, and to show just cause why he was held in illegal custody. The writ was ignored.

Governor Johnson ordered Sherman, as major general of the militia, to enforce the law. Since the militia existed only on paper, Sherman issued a call in the newspapers for volunteers. About 800 men came forward and were mustered into companies and regiments. The newspapers throughout the city supported the committee and poured invectives on Sherman and all who were in agreement with his position.

In Sacramento the governor sent his aide to General Wool with a letter requesting him to issue the necessary arms and ammunition to the militia. Wool replied that it was unsafe to ship arms to San Francisco. Sherman was furious, as he had relied on the general's promise of support.

San Franciscans believed that bloody civil war would erupt at any minute. A group of "the best men" of the city, representing the moderates from whom Sherman and the governor derived their main strength, sought an interview with Johnson to see if the matter could be settled without an appeal to arms. Sherman escorted them to Benicia, where they met with the governor and his advisers. There were heated arguments and counterarguments, and the moderates finally left in a huff.

After the interview, Sherman informed the governor that he had exhausted his efforts to help and wanted to resign. He resented the fact that arms had been refused. He had a militia commission to quell civil strife but was powerless to act. As the governor expressed no objection, Sherman wrote out his resignation, walked out of the hotel, and caught the steamer for San Francisco.

"I believe that night, through the instrumentality of that [moderate] committee," Sherman wrote Thomas Ewing later, "I would have brought the Vigilantes to a dead standstill, with absolute submission to the law, or could have so placed them in the wrong that all good and moderate people would have joined us."

With Sherman's resignation, all show of resistance against the committee ceased. Nobody but the most active supporters would serve under the new major general, and nobody would enforce the governor's proclamations. Sherman was deeply troubled. The existence of the committee was treason. Honest men were applauding its actions; even the moderates now were approving what had been done and what was intended.

Sherman knew the men who had usurped authority: they were "very ordinary men." "Here in this country," he wrote John, "the Democratic—a mob—element prevails to such a degree that, as you will have observed, the influence of governor, mayor, and all the executive authority has been utterly disregarded. For three months here we have been governed by a self-constituted committee, who have hung...men, banished...others, imprisoned, and ironed many more.... if we are to be governed by the mere opinion of the Committee, and not by officers of our own choice, I would prefer at once to have a Dictator."

Sherman's observation of the Vigilance Committee reinforced his loathing of mob rule, his scorn for politicians, and his contempt for popular opinion. He distrusted the public mood, which could be manipulated by the press and unprincipled demagogues to sanction excesses.

"I am sick of this whole matter," Sherman wrote Turner, "and I believe the community is fast becoming so, and therefore I will drop the subject, leaving the newspapers to keep you advised. . . . I am out of it, and believe that I have lost nothing in public estimation in what I did. At all events it is a lesson I will never forget—to mind my own business."

In the days that followed he remained aloof from all parties, but he was disgusted with the Vigilance Committee's secrecy, street forts, parades, and mock trials. Gradually, however, the work of the committee subsided, and the city was calm again.

As the local crisis faded, Sherman became increasingly concerned over national politics in which he had taken a much keener interest since John Sherman's election to the House of Representatives. He watched with deep anxiety the North-South struggle. He felt the politicians were so complicating the situation that the Southern states would eventually secede and precipitate a civil war.

To John, he wrote: "Unless people, both North and South, learn more moderation, we'll see sights in the way of civil war. Of course, the North have the strength, and must prevail, though the people of the South could and would be desperate enough. I hope in Congress you will resolve yourself into the fighting branch and work off some of the surplus steam that is threatening to blow up the Union."

The Vigilance Committee episode had distracted Sherman's attention from his own financial affairs. Everything he earned, it seemed, was spent immediately. Ellen attempted greater economy, but it was no use. Neither Ellen nor Cump could change their living habits. They had to keep up a degree of respectability, and they entertained on a grand scale. "I don't think I am one dollar's richer this day than when I left New Orleans," Cump lamented. Although the bank had a splendid reputation, it was not earning profits as large as had been calculated. The exchange business was losing money, and deposits were small.

San Francisco had overbuilt. Property values had plummeted. Rents were low; profits were almost nonexistent. The home office hinted at closing the San Francisco branch, but Sherman would not hear of it. It was bad policy to quit during a period of adversity.

Adding to his worries was his concern over the accounts of his army associates who had trusted him with their savings. Many officers, upon arrival in California, had deposited their money with Lucas and Turner and asked Sherman to invest it for them. From across the country he had received letters from old friends with similar requests. From Carlisle Barracks, in Pennsylvania, one man wrote: "As I do not know much about such matters I confess according to the existing rumors I feel more safe with my affairs in your individual hands than to have them in any House under the sun." Altogether, Sherman had invested more than $100,000 for friends.

When Page and Bacon and other institutions failed, many of these investments became worthless. Although he was not legally responsible for the losses, Sherman felt it a point of honor to repay in full those who had trusted in him. To accomplish this, he drained his own savings.

Braxton Bragg, a friend from the days at Fort Moultrie who had resigned from the army, realized that Sherman, amidst his own financial difficulties, was trying to defray his friends' losses. "Your feelings and actions for your friends, my dear Sherman," he wrote, "are most fully appreciated and believe me sincere in the assurance that you are not [only] sustained in all you have done for me, but I feel an obligation I can never forget.... It will not be forgotten." Other grateful comrades wrote similar letters.

Ellen still badgered Cump to leave California, as did her father, who kept urging the Shermans to come back to Ohio. Once he offered to pay all the traveling expenses. "If you were free from your engagement I assure you could soon make a handsome fortune here," he wrote Cump. The uphill struggle in San Francisco seemed not worth the effort. But, Sherman told Mr. Ewing: "You can understand I am in a tight place. I am bound in honor to stay here as long as I agreed, and then if nothing material is found, necessity will force me to continue. . . . I had no right to come here unless I intended to stay and interests of too great importance have been placed in my hand which do not admit of shifting without great detriment so all I can do is to go on and do my best trusting to luck in the future."

That fall a second son was born to the Shermans. Father Gallagher baptized him Thomas Ewing Sherman after his grandfather. "I hope," Cump wrote Mr. Ewing, "he will grow up a strong healthy man and do credit to his name."

Early in 1857, the decision was made to close the San Francisco branch, despite Sherman's pleas. Lucas decided he did not want his money tied up in a distant and financially precarious region. In March Sherman received final instructions to wind up affairs and return east to represent the firm in New York City. The offer was so attractive that he could not decline.

Sherman and his associates set to work reducing credits and loans; then they gave public notice to all parties having deposits with Lucas and Turner to withdraw them. The bank was leaving California.

"On the whole," Ellen wrote Maria Ewing, "I think Cump feels great regret at leaving here and he had fully made up his mind to spend his life here, and would rather do that than relinquish his undertaking. I feel like one relieved of a terrible burden and I cannot feel any sympathy for Cump's disappointment—for it would have been at too great a sacrifice on my part that he would have staid here."

"...wherever I go there is a breakdown...."

IN THE SPRING of 1857, the Shermans arrived back in Lancaster almost penniless. Cump was forced to leave his family in Ohio while he went on to New York. He left Lancaster asserting that if the family followed him east it would destroy his peace of mind. To Ellen, this was a mean and harsh statement as it was not accompanied by any regret of separation or evidence of affection. "It is against my will and judgment, and inclination," she wrote, "that we live apart for any lengthy period, but if I cannot help it I must bear it as well as possible. Let me persuade you against too great a despondency as to your business affairs."

The New York office of Lucas and Turner opened its doors on Wall Street on July 21, 1857. At first Sherman boarded at the Metropolitan Hotel but later moved to a Mrs. Van Nostrand's at 100 Prince Street along with an old friend, Maj. John G. Barnard of the Army Engineer Corps.

The new surroundings failed to lift Sherman from his black mood. He was in deep debt. His property investments in California, his house and lot, and other real estate he owned were "dead losses." Family expenses far exceeded his income even with the family living in Lancaster.

As the California depression worsened, more army officers for whom he had invested savings were requesting their money. By the summer of 1857, Sherman had repaid all but $20,000 of the $130,000 entrusted to him. "I was not bound by this," he explained, "but I did it rather than feel that I had been party to their losses." He wrote John that he was "used up financially" and forced to sell his property in Saint Louis.

His analysis of business conditions in New York City con-

121

vinced him that "banking was overdone." Competition was keen and the smaller banks operated at a disadvantage. Lucas and Turner was forced to rent expensive offices, hire high-salaried clerks, and offer inducements to the western banks to use their services at low commission rates. "In my judgment the business is not lucrative, while at the same time we have to hold out the appearance of great prosperity," was Sherman's dejected appraisal. He was concerned about the number of bank failures in the city and the unsettled condition of business generally.

More and more banks and investment houses were collapsing as depression gripped most of the country. "It seems that I am the Jonah of Banking," he wrote John, "wherever I go there is a breakdown."

"Of all the lives on earth," he told Ellen, "a banker's is the worst, and no wonder they are specially debarred all chances in heaven. . . . If I were a rich man—of which there is not the re-motest chance, I would as soon try the faro table as risk the chances of banking."

One October morning in 1857, a friend burst into Sherman's quarters and excitedly pointed to a newspaper notice. James H. Lucas's company of Saint Louis had failed. Cump refused to believe it, but at his office he found a dispatch confirming the account. The following day, he was called to Saint Louis. There he found the situation more serious than he had expected. Merchants and bankers for some time had been selling on long credit and were now reaping the consequences. By borrowing heavily upon his rich real estate holdings, Lucas paid off all the depositors, but the banking business was finished.

Sherman volunteered to return to California to try and collect debts and realize as much as possible from the real estate holdings. "What I will finally settle down to do, I do not yet know, but in the spring I must do something for I will be completely out of money, property and employment," he said.

"If I had no family," he told Hugh Boyle, "I would stay in California all my life, or go to some of the Pacific countries, but though I see mighty slim prosperity in the future, I will return & try something God knows what." The army was one possibility. If new regiments were raised, he thought he had a chance for a commission, perhaps a lieutenant colonelcy. Life in the army would be far better than unemployment or undertaking new and indefinite schemes. He felt sure in the next ten years the army would have "plenty to do in the war line."

When Ellen received word from him that he was going to California, she broke into tears. "I am entirely unwilling for you to go out there at all," she wrote. "I don't care what Mr. Lucas has at stake." She was angry too at the idea of returning to the army. "I have wandered enough with my children and I trust and pray that you may be willing to attempt something besides California and the army."

But when Cump returned to Lancaster for the Christmas holidays, he was so low in spirits that Ellen made an effort to be cheerful. "I'm beginning to lose what little self-respect I ever had," Cump confessed.

In San Francisco Sherman searched through the records. Lucas and Turner held $100,000 in real estate and $200,000 in notes, bonds, and mortgages, but so rapidly had property values declined in California, that he could neither determine its worth nor could he estimate the loss or gain. If he forced sales he might incur a great loss. Those who were indebted to the bank, if pushed, might resort to the Bankruptcy Act. After several weeks in San Francisco, he wrote to John: "I fear my stay here must be prolonged much beyond my private interest, for after I get through here I will be absolutely penniless, and I don't know how I shall earn a living. I trust therefore if it be possible my friends in Washington would get me a commission in a new regiment if one be raised, as that would play into my hands at once.

"Whilst out here I get no salary further than personal expenses, so that the longer I stay the worse I am off. I suppose I am justly punished for giving up my commission for which I was well qualified for this place, for which no amount of natural sagacity will suffice."

Completely discouraged, homesick, and longing for sympathy, Cump wrote Ellen: "It is too bad to oppress your mind with sad pictures, but you can easily imagine me here—far away from you —far away from the children—with hope almost gone of ever again being able to regain what little self-respect or composure I ever possessed. I envy the nonchalance of business men generally who wipe out these old sums, like the marks on a slate, and begin anew with no feeling of regret for the past."

Ellen replied: "I am distressed to find that you allow your mind to be so harassed by business and the disagreeable circumstances connected with it. After having done your part so well and being conscious only of the purest motives, you ought to be calm and content and be able to bear with fortitude and equanimity whatever happens.

"I know it is easier to say all these things than to practice them, but you have a strong will, so much intellect and such power over yourself that I am surprised to see you yield in this. A good conscience should sustain you. As for me, I feel that I have never loved and admired you as much as now. That I believe is natural, where love has the solid foundation of esteem mine has had."

Ellen's letter failed to rouse Cump from his despondency. One evening he wrote to Thomas Ewing concerning a standing offer to work in Ohio, superintending the Chauncey saltworks. He said that rather than face an uncertain future, for the sake of his family, especially Ellen, he was willing to return to Lancaster. "Though I assure you of my willingness to undertake what you propose, the smaller the beginning the better I will be pleased —only so that I may feel I am not a burden on anybody. . . . All I need to say is that this Fall I will be adrift, and will be happy to have the honest employment you suggest—provided you think I can earn a living for my family."

Then he added: "I have been Captain so long that subordination will come a little hard, but I hope I can fill any post as my natural temper will admit. I must be either on the go or out doors. I prefer that to any sedentary work."

Sherman was humbled. He sought an inconspicuous job, free of responsibility. At no time during this period did he write of his hopes and ambitions. Instead, his letters stress his failure and loss of self-respect. "I am between two fires," he told John. "I expect at all events to come to Ohio in the fall, when necessity will probably compel me to stay at or near Lancaster."

By accepting Thomas Ewing's offer, he felt he was surrendering any hope of regaining his self-esteem. "You can understand, what Ellen does not," he told Mr. Ewing, "that a man needs a consciousness of position & influence among his peers. In the Army I know my place, and out here am one of the Pioneers and [one of] the big chiefs—at Lancaster I can only be Cump Sherman."

He could not, unlike many other men, harden his conscience and say that he could no more have stemmed the financial downfall than he could have "side-stepped a cannonball." Although he knew personally that he had worked as hard as anyone, he wrote: "What I failed to do, and the bad debts that now stare me in the face, must stand forever as a monument of my want of sense of sagacity."

Although Ellen professed a willingness to "live in a log hut, feed chickens and milk the cow," Cump knew that she required, even demanded, certain comforts which to another woman would be unnecessary. Whatever scheme he embarked upon, her wants and those of the children had to be considered first.

When Ellen learned that Cump had decided to settle in Ohio and superintend the saltworks, she was overjoyed. Her own self-interests blinded her to his despair and his profound sense of failure. All the Ewings rejoiced when, in the summer of 1858, he finished his business in San Francisco and rejoined his family.

A bitter quarrel between Ellen and Cump's sister Elizabeth Reese, who was then living in Lancaster, added to his despondency at being back in Ohio. Elizabeth had accused Ellen of forcing Cump to leave California and had further antagonized her by injecting Ellen's Roman Catholicism into the argument. Ellen could not tolerate any derogatory references to her religion. "I see plainly," Cump wrote Tom Ewing, "that in coming here to Lancaster for a peaceful retreat, and shelter from the storm of ocean, I find myself like to be involved in danger far more disagreeable."

Tom Ewing was then living in Leavenworth, Kansas Territory, practicing law. With the passage of the Kansas-Nebraska Act in 1854, which lifted the ban against slavery in the western territories, both North and South were determined to have Kansas, and both sides refused to permit Kansans to work out their own destiny. The territory became a testing ground, then a battlefield. In November, 1854, an election was held to pick a territorial delegate to Congress. A host of Missourians, who crossed over to elect a proslavery man, carried the election easily. In March, 1855, an estimated 5,000 Missourians entered the territory again and elected a legislature which quickly enacted a slave code and

strict laws against abolitionist agitation. Antislavery settlers refused to recognize this regime and held their own elections. By
January, 1856, two governments existed in Kansas, one based on
fraud, the other extralegal.

By denouncing the free-state government, located at Topeka,
President Franklin Pierce encouraged the proslavery Kansans to
assume the initiative. In May they sacked the antislavery town
of Lawrence. This inspired a Free-Soiler named John Brown to
take action. He and his little band of men stole into the proslavery
settlement on Pottawatomie Creek, dragged five settlers from their
cabins and murdered them. This slaughter brought men on both
sides to arms by the hundreds. Irregular warfare broke out and
by the end of 1856, some 200 persons had lost their lives.

In Washington Rep. John Sherman espoused the cause of the
Kansas Free-Soilers and berated President Pierce for his proslavery
utterances and for arguing that sectional prejudice had called the
Republican party into being. In contradicting this allegation, John
Sherman ascribed the origin of the existing agitation to the Kansas-
Nebraska Act and added: "Sir, the very existence of the Republican party, which the President so much deplores, is one of the
effects of this measure." Sherman, who, like all other Republicans,
opposed the extension of slavery in the territories, was also against
any interference by the United States government with slavery in
the slave states: "If I had my voice, I would not have one single
political Abolitionist in the Northern States." A member of a
House committee investigating the events in Kansas, John Sherman wrote a report which scored the Democrats for their actions
in Kansas, and this was distributed as Republican campaign
literature.

Cump Sherman cautioned his brother to take a middle course
and not to become too sectional, as most Republicans were. He
thought the Republican party's stand to restrict the extension of
slavery in the territories was good, but the extinction of slavery in
the South was both undesirable and unthinkable. "The Negroes of
our country should remain slaves. I would prefer to have them
subject, than in any other political position, where in numbers
they approach in equality the whites.

"The Southern states," Cump said further, "should be more

likened to a man having a deformity, like the fox who lost its tail and wanted all others to cut theirs off. They think they are best off, or at least are bound to think so, and instead of thrusting the fact before them all the time I would indulge them in their delusion, with all the philosophy and complacency of a strong man. If they attempt to abolish the laws about slave trade vote them down without unnecessary debate. If they in committee frame a Bill to restrain Territorial legislation from restricting slavery vote them down.

"They have not the Physical or Political power to oppress the Free States. Nor can they afford to dispense with the slave any more."

When John Sherman was reelected to a second term, his brother wrote: "Politicians are of course corrupt, have been, are now, and always will be when the motive is so natural. When the mass of People divide into two Great Divisions of nearly equal vote, a few can turn the scale. Anything in war or politics seems to be justified by success, and success can be achieved by buying up a small knot of lazy worthless idlers of cheap price, whose votes can turn the scale.

"As long as rabble in cities have votes, so long will these votes be bought & sold, like any other cheap & valuable commodity, and the party in power can buy for it most readily by patronage.... As to reforming Politicians or the human Race, that is simply impossible. Every now and then there may be spasmodic changes such as we had in San Francisco, forcing property holders to rebel, & do more harm than good."

Cump then went to Leavenworth to see Tom Ewing, who urged him to join the law firm he was forming in partnership with a friend, Dan McCook. Cump could manage the collection notes, rents, and outside business. It was either this or Thomas Ewing's saltworks, and Sherman chose Leavenworth.

When Ellen heard that they were to live in Kansas, she wrote her husband: "I shall be ready to start at the word and only wish it may come soon. I suppose it will be a long time before I shall see home again as I have now too many children to be lugging back and forth and the rest of the family can more easily visit me.

I believe I can now content myself anywhere out of California away from home for years at a time.

"I have never loved you as I do now," she assured Cump.

Sherman was admitted to the Kansas Bar without an examination "on the ground of general intelligence and reputation." The new firm rented an office on the second floor of a frame building and furnished it with "two-ply" curtains, carpeting, and a few pieces of furniture. In late autumn Cump hung out a sign, "Sherman, Ewing and McCook." In the first week the partners received three cases, one bringing a fee of $300.

"On the whole," Tom wrote his wife, who was visiting in Ohio, "the sky is brightening rapidly, and I feel cheerful as to the future. It will be all right. The prospect for law business is first rate. It will give me a good living by next summer." Although Ewing was optimistic, Sherman was surprised to learn that Tom was in debt $25,000 from speculative ventures.

Ellen, Lizzie, Willy, and Tommy Sherman reached Leavenworth on November 12. The steamboat's whistle brought Cump, Hugh Boyle, and Tom hurrying to the dock. Ellen beamed with happiness to see them all again, after a tedious eight days on the river. Cump, however, was terribly upset that Minnie had remained in Lancaster with the Ewings.

They drove to Tom Ewing's beautiful house on the corner of Third and Pottawatomie streets, where the Shermans were to have two upstairs rooms as temporary quarters. Tom's wife, Ellen, would return to Leavenworth that winter, while the Hugh Boyle Ewings were going back to Ohio in another week. Ellen Sherman was favorably impressed with the living arrangements and thought it best to stay in "Uncle Tom's Cabin" until spring. Then the Shermans would build their own home.

The day after Ellen's arrival, Cump received a letter from Minnie, whom he hardly knew anymore:

Lancaster
Nov. 5th '58

My Dearest Papa,

I hope you are not displeased that I did not go to Leavenworth but indeed I could not feel willing to leave Grandma and she could not feel willing to spare me.

I go to school in Aunt Sissy's room. I spell and read and write. I am writing this letter now in school. I am going to commence my geography lessons again next week ....

Your own little
Minnie

Cump replied: "I was, of course, much disappointed that you decided to stay in Lancaster all winter, instead of coming out to Kansas, but I am perfectly willing you should if you are a good child & a comfort to your grandma and grandpa. As loving as you are and so attached to each other I must be contented though you must not forget Lizzie & Willie—but remember them & be ready to come out to this Bloody Kansas as Tommy calls it."

In December business was dull. The courts were not in session and clients were few. In desperation Sherman became a notary and picked up a stray 50 cents occasionally. "If I can see fair prospects for making a living here," he wrote Mr. Ewing, "I shall not look elsewhere, but I am not content to stay here or anywhere, unless I can be independent of assistance from any quarter. You can well understand that I am far from easy to receive even from you, and it is only in the start that I am willing to think of it."

Christmas, 1858, was a poor day for Ellen, remembering the previous year's festivities in Lancaster. There was no money for presents, but the children were happy with their stockings full of nuts, candy, cake, and apples. Mr. Ewing had sent his daughter $100, but Ellen put it aside for emergencies.

After the Hugh Boyle Ewings left for Lancaster, Ellen rearranged the house. In one corner of their bedroom, she placed the narrow bed which she had bought for Lizzie. During the nights that followed, when bad dreams awakened the child, she would run over and climb into bed close to her father.

Ellen began flattering herself that she was free from homesickness. The children seemed happy, although they often talked of Lancaster. But Ellen's high spirits quickly evaporated. She was pregnant again, unwell, and soon became depressed, refusing to believe there was a competent physician in Leavenworth. There was little money coming in, and she tried to economize, fearful that they would be bankrupt by spring. "Life seems a burden, which I feel that I would thankfully lay down were it not for the sole desire to save my children from evils which without me might befall them," she wrote Maria. Already she was looking forward to the summer and a visit from her parents.

During his leisure hours at the office, Sherman began to explore the possibilities of a railroad through Leavenworth, and at John Sherman's request, he prepared a lengthy paper on a proposed railroad to the Pacific and the best routes. The cost of building such a railroad would be astronomical. "It is a work of giants," he wrote, "and Uncle Sam is the only giant I know who can or should grapple with the subject." He had a fine imagination and predicted correctly the route that was just ten years away from realization. His notes, written in January, 1859, so impressed John Sherman that he published them in the *Washington National Intelligencer*.

The discovery of gold in the vicinity of Pikes Peak in the Rockies forecasted a huge migration through Kansas in the spring and summer of 1859. Leavenworth, Kansas City, and Atchison, in Kansas, and Saint Joseph and Kansas City, in Missouri, all vied with one another to outfit prospectors, each maintaining that it was the terminal of the best route across the western plains.

In this rivalry Leavenworth had distinct advantages. For years the town had been the jumping-off place for emigrants to California and Salt Lake, and it was the headquarters of the famous freighting company Russell, Majors and Waddell. Sherman became fascinated with the speculative possibilities. Thomas Ewing too believed that the rush westward through Kansas spelled prosperity for Leavenworth.

In a detailed letter to his father-in-law, Sherman predicted that thousands of emigrant trains would send to Leavenworth for provisions and feed. Vast numbers of horses and cattle would be driven into town and sold cheap, herds which would be fattened up and later sold on the road for a profit. The best route to the gold mines, he explained, was by way of Fort Riley. All the roads, whether to Saint Joseph, Leavenworth, or Kansas City, passed within four miles of the Ewing property at Indian Creek.

Sherman had decided he would ask Ellen to sell her Saint Louis property to finance a provisioning venture, but he was unwilling to risk everything unless Thomas Ewing came in with $5,000. He believed the investment could be doubled in six months.

Ewing answered promptly. "I think well of your scheme, and that it ought to be attended to immediately." He suggested that Cump contract for corn and oats. If the Pikes Peak fever had not yet filled the Kansas farmers with speculative ideas, Ewing hoped that corn could be bought cheap and sold to the emigrants at exorbitant prices.

Sherman went to work. On the Ewing land at Indian Creek, which already had one frame house, he put up another two-room shanty with the help of a hired hand and negotiated for the ploughing and fencing of a hundred acres. He built stables, had a well sunk, and bought a fractional quarter of land to complete the Ewing farm. He throve on the outdoor work.

After spending $2,000 of Mr. Ewing's money, Cump went to Saint Louis and sold one of Ellen's lots. Some of the cash went into interest-bearing securities, but the majority was invested in 5,000 bushels of corn. Mr. Ewing was pleased with the way Sherman had taken charge. He urged him to open a provision store along the road, where passing emigrants could stock up on groceries for the long trek.

Leavenworth now resembled a boomtown. Steamboats loaded with gold seekers arrived in two's and three's each day. The streets were jammed. All around the town emigrant camps were preparing for the push west, but although business was brisk, there was little speculation in real estate and less in corn.

At Indian Creek Sherman directed the corn deliveries. "If there is gold at Pike's Peak, or if this mass of people tarry there, they must be fed somehow, and the trains which transport them must have corn all summer," Cump wrote elatedly. By mid-April, he had already contracted for the delivery of 7,200 bushels.

But as the spring wore on, Sherman's luck began to fail. There was no demand for corn. Prices failed to rise. The new stage lines contracted for corn at their own stations. The quartermasters at Forts Leavenworth and Riley informed Sherman they had full supplies. The emigrant parties passing through the area of Indian Creek had spent all their money before taking the road and therefore purchased little corn. By mid-May, the grass was growing fast, and the horses, mules, and oxen preferred it to grain.

Sherman was forced to write Mr. Ewing that the purchase of corn was "a mistake." He had invested $2,000 and Ewing $3,340.

"It was rather a bold adventure to come out here to Indian Creek, and attempt so large a purchase," he said. Thomas Ewing urged Sherman to unload the corn quickly, to sell it at any price. He did so with some success, but he still had 4,000 unsold bushels.

Ellen Sherman, who had returned to Lancaster for the summer, urged her husband to come home to Ohio. "How can you stay there when you do not make even enough for your own board?" she asked. "As it is certain that your earnings will be inadequate to our wants in Leavenworth (where expenses must *always be high*) why not consent to live where our moderate income will support us? We can live here [in Lancaster] on what we would spend for *fuel* in Kansas.

"I could not be happy to have you come here to live were there any *reason* why you should hate the place but as it is a mere preference you have for any other place over this, and as my choice did not make you averse to living else where or make you unhappy you ought to be able to understand why I should be glad to have you live where we have both grown up, where we are known and respected (no matter how poor we may be)."

"Disunion and Civil War are synonymous terms."

WHEN SHERMAN ARRIVED back in Lancaster in mid-July, 1859, a letter was waiting for him from an old army friend, Don Carlos Buell, reporting that there was a vacancy as superintendent of a new military institute in Alexandria, La. The salary was $3,500 a year plus living accommodations. At present there were no family quarters, but a house would be built for the superintendent as soon as possible.

The president of the board of supervisors of the new school, G. Mason Graham, a rich Louisiana planter, was the half-brother of Colonel Mason, who had been Sherman's commanding officer at Monterey. Graham had written Buell asking for recommendations.

Sherman immediately applied for the post. His application consisted of a half-page note, and for recommendations, he referred to Braxton Bragg, P. G. T. Beauregard and Richard Taylor, all living in Louisiana. No sooner was his application read, so the story goes, than one member of the board of supervisors exclaimed, "By God! he's my man. He's a man of sense. I'm ready for the vote." In August Sherman received word that he had been appointed and that the school would open on January 1, 1860.

In the interim he had been offered a job by William R. Rodolfson, a Cincinnati banker, to set up a banking house in London, England, at a salary of $7,500 a year. However, the men behind the scheme were comparative unknowns in the financial world. After seriously pondering both possibilities, Sherman finally settled upon the military offer. "I have nothing to overcome but the natural repugnance to teach youngsters," he told John Sherman.

Cump tarried in Lancaster throughout September, when his fifth child was born, a girl, who looked exactly like Cump. Ellen wanted to name her for one of the Shermans, but was overruled, and the baby was baptized Eleanor Mary Sherman.

During that fall, Sherman prepared for his new job by writing letters to army friends asking advice on policies and visiting the military academy at Frankfort, Ky. Urged by the governor of Louisiana to come early to Alexandria in order to prepare the school for its opening, Cump left Lancaster in mid-October. Just before departing, he wrote a hasty note to his brother in Washington, concerning John's increasingly strong stand against Negro slavery. "As you are becoming a man of note and are a Republican," he said, "and as I go South among gentlemen who have always owned slaves, and probably always will & must, and whose feelings may pervert every public expression of yours, putting me in a false position to them as my patrons, friends and associates, and you as my Brother, I would ... [want] to see you take the highest ground consistent with your party creed. . . . All I ask of you is not to be drawn into too strong expressions against slavery, that will be calculated to commit me in the South."

After Cump left, Ellen and the children moved from the Ewing mansion to a house of their own. At first Mr. Ewing objected, but Ellen persisted. "I enjoy a peace, which I never can feel again in Father's house while mother's health and strength are so feeble," she wrote Cump. "We will have a fine winter of comfort even if a lonely one. The house is fine, but, of course, there is a sad want; it is a poor home with the father gone."

Upon his arrival at Alexandria, Sherman took rooms at a tavern, then rode the four miles out into the pine woods to inspect the new building which had been erected for the institute. He also visited G. Mason Graham, who was deeply interested in the success of the new academy. It was in origin and organization similar to the publicly supported universities of other states; its endowment, realizing $8,000 annually, was derived from the sale of public lands donated in 1810 and 1811 for educational purposes.

In the days that followed, Sherman held several sessions with the academic board at Graham's plantation. Present at those meetings were Professor of Mathematics Anthony Vallas, a noted Hungarian scholar exiled for his connection with the revolution of

1848, and Professor of Modern Languages E. Berte St. Ange, a former French naval officer. Together they drew up rules and regulations based on the code at Virginia Military Institute and on Sherman's experience at West Point.

The teaching staff was increased by the arrival of Profs. Francis W. Smith and David French Boyd, both young Virginians and graduates of the University of Virginia. Professor Boyd well remembered his first meeting with Sherman. "He was then, as he ever was, a prince of talkers. I fell in love with him at first sight. The superintendent's appearance was striking—tall, slender with a figure slightly bent, bright hazel eyes and sandy hair."

From Thibodaux, La., Braxton Bragg, now a prosperous planter, wrote a lengthy letter of advice to Sherman. Bragg, from the first, was convinced that the school needed additional financial support. The people of the country were not yet sufficiently aware of the institute to patronize it. But he was confident that if his friend could nurture the school through its infancy, it would become popular and self-supporting in the future. "High literary institutions" were sprouting up everywhere, but Louisiana remained sadly deficient in scientific and military schools. No class of people was more dependent on science and discipline for success than Southern planters, for, Bragg emphasized: "Every plantation is a small military establishment—or it ought to be. By military, I don't mean the old fogy notion of white belts, stiff leather stocks, but discipline by which we secure system, regularity, method, economy of time labor and material." In closing, Bragg urged, "Give us well-disciplined masters, managers, and assistants, and we shall never hear of slave insurrections."

That fall while Sherman was preparing the institute for its formal opening, John Brown and a group of 18 devoted followers attacked Harpers Ferry, Va., a town on the Potomac upriver from Washington. Brown planned to seize the federal arsenal there, arm the slaves who he thought would flock to his colors, and then press ahead with a sort of private war against the South. Federal troops, however, quickly crushed the revolt.

John Brown's raid generated intense controversy in every section of the country. Virginia authorities charged Brown with treason and murder. He was tried, convicted, and hanged. Northerners were impressed by Brown's calm while awaiting execution and by his insistence that he had acted throughout as God's agent. The *New York Tribune* proclaimed: "the consistent devotion to the rights of human nature prompted his desperate undertaking" and "has elevated him to the position of hero."

The Harpers Ferry insurrection stirred the South even more violently than it did the North. Something more vital, more basic had been touched. Physical invasion of the South and the stirring of a slave revolt, even when attempted by a handful of men, were no trivial matters. Harpers Ferry proved that Northern fanaticism extended beyond words. Southerners feared "the destiny which awaited them if they stayed in the Union, under the control . . . of the Republican antislavery party in the free states." If the South did not win the presidential election of 1860 and a Northern party proved victorious at the polls, there was only one step left—secession.

Thomas Ewing wrote Cump that he and Ellen thought he ought to reconsider the English banking house proposition, which was still open. He felt that Cump, as head of a Louisiana military academy with an antislavery brother in Congress, was in an extremely vulnerable position. Already Southerners enrolled in Northern colleges were withdrawing and returning home, and Northern teachers were being banished from Southern institutions. There was growing feeling in the slave states against Northerners.

Sherman realized that his position was increasingly threatened and that he would be watched and suspected. On the question of Negro slavery, he wrote Tom Ewing: "I would not if I could abolish or modify slavery. I don't know that I would materially change the political relation of master and slave. Negroes in the great numbers that exist must of necessity be slaves. Theoretical notions of humanity & Religion cannot shake the commercial fact that their labor is of great value, & cannot be dispensed with.

"Still of course I wish it never had existed, for it does make mischief. No power on earth can restrain opinions elsewhere, and these opinions expressed beget a vindictive feeling. . . .

"I of course do not debate the question and moderate as my views are, I feel that I am suspected, and if I do not actually join in praises of slavery I may be denounced as an abolitionist."

To make sure Graham knew exactly how he stood on the

political situation, Sherman wrote: "I think Southern politicians are almost as much to blame as mere theoretical abolitionists. The constant threat of disunion and their enlarging the term *abolitionist* has done them more real harm than the mere prayers and preachings, and foolish speeches of distant preachers. . . .

"The true position for every gentleman North and South is to frown down even a mention of Disunion. Resist any and all assaults calmly, quietly like brave men, and not by threats. The laws of the States and Congress must be obeyed, if wrong or oppressive they will be repealed.

"Disunion and Civil War," Sherman said, "are synonymous terms." Peaceful secession from the Union was impossible. "It would be war eternal, till one or the other were conquered."

Sherman was determined to organize and establish the school. He hoped to escape the misfortune which had dogged him in California, New York, and Kansas and dreaded the possibility that at any moment some "fool" in the Louisiana legislature might brand him a Northern abolitionist or spy.

On January 2, 1860, Sherman opened the doors of the Louisiana State Seminary of Learning and Military Academy to 53 cadets. Soon after, he wrote a letter to his beloved Minnie:

January 22, 1860

Dear Little Minnie:

I will soon have a good house, so next year you and Mama, Lizzie, Willy, Tommy and the baby will all come down to Louisiana, where, maybe, we will live all our lives. I think you will like it very much. There is no snow here now. We had snow only two days this winter, and there is plenty of wood—but today it was so warm that we did not need fires at all.

The grass is beginning to grow and the trees begin to look as though we would soon have flowers, but generally the leaves do not sprout till about March.

Your Mama tells me that you all expect me this winter, but I am counting on staying here, and bringing you all down next winter. Give my love to all. Tell Willy that as soon as he can read I will write him very often, for I know he loves me very much—more than he does anybody else unless he has changed . . . .

When he comes here he will have no sled, but I will get a pony for him to ride. You may believe I would like to see you all in your snug little house, but I know I am too far off, and there is no chance of my coming for a long time yet.

During the first months at the institute, Sherman was popular with the cadets, despite the harsh discipline he imposed upon them. "When occasion required," recalled a student, "he knew how to reprimand, and words of kindness and encouragement often fell from his lips."

One of his colleagues wrote later: "He made every professor and cadet ... keep his place and do his duty; at the same time, he was the intimate, social companion and confidential friend of the professors, and a kind loving father to the cadets. All loved him. ... Often I have seen his private room full of boys, listening to his stories of army or western life, which he loved so well to tell them. ... Nothing seemed to delight him so much as to mingle with us freely, and the magnetism of the man riveted us all to him very closely, especially the cadets."

By February the novelty of the school had worn off, and cadet discipline became more of a problem. But Sherman maintained a firm command, expelling several students. He demanded high standards, both from cadets and professors, and often visited the classrooms unexpectedly. One member of the faculty remembered: "Sherman looked well not only to the happiness and health of his charges and to the military discipline and drill, but especially to the progress of the cadets in their academic studies. He had no patience with inefficient teaching, whether from want of ability, or too much ability, rendering it difficult for the savant to come down to the plane of comprehension of beginners. Yet he himself was no scholar in the professional sense—not a man of varied and extensive literary and scientific acquirements nor even a general reader. He was rather a tough, unpolished diamond, made great by nature of deep discernment, needing little the ideas of other men. But brilliant and original as he was in thought, he had not the usual accompaniment of genius—want of practicality. Sherman was eminently practical."

Sherman abhorred complicated explanations. "Once I remember," wrote a professor, "he asked me my opinion of something. I gave it and then began to give my reasons when he stopped me with this remark: 'I only wanted your opinion. I did not ask for your reasons, and remember, never give your reasons for what you do until you must. Maybe after a while a better reason will pop into your head!'"

Despite his firm hold over the faculty, there was little friction. He won the respect of the professors, and after a few months, their affection. Many a winter evening the unmarried professors, who lived in the main building with him, congregated in his quarters to smoke and converse. "What a charming and instructive companion he was. . . ." recalled Professor Boyd. "To me certainly was it a treat to listen to his clean cut and original views on nearly every subject that came up. . . . When the world knew but little of him, I looked up to Sherman as a singularly gifted man, his mind so strong, bright, clear, original, and quick as to stamp him a genius; and his heart under his stern, brusque, soldierly exterior, the warmest and tenderest. Of happy nature himself, he strove to make all around him happy."

Cadets enjoyed his Friday lectures on history and began stopping by his quarters to hear more of them. Often Sherman was seen on the academy grounds surrounded by attentive students.

"Much time was given to silence and the keeping of his own counsel," remembered a cadet. "He was fluent and eloquent when he spoke. I have heard him lecture charmingly to the assembled students on the history of his country, selecting by preference chapters of exploration and adventure, or heroic struggle and enterprise, such as gave to the Union the territory of Texas and the great West. Upon me and others he made the impression of an ardent, powerful man, governed by duty and a sense of devotion to his country and humanity."

Sherman was beginning to feel an attachment for the seminary, its professors, and cadets when, during the spring, Thomas Ewing again pressed him to take the London banking job. Ellen too felt that to stay in Alexandria would at best be "an honorable exile," where she would be cut off from all social intercourse. She kept pestering her husband to accept the London offer, bombarding him with letters and telegrams. Cump exploded. "Again we give up a certainty for an uncertainty," he wrote. "As to you going to

London you know well you wont, the alternative is you must remain at Lancaster two years till I can save the means to return and
settle in Ohio.

"I feel very much like an antelope—not a sheep or goat, but
something of that order of beast. The hunter hides himself and ties
a rag to the rammer of his gun. The antelope runs off as far as
possible, but fate brings him back. Again he dashes off in a new
direction, but curiosity or his Fate lures him back, and again off he
goes but the hunter knows he will return and bides his time.

"So have I made desperate efforts to escape my doom—Ohio.
I have made desperate efforts to escape but I see it is inevitable,
and so might as well surrender."

"Mr. Ewing writes me urgently to go [to London] and even
Mrs. Sherman prefers it to coming South," Sherman wrote
Graham. "Still I mistrust all Financial Schemes. Just 7 years ago I
was similarly situated in New Orleans, Commissary, U.S. Army,
when Mr. Lucas and Henry Turner . . . came and prevailed upon
me to go to California as Banker, with prospects more brilliant
than those now offered me. I went, and without any fault, negli-
gence, or want of ability, I was involved by the losses of others, so
that I am mistrustful of Finance and Financiers."

He went on: "I would do myself and family an injustice to
prefer this [the seminary] to the other, for by the other I am
certain of 15,000 for two years, of which I could save a large
fraction, whereas here all I would look for would be an honorable
position, and pleasant future for my family and children."

In closing, Sherman added that he might stay on at the
academy if the board of supervisors guaranteed a house for his
family and raised his salary to $5,000.

Graham immediately sent a letter to the governor. "I am convinced that unless we meet his demands we are going to lose our
irreplaceable superintendent, the apprehension of which kept me
awake for more than half the night.

"In the words of Dick Taylor," Graham continued, " 'if you
had hunted the whole army, from one end of it to the other, you
could not have found a man in it more admirably suited for the
position in every respect than Sherman.' "

Rodolfson, the Cincinnati banker, arrived in Alexandria at a moment when Sherman, because of the pressures of Thomas Ewing and Ellen, was reluctantly leaning toward the London proposition. But he felt that under no circumstances could he walk out in the middle of a term without the blessing of the board of supervisors.

Graham and five members of the board, who were meeting informally, passed a resolution that they regretted the prospect of losing the valuable services of Captain Sherman as superintendent. Then Graham sat down with Rodolfson and discussed the academy's situation and Sherman's position. They both agreed to give him ten days to make a decision; then the banker returned home.

Sherman traveled to Baton Rouge to confer with the members of the state legislature, who gave him assurances that they would provide handsomely for the institute. Considering the alternatives, Sherman decided to accept the London job, but only if Rodolfson secured the $15,000 in advance. His request was refused, and the difficult question was settled.

"It is dull enough here in the Pinewoods," he told Thomas Ewing, "but my salary is paid regularly, and as I get monthly, more than a whole year's earnings in Kansas, I am content." Ellen accepted resignedly her husband's decision. "I want you to write me more about your companions, the professors," she wrote him, "so that I shall not feel them strangers when I get there. I find myself thinking constantly of the house you are going to have for us, which is to be *our own* and where we are to spend so many of our coming years, together. For the first time I look forward to all my arrangements connected with it, with the zeal & interest of a child. . . . We have had a good many ups and downs & have been tossed about heretofore in such a way that we will both hail a quiet resting place as a weary traveler in the desert would hail a spring of water."

On the first of May, their wedding anniversary, Ellen wrote: "Ten years ago this evening, dearest Cump, we were married. You cannot have forgotten how delightful the weather was, nor how propitious everything seemed to us then.

"And in looking back I cannot help feeling that we have been particularly blessed notwithstanding all our cares and trials and disappointments. Our children are healthy and good; they are as bright and pretty as we need wish them to be.

"We ourselves—I speak from my own heart—are more attached, love more fondly and more truly esteem one another than ever before and are more necessary to each other's happiness. My prayer today shall be a thanksgiving for the blessing of a *good* husband."

When Sherman received final authorization from the legislature, he immediately contracted for a house to be built by October 15 and sent the plans to Ellen.

When he wrote that servants other than slaves were difficult to secure, Ellen replied angrily: "I could never consent to buy or sell a slave—so if I am to be consulted we never can own property of that sort but must depend upon labor of some other kind." Six days later she wrote: "Your suggestion about servants alarms me a little for I shall be helpless if left without them, and I must change considerably before I can consent to buy slaves. I am *unwilling* now to invest in that way."

Sherman was sure that Ellen would change her mind. "What will you think of that, our buying niggers, but it is inevitable," he explained to Tom Ewing. "Niggers won't work unless they are owned, and white servants are not to be found in this Parish. Everybody owns their own servants.

"All the Congresses on earth could not make the Negro anything else than what he was. He has to be subject to the white man or he must amalgamate or be destroyed. The two races could not live in harmony save as master and slave."

The nation was on the brink of disunion. Radicals, North and South, were heedlessly provoking one another. In the Deep South more and more people talked of leaving the Union. The North was growing at a much faster rate than the South, and if nothing were done, Southerners feared that a flood of new free states would soon be able to amend the Constitution and emancipate the slaves.

The Democratic senator from Illinois, Stephen A. Douglas, was probably the last hope of avoiding a rupture, but when the Democrats met to choose their presidential candidate at Charleston in the spring of 1860, it became clear that the slave state delegates

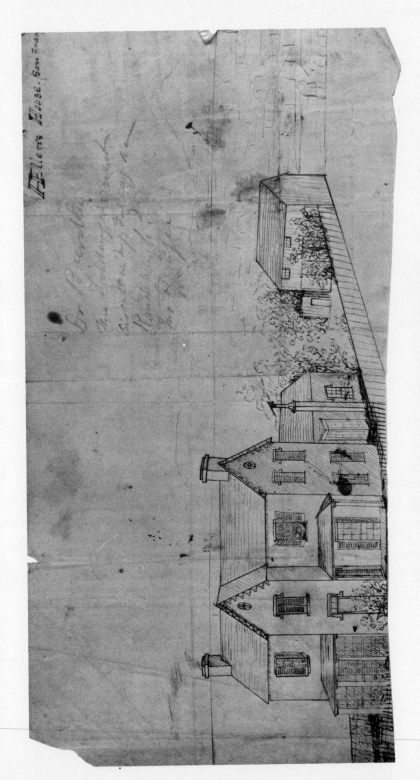

Sherman's sketch of the family's home in San Francisco

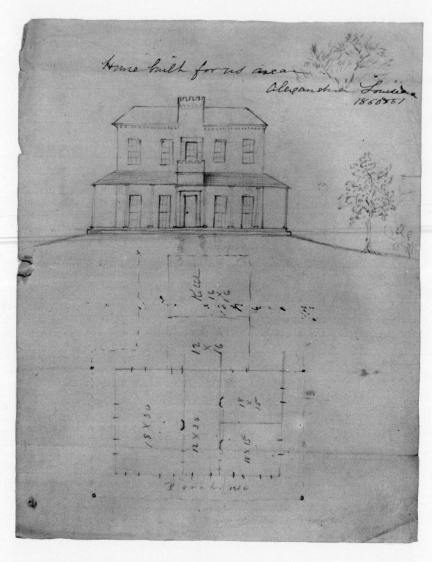

Sherman's sketch for his family of the "home built for us" near
Alexandria, Louisiana, 1861

would not accept him unless he promised not to interfere with slavery in the territories. When Southern demands were voted down, most of the delegates from the Deep South walked out of the convention. Douglas could not obtain the required two-thirds majority, and the convention adjourned without naming a candidate.

In June the Democrats reconvened at Baltimore but failed again to reach an agreement. The two wings of the party met separately, the Northerners nominating Douglas; the Southerners, John C. Breckinridge of Kentucky. At last sectionalism had divided the Democratic party.

Meanwhile the Republicans met in Chicago and skillfully drafted a platform attractive to all classes and all sections of the free states. As to slavery in the territories, the party did not equivocate: "The normal condition of all the territory of the United States is that of freedom." Neither Congress nor local legislatures could "give legal existence to Slavery in any Territory." The convention chose Abraham Lincoln of Illinois as its standard-bearer.

With the Northern and Southern wings of the Democratic party and the Republicans already in the race for the presidency, a fourth party entered the campaign, the Constitutional Union party. Most of its members were former Whigs, who nominated John Bell of Tennessee. "It is both the part of patriotism and duty," they resolved, "to recognize no political principle other than the Constitution of the country, the Union of the states, and enforcement of the laws."

During the ensuing campaign, statesmen of the Deep South threatened that if Lincoln were elected the South would secede from the Union. But Sherman was "convinced that Lincoln's success would be attended with no violence. He is a man of nerve, and is connected by marriage and friendship with the Prestons of Kentucky and Virginia and have no doubt he will administer the Government with moderation." Privately, Sherman championed the cause of John Bell for the presidency as "he would give us four years [of] truce, but I fear it is not to be."

"I keep aloof from all political cliques and knots," he told Graham, "and only express an opinion occasionally to the effect, that there are many men of action and ability at the South, who will act with prudence and decision when the time comes, but danger does exist from the growing suspicion and mistrust, between the two Great sections of our country."

At the academy Sherman was busy with accounts, finances, and housing. During the last days of June and early July the closing of the seminary's first semester was celebrated with drills, speeches, and a fancy-dress ball. When the last examination was finished, Cump headed for Ohio. Except for brief trips to Washington to purchase muskets for the academy and to New York to invest the money appropriated by the Louisiana legislature in books and chemical apparatus, he spent his vacation with his family, making arrangements for them to go to Louisiana.

The Republican party was active in Lancaster. One Saturday evening there was a torchlight parade through the streets, and John Sherman and others gave rousing speeches for Lincoln in the square. Afterward, Mr. Ewing entertained lavishly at his house and promised to vote for Lincoln.

On the last day of Cump's vacation, there was an encampment of the Ohio Militia, and Charlie Ewing urged Cump to don his uniform and review the company, which he did, to the great delight of the children.

When he arrived back in Alexandria in October, he moved into his new house. He pushed the carpenters to complete the finishing touches, although he doubted that Ellen and the children would ever live there.

Louisianians were already talking as though disunion were inevitable. Men said bluntly that as long as the danger of abolitionism existed, they would prefer establishing a Southern Confederacy to remaining in the Union. Sherman was closemouthed and tried to mind his own business. But if Lincoln were elected and his brother, the outspoken opponent of slavery in the territories, accepted a high post in the administration, his position in Louisiana would be untenable.

Election day came to Alexandria, cold and stormy. The majority there voted for Breckinridge; not a single vote was cast for Lincoln. The returns for the entire country were slow in reaching Louisiana. When finally news came of Lincoln's victory, Sherman wrote Ellen not to come south: ". . . . prudence dictates some caution, as political events do seem portentous. . . . I also notice that many gentlemen who were heretofore moderate in their opinions now begin to fall into the popular current, and go with the mad, foolish crowd that seems bent on a dissolution of this confederacy. . . . I have no doubt that the politicians have so embittered the feelings of the people, that they think the Republican party is bent on abolitionism, and they cease to reason or think of consequences."

"What I have been planning so long...
is about to vanish...."

WITH LINCOLN'S ELECTION it appeared certain that South Carolina would secede. Alabama, Georgia, Florida, and Texas would probably follow. These states could go and it would still leave the Union strong, Sherman believed, but if Louisiana, Mississippi, and Arkansas, those states resting on the Mississippi River and controlling its mouth, were to withdraw, it would be war.

By Thanksgiving Day it looked as if Louisiana would follow South Carolina out of the Union. "I am sick of this everlasting subject," Sherman wrote Ellen. "The truth has nothing to do with this world. Here they know that all you in Ohio have to do is to steal niggers, and in Ohio, though all the people are quiescent, yet they believe that the South is determined to enlarge the area of niggers."

At Baton Rouge Gov. Thomas Moore ordered the legislature to convene on December 10, and called a convention to consider secession. Cump, who had hoped to reunite his family by the first of the year, wrote a long letter to Minnie:

Alexandria
December 15, 1860

Dear Minnie,

The house is all done, only some little painting to be done. It looks beautiful; two front porches and one back one. All the windows open down to the floor like doors, so that you could walk out on the porch either up the stairs or down stairs. I know you would all like the house very much; but my dear little Minnie, man proposes and God disposes.

What I have been planning so long and patiently, and thought we were on the point of realizing the dream and hope of my life,

148

that we could all be together once more in a home of our own, with peace and quiet and plenty around us all, I fear is about to vanish, and again I fear I must be a wanderer, leaving you all to grow up at Lancaster without your Papa.

Men are blind & crazy ... the people in the South are going ... to break up the government under which we live. You cannot understand this, but Mama will explain it to you. Our governor here has gone so far that he cannot change and in a month or so maybe, you will be living under one government and I under another. This cannot last long, and as I know it is best for you all to stay in Lancaster, I will not bring you down here at all unless some very great change takes place.

If this were only a plain college I could stay with propriety, but it is an arsenal, with guns and powder and were I to stay here I might have to fight for Louisiana against Ohio—that would hardly do; you would not like that, I know, and yet I have been asked to do it. But I hope still this will yet pass away, and that our house and garden will yet see us all united here in Louisiana.

Your loving father

Sherman felt that the national situation in 1860 paralleled the vigilante disorders in San Francisco in the 1850s. The United States had become so democratic that mere popular opinion stood above the law. Men had discarded constitutions, lawbooks, and statutes to follow the popular clamor of the barrooms and newspapers. "And now things are at such a pass," he observed, "that no one section believes the other and we are beginning to fight. The right of secession is but the beginning of the end."

If the will of the South does not conform "to the Interest of the Great Whole," he said, then "it must be made to conform." Force and compulsion "are as necessary in government as in the administration of the courts."

"What effect would a sentence of death and imprisonment be without the scaffold and penitentiary?" he asked Tom Ewing. "I think the People have done as they d——n please so long that they think their sovereign will is the law—Every state, county, village, family is the sovereign, and can defy all mankind. Time this farce should cease—if the People are incompetent to Rule, some remedy must be devised. Those who pay the Taxes and Expenses will soon clamor for help and protection...."

"My opinion is that this Question [of secession] has gone so far it *must* be met. Secession is Treason."

On several occasions Sherman announced a preference for monarchy over democracy. He thought· the "self-interest of one man" was a far "safer criterion than the wild opinions of ignorant men."

Although he had written Ellen not to come south, he was annoyed when he learned that she had rented a large house in Lancaster in anticipation of his resignation. "As to our own situation," he said, "it is too bad to think of. I have got pretty near the end of my rope. I have neither health, strength, or purpose to start out life anew or can you afford it. When you knew any day might throw me out of employment and when necessity may force me to go abroad to seek a mere maintenance you engage a new house and begin steps that will result in spending a few more hundred dollars. I won't find fault because I admit that your reasons are good, but it would have been more prudent and respectful to wait awhile.

"As to my coming to Lancaster, and laying around doing nothing, I say without fear of being adjudged blasphemous I would rather be where your damn sinners [are]. Tis your part to follow me, without imposing conditions that cripple my actions."

On December 20, Sherman was in his room talking with Professor Boyd when the news came that the South Carolina convention had voted unanimously for secession. Tears welled up in his eyes. Nervously, he began pacing the floor and, turning to his friend, exclaimed, "Boyd, you people of the *South* don't know *what you* are doing! You think you can tear to pieces this *great Union* without war! But, I tell you there will be *bloodshed*, and plenty of it!"

For more than an hour, Boyd recalled, Sherman poured out "his great patriotic heart in the agonies of grief, over what he then so clearly foresaw!"

On Christmas Day, Sherman wrote Graham: "As long as Louisiana is *in* the Union, and I occupy this post, I will serve her faithfully against internal or external enemies. But if Louisiana secede from the Genl. Government *that* instant I stop.

"I will do no act, breathe no word, think no thought hostile to the Government of the United States. Weak as it is, it is the only semblance of strength and justice on this continent, as compared with which the State governments are weak and trifling."

In another letter to Graham, he stressed that the laws and the Constitution of the United States had to be obeyed "not because it meets our approval, but because it is the law, and because obedience in some shape is necessary to every system of civilized government."

Sherman warned that if South Carolina in any way injured his friend, Maj. Robert Anderson, who commanded Fort Sumter in Charleston Harbor, "I say Charleston must be blotted from existence. 'Twill arouse a storm to which the slavery question will be as nothing, else I mistake the character of our people."

Sherman revealed his feelings to Braxton Bragg, who replied: "You are acting on a conviction of duty to yourself and your family and friends. A similar duty on my part may throw us into an apparent hostile attitude." The Union was dissolving. "The only question now is," said Bragg, "can we reconstruct any government without *bloodshed?* I do not think we can."

In January and February, 1861, the other states of the lower South, including Louisiana, followed South Carolina out of the Union. Delegates were sent to Montgomery, Ala., to plan the course of secession and to establish the Confederate States of America. Jefferson Davis of Mississippi was chosen president; Alexander H. Stephens of Georgia, vice-president.

"It may be that Louisiana's honor compelled her to this course," Sherman wrote Graham, "but I see it not and must think it is the rash result of excited men. Men here ceased to reason, and war seems to be courted by those who understand not its cost, and demoralizing results. Civilians are far more willing to start a war than military men—and so it appears now."

At Baton Rouge the United States arsenal surrendered to Louisiana troops. Sherman was notified that 3,300 muskets and 70,000 cartridges, which had been seized, were being sent to the institute.

Throughout the lower tier of slave states Southerners occupied post offices, customhouses, and hospitals; took over the mint at New Orleans; and captured United States revenue cutters, and other ships. Of the forts in the seceded states the only ones remaining in Union hands were Fort Sumter in Charleston Harbor,

Fort Pickens in Pensacola Bay, and two minor forts off the Florida coast. These seizures, however, had occurred before Abraham Lincoln took office in March, 1861, and until then, the president-elect had deliberately avoided threatening the repossession of places already taken.

To Sherman, these were unjustifiable acts of war, and he could no longer remain silent. In his office at the academy, he wrote out his official resignation to the governor, and then in a note marked "private," he added: "I have never been a Politician and therefore undervalue the excited feelings and opinions of the Present Rulers, all over the Land, but I do think if the People cannot execute a form of Government like the Present, that a worse one will result. . . . When I leave, which I now regard as certain . . . I entertain the kindest feelings to all, and would leave the south with much regret—only in Great Events we must choose one way or another."

Governor Moore answered promptly and politely, authorizing him to turn over all property in his charge to the commander of cadets.

Sherman cut his tie with the South, finally and completely. His responsibility was to Ohio, the Union, but above all, to law and order. But his feelings were ambivalent and he still placed the onus of blame primarily on nearsighted politicians and over-zealous newspaper editors, both in the North and in the South, who allowed sectional feeling to influence their actions.

For a few weeks longer, Sherman remained at the academy to settle his affairs. To Graham, he wrote a long letter explaining why he had resigned his post. He then added: "My opinion is that Lincoln will be installed in office, that Congress will not repeal the Union, that the Revenues will be collected. The consequence is inevitable—War and ugly war. . . .

"The storm is upon us, and we must each to our own ship. I hope I may see you again, but if not accept the assurances of my . . . affection, respect, and admiration, and my earnest prayer that you and yours may long survive to look back with satisfaction to the time when we started the Seminary in the vain belief that we were serving the cause of our common country."

On his last day the corps of cadets formed, and he made a short speech. Then passing along the line shaking hands, he said good-bye to each cadet and officer. After the ceremony, he walked over to the professors, attempted to speak, but broke down. With tears in his eyes, his voice choked, he could only mutter, "you are all here." Turning quickly, he strode off to his waiting carriage.

He traveled south to New Orleans, where he audited his accounts and presented the president of the board of supervisors with a certificate saying he had faithfully accounted for every cent. On the following day a huge procession of armed volunteer companies paraded through the streets of the city, hurrahing and waving flags honoring Southern independence. Sherman lunched with Col. and Mrs. Braxton Bragg and discussed the secession crisis. Bragg had a commission in the First Louisiana Artillery and was engaged in enlisting the regiment.

While in New Orleans, Sherman received a letter from Ellen. "I have for some time past been convinced," she said, "that you will never be happy in this world unless you go into the Army again. *I have believed* that John Sherman ... would procure for you a high position either in some new regiment or in the place of some one resigned. ...

"I will own that I am the less reluctant to have you go into the Army again because I believe that if war should rage you will be impatient of any other employment & join some volunteer regiment. I am proud and happy in the knowledge that you have so promptly declared your disapproval of their rebellion & that you have so distinctly announced your opinion & position in the terrible state of affairs."

After concluding his business, Sherman returned to Lancaster in early March. He had decided that if civil war broke out, he would accept a commission only if the rank were high enough to permit him to have a word in the councils of the army, for he had no confidence in the military ability of the Lincoln Administration. He preferred a government position, perhaps an assistant treasurer's post in Saint Louis, in some other city, or in a railroad agency. "If I could once more get a foothold," he told John Sherman, "then I think I could again build myself up." He urged his brother to ask the secretary of the treasury to secure a position for him. "Otherwise," he concluded, "I fear I am doomed to the Salt Works."

John Sherman had been chosen to succeed Sen. Salmon P. Chase, whom Lincoln had selected secretary of the treasury. "My brother John," Cump wrote a friend, "is now a senator and quite a man among Republicans, but he regards me as erratic in politics. He nor politicians generally can understand the feelings and opinions of one who thinks himself above parties and looks upon the petty machinery of party as disgusting."

After spending a few days with his family, Sherman went east to see John. Arriving the day after Lincoln's inauguration, Sherman later remembered: "I was amazed at what appeared to me the apathy of the country. The south had done a hundred acts of open war and treason in the seizure of forts, mints, arsenals, revenue cutters, and whatever of government property they could lay their hands on, and yet at the north no attention seemed to be paid at it. Everybody was attending to his business as in time of profound peace. I confess it looked to me as though the Secession of the South would be submitted to without a struggle."

John explained to his brother that a treasury job in Saint Louis was out of the question, as it was a political appointment. Also there was no chance of entering the army as a brigadier general until the military establishment was materially increased.

John had conversed with the secretary of war, the secretary of the treasury, and the postmaster general, all of whom had a high regard for his brother's abilities. They had promised to do everything they could in "a military way," but they could scarcely settle Sherman in a political post as he was a military man. John urged his brother not to rebuff the Republican party or President Lincoln over "temporary difficulties." "You and I have our futures to make," he counseled. "We can aid each other."

The two of them called on President Lincoln at the White House. "Mr. Lincoln," John remarked, "my brother is just up from Louisiana and may be able to give you some information of things down there."

Turning to Sherman, Lincoln said, "Well, how are folks down there?"

"The folks looked to me like they were expecting and getting ready for a fight," replied Sherman.

"Well," said the president, "I guess we will manage to keep

the house." Lincoln also expressed the hope that the danger would pass and that the Union would be restored by a peaceful compromise.

Such optimism disturbed Sherman as he knew the South was united and already was recruiting the best officers it could secure. He shied away from expressing himself further, but once outside the White House, he told John: "The North just don't care a damn, you politicians have got things in a hell of a fix, and you may get them out as you best can."

He had no sooner returned to Lancaster when his old friend, Major Turner, offered him the presidency of a street railroad in Saint Louis at a salary of $2,500 a year. Both Turner and Lucas owned large shares in the company. Accepting this offer gratefully, Cump packed up his family and all his household effects, moved to Saint Louis, and bought a house, "a home too costly for us," at 226 Locust Street.

Although he received a good salary with the prospect of an increase, fixed expenses totaled $200 per month, which left little for contingencies. With what little money they had in reserve, Ellen bought a carpet "of the best Brussels and a beautiful pattern" for the parlor, an oilcloth for the hall, a stair carpet, and for her room, a good quality ingrain carpet. She also brought home furniture and bathroom fixtures and hired a cleaning woman.

The Shermans were just getting settled when Cump received a telegram from Postmaster General Montgomery Blair: "Will you accept the chief clerkship in the War Department. We will make you assistant secretary [of war] when Congress meets." He answered negatively. Since he had incurred certain obligations in Saint Louis, he explained, he was not at liberty to make a change. Thanking Blair for his trouble, he wished the administration success in the work ahead. Much later he was to learn that the cabinet took offense at his curt refusal.

In April, 1861, the nation's attention swung to Charleston Harbor and Union-held Fort Sumter. On the 12th, Confederate guns opened fire on the bastion, triggering the Civil War. Within an hour after the arrival of the news in Saint Louis, all ordinary business came to an end. Crowds of cheering, singing men swarmed through the downtown district; the bars and restaurants were thronged; the mayor delivered three speeches from the steps of his office; storefronts were decorated with bunting and streamers; firecrackers exploded; guns and revolvers were fired into the air; and steamboat whistles were tied down.

In Washington President Lincoln called forth "the militia of the several States of the Union, to the ... number of seventy-five thousand," to suppress "combinations" in the Southern states "too powerful to be suppressed by the ordinary course of judicial proceedings."

The militia, though subject to federal call and referred to in national laws, was in peacetime a state institution so far as it had any existence at all; and in most of the states it was a nebulous, ineffective organization. The Regular Army of the United States, though extremely well trained, had a strength of only 16,000 in March, 1861.

Popular response was enthusiastic. Mass meetings were held where orators played upon popular emotion and prejudice. Anyone who wished could advertise his purpose to "raise a company," or even a regiment, and invite "all willing to join to come on a certain morning to some saloon, hotel or public hall."

Although Sherman approved of Lincoln's determination to use force to defend and maintain federal authority, he knew that 75,000 volunteers were not enough to quash the rebellion. "You might as well attempt to put out the flames of a burning house with a squirt gun," he wrote. "I think it is to be a long war—much longer than any politician thinks."

"The first movements of our Government will fail," he told John, "and the leaders will be cast aside. A second or third set will rise, and amongst them I may be, but at present I will not volunteer as a soldier or anything else. If Congress must, or if a national Convention be called, and the Regular Army be put on a footing with the wants of the country, if I am offered a place that suits me I may accept. But in the present call I will not volunteer. . . .

"The time will come in this country when Professional knowledge will be appreciated, when men that can be trusted will be wanted, and I will bide my time. I may miss the chance, and if so all right, but I cannot & will not mix myself in this present call. . . . volunteers & military men never were and never will be fit for invasion and whenever tried it will be defeated & dropped by Lincoln like a hot potato . . . .

"As to abolishing slavery in the south or turning loose 4 million slaves," he continued, "I would have no hand in it. The questions of national integrity and slavery should be kept distinct, for otherwise it will gradually become a war of extermination."

From his home in Mansfield John Sherman wrote Cump that he thought Gov. William Dennison of Ohio would offer him the top military post in the state, major general of volunteers. But instead the governor appointed George B. McClellan and offered Sherman a subordinate commission. Cump refused, but he was not surprised that another had been selected for high command. He believed he had received less mark of approval in Ohio than in any other state where he had lived.

Sherman also politely but firmly declined a commission as brigadier general to command the Saint Louis volunteers as he considered them too raw and undisciplined to invade enemy country. Tom Ewing told him he had made a drastic mistake in refusing this offer. A letter from James B. Fry, the assistant adjutant general, urged him to reconsider and join a volunteer outfit.

John Sherman's letters to his brother implied that now was the opportune time to redeem himself in his own estimation. "I feel earnestly about it, as I fear circumstances by which you are surrounded may lead you to neglect the golden opportunity." John's letters made no appeal to a sense of patriotism but underscored the possibility of self advancement, which might be realized by raising a volunteer regiment.

To Tom Ewing, Sherman wrote: "I know a good many will be displeased with my apparent apathy. I am and always have been an active defender of Law & the Constitution. Twice have I sacrificed myself thereto. In San Francisco to a Northern mob, and in Louisiana to a southern Rebellion. I believe now I am a more zealous friend of Govt & order, than others who will find fault with me. . . . I came north prepared to act any part which might be assigned me. I went to Washington & saw the President and heard him say that military men were not wanted. I asked for civil employment here in St. Louis, but it was denied me and when I reached Ohio necessity forced me to seek work, and I found it here.

"Had Lincoln intimated to me any word of encouragement," he added, "I could have waited awhile, but I saw in Washington not a spark of encouragement, & therefore my coming here."

Sherman wrote his friend Professor Boyd at the seminary: "We are now by Declaration of the Confederate Congress, and by Act of our own Constituted authorities, enemies, and I cannot realize the fact. I know that I individually would not do any human being a wrong, take from him a cent, or molest any of his rights or property, and yet I admit fully the fact that Lincoln was bound to call on the country to rally and save our Constitution and Government.

"Had I responded to his call for volunteers I know that I would now be a Major General. But my feelings prompted me to forbear and the consequence is my family and friends are almost cold to me, and they feel and say I have failed at the critical moment of my life.

"It may be I am but a chip on the whirling tide of time destined to be cast on the shore as a worthless weed. But I still think in the hurly-burly of strife, order and system must be generated, and grow and strengthen till our people come out again, a Great and purified nation.... No matter what happens I will always consider you my personal friend, and you shall ever be welcome to my roof."

Dr. S. A. Smith, then president of the board of supervisors at the seminary, wrote condemning Lincoln's actions and pressing Sherman to come south and put his talents to work for the Confederate army. "How freely we would furnish you with the men and means to do *anything possible* in line of your profession."

By early May President Lincoln, realizing that calling forth the militia was inadequate for the emergency, called for 42,000 United States volunteers to serve for three years and directed that large additions be made to the Regular Army.

Tom Ewing was in Washington on official business. His rise in Kansas politics had been meteoric, and now in 1861, he was chief justice of the Kansas Supreme Court. And he had strong ambitions for a seat in the United States Senate. With Sen. John Sherman he paid a call on President Lincoln to urge him to offer his brother-in-law a commission in the Regular Army. Lincoln, expressing a high regard for Sherman based on statements of General

Scott and other military leaders, said he would second his appointment to any high post.

After the interview, John went straight to the War Department and saw Secretary Simon Cameron, who promised that Sherman could have a commission as a colonel in the Regular Army with authority to raise a double regiment: 2,200 men. The promise was unconditional.

Tom Ewing then wrote Cump, suggesting that he tender his services to General Scott and Secretary Cameron. By this time Sherman had finally concluded that if a long civil war was inevitable, he might as well take part as a Regular. He had drastically reduced the operating expenses of the railroad and had so reorganized the company that he could leave on short notice without serious detriment to his interests. Deep down he believed that in justice to his family he should stay in Saint Louis, where he could better provide for them. But, being under "a species of honorary obligation" to tender his military services, he did so, unreservedly.

To Secretary of War Cameron, he wrote on May 8: "I hold myself now, as always prepared to serve my country in the capacity for which I was trained. I did not and will not volunteer for three months, because I cannot throw my family on the cold support of Charity but the three years call of the President would enable an officer to prepare his command and do good service.... Should my service be needed the Record of the War Department will enable you to designate the section in which I can render best services."

Early in May Southerners in Saint Louis were openly displaying Rebel flags at their headquarters. They boasted of what they would do should President Lincoln coerce Missouri into staying in the Union and talked of marching on the arsenal.

On the outskirts of the city, at Camp Jackson, was an encampment of militia and state guards, 1,000 strong, under the command of Gen. Daniel M. Frost, a former army officer and a prominent Missourian. This force was regarded by Saint Louis as the nucleus of the Rebel organization in the state. It was rumored that they were receiving guns and ammunition from the arsenal at Baton Rouge.

On the morning of May 10 Sherman heard that Gen. Nathaniel

Lyon and a group of Union volunteers and Regular troops had marched from the Saint Louis arsenal out toward Camp Jackson to confiscate the arms and ammunition.

Learning that the Rebels had surrendered to Lyon, Cump took Willy and walked out Olive Street toward Camp Jackson. Suddenly, they saw a crowd and a regiment of United States troops and volunteers with the disarmed Confederates moving down the street amid cheers. Someone yelled, "Hurrah for Jeff Davis! Hurrah for Jeff Davis!" A gun was fired. The crowd surged forward. The ranks of the undisciplined volunteers lowered their muskets, fired into the bystanders, and reloaded. Cump grabbed Willy and hurried toward home.

Later that evening he heard that a woman had been killed and ten people wounded. The incident further convinced him that the military could not depend upon untested volunteers. The greatest difficulty facing the nation was not to conquer but "so conquer as to impress upon the real men of the South a respect for their conquerors." Regulars were the only force that should be employed for invasion.

It was his belief that Lincoln should use the officers who had been serving on the western frontier. These men had practical experience which fitted them for commands. He was unimpressed by the president's recent choice of generals—Nathaniel Banks, John C. Frémont, John Pope, and others. "Lincoln's present appointments do so plainly indicate a political bias that none but Union prone republicans should expect anything," he wrote Tom. "The appointment of Pope . . . . etc. will afford to Bragg & David & Beauregard the liveliest pleasure. The north has so decided an advantage in men for the ranks that it is a pity to balance the chances by a choice of leaders . . . I know of no one competent unless it be [George B.] McClellan. But as soon as real war begins, new men, heretofore unheard of will emerge from obscurity, equal to any occasion."

On June 5 Tom Ewing wired Cump from Washington: "Come forthwith important." Parting with the family was difficult, for Ellen was pregnant again. Although she wanted to go with her husband, this was impossible, and she and the children prepared to go to Lancaster for the duration.

Sherman left for Washington. It was almost to the day, 21

years before, that he had graduated from West Point. His life since then had been a record of petty successes, frustrated ambitions, and failures. He was deeply indebted to Thomas Ewing, but at the same time, he looked upon his father-in-law as an antagonist who was constantly urging him against his instincts to live in Lancaster, to work at the saltworks, and to accept financial aid.

Ellen continually turned to her father rather than to her husband for counsel. It was mainly because of Thomas Ewing that Sherman was driven to make good, to show the Ewing family what he could do. But as he headed eastward, he was determined to keep himself in the background for awhile because "I saw [that] the controlling powers underrated the measure of hostility, which I reasoned would lead to the sacrifice of the first [military] leaders."

Bull Run and Muldraugh's Hill

IN THE WAR between the Union and the 11 states within the Confederacy, the former possessed tremendous advantages. There were over 20 million people living in the North, excluding Kentucky and Missouri, where loyalties were divided; only 9 million in the South, and of these about 3.5 million were slaves, whom the Southerners were unwilling to have serve in the armies. The North's economic and financial capacity to wage all-out war was even more overwhelming, for it had seven times as much manufacturing and a far larger and more efficient railroad system than the South. In 1860 the North produced firearms valued at $2,270,000; the South's output was only worth $73,000. Northern control of the merchant marine and the navy made possible the blockade of the Confederate states, a particularly potent weapon to hold over a region so dependent upon foreign markets.

The South, however, discounted its liabilities. It seriously doubted that public opinion in the North would sustain President Lincoln if and when he attempted to meet secession with force. Northern manufacturers and merchants depended on Southern markets. Should the Union try to cut Europe off from Southern cotton, Great Britain and France could be relied upon to pry open Confederate ports and provide the South with the tools of war.

Southerners also possessed certain military advantages. The new nation need only hold on to what it had. Southerners would not only be defending their social institutions, but also their homes. The South was infused with a martial spirit, its young men having given more attention to military training than had their Northern counterparts. Its generals were among the finest products of West Point. With many Federal forts and arsenals in their hands, Southerners were not unreasonable in their hope of winning the war, if it should not be too drawn out. The imbalance of resources between the Confederacy and the Union was not as great as it had been between the American colonies and Britain.

On June 11, 1861, Sherman reached Washington. He watched the militia pouring into the city and was appalled at the greenness of the men. "Their arms," he remarked, "were ... of every pattern and caliber; and ... [the men] were so loaded down with overcoats, haversacks, knapsacks, tents and baggage that it took twenty-five to fifty wagons to move the camp of a regiment from one place to another."

At the War Office he learned that he had been appointed colonel, Thirteenth United States Infantry. Temporarily, he was attached to the army headquarters in Washington, while his regiment was being recruited.

In mid-June Colonel Sherman went to Williamsport, Md., to see John Sherman, who was temporarily a volunteer on the staff of Gen. Robert Patterson. In a country tavern he met his brother and renewed his acquaintance with an old classmate, Col. George H. Thomas, then commanding a Regular regiment. The conversation revolved around the war and overall strategy. The two colonels spread a big map of the United States on the tavern floor, and on their hands and knees, discussed the probable strategic importance of Richmond, Vicksburg, Nashville, Knoxville, and Chattanooga. At a much later date, John Sherman was to recall how these two had designated correctly the exact lines of operations and had pinpointed the strategic areas of a war which was just beginning.

On June 28 Sherman was ordered to report to Gen. Irvin McDowell, whose army of 30,000 guarded the capital from a position near Centreville, Va., about 20 miles southwest of Washington. The main Confederate army under P. G. T. Beauregard was camped nearby at Manassas.

Sherman received orders to take command of the Third Brigade of the First Division under Gen. Daniel Tyler. The brigade was composed of the Thirteenth New York, Sixty-ninth

New York, Seventy-ninth New York, the Second Wisconsin, and a battery of Regular artillery. These units were all scraggly. They had come into camp almost straight from the enlistment offices, had been formed into regiments, and had been shipped off to Washington before they had learned which end of the rifle went off. The newly commissioned officers and noncoms simply did not know their jobs. It was Sherman and his handful of Regulars who drilled them, inspected them, and taught them how to fire their muskets.

Under the constant pressure of "On to Richmond," McDowell planned a forward movement against the enemy. He had under him an aggregation of civilians in uniform leavened by a few Regulars. His opponent's army was as raw as his own. McDowell's campaign was based on the assumption that General Patterson would engage the Confederate force under Gen. Joseph E. Johnston, then at Winchester, Va., and prevent Johnston from joining with Beauregard. Patterson failed to keep Johnston occupied, and the Confederates at Winchester slipped away and joined General Beauregard on July 20.

Several days before McDowell started the advance, Cump learned that Ellen had given birth to another daughter, Rachel. To Minnie, he wrote a long letter:

Sunday, July 14, 1861

My Dear Minnie: I received your good letter the other day and have got up early this morning before I have to go out on duty to write to you.

War is a terrible thing, especially when, as now, we are fighting people like Mrs. Turner and thousands of others whom I used to know as kind, good friends, and they thinking they are defending their country, their houses and families against foreign invaders.

So, my dear child, don't get in the habit of calling hard names, of rebels, traitors, but remember how easy it is for people to become deceived and drawn on step by step till war, death and destruction are upon them . . . .

All around for miles fences are torn down and hogs, horses and cattle roam at will through clover and wheat and corn fields. No matter how much officers may wish to protect, soldiers will take rail fences for their campfires, and it is miraculous how soon a fence disappears and yet nobody did it. Thus wherever an army goes there will be destruction of property . . . .

We must fight and subdue those in arms against us and our government, but we mean them no harm. We have not disturbed a single slave; even the slaves of Colonel [Robert] E. Lee are at Arlington cultivating the farm and selling vegetables and milk to the soldiers for their master and mistress, who are with the Virginians.

This is a strange war, and God grant it may never be felt near you all. In the quiet of Lancaster I believe you are better off than anywhere else and I am glad you all like it so.

Tell Willy I would like to show him some real soldiers here, but he will see enough of them in his day. Love to all

Your papa.

On July 16, the day on which McDowell's army marched, Cump wrote hastily to Ellen: "I still regard this as but the beginning of a long war, but I hope my judgment therein is wrong, and that the people of the South may yet see the folly of their unjust rebellion against the most mild and paternal government ever designed by man."

And, he added: "Tell Willy I will have another war sword he can add to his present armory. When I come home again I will gratify his ambition on that score, though truly I do not choose for him or Tommy the military profession. It is too full of blind chances to be worthy of a first rank among callings."

The march of McDowell's army through the Virginia countryside was like a holiday parade, with many of the companies and regiments resplendent in brilliant uniforms. But there was a lack of discipline everywhere. "With all my personal efforts," Sherman remembered, "I could not prevent the men from straggling for water, blackberries or anything on the way they fancied."

On July 21 McDowell attacked the Confederates at Bull Run. The rank and file and many officers of both armies heard the roar of cannons for the first time. Up until midafternoon the Federals had the better part of the battle, fighting extremely well for raw troops. During the early stages Tyler's division guarded the Stone Bridge against any attempt of the Rebels to cross and mount a counterattack. The sound of McDowell's advance could be heard, but at noon the roar of battle became stationary.

General Tyler ordered Sherman, with his brigade, to support. Crossing by a ford, they marched toward the sound of the guns and reported to McDowell in the field. The cannon were louder now, a steady rumble. The brigade was ordered to attack over ground swept by artillery and musketry. Quickly, Sherman sent his regiments in, one by one, against the storm of shot and shell. The losses were fearful.

For four hours Sherman was under fire. He was grazed on the knee and shoulder as his horse faltered, shot through the leg. This was his first day in a practical school, but he soon grew accustomed to the sight of corpses. The mangled bodies of soldiers around their guns brought home to him the enormity of battle and sickened him.

With the arrival of reinforcements, the Rebels charged. By short, quick thrusts and desperate fighting, they dislodged the Federals from their position on Henry Hill. McDowell was forced to retreat in the direction of Washington.

After having advanced toward the enemy, the men in Sherman's regiments, exposed to a devastating fire, suddenly faltered. With hoarse shouts, the noncommissioned officers tried to call forth some sort of order from the demoralized recruits, who were scurrying like hysterical chickens through the dust and smoke. Sherman and his officers quickly re-formed what was left of the regiments and withdrew with deliberate caution across Stone Bridge.

The retreat of McDowell's army was at first orderly, and at Centreville the Federals blocked what limited pursuit the Confederates could muster. But when the soldiers were fired upon in the road after becoming entangled in a mass of camp followers and spectators, control was lost and the army disintegrated into a mob rushing for Washington.

"There was never anything like it for causeless, sheer, absolute, absurd cowardice, or rather panic, on this miserable earth before," wrote a congressman-spectator. "Off they went, one and all; off down the highway, over across fields, towards the woods, anywhere, everywhere, to escape. Well, the further they ran the more frightened they grew, and although we moved on as rapidly as we could, the fugitives passed us by scores. To enable them better to run, they threw away their blankets, knapsacks, canteens, and finally muskets, cartridge-boxes, and everything else.

"We called to them, tried to tell them there was no danger,

called them to stop, implored them to stand. We called them cowards, denounced them in the most offensive terms, put out our heavy revolvers, and threatened to shoot them, but all in vain; a cruel, crazy, mad, hopeless panic possessed them, and communicated to everybody about in front and rear. . . ."

Sherman had read of retreats and had seen the confusion of men at fires and shipwrecks, but nothing compared to this rout.

Exhausted and dirty men poured into Fort Corcoran. It began to rain hard. Finding no tents available, the soldiers crowded into a barn. Their grumbling assumed a threatening tone. Appalled by the "whole God-damned retreat," repelled by their complaining, worried by the possibility of mob violence and revolt, Sherman ordered them out into the storm.

"Many of the men were desperate," recalled Lt. William T. Lusk, Seventy-ninth New York. "They became clamorous for food. Sherman sneered at them for such unsoldierly conduct. They begged for some place to rest. He bade them sleep on the ground. They had no blankets, many not even a jacket, and all were shivering in the wet. The soil was oozy with water, and deep puddles. The men became quarrelous. Sherman grew angry, and called them a 'pack of New York loafers and thieves.' "

Several days later Sherman's regiments were almost in a state of mutiny because of the War Department's order extending the men's enlistment from three months to two years. Soldiers threatened to spike the guns. Sherman's reaction was quick and decisive. He readied an artillery outfit and prepared to open fire if necessary to quell any irresponsible action, and for several hours it looked as if he might have to. When the tension finally subsided, he arrested 100 ringleaders and placed them in irons on board a warship in the Potomac. "This is a bad class of men to depend on to fight," he wrote Ellen. "They must eat their rations and go on parade, but when danger comes they will be sure to show the white feather." He was so incensed that he went to Washington and complained to President Lincoln and Secretary of State William H. Seward.

"I saw both Seward and Lincoln and they are perfectly powerless in this emergency," he wrote Ellen. "The Administration appeal to military men to save the country. . . I know not if it be possible. Newspapers will lay the blame on the officers and shield the men. The People can do no wrong. This fallacy must be obliterated before the United States can claim to be a Power on Earth. . . .

"Are you not glad at least that I persisted in keeping in the background? I want not to be a Leader till I see some clear distinct end to this muddle. I dislike to witness the downfall of a country, but the want of organization and subordination to our People is a more dangerous enemy.

"Our rulers think more of who shall get office, than who can save the country," he went on. "Nobody, no man, can save the country. The difficulty is with the masses. Our men are not good soldiers. They brag, but don't perform, complain sadly if they don't get everything they want, and a march of a few miles used them up. It will take a long time to overcome these things, and what is in store for us in the future I know not.

"Our adversaries have the weakness of slavery in their midst to offset our democracy, and 'tis beyond human wisdom to say which is the greater evil."

Though Bull Run appeared to have been a smashing defeat for the Union, it was indecisive and gave no serious military advantage to the South. The Union army remained in camp outside Washington.

One afternoon in late July, standing by a grove near Fort Corcoran, Sherman watched an open carriage jolt down the road and recognized President Lincoln and Secretary of State Seward. When the carriage stopped, Sherman asked if they were going to Fort Corcoran.

Lincoln replied, "Yes, we heard that you had got over the big scare, and we thought we would come over and see the boys." He asked the colonel to get in and show them the way.

Sherman, realizing that Lincoln wanted to speak to the men, said: "Please discourage all cheering, noise or any sort of confusion; we had enough of it before Bull Run to ruin any set of men; what we need is cool, thoughtful, hard-fighting soldiers—no more hurrahing, no more humbug."

Reaching the first group of tents, Lincoln stood up in the carriage and made, as Sherman described it, "one of the neatest, best and most feeling addresses I ever listened to, referring to our late disaster at Bull Run, the high duties that still devolved on us and the brighter days yet to come."

At one or two points the soldiers began to cheer, but the president checked them: "Don't cheer, boys. I confess I rather like it myself, but Colonel Sherman here says it is not military; and I guess we had better defer to his opinion."

At Sherman's brigade camp, the men still smarted from their treatment on the night after Bull Run. As Lincoln drove up "they besieged the carriage," said Lieutenant Lusk, "hooted him, and reminded him who it was that first basely deserted us on the battlefield, by turning his horse's head from us, and leaving us to our fate." Lincoln, seeing the men's malice, ordered his coachman to drive on.

In the days that followed Gen. George B. McClellan was summoned to Washington and elevated to McDowell's command. He began to reorganize the Army of the Potomac. McClellan was the North's first military hero. His forces had driven the Confederates from the western counties of Virginia, where Union sentiment was strong. The fighting had been on a small scale, but McClellan had managed to inflate its importance.

In early August Sherman was still in command of the regiments of volunteers. He drilled them hard and worked to strengthen the fortifications at Forts Corcoran and Bennett and the redoubt on Arlington Road. It was rumored that Lincoln would select Colonel Sherman as one of the new brigadier generals in the Regular Army. Later Sherman was told that the president would make no new appointments. "This will still keep me where I want, in a modest position till time and circumstances show us daylight," he wrote Ellen. His distrust of volunteer troops made him shun the responsibility of a brigadier general. "I know not why I feel no ambition," he confessed. "If we could handle volunteers so that our plans could be carried out I would launch out, but I know that they will mar any plan and blast the fair fame of anybody. They, of course, the People, can't do wrong." He was convinced that the generals would eventually become national scapegoats, blamed for the shortcomings of untrained and undisciplined troops.

Two weeks after writing this, he was sworn in as brigadier general of volunteers.

One evening in mid-August Gen. Robert Anderson, the hero of Fort Sumter and Sherman's artillery instructor at West Point, asked the new brigadier general to meet him at Willard's Hotel in

Washington. When Sherman arrived, he found Anderson dining with Sen. Andrew Johnson of Tennessee. Johnson was a vigorous Southerner who had opposed secession and had displayed great courage in his opposition to the Confederate movement.

President Lincoln, Johnson told Sherman, had decided to aid the Union men in Kentucky and Tennessee and had appointed General Anderson to command the troops. Anderson had selected Sherman as second in command, and together they were to go to Kentucky and Tennessee to organize an army. Sherman was impressed and came away from the meeting believing that this duty was of vast importance to the Federal government.

"War like a . . . monster demands its victims, and must have them," he wrote Ellen. "How few realize the stern fact I too well know. Unless we can organize a large armed party in Kentucky & Tennessee, there is a danger that our old Govt may disintegrate and new combinations formed. . . . There should be only three |armies| East, Center, West and each should be over 100,000 effective men. But our People won't realize the magnitude of opposition till we are whaled several times a la Bull Run.

"I hardly know my sphere in Kentucky," he continued, "but it will be political and military combined. I think Anderson wanted me because he knows I seek not personal fame or glory, and that I will heartily second his plans and leave him the fame. Most assuredly does he esteem my motives. Not till I see daylight ahead do I want to lead. But when danger threatens and others slink away I am and will be at my post."

Before leaving Washington for the west, Sherman extracted a promise from President Lincoln that under no circumstance would he be asked to replace General Anderson, explaining that he was not then ready for such responsibility. Dogged by his failure to establish himself in California, Kansas, and Louisiana, he refused to gamble away what he believed was his last chance to realize himself. Driven by ambition, restrained by apprehension, he adopted a false humility to rationalize his unwillingness to devote himself wholeheartedly to the Union. He refused to face the issue, for he could not admit that he lacked the patriotism to court public censure by leading undisciplined men. But he could not hide his true feelings completely from himself, and in his letters he frequently complained of the quality of the recruits.

"Officers hardly offer to remonstrate with their men, and all devolves on me," he wrote. "Had I some good regulars I could tie them down. As it is, all the new Brigadiers must manufacture their Brigades out of raw material. Napoleon allowed three years as a minimum. Washington one year. Here it is expected in nine days.

"With Anderson," he confided to Ellen, "I suppose we will have to go into Kentucky and Tennessee to organize an army in the face of that [Confederate] prejudice which you complained so much about in Missouri. That prejudice pervades the public mind and it will take years to overcome. In all the southern States, they have succeeded in impressing the public mind that the North is governed by a mob (of which unfortunately there is too much truth) and in the South that all is chivalry and gentility. Out of this chaos some order in time must arise, but how or when I cannot tell."

So precarious was the balance between North and South in Kentucky that even a slight alteration in events might have jostled the state into the Confederacy and made the Ohio River the boundary between the two warring sections. Although as a state Kentucky stayed with the Union, its citizens were sympathetic to the cause of the Confederacy.

From May to September, 1861, Kentucky had remained neutral, but the rush of events forced an abandonment of this policy. Both belligerents were actively recruiting in the state. Kentucky Unionists established Camp Dick Robinson near Danville. The Rebels seized Columbus, and directly afterward the Unionists marched into Paducah. On September 11 the ghost of neutrality was laid when the legislature demanded the withdrawal of the Confederates. On the 18th of September it created a military force to expel the Rebels, thus placing Kentucky in the Union.

Tennessee also had divided sympathies. The various sections of the state had never lived happily together, for the mountainous east resented the planting regions. The middle and western areas took the state into the Confederacy, giving the South control of the Virginia and Tennessee Railroad, the only direct rail link between Virginia and the Mississippi River. When a powerful Unionist movement developed in the mountains of eastern Tennessee, the Confederacy tried, but failed, to suppress it entirely.

Sherman and Gen. George H. Thomas reported to General Anderson in Cincinnati, where they met with a group of Kentuckians. The situation was alarming. The Unionists in Kentucky were without muskets and ammunition. Tennesseans were ready to invade the commonwealth at any moment and destroy the railroads. "I hardly apprehend that Beauregard can succeed in getting Washington," Sherman wrote John, "but should he, it will be worse to us than Manassas [Bull Run], but supposing he falls back, he will try to overwhelm [General William S.] Rosecrans in Western Virginia and then look to Tennessee. We ought to have here a well appointed Army of a hundred thousand men. I don't see where they are to come from, but this is the great centre. I still think that Mississippi will be the grand field of operations."

If the Confederates could hold the river from Columbus, Ky., to the Gulf, the Federals could never subdue them. "To secure the safety of the Mississippi," Sherman said, "I would slay millions. On that point I am not only insane but mad."

General Albert Sidney Johnston assumed command of Confederate forces in Tennessee and organized the army into two divisions, the first under William J. Hardee, the second under Simon B. Buckner. Hardee's division was ordered forward to the Green River. Buckner's force was held in reserve. Johnston lacked the strength to attack, so he massed his units on the east side of the Mississippi to meet anticipated Federal advances against Bowling Green, Ky., Cumberland Gap, Tenn., and along the line of the Mississippi.

Johnston hoped to convince the enemy that his army was larger than it really was—and he did. General Anderson was positive that the Confederates were posed to attack, so he did not launch his own offensive for lack of troops.

Hurriedly, General Sherman wired Washington for more regiments. "Whatever I can do I will move willingly to sustain you all," wrote Secretary of the Treasury Chase. "The loyalty of Kentucky is a great point." Four thousand muskets were ordered, but as far as more troops were concerned, Lincoln calculated that Anderson already had enough near Louisville. In fact Washington had ordered five regiments of Frémont's command in Missouri to the east to bolster McClellan's army.

From Camp Dick Robinson, General Thomas reported that

his troops were "just a mob of men." "I almost despair of putting it in a fighting condition," he wrote to Sherman. "There are so many things which require immediate attention and which would require so lengthy a letter to make you understand their bearing that I hope you will take time to come down to see me so that I can lay them before you."

Detachments of Confederates pushed forward and burned a railroad bridge within 30 miles of Louisville. The city was thrown into panic. It was reported that the enemy was approaching Muldraugh's Hill, 40 miles from Louisville, near the point where the Louisville and Nashville Railroad crossed the Salt River.

General Sherman, the Louisville Home Guards, and Gen. Lovell H. Rousseau's men, 1,800 strong, moved to the front. It was quickly ascertained that the enemy was not advancing. Sherman deployed his men about Muldraugh's Hill and waited for more troops to arrive. Finally, they straggled in, the Forty-ninth Ohio and three Indiana regiments, raw and untrained, without blankets, haversacks, or tents.

Confederate forces were operating in the area with superior numbers, and Kentuckians were flocking to the Rebel standard. Sherman estimated that the enemy had from 7,000 to 20,000 men under arms, and he was sure that if they took Kentucky, they would cross the river and lay waste to Ohio.

"If the Confederates take St. Louis and get Kentucky this winter," he told John, "you will be far more embarrassed than if Washington had fallen into their possession, as whatever nation gets control of the Ohio, Mississippi, and Missouri Rivers will control the Continent. This they know and for this they will labor. You of the North never fully appreciated the energy of the South. My health is good, but . . . I am far from easy about the fate of Kentucky."

Sherman sent telegrams to President Lincoln and to the governors of Kentucky, Ohio, Indiana, and Illinois. "I hope you will send off all the troops you can raise."

In Lancaster Mr. Ewing wrote to General Scott complaining about the lack of support for Sherman and then went to Columbus to see the governor about more troops for Kentucky. "I feel so nervous & uneasy," Ellen wrote Cump, "that I am fit for nothing & cannot even write with a steady hand. But my hope is steady yet notwithstanding my fears and my trust in God is unshaken & are you not fighting for justice and legitimate authority against the foulest usurpation that ever ambitions sought to impose upon a free people?" Fearful that Ohio might be overrun by Southern marauders, Ellen wrote John Sherman in Washington to intercede for his brother at the War Department.

Enfeebled by poor health and by the "mental torture" of the Kentucky campaign, General Anderson relinquished the reins on October 8, and Sherman, over his own protests, assumed command of the Department of the Cumberland. "I am forced into the command of this department against my will," he told a friend, "and it should take 300,000 men to fill half the calls for troops."

Kentuckians, instead of assisting the Federals, were clamoring for protection against the local secessionists. Volunteers in Ohio and Indiana were ready to pour into Kentucky, but lacked arms and clothing. McClellan in the east and Frémont in the west had made such heavy drafts that supplies were scant.

Sherman telegraphed to Lincoln: "I am ordered to command here. I must have experienced brigadiers. I will not be responsible for events but will do my best." He felt the administration was unresponsive to the needs of the region. Secretary of the Treasury Chase warned him: "Do not overestimate your enemy's force so much as to delay greatly your aggressive movements. In my judgment we have lost much this way."

Lorenzo Thomas, the adjutant general, urged him to take the offensive and seize Cumberland Gap, which would protect the Unionists in eastern Tennessee. With untrained men, few officers, and a lack of supplies, this plan seemed preposterous to Sherman. In consultation with officers of the Tennessee troops, he estimated that it would take more than 10,000 men to mount an offensive into Tennessee. He had no intelligence service, and so he was constantly exaggerating the strength of the enemy forces opposing him.

In Louisville he worked day and night. "He lived at the Galt House on the ground floor," said a reporter, "and he paced the corridor outside his room for hours, absorbed." He was terribly nervous, smoking too many cigars and drinking too much whiskey.

It was a dirty, ill-omened campaign, a campaign of sniping and scouting, in which Sherman and his army groped almost hopelessly for the enemy. It was a campaign doomed to obscurity in the public mind, a campaign in which Sherman stood to gain little and had everything to lose.

On the evening of October 16 Secretary of War Simon Cameron stopped off in Louisville on his way back to Washington from Saint Louis. Cameron was an ineffectual man, whom Lincoln had appointed in compliance with a prenomination bargain. Traveling with him was Adj. Gen. Lorenzo Thomas.

Cameron and Thomas and a handful of newspaper reporters arrived at Galt House, ordered food and liquor sent to their rooms, and then called for General Sherman. When Sherman arrived, he found Cameron stretched out full-length on his bed. Glancing up, Cameron smiled and said, "Now General Sherman, tell us your troubles."

Sherman objected vehemently to any such discussion before newspapermen. The secretary replied, "We are all friends, here."

Locking the door and striding up and down the room, Sherman gave his appraisal of conditions and recited his needs. The western part of Kentucky was already in Confederate hands. General Buckner was in advance of the Green River with a heavy force on the road to Louisville, and an attack could be expected daily. Federal units could not resist a major offensive.

"You astonish me!" Cameron exclaimed. Sherman insisted that since Kentucky had a frontier of nearly 1,000 miles and had railroad communications with the entire South, he needed 60,000 men to defend it and 200,000 to take offensive action.*

"Great God!" Cameron exclaimed. "Where are they to come from?"

Cameron felt sure that Sherman was overestimating the power of the Rebels, but the general stood his ground, and as the interview was about to break up, Cameron promised more arms and 10,000 men.

The same night Cameron wired Lincoln: "Matters are in much worse condition than I expected to find them. A large number of troops are needed here immediately."

---

* After the war, General Sherman claimed he meant it would take 200,000 troops to clear the entire Mississippi Valley, not just Kentucky. General Thomas J. Wood, who was present at the Sherman-Cameron interview also contended that Sherman specified the 200,000 for the Mississippi Valley.

It was unfortunate that the Cameron-Sherman interview had taken place in the presence of newsmen. Sherman had a long-standing dislike for the press, and in Kentucky, he had imposed censorship, claiming that news columns revealed valuable information to the enemy.

In Harrisburg, Pa., on his way to Washington, Cameron remarked to newsmen that General Sherman was "absolutely crazy." One reporter, whom Sherman had once threatened to hang as a spy, wrote up a story with great embellishment for a New York paper. The press throughout the nation carried accounts of General Sherman's "insane request." They contained half-truths, distortions, and falsifications. It was said that Sherman had asked for 200,000 men to save Kentucky, that he was suffering from "nervous fear" and "took a frightened view of things"; that he had made absurd demands on the secretary of war. Cameron was rumored to look upon Sherman as an officer whose mind had become unbalanced.

"Mr. Cameron," recalled Sherman later, "... never to my knowledge, took pains to affirm or deny it. My position was therefore simply unbearable, and it is probable I resented the cruel insult with language of intense feeling. Still I received no orders, no reenforcements, not a word of encouragement or relief." It was true that Sherman was depressed by Washington's neglect of his army and by military affairs in Kentucky, but while he over-estimated the strength of the Confederates, his judgment was basically sound.

Deeply concerned, Sherman wrote General Thomas: "I am told that my estimate of troops needed for this line, via 200,000 has been construed to my prejudice, and therefore leave it for the future. This is the great center, on which our enemies can concentrate whatever force is not employed elsewhere."

"I feel that I am to be sacrificed," Cump told John. "I tell you and warn you of the danger so far as my power goes. I cannot promise to prevent the enemy reaching the Ohio River at a hundred different places."

Sherman realized that he was taking a pessimistic view and "hoped to God" that he had incorrectly analyzed military conditions in Kentucky. Loyal Tennesseans, including Senator Johnson, kept pressuring him to mount an all-out offensive and capture Knoxville. Sherman refused to march into Tennessee until Kentucky was secure. Senator Johnson, returning to Washington from Tennessee, discussed the situation with cabinet members and reported that there was nothing to prevent a Union advance into Tennessee. General Sherman, he said, was so intimidated by the alleged strength of the Confederates that he was "much of the time incapacitated for command."

"To advance," Cump wrote Ellen, "would be madness and to stand still folly.... The idea of going down in History with a fame such as threatens me nearly makes me crazy, indeed I may be so now.

"I have so much to do and a dread of danger so hangs around me that I can hardly write to you with any degree of satisfaction," he continued. "I am doing all I know how, but to be in the midst of people ready to betray is the most unpleasant of all feelings."

In late October Sherman was momentarily encouraged when Thomas's units won a decided victory, repulsing the enemy on nearly equal terms. This enthusiasm, however, evaporated when he learned that a band of his men, burning Confederate bridges in eastern Tennessee, had been captured and hanged. The execution of the bridge burners, who had been sent out in the expectation that Thomas would advance across the mountains and invade Tennessee, caused Sherman great pain. After the raiders had entered enemy territory, Sherman had refused to risk an offensive that late in the season. He felt that he had let these men down, and his grief was exacerbated by feelings of guilt.

Upset, ignored by the decision makers in Washington, Sherman wanted to resign. "Do not conclude as before," he confided to General Thomas, "that I exaggerate the facts. It would be better if some more sanguine mind were here, for I am forced to order according to my convictions."

On November 1, 1861, Gen. Winfield Scott retired, and General McClellan wired Sherman, asking for an estimate of the Kentucky situation. Sherman's response ended, "Our forces are too small to do good, and too large to be sacrificed."

Again McClellan telegraphed. Were the Confederates moving on Louisville? Were they crossing the Green River? McClellan demanded that Sherman wire him daily and report on military activities. Sherman resented this close supervision. It was impossible to send daily reports.

The Confederates had a great advantage. Within Federal lines, in the camps and along the highways, the enemy had active partisans, ordinary citizens, who acted as spies. They reported all Union movements to Rebel headquarters, while Federal officers had to procure their information through circuitous and unreliable means.

To gain a better picture of the Kentucky situation, McClellan sent his close adviser, Col. Thomas M. Key, to Louisville. Key reported that Sherman's mind was not sufficiently steady for command. This was interpreted by some to mean that Key believed Sherman was unbalanced, and this rumor began to permeate the War Department.

Sherman despaired when Adjutant General Thomas's report of military conditions in Kentucky was published. The report strongly underscored Sherman's fear of a Confederate attack, his unwillingness to assume the offensive, and the secretary's belief that Sherman had vastly overestimated the enemy's strength.

Sherman telegraphed McClellan, asking to be relieved of command, fully conscious that he was doing irreparable damage to any remaining chances he might have had for immediate advancement. By surrendering the command in Kentucky, he was confirming his inability to manage it. "I asked to be relieved," Sherman wrote Thomas Ewing, "because I felt my opinions were not heeded, and that they in Washington believed I overrated the forces of the Rebels. . . . There is no doubt my mind is deeply moved by an estimate of strength and purpose on the part of our enemies much higher than the Government or People believe to be true. I am perfectly willing to leave its solution to time and will be much relieved to find I am wholly wrong."

McClellan answered: "In compliance with your request to be relieved, General Buell will take command in Kentucky."

Like many of the other Northern generals early in the war, Sherman was inexperienced. Erstwhile army lieutenant, banker, lawyer, speculator, and railroad president, Sherman had never seen battle or commanded large groups of men until July, 1861. Although the president, the War Department, and Northerners in general demanded an offensive in Kentucky, as well as elsewhere, Federal troops were simply unprepared for the task. "I knew the impatience of the country for results," Sherman wrote Thomas Ewing, "but to expect us in Kentucky with troops many of which had come unarmed to assume . . . the offensive while a well organized army lay at Washington, D.C. was unfair."

The political situation in Kentucky was complicated, and it was difficult to gauge which way the commonwealth was headed. Sherman, however, was off the mark in his estimation that Kentucky was overwhelmingly Confederate in sentiment.

In his interview with Cameron, he had overestimated the military posture of the enemy. His original estimate of 200,000 was based not on analytical calculations, but on a vivid imagination. This quickness of mind, this ability to grasp instantly all possibilities, was eventually to lead Sherman to greatness, but from September to November, 1861, it led him to errors of judgment.

Sherman offended members of the administration by his unequivocal demand for reinforcements, and he alienated the press. He had exposed himself to public censure. "God knows that I [wish]," he wrote Ellen, "that we might hide ourselves in some quiet corner of the world."

"I prefer to follow not to lead...."

AT HIS HOME in Mansfield, Ohio, Sen. John Sherman was annoyed when he learned that his brother had resigned his command. "Your view [of things in Kentucky] was so gloomy that if I could entirely rely upon its correctness it would induce me promptly to go to Washington," he wrote Cump. "But conversations with others, my own observation, and the reason of things convince me that you are not only in error but are laboring under some strange illusion. I am the more convinced of this from your manner ... to overestimate difficulties. You have been so harrassed with the magnitude of your labors and have allowed yourself so little rest and such that your mind casts a sombre shadow upon everything.

"This is my conviction confessed to you with the pardon of a brother. Beside your manner is abrupt and most repulsive. This is so unlike your usual manner as to occasion complaint from your warmest friends."

In Louisville, awaiting General Buell's arrival, Cump answered: "I blame nobody during this awful Civil War. All I say is that an expedition into East Tennessee with my force was impossible .... If anybody can do better than I can for God's sake let him. I prefer to follow not to lead, as I confess I have not the confidence of a Leader in this war, and would be happy to slide into obscurity."

Again he wrote: "It is easy enough for you politicians to sit and calculate what more I should do, but this force in the west was half armed and increased little by little so that at no time could we pretend to have superior numbers."

Sherman was mentally and physically spent, and informing

Ellen of his resignation, wrote: "I am almost crazy," and "worried to death with the multitudinous duties of command." One of Sherman's officers was so concerned over his condition that he wrote Thomas Ewing: "Send Mrs. Sherman and the younger boy down to relieve General Sherman's mind from the pressures of business—no occasion for alarm." Within 24 hours, Ellen and Phil Ewing, along with Willy and Tommy, were on their way to Louisville.

When she arrived at Galt House, Ellen was greatly disturbed by Cump's drawn face and heavy eyes. His black mood was expressed in long, glum silences, and if anyone spoke to him, he answered with startling brusqueness. Everyone who was not strongly for the Union, he told her, "wanted to turn assassin and shoot us all down like dogs!"

Ellen thought this was nonsense. "You should make up your mind to be calm, and be satisfied that you have done your best." His worried servant boy confided to Ellen, "General Sherman has seldom taken a meal lately. Sometimes he eats nothing all day."

Ellen was convinced that Cump's despondency over the executions of the bridge burners was the principal reason for his resignation. She was disturbed that Washington had failed to support him.

"I am glad you are with your husband," Thomas Ewing wrote Ellen. "He has felt too deeply the responsibility of his situation; and incessant watchfulness and the thousand harassing cares that he has suffered to press on him too closely have broken his health and spirits. No man ever did or ever can stand up against such an accumulation of toils and cares without casting them off for many hours in the day by some kind of relaxation. . . .

"The enemy is no doubt formidable but he over-estimates their forces, as *they* no doubt do his. *He* knows the defects of his own army, but has no means of knowing the deficiencies of theirs, which are quite as formidable. On the whole I do not think an advance on their part probable, and if made I have no doubt it will be successfully repelled."

From Louisville Ellen wrote John Sherman begging him to come to Kentucky. "I am," she said, "distressed by his melancholy forebodings. I do not participate in them, to any extent, but on the contrary I believe if he would keep his present command & preserve his health, he would ultimately win laurels inferior to no man's and drive the rebels into the Gulf of Mexico before another year rolls around. . . .

"For God's sake do what you can to cheer him up and keep him in the position most advantageous to his mind & reputation. If he only had troops enough to gain a victory it would have a great effect on his mind. No man is better qualified to direct and govern men."

John Sherman went to Louisville. Cump began to improve in looks and spirits. When Ellen decided that he was all right, she sent Phil and the children home, and several days later she and John departed for Ohio.

Almost three weeks after Sherman had sent in his resignation, General Buell arrived in Louisville. Buell analyzed conditions in Kentucky and wrote McClellan that Sherman was still insisting on 200,000 men, but that he was "content to try with less." It was not difficult, he said, to ascertain the enemy's movements, and he was convinced that they would not attack.

After reviewing the troops, Sherman turned over the command to Buell and departed for Saint Louis, where he was ordered for duty under Gen. Henry W. Halleck, commanding the Department of Missouri.

President Lincoln was concerned over Sherman's resignation. He liked the general and endorsed a letter from a pro-Union railroad president in Kentucky, James Guthrie, suggesting that Sherman remain in the state and serve under Buell. The president's endorsement was qualified and read: "If General McClellan thinks it proper to make Buell a major-general, enabling Sherman to return to Kentucky, it would rather please me." But General McClellan had no such plans.

At Planter's House in Saint Louis, Sherman reported for duty to his long-standing friend, General Halleck. Though their temperaments were different, Sherman had always admired him since their days at West Point, when Halleck, the honor student, had taken an interest in the young cadet from Ohio. Their friendship had matured during their voyage to California and during the months they had messed together in Monterey. Halleck had retired from the army to become a lawyer.

Halleck's main job in Saint Louis was to reorganize completely

General Frémont's command. Military conditions in Missouri were in complete chaos. The troops were unpaid and many were without arms or clothing. They were demoralized. Hospitals were overflowing.

Sherman was still fatigued when he arrived in Saint Louis and "felt and saw, and was deeply moved to observe that manifest belief that there was more or less of truth in the rumor that cares, perplexities, and anxiety of the situation [in Kentucky] had unbalanced my judgment.

"I could not hide from myself," he said, "that many of the officers and soldiers subsequently placed under my command looked at me askance and with suspicion."

Halleck, however, ignored all rumor surrounding his friend and ordered him into the field to visit different posts throughout Missouri, to report the effective strength of the various units, and to take command, if he desired, of the three divisions camped at Sedalia, Syracuse, and Tipton. On November 28 Sherman wrote to Halleck to "look well to Jefferson City" as Gen. Sterling Price with a vast Confederate army was moving in that direction. Another enemy force was marching on Rolla, and after capturing that town, it would join forces with Price, and this combined army would threaten Saint Louis. Overestimating the enemy's strength once again, Sherman maneuvered his troops into defensive positions.

Ellen, worried about her husband, decided to go to Saint Louis and remain with him as long as possible. When she arrived at Planter's House, she was disappointed to learn that he was in the field, but she met and was favorably impressed with General Halleck. He was obviously treating Sherman with courtesy and consideration, a marked difference, she thought, from the way Washington had used him in Kentucky.

Halleck, however, exercising caution, had checked with Gen. John Pope at Syracuse, Mo., on Sherman's reports. Discovering no trace of the enemy, Pope wired Halleck that there was no possibility of General Price marching northward. Halleck then ordered Sherman back to Saint Louis to report in person on his observations of military conditions in Missouri.

When Sherman arrived in Saint Louis, he was happy to find Ellen waiting. But his high spirits rapidly vanished when his recall was interpreted by the press as a further indication of his emotional unbalance. One newsman reported that "his eye had a half-wild expression. . . . He looks rather like an anxious man of business than an ideal soldier, suggesting the exchange and not the camp. He sleeps little; nor do the most powerful opiates relieve his terrible cerebral excitement."

Realizing that his efforts in Missouri were now temporarily useless, Sherman asked for a 20-day leave to accompany his wife back to Lancaster and "to allow the storm to blow over." Before departing, he told Halleck that he wished to waive his right to command a division upon his return.

Halleck wrote McClellan that Sherman's movements of troops in and around Sedalia had been unsatisfactory. "I am satisfied," he went on, "that General Sherman's physical and mental system is so completely broken by labor and care as to render him for the present entirely unfit for duty. Perhaps a few weeks' rest may restore him. I am satisfied that in his present condition it would be dangerous to give him a command here."

Ellen took Cump to the house she was leasing near the Ewing mansion. Relieved from the anxieties of command for the first time since June, his health and spirits improved.

Picking up the newspaper on December 9, Cump noted a small item, "Special to the New York *Times*," which reported, in part: "General Robert Wilson, President of the Missouri State Convention, arrived here last evening. He says that the federal troops still occupy Sedalia. . . . General Sigel· is now in command in place of General Sherman, whose disorders have removed him, perhaps permanently, from his command."

Two days later, the *Cincinnati Daily Commercial* headlined: "General William T. Sherman Insane." "It appears," the column said, "that he was at times when commanding in Kentucky stark mad. We learned that he at one time telegraphed to the War Department three times in one day for permission to evacuate Kentucky and retreat into Indiana." While in Missouri, the report continued, he was placed "at the head of a brigade at Sedalia, where the shocking fact that he was a madman was developed by orders that his subordinates knew to be preposterous and refused to obey. He has, of course, been relieved altogether from command. The harsh criticisms which have been lavished upon this gentleman, provoked by his strange conduct, will now give way to feelings of the deepest sympathy for him in this great calamity. It seems providential that the country has not to mourn the loss of any army through the loss of the mind of a general into whose hands were committed the vast responsibilities of the command in Kentucky."

The *Saint Louis Missouri Democrat* carried the same story, and the *Cincinnati Gazette* published a telegram from Frankfort, Ky., which said, in part: "The family and friends of Sherman desire to keep his insanity a secret."

The Ewing family was in an uproar. Phil Ewing left immediately for Cincinnati to confront the editor of the *Daily Commercial*. In Washington Thomas Ewing was convinced that there was an army conspiracy against his son-in-law. "A political personality or the devil can live down a slander," he exploded, "but not a military man."

"You have political power, you ought to use it and I know you will protect him," Ellen wrote John Sherman. "And why," she went on, "were re-enforcements now pouring into Kentucky to sustain General Buell, when Sherman's requests had gone unheeded?"

Ellen detested General McClellan. "He not only did not attempt any active service himself," she wrote, "but he paid no attention to the interests of the country in Kentucky, ignored Cump, refused him any regular troops or men that had had any discipline and suffered him to be driven out of the position by his neglect without raising a finger."

Although John Sherman was irked at his brother's resignation, he resented the news stories charging insanity. He called on President Lincoln. "I had a long interview about Cump with the President," he wrote Ellen. "The conversation was a very free one. It was manifest that the President felt kindly to him and when he went to Kentucky relied upon him more than upon Anderson. All his early movements were highly extolled."

The president explained to John why reinforcements were not sent into Kentucky. He told him about the letters to the

White House from persons "high in the army and in civil life" attesting to Sherman's extreme depressions and his physical exhaustion.

"These were unluckily supported," John continued, "by letters and dispatches from him of which were proven by subsequent events to be entirely erroneous and all were desponding, complaining and almost insubordinate. He constantly exaggerated the number and resources of the enemy and looked upon all around him with distrust and suspicion. This condition of affairs was supported by what Cameron . . . said, and led to the prompt compliance with his request to be recalled. . . .

"The President has the kindest feeling for him and suggested that he come here on a visit. . . . On the whole I am well convinced that Cump made serious mistakes in Ky.—1) in overrating the enemy and underrating his own force and position, 2) in hasty and inconsiderate demands here and in unreasonable impertinance for compliance, 3) in repelling too hastily newspaper reporters and others who have at least the power to create prejudice against him.

"If I was in Cump's place I would disregard them [the newspaper attacks] quietly, perform his duty wherever sent, and justify the President's remark that there was more fighting qualities in Gen. Sherman than in any Brigadier he had appointed. . . . If he had the self confidence of [General Nathaniel P.] Banks and the Hope and faith of many others he would be the best general in the Army."

Despite this interview with Senator Sherman, neither Lincoln nor members of the cabinet nor General McClellan publicly contradicted the newspaper stories that Sherman was "insane." Learning of Sherman's resignation, a Pennsylvania politician, Alexander K. McClure, went to the War Department and asked Assistant Secretary of War Thomas A. Scott what it meant. Scott's answer was short: "Sherman's gone in the head." On further inquiry McClure discovered that "Scott simply voiced the general belief of those who should have been better informed on the subject."

However, Sherman still had friends whose confidence in him was not swayed. Halleck's assistant adjutant general, J. A. Hammond, wrote Sherman from Saint Louis: "I hope you will not seriously think of waiving your right to a division. Do you remember the parable of the talents? Now with your powers, and position, you may in time to come, do immense good, protect the innocent, etc. Reflect I beg of you that as you curtail your power —and position measures the power now—you curtail your opportunities of doing good; to say nothing of punishing outrage, & removing abuses. You owe it to yourself, friends, and the cause, to increase your power."

General Hugh Boyle Ewing, writing from Washington, explained that a number of army officers considered Sherman second only to McClellan, while Lincoln had the highest regard for him. Whether Cump believed him or not, this was the truth. Many Washington authorities were convinced the "revenge of disappointed and angry reporters" had caused the press attacks.

Much later in the war, when someone sought to win Sherman's favor by speaking disparagingly of General Grant, Sherman remarked: "It won't do, sir. It won't do at all. Grant is a great general, he stood by me when they said I was crazy."

In Lancaster the Sherman children became embroiled in the controversy. Ellen was shaken one day when Tommy burst into the parlor saying that a boy down the street had told him, "Your Papa is crazy."

Cump vigorously denied the newspaper charges. "That damn column," he was sure, was the handiwork of that rascal of a correspondent whom he had threatened to hang as a spy in Kentucky. He was deeply troubled at the effect of this publicity on the Ewing family, particularly on his father-in-law. "Among the keenest feelings of my life is that arising from a consciousness that you will be mortified beyond measure at the disgrace which has befallen me," he told Mr. Ewing.

He wrote General Halleck a long letter, relating the charges and asking him if he thought that his actions at Sedalia displayed any "want of mind." He stated that he saw a much greater danger in the acts of the Confederate sympathizers in Missouri than most officers. Having lived in the South, he knew well that they were more hotheaded than Northerners. In his judgment, the enemy force could do more harm scattered than united. He concluded that the newspaper attacks would destroy his usefulness by depriving him of the confidence and respect of the men in the ranks.

General Halleck was not surprised that his friend had been attacked in the press. He recalled how extremely upset and nervous Sherman had appeared. Anyone could have gained the wrong impression from his "broken down appearance."

Halleck wrote to the *Missouri Democrat*, stating that General Sherman was far from crazy and had, in fact, been employed on duties of the highest importance on the day he left on leave.

In a letter to Ellen, Halleck, who had also been criticized by the newspapers, said: "These things never disturbed me & I hope that the Genl will not let them annoy him. Tell the Genl I will make a Yankee trade with him—I will take all that is said against him, if he will take all that is said against me. I am certain to make 50 per cent profit by the exchange.

"I treated the whole matter as a joke," he continued, then added, candidly, "He certainly acted insane." However, as Halleck pointed out to Phil Ewing, anyone who knew Sherman as well as he did "thought nothing was the matter with . . . [him] except want of rest."

Ellen's anger turned to depression. She was apprehensive about Cump's return to Saint Louis for duty. She had seen her husband in periods of great stress, but she had never seen him as black and silent as now.

The newspaper charges, she wrote John, "will fasten upon him that melancholy insanity to which your family [Hoyt-Sherman] is subject, but which is so far removed from that they have represented."

Referring to the despondency Cump had experienced in California, Ellen knew that "the insanity" which affected the Hoyt-Sherman families, was rather "a depression of spirits," or "a morbid melancholy."

Ellen wanted her husband to remain at home until early spring, resting and looking after her father's financial affairs. But despite her efforts, he left Lancaster on December 18. He was readier to face the suspicions of his fellow officers in Missouri than to work at the saltworks, which had been waiting for him for years, "like purgatory."

On Sherman's arrival in Saint Louis, General Halleck decided that although he looked much better, he was still not ready to take the field against the enemy. Halleck assigned him to command Benton Barracks and there to instruct over 12,000 recruits in the art of war. Immediately Sherman went to work drilling volunteers, and by late December, had ready for action four infantry and two cavalry regiments. Halleck wrote McClellan that Sherman would soon be fit enough for a field command.

His careful handling of Sherman would ultimately reap personal rewards. Sherman came to regard Halleck as his benefactor, who had saved him from obscurity. By gradually increasing Sherman's responsibilities, Halleck helped him regain his lost confidence.

Sherman, however, continued pessimistic. The longer he was in Saint Louis, the more convinced he became that two-thirds of its population were secessionists. "The people are against us, some from southern connections and many from self-interest— the South holding the River, and the River being the life of the country," he wrote John. "Could we open the navigation of the Mississippi, this class would be loyal enough." In Kentucky General Buell had now doubled the manpower of his army, yet he had done nothing.*

Sherman wanted to remain in obscurity at Benton Barracks until he saw some hope of the Union winning the war. He realized that while he was in a subordinate position, others less fit were in posts that he was well suited to occupy. Yet he could not claim these, for he had failed in Kentucky.

He felt disgraced for having surrendered his command. The actions of the bridge burners in Tennessee and their subsequent executions were "the chief source of my despondency." Sherman's almost unbearable frustration and feelings of inadequacy caused him to confide in John: "I do think I should have committed suicide were it not for my children."

To Ellen he wrote: "I certainly have not the same character I would have had, had I not lived so much in the South and experienced so much of their peculiar hospitality. I also wanted to

* Later in the Civil War, when the Union placed in the west total forces approximating those asked for by Sherman, it appeared that his estimate had been correct. But as the military situation developed, it did not follow the pattern he predicted. Union forces in the west operated in subtheaters—the two principal ones were the Mississippi River line and the Tennessee River line. They acted as two armies, and the numerical strength of neither was near the 200,000 demanded by Sherman in November, 1861. See T. Harry Williams, *McClellan, Sherman and Grant* (1962), pp. 55–56.

keep out of the war and knew the first set could be swept away in the tempest of passion, besides in Louisiana I said I would keep in the background and before I was aware of it I found myself in the prominent position in Kentucky. I ought to have called about the best men I could find & trust to events. . . . When [Adjutant General] Thomas's letter came out I felt so discouraged I asked relief. It looks very different to me now, although I would not resume the place for the world—but being in it I should have stayed.

"I have given you pain, when it should have been pride, honor and pleasure," Cump said, "but this unnatural war does weigh heavy on my mind & heart."

Ellen could not understand why her husband was abusing himself. He had brought no disgrace on anyone. "So let me beg you, my dearest husband, for the sake of your family," she wrote, "to put away all such depressing thoughts & stand calm—and undisturbed in the brightness of your superior intellect and your admirable virtues. In giving way to these feelings you may bring on that more serious melancholy that afflicted your Uncle Charles. Do try to drive them away and submitting your will to that of our Good God, keep your soul calm and hopeful."

Mr. Ewing had seen President Lincoln and had come away convinced that he felt most kindly toward Cump.

Ellen decided to write the President herself:

Mr. Lincoln, Dear Sir: Having always entertained a high regard for you & believing you to possess the kindest feelings as well as the truest honor, I appeal with confidence to you for some intervention in my husband's favor & in vindication of his slandered name.

Left, for several weeks, in an enemy's country, with but thirty thousand raw recruits to protect an extent of territory larger than that which Genl McClellan held his choice & immense force, to protect; and with no muskets to give the miserable East Tennesseeans could he have sent a force through Cumberland Gap?

Ellen went on, relating in detail the events of the past month: "I beseech you, by some mark of confidence, to relieve my husband from the suspicions now resting on him. He is now occupying a subordinate position in Gen. Halleck's department, which seems an endorsement of the slander. I do not reproach Genl Halleck for Gen. Sherman's enemies may have shaken the confidence of the men, in him, by the suspicions that he is insane & thus rendered it impolitic to appoint him to a command there. His mind is harassed by these cruel attacks. They originated in the West; he is under their influence there, & his subordinate position gives sanction to the belief."

Ellen urged Lincoln to transfer her husband to the eastern theater of operations and then added: "As malice cannot prevail, where justice rules, I look for a speedy relief from the sorrow that has afflicted me in this trial to my husband." If Lincoln ever answered her letter, there is no record of it.

In January Ellen went with her father to see the president to plead Cump's case in person. One evening she and Mr. Ewing had a long and satisfactory interview at the White House. Lincoln praised Sherman and told Ellen that he and Secretary of State Seward had been strongly impressed with her husband when he was commanding the brigades at Fort Corcoran.

He had been sorry when Sherman was sent to Kentucky, but he felt that Kentucky was much safer after the general had assumed command. The dispatches from the commonwealth, however, made him feel less comfortable, less sure of the military situation.

"He seemed anxious for us to know, and said that he wanted *you* to know," Ellen told Cump, "that he had entertained the highest and most generous feelings towards you, and that he still entertained them; and he intimated that ... recent reports were unfounded [and that] your abilities would soon secure promotion. ... He seemed anxious that we should believe that he felt kindly towards you. He and father are great friends just now.

"I look forward with great confidence to the future," Ellen added. "The President is very friendly to you. ... A little time will wear away this slander and then you stand higher than ever."

In another letter to her husband, Ellen wrote: "Truly did father say to Lincoln that the only trouble with you was that you saw too far and too accurately into the future. I want you to banish the spirit of self distrust that you have admitted lately and do not allow yourself to believe that you have been mistaken for you have not in anything."

In Missouri, meanwhile, Gen. Sterling Price's Confederate forces had fallen back to Springfield and were scattered. Although Halleck had 80,000 men and the Rebels but one-fifth that number, Missouri swarmed with secessionist sympathizers who destroyed railroads and other lines of communication. "Our Army here," said Halleck, "is as much in a hostile country as it was in Mexico." Both Halleck and Sherman were coming to believe that the military forces in Missouri should be employed against the civilian population as well as the Rebel armies.

Halleck continued to observe Sherman closely. His health and spirit seemed greatly improved, and one day Halleck decided to explain to him in a letter why he had assigned him to Benton Barracks. "When you came here ... your health was so broken & your nervous system so shattered by hard labor, anxiety & exposure, as to unfit you for *field* service, [that] I thought that Benton Barracks was, under the circumstances, best suited to your health. I did not consider it a subordinate one, but one of the most important in this Dept.

"I believe you can and will render important service in this Department," he continued, "and the time may soon come when we must all take the field. When it does come there is no one who I had rather have with me than yourself."

More and more Halleck took Sherman into his confidence and invited him to participate in strategy conferences. One evening Halleck met with his chief of staff, George W. Cullum, and with Sherman. The Confederates had fortified Columbus, Ky., and controlled the Mississippi River southward to New Orleans. Westerners, Halleck complained, were insisting on a Federal advance down the Mississippi River. Generals Gideon Pillow and Leonidas Polk commanded a minimum of 20,000 Confederates, equipped with heavy cannons planted high on the river bluffs.

Suddenly, Halleck got up from his chair and went to a large map on the table. "Where is the Rebel line?" he asked.

Sherman drew the pencil through Bowling Green, Ky., Fort Henry, on the Tennessee River, and Fort Donelson, on the Cumberland.

"Now," mused Halleck, "where is the proper place to break it?"

Sherman replied: "Naturally, in the center."

Halleck drew a line perpendicular to Sherman's line, near its middle. It coincided with the general course of the Tennessee River. "That's the true line of operations," he said.

The three studied the map. Halleck was not impressed with the strategy of sending Union gunboats down the Mississippi River. He preferred an army-navy expedition up the Cumberland and Tennessee rivers, against Forts Henry and Donelson, which protected the primary target, Nashville. Such moves would force the Rebels to abandon Columbus and Bowling Green. "This line of the Cumberland or Tennessee," Halleck reported to McClellan, "is the great central line of the western theater of the war."

As a result of this and other conferences among Halleck, Cullum, and Sherman, General Grant's forces in early February, 1862, boarded transports at Cairo—at the confluence of the Mississippi and Ohio rivers—and, escorted by Union gunboats, maneuvered up the Tennessee toward Fort Henry.

Before his army could attack Fort Henry, heavy firing from the gunboats forced the Confederates to surrender. With the fall of this bastion, Grant planned to march overland and assault Fort Donelson on the Cumberland.

Until this time the career of General Grant, who was nearing 40, had not been such as to create great expectations. It seemed that this stubby man with his unkempt beard had been marked for failure. Although a West Pointer, who had served capably under Zachary Taylor and Winfield Scott during the Mexican War, he tried to escape chronic ague and the boredom of peace by drinking. His excesses led to a warning from his commander, to which Grant reacted by presenting his resignation. He subsequently earned a precarious living for his family by a variety of occupations, some of them of the most menial type.

Soon after the Civil War broke out, he became a colonel of Illinois volunteers, and a couple of months later, much to his surprise, was made a brigadier general. A professional among amateurs, he had already proved an effective organizer when, in the fall of 1861, he was in command at Cairo.

General Halleck, who now had "every confidence in Sherman," assigned him to command the District of Cairo, a part of Grant's rear zone. From Paducah, Ky., Sherman forwarded troops to Grant at the front, handled the wounded, and guarded prisoners of war.

On February 16 after a short siege, Fort Donelson capitulated to Grant's army. Sherman considered this victory "most extraordinary and brilliant," but however impressed he was with Grant's tactics in Tennessee, he still believed that Halleck was the best strategist in the Union. "I have the most unlimited confidence in Halleck," he wrote John. "He is the ablest man by far that has thus far appeared—more rapid than McClellan."

After months of discouragement, news from the west buoyed the hopes of the North, and many thought that the end of the war was near at hand. "After this, it certainly cannot be materially postponed," declared the *New York Times*. "The monster is already clutched in his death struggle." And in Washington Secretary of the Treasury Chase wrote: "The underpinning of the rebellion seems to be knocked out from under it."

The victory at Fort Donelson was followed by the evacuation of the Rebel position at Columbus and the retreat of Albert S. Johnston, ranking Confederate general in the west, who was forced to abandon his Kentucky front and to pull out of Nashville as well.

Sherman had been active in exploring the military situation in Columbus and was one of the first to ascend the bluffs and plant the Stars and Stripes over the city. He was in high spirits. From Washington John wrote congratulating his brother on his actions at Columbus, saying that this was but "a prelude to new laurels."

Grant, who had been promoted to major general, sought to consolidate the results of the victories at Forts Henry and Donelson. He had expected that a decisive Federal victory, such as Donelson, would cause the rebellion to collapse in the west. He soon discovered, however, that a new Rebel line was forming farther south, and a powerful enemy effort was to be launched to regain the lost ground.

General Albert S. Johnston was concentrating his army in and around Corinth, Miss. Grant sent his forces to Pittsburg Landing, Tenn., on the Tennessee River, and on orders from Halleck, General Buell and his 37,000 troops began moving to reinforce him.

"...somehow I am forced into prominence...."

GENERAL SHERMAN arrived at Pittsburg Landing in mid-March, commanding his newly organized division. His moodiness had all but disappeared. Officers who came into contact with General Sherman described him almost uniformly. One general related: "He talked and smoked cigars incessantly, giving orders, dictating telegrams, bright and chipper." Another recalled: "If I were to write a dozen pages I could not tell you a tenth part of what he said, for he talked incessantly and more rapidly than any man I ever saw. General Sherman is the most American man I ever saw, tall and lank, with hair like thatch, which he rubs with his hands. ... It would be easier to say what he did not talk about than what he did.... At his departure I felt it a relief and experienced almost an exhaustion after the excitement of his vigorous presence."

Similar descriptions run through most of the pen sketches of Sherman—the nervous energy, the rich imagination, a mind running restlessly on all sorts of subjects. "To say the least," one general declared, "Sherman is *very erratic*. I don't believe him guilty of *vaulting ambition*, but I have never been entirely willing to trust his mental processes and special idiosyncrasies."

Sandy-headed and gaunt, with a grizzled, short-cropped beard, Sherman still had that "wild expression about his eyes." "I never saw him but I thought of Lazarus," one observer reported. His shoulders twitched, and his hands were never still, always drumming them on a table or fiddling with his beard or fidgeting with the buttons on his coat. The men under his command, most of them just out of training camp, did not relish tasting combat for the first time under a man who had been, but a short time ago, suspected of "insanity" and "emotional imbalance."

A friend of Tom Ewing's, S. M. Dayton, visited Sherman at his headquarters and came away from the interview believing that the general was the most self-effacing man he had ever met. Sherman discussed in detail the war and his own status in the army. He indicated that he was entirely satisfied with his present command and that he desired nothing more from Washington except to be left alone. "I aspire to nothing and will ask for nothing." Dayton did not suspect that Sherman's repeated denials of ambition masked his urgent need to lead. Haunted by self-doubt, Sherman had a compulsion to prove his superior quality. Once, late in the war, he wrote: "Life is a race, the end is all that is remembered by the Great World. Those, who are out at the end, will never be able to magnify the importance of intermediate actions, no matter how brilliant and important." His depressions, his reluctance to accept responsibility when he saw no hope of victory arose out of his deep fear of failure.

After his conversation with Dayton, Cump ended a letter to Tom Ewing: "Give my love to everybody, and all I ask is to be allowed to fill a subordinate place in this war. The issues involved are too great to be the subject of personal ambition."

General Grant's headquarters were at Savannah, Tenn. He had five divisions camped at Pittsburg Landing, nine miles upriver, and Gen. Lew Wallace's division at Crumps Landing, five miles away.

Grant looked daily for General Buell and his army from Nashville. Once they came the Federals would move against the enemy at Corinth, 19 miles to the south. The Union forces were well fed, and clothed and anxious to fight. However, Sherman suspected that only a few appreciated the difficulties and dangers which lay ahead. Only his division was composed entirely of new regiments.

During the first days of April Sherman's units began probing Rebel lines. In one report, he wrote: "The enemy is saucy but got the worst of it yesterday, and will not press our pickets far... I do not apprehend anything like an attack on our position." Confidently, Grant wired Halleck: "I have scarcely the faintest idea of an attack [a general one] being made upon us."

On Sunday morning, April 6, a cannon resounded at 5:14 A.M., the prelude to a vigorous Confederate surprise assault. "We were more than surprised," one Illinois officer admitted. "We were astonished!"

Grant's forces had no line or order of battle, no defensive works of any sort, no outposts, properly speaking, to give warning or to repulse the advances of the enemy.

The most exposed position, at Shiloh Church, three miles west of Pittsburg Landing, was held by the rawest of troops, commanded by Sherman. The Rebels struck this point. "About 8 A.M.," Sherman wrote later, "I saw the glistening bayonets of heavy masses of infantry to our left front . . . . and became satisfied for the first time that the enemy designed a determined attack on our whole camp."

By 10:00 A.M. Sherman's and Gen. John A. McClernand's camps had been overrun by the enemy. A hot and confused battle raged all day. Sherman was twice wounded and had three horses shot from under him, but despite his wounds, he kept trying to get his troops into some semblance of order.

At the close of the day, the Confederates had pushed a mile behind the position Sherman had held in the morning. In the disorganized fighting, the scattering bluecoats lost touch with their units; fragments of broken regiments and companies joined such commands as they chanced to fall in with; only one of Sherman's brigades retained its organization. Some of his regiments had broken at the first fire. Others behaved better, and he managed to keep enough to form a command.

Grant was at Savannah when the firing began, and when he arrived on the battlefield, having suffered a painful fall from his horse, his generalship was of little avail.

As the evening wore on, the fighting ceased. "The battle . . . was very severe," Cump wrote Ellen. "The scenes on this field would have cured anybody of war. Mangled bodies, dead, dying, in every conceivable shape, without heads, legs; and horses! I think we have buried 2,000 since the fight, our own and the enemy's; and the wounded fill houses, tents, steamboats and every conceivable place."

Although victorious in the first day's battle, the Confederate troops sustained a severe loss in the death of their commanding general, Albert S. Johnston, who was hit in a leg artery and died from loss of blood. At his headquarters near Shiloh Church, a log cabin where Sherman had spent the previous night, General Beauregard assumed command of the Rebel army.

It rained hard. "Night closed upon the scene amid the thundering of artillery and the bursting of shells," wrote Lt. George Crosley, Third Iowa Infantry. "The scene became one of intense and thrilling Grandeur. Our heavy guns would belch forth a blazing stream of fire and the tremendous reports would shake the ground like an earthquake and the forest around was lighted up with the blazing of guns. . . . Many shells struck and exploded near me, solid shot came tearing through the trees above our heads, cutting off limbs and hurling them down to the ground. Men fell around me almost every moment."

While Sherman spent most of the night questioning prisoners, ruling on problems concerning care for the wounded of both sides, and arranging for the burial of the dead, General Buell's army struggled into Pittsburg Landing to reinforce Federal units.

Later on word came to Sherman that one of his old cadets from Louisiana, taken prisoner, had asked for him. At the prisoners' compound, he discovered Lieutenant Barrow, and they reminisced together about the days at the seminary, while Barrow told of other former cadets who were in the battle. Before leaving, Sherman gave Barrow an extra pair of socks, some drawers, and a shirt.

On the next day, Monday, April 7, Grant's troops, now reinforced by Buell's well-disciplined units, attacked the Confederates and drove them from the field. Badly demoralized, Beauregard's army retreated and dug in at Corinth.

In his official report of the two-day battle, General Grant wrote: "I feel it a duty . . . to a gallant and able officer, Brig. Gen. W. T. Sherman, to make a special mention. He was not only with his command during the entire two day action, but displayed great judgment and skill in the management of his men. Although severely wounded in the hand the first day his place was never vacant."

General Halleck, reading all the dispatches, noted in his report to the War Department: "It is the unanimous opinion here that Brig. Gen. W. T. Sherman saved the fortune of the day of the 6th and contributed largely to the glorious victory of the 7th. He was in the thickest of the fight on both days." Halleck requested that Sherman be made major general of volunteers.

Sherman was exceedingly pleased. His actions in battle had restored his reputation and had vindicated him. His pride in himself returned. He now knew that he was capable of leading forces into battle, and he had seen firsthand that the Union armies could battle the Confederates on equal terms. "I have worked hard to keep down," he wrote Ellen, "but somehow I am forced into prominence and might as well submit."*

Sherman's sensitive mind dwelled "on the horrid nature of this war, and the piles of dead and wounded and maimed makes me more anxious than ever for some hope of an end, but I know such a thing cannot be for a long, long time. Indeed I never expect ... to survive it."

"This war," he wrote, "will have more objects than one to accomplish and this is one, to make all men North and South obey and revere the written Law and despise the mere popular impulse in the Law.... This war will instill in our people the conviction that we must obey the Law, not because we like & approve it, but blindly because it is Law."

To his son Willy, he wrote: "Mama has told you all about the Big Battle; we had a hard fight and beat the Rebels back, but they are not afraid and we must have more battles. I have picked up some cannon and musket balls which I have pushed in a box and will send for you & Tom. Some of them have powder in them and you must keep them away from the fire. Else they might burst and kill somebody ....

"These things will remind you of battle. I am now living in a small tent and have a poor bed and clothes because the Rebels took my camp and carried off my bed, and some of my clothes. All my horses (3) were killed in the battle and have now two poor horses I got from the Cavalry soldiers whose riders were killed.

"We have here now a very large Army ... and must soon move toward Corinth."

* Years later, on the anniversary of the bloody conflict, Ellen told Cump: "This ... is the anniversary of the battle of Shiloh, the battle of Sunday when you had your opportunity to vindicate your name & prove the slanders of your enemies, to be false—and gloriously you did it. From that day forth, I had not a doubt of your continued success & good fortune."

The Ewing and Sherman families were overjoyed at Cump's success at Shiloh. Both Tom Ewing and John Sherman, on receiving a copy of Halleck's letter, called on Secretary of War Edwin M. Stanton, who had replaced the inept Simon Cameron. He had not seen the dispatch, but was pleased when he read it and promised that as soon as his copy arrived he would publish it in all the newspapers. Already he had sent Sherman's name to President Lincoln for promotion.

The major general's commission was not long in coming. When Sherman learned the news, he hurriedly informed Ellen: "I received today the commission of Major General, but, I know not why, it gives me far less emotion than my old commission as 1st Lieutenant of Artillery. The latter, I know, I merited; this I doubt, but its possession completes the chain from cadet up, and will remain among the family archives when you and I repose in eternity."

Ellen thought the promptness with which the commission came through as complimentary as the promotion itself. She was especially pleased that Cump repeatedly said that he could not have borne all the trials of the past had it not been for her support. "It was for relief for him that I troubled others so much," she told John Sherman, "and now that the cloud is lifted, let me thank you John for all you have done. . . . The terrible calamity that seemed to threaten me in November & the subsequent anxieties & troubles I have had on Cump's account have united me more nearly, by sympathy, to his family & I now feel more than I ever felt before that his people are my people. The peculiar affection and pride with which Cump has regarded you must henceforth endear you to me."

The *Cincinnati Daily Commercial* shifted from its anti-Sherman posture, and even Ellen admitted that it was now disposed to do her husband justice. One of its publishers acknowledged to Tom Ewing the gross wrongs the newspaper had inflicted on his now famous brother-in-law.

While Sherman was enjoying a triumph of his own, reaction in Washington and around the country was building up against the large losses of Union troops at the battle of Shiloh. Hearing rumors that Grant had been drunk on the battlefield and thinking that this was why the attack was a surprise, Secretary of War

Stanton telegraphed Halleck: "The President desires to know ... whether any neglect or misconduct of General Grant or any other officer contributed to the casualties that befell our forces on Sunday."

"The sad casualties," replied Halleck, who had hurried to Pittsburg Landing, "were due in part to the bad conduct of officers who were utterly unfit for their places, and in part to the numbers and bravery of the enemy.... A great battle cannot be fought or a victory gained without casualties.... the enemy suffered more than we did."

Sherman was irate at the newspapers for attacking Grant on his handling of the troops and for telling and retelling the old story of his fondness for whiskey. Sherman loathed that "set of dirty newspaper scribblers who have the impudance of Satan" and publish rumors as facts. "They are a pest and shall not approach men," he wrote, "and I'll treat them as spies which in truth they are." He swore "to get even with the miserable class of editors."

Worse still in his eyes was the professional jealousy of some officers. When Washington assigned someone to a top field command, they maneuvered the press to malign him, to destroy his usefulness, to pull him back into obscurity. He had seen himself assassinated in print, and now it was happening to Grant. "The very object of war is to produce results by death and slaughter," he wrote Ellen, "but the moment a battle occurs the newspapers make the leader responsible for the death and misery, whether of victory or defeat. If this be pushed much further officers of modesty and merit will keep away, will draw back into obscurity and leave our armies to be led by fools or rash men."

Sherman believed that Grant was not brilliant, but rather a good, brave soldier—sober, industrious, and "as kind as a child," in fact "a good, plain, sensible, kindhearted fellow" in whom he could place "absolute faith."

About Grant's drinking, Sherman wrote, long after the war, that Grant "always encouraged me to talk to him frankly on this and other things and I always noticed that he could with an hours sleep wake up perfectly sober and bright, and when anything was pending he was invariably abstinent of drink.... Grant did drink but never when anything important was pending."

To the lieutenant governor of Ohio, Benjamin Stanton, who

had openly criticized Grant and others for "blundering stupidity," Sherman composed a blistering letter. "I hold you responsible for a deliberate & malicious falsehood and calumny against officers and gentlemen."

Before he sent it, Cump forwarded a copy to Thomas Ewing and asked his advice. Ewing advised Cump to reconsider, to write with greater care a letter not only for the present but for future history. Cump reworked the letter and sent it to Ewing, who dispatched it to the newspapers to be published. Cump's family and friends were delighted to see him so defiant.

Sherman himself did not escape newspaper censure for his actions at Shiloh. The *Cincinnati Gazette* held him directly responsible for the bloodshed. In a letter to the *Louisville Journal*, Thomas Ewing claimed that the *Gazette* gained its information only from deserters. "I see newsmen are fighting you again," John Sherman wrote Cump. "Why can't you keep on good terms with them? They are very useful if you allow them to be, but if not they have a power for evil that no one can stand against. I see no reason for you to quarrel."

Military critics who examined the battle of Shiloh have agreed that Grant's arrangements at Pittsburg Landing were faulty and have criticized his failure to guard against surprise by entrenching. These arguments are pertinent, but Grant's errors were due primarily to his lack of experience.

General Halleck assembled a huge army at Pittsburg Landing: Grant's army, Buell's army, and Gen. John Pope's army, which had been opening the upper Mississippi with Union gunboats. Halleck had decided to take active field command—for the first and only time in the war—and he had given Grant the dubious promotion of becoming second-in-command, depriving him of any actual command of troops.

Grant chafed and asked more than once to be relieved from duty under Halleck. One evening Sherman went to Grant's quarters and discovered him packing.

"What are you doing? Where are you going?" questioned Cump.

"You know. There is nothing here for me. I am not allowed to do anything here. I am going to Saint Louis," said Grant, visibly shaken, tears coming to his eyes.

"Don't, you must not go! If you go, you are forgotten. We are your friends," Cump reassured Grant, persuading him to stay.

A close friendship, a deep mutual understanding was beginning. Once Sherman compared himself to Grant and General McClernand. The latter saw clearly what was near, but little beyond. "My style is the reverse. I am somewhat blind to what occurs near me, but have a clear perception of things and events remote. Grant possesses the happy medium, and it is for this reason I admire him."

The admiration was mutual. Grant, in a letter to Ellen, wrote: "Having known General Sherman for a great many years, and so favorably too, there is nothing he, or his friends for him, could ask that I would not do if it were in my power. It is to him and some other brave men like himself that .... our cause has triumphed to the extent it has."

The Union army under General Halleck pushed slowly and cautiously toward Corinth, a position Beauregard had held since Shiloh. By the end of May, the Confederates had evacuated the area, and the Federals marched in and occupied it.

To the men in the ranks of the Fifth Division, Sherman issued his congratulations on a job well done and finished by telling them: "We are not here to kill and slay, but to vindicate the honor and just authority of that Government which has been bequeathed to us by our honored fathers, and to whom we would be recreant if we permitted their work to pass to our children marred and spoiled by ambitious and wicked rebels.

"The General commanding while thus claiming for his division their just share in this glorious result, must at the same time remind them that much yet remains to be done, and all must still continue the same vigilant patience, industry and obedience till the enemy lay down their arms and publicly acknowledge that for their supposed grievances they must obey the laws of their country and not attempt its overthrow by threats, by cruelty and by war. They must be made to feel and acknowledge the power of a just and mighty nation."

Throughout the Corinth campaign Sherman's admiration for

Halleck increased. "Halleck is entitled to all the praise," he wrote Ellen. "He ever astonishes me by his sagacity. Our movement has been slow, deliberate and methodical and doubtless Bragg & Beauregard felt like the fly on the approach of the spider." Again Sherman wrote, Halleck "merits the confidence reposed in him. He . . . is a man of intellect, high education and calm determination. He is the only real Great Man thus far."

The Union troops were cheered by the news that New Orleans had fallen to the Union navy and that an army, now set free, would come to support Halleck's forces.

In mid-June Sherman and his division marched to LaGrange, Tenn., to cover the reconstruction of the Memphis and Charleston Railroad, which would open up communications from Corinth and Grand Junction to Memphis. He sent an expedition to Holly Springs, Miss., to scatter the fragments of the enemy and push them toward Grenada, Miss.

General Halleck was made general-in-chief of all the armies of the United States, with headquarters in Washington. This brought promotion to General Grant. He was now in command of the forces in western Tennessee and northern Mississippi, and while still leading his own Army of the Tennessee, he had authority over William S. Rosecrans, commanding the Army of the Mississippi. Buell, commanding the Army of the Ohio, was entrusted with operations in central and eastern Tennessee.

Just before leaving for Washington, Halleck dropped Sherman a note, which ended: "I am more than satisfied with everything you have done. You have always had my respect, but recently you have won my highest admiration. I deeply regret to part with you."

"I thank you for the kind expression to me," Sherman answered, "but all I have done has been based on the absolute confidence I had conceived for knowledge of national law and your comprehensive knowledge of things gathered, God only knows how." Sherman felt that the Mississippi River was the key to victory and regretted Halleck's departure. Although he had a fine relationship with Grant, he wrote Halleck: "You cannot be replaced here. . . . We are all the losers; you may gain [in your new post], but I believe you would prefer to finish what you have so well begun."

"Halleck now that he is East," Cump wrote Ellen later, "will naturally look to that sphere and there is no one here qualified to control large movements. Scattered as our troops are they can affect no great results and I suppose we are on the defensive."

In July Grant ordered Sherman north to Memphis to put that city, recently won from the Confederacy, in a state of defense. When Sherman and his troops arrived on July 21, they found Memphis all but dead. Churches, schools, and stores were shut tight. The citizens, sympathetic to the Confederacy, either stayed indoors or moved about the streets with resentful faces.

Sherman ordered everything reopened, reorganized the police force, restored the city government, and took other steps to return Memphis to normal, everyday life. Meeting its citizens more than halfway, he issued an order permitting trade, without military or Treasury Department passes, over the five roads leading into the city from the surrounding areas. Quickly, business activity was restored.

In Sherman's occupation of Memphis, his first experience with conquered civilians, he displayed a high regard for the rights of citizens and was deeply concerned for their welfare. His actions indicate a consideration for ethics and a sensitiveness rare among the military. For buildings destroyed in constructing Memphis's defenses, he authorized fair compensation. To aid the needy, he established a form of poor relief and donated $1,000 and 25 cords of wood a week to get it started.

Yet Sherman viewed the city as a military post and was determined it would be treated as such. He impressed all packet steamers for army use and at first maintained his headquarters at a camp outside Memphis. One Sunday, when an Episcopalian priest omitted the standard prayer for the president of the United States, Sherman stood up, and in a loud voice, recited it himself.

The people of Memphis took no pains to hide their hatred of the Yankee invader. But Sherman believed that he was getting things under control and wrote Ellen: "The streets are here lively [again], the theatres crowded and really the town looks prosperous." He told Grant: "I find [the people] much more resigned and less presumptuous than at first."

Sherman worked tirelessly at rehabilitation, sponsoring Union clubs and militia outfits, helping the city's police fight crime, caring for the poor and homeless. He put Memphis Negroes to work on fortifications and in return gave them food, clothing, and a pound of tobacco a month. He hoped that by a policy of justice and mercy he might nurture in the citizens of Memphis a renewed loyalty to the Union.

Any hostile acts of the inhabitants, however, Sherman suppressed, and in so doing, he expected and tolerated unfriendliness. "If all who are not our friends are expelled from Memphis," he wrote, "but few will be left." He also did not hesitate to use harsh measures when bands of guerrillas began operating. Such attacks deeply affected the general, and he began to realize the difficulty faced by a conquering army operating in a hostile country. He saw how easily Rebel units maneuvered in the area without having to guard against the civilian population. At the same time his larger force was made impotent by the superior flexibility and rapid movement of the Confederates. Surprise attacks created a sense of frustration. "All the people are now guerrillas," he notified Grant, "and they have a perfect understanding." To John Sherman he wrote: "It is about time the North understood the truth. That the entire South, man, woman, and child is against us, armed and determined."

He could foresee that civilian resistance would result in total war. "The North may fall into bankruptcy and anarchy first, but if they can hold on the war will soon assume a turn to extermination, not of soldiers alone, that is the least part of the trouble, but the people."

Again and again guerrilla bands disrupted the passage of unarmed steamboats down the Mississippi. Sherman issued orders to Col. Charles C. Walcutt of the Forty-sixth Ohio: "The object of the expedition you have been detailed for is to visit the town of Randolph where yesterday the packet *Eugene* was fired upon by a party of guerrillas. Acts of this kind must be promptly punished, and it is almost impossible to reach the actors, for they come from the interior and depart as soon as the mischief is done. But the interest and well-being of the country demands that all such attacks should be followed by a punishment that will tend to prevent a repetition." He added: "I think the attack on the *Eugene* was by a small force of guerillas from Loosahatchie, who by this time have gone back, and therefore you will find no one at

Randolph, in which case you will destroy the place, leaving one house to mark the place."

He wished to make an example of Randolph simply because it lay near the scene of the trouble. Gradually, he was evolving a theory of collective responsibility, based on the assumption that everyone in the Confederacy was armed and at war.

He believed that partisans were not entitled to the protection of the laws of civilized warfare, especially when they struck unarmed steamers carrying women and children. If they were captured, he promised to try, convict, and execute them.

On September 27, 1862, three days after his order to burn Randolph, Sherman issued Special Order No. 254:

Whereas many families of known rebels and of Confederates in arms against us have been permitted to reside in peace and comfort in Memphis, and whereas the Confederate authorities either sanction or permit the firing on unarmed boats carrying passengers and goods for the use and benefit of the inhabitants of Memphis, it is ordered that for every boat fired on, ten families must be expelled from Memphis.

In a report to General Grant, he summed up his views: "We cannot change the hearts of the people of the South, but we can make war so terrible that they will realize the fact that, however brave and gallant and devoted to their country, still they are mortal and should exhaust all peaceful remedies before they fly to war." He reiterated that while Southerners "cannot be made to love us, they can be made to fear us."

"I have," he wrote to Minnie, "been forced to turn 'families' out of their houses and homes and force them to go to a strange land because of their hostility, and I have today been compelled to order soldiers to lay hands on women to force them to leave their homes to join their husbands in hostile camps. Think of this, and how cruel men become in war when even your papa has to do such acts. Pray every night that the war may end.

"Hundreds of children like yourself," he continued, "are daily taught to curse my name and every night thousands kneel in prayer & beseech the Almighty to consign me to perdition."

The people of Memphis pleaded with Sherman to cancel his

order removing families. He replied that he would suspend the order 15 days so that they might beg Confederate guerrillas to cease their activities. To Miss P. A. Fraser of Memphis, one of those who had appealed to him, he wrote: "When the time comes to settle the account, we will see which is more cruel—for your partisans . . . to shoot down the passengers and engineers with the curses of hell on their tongues, or for us to say the families of such men engaged in such hellish deeds shall not live in peace where the flag of the United States floats."

Since, to Sherman, this episode had served his purpose, he revoked the order expelling Memphis families. Sporadic guerrilla actions continued, however.

Sherman was also concerned at this time about the cotton-buying policy of the United States government. Memphis was becoming a center for cotton purchases for Northern markets and for the distribution of supplies received in exchange. Sherman believed these supplies were passed on to the Rebel armies by the civilians. As in Kentucky and Missouri, he suspected the population of Memphis of collaboration with the enemy. To the secretary of the treasury he wrote: "When one nation is at war with another, all the people of the one are enemies of the other: then the rules are plain and easy of understanding. . . . The Government of the United States may now safely proceed on the proper rule that all in the South *are* enemies of all in the North; and not only are they unfriendly, but all who can procure arms now bear them as organized regiments or guerillas."

Rebels assaulted more river steamboats. In retaliation Sherman ordered Walcutt's volunteers to destroy all the houses, farms, and cornfields for a distance of 15 miles along the Arkansas bank of the Mississippi.

"Our enemies are even worse than we are," he wrote Minnie, "for they shoot our men if they go outside our lines and fire on steamboats and they go up and down the river. . . . Your Mama and Grandpa think it is a great thing to be a high general. I would in any war but this, but I cannot but look on these people as my old friends. Every day I meet old friends who would shoot me dead if I were to go outside of camp and who look on me as a brutal wretch."

Two years later while analyzing the application of his theory of collective responsibility, he concluded that the terror inspired by his troops had crippled the people as much as their actual loss of property: "It was to me manifest that the soldiers and people of the South entertained undue fear of the Western men.... This was a power, and I intended to utilize it."

An incident related by Gen. Benjamin H. Grierson, the cavalry commander, in his autobiography illustrates another principle which Sherman was later to expand and exploit. Grierson overheard Sherman, then about to leave Memphis, bawling out his quartermaster for not supplying his transportation needs. The quartermaster argued that horses and mules were unobtainable. Grierson interrupted. "There is no need for any trouble in the matter for I can get you 2,000 mules and horses by tomorrow night, and more."

Sherman, turning toward him in amazement, asked: "How? Where in the world can you get them?"

"Take them from the rebels wherever they may be found," responded Grierson.

Sherman said, "We must have them. Do it, Grierson—do it!"

From recent scouting expeditions Grierson knew where the animals could be found. "I sent my men throughout the country," he wrote, "and swept them in by tens, twenties, fifties, and hundreds. I stopped wagons and carriages and took the mules and horses from the traces, and scoured the plantations, and thus quickly obtained the animals from barns, corrals, and pastures." Sherman had his transportation.

By late summer and fall the "Negro question" became important in discussions concerning the military and political situation. On August 8 Sherman issued regulations for the treatment of slaves in his jurisdiction. It was "neither his duty nor pleasure to disturb the relation of master and slave." Loyal masters would continue to recover their slaves, while the disloyal ones would lose them. No enticement of slaves from their masters was permitted, but Sherman would employ no force to return runaways. In substance, the general wanted the status quo.

Although Congress had declared at the start of the conflict that slaves were "contraband of war," Sherman did not permit his soldiers to interfere with the relationship between master and slave. "Have nothing to do with the Negro," he ordered. "As to freeing the Negroes," he wrote Ellen, "I don't think the time is come yet. When Negroes are liberated they or their masters must perish. They cannot exist together except in their relationship."

When President Lincoln issued his Emancipation Proclamation on September 22, 1862, giving notice to the Confederacy that he would free the slaves on January 1, 1863, Sherman declared: "Are we to feed all the Negroes, men, women, and children?" The president has freed them, he said, "but freedom don't clothe them, feed them, & shelter them. I admit these things are beyond my comprehension."

"My spirits are on Chickasaw Bayou...."

DURING THE LATE AUTUMN of 1862, while most of the Sherman children were in school at Notre Dame in Indiana, Ellen and Tommy visited Cump in Memphis. In the previous months the general had thought much of his family, and it had pained him to be separated from them for so long a time. Ellen found him extremely well and cheerful, although he was now much thinner, his face more wrinkled.

Every few nights Tommy took his blanket over to the army camp and slept in a tent with the soldiers. The men were fond of the boy, and the tailor of one of the companies made him a uniform and stitched on corporal's stripes.

Despite his heavy schedule Sherman always found time to correspond with Minnie: "I am most happy that this war does not reach you. In after years you will know all about this war from books, and may remember that I was one of its actors, but do not think that I feel in this war as I would if England were the enemy opposed to us in battle. I feel that we are fighting our own people, many of whom I knew in earlier years, and with many of whom I was once very intimate."

He advised Minnie on deportment and study habits: "When you study, study hard; learn to apply yourself so that when you are at work you think of nothing else, and when you are done with your books let your mind run free. I have seen a great many young ladies, and know that such are most interesting who are not forward or bashful—the truth lies between. Modesty is the most beautiful feature in a young girl, but should not degenerate into bashfullness. Think yourself as good as any, but never think yourself better than the poorest child of all."

In Washington Thomas Ewing had many conversations with Secretary of War Stanton. Lately the secretary had had much correspondence from Sherman and told Ewing that he believed the general was by far "the best officer, both in administration and in the field, that we have in our army." Stanton had promised John Sherman that "no effort of mine will be spared to secure to the government the fullest exercise of his abilities." General Halleck told Ewing that he wanted to give Sherman the command of a district, which would include the Mississippi.

At this time, General McClernand was in contact with President Lincoln, a neighbor from Springfield days. A former Democratic congressman from Illinois and currently major general of volunteers with a good combat record, McClernand was ambitious. Thoroughly versed in Midwest politics, he realized that a political crisis was mounting in the prairie states, which demanded a military remedy. However, in a year and a half of civil war the professional soldiers had not managed to break through Rebel barriers on the Mississippi River. This failure to open the river trade might ultimately destroy the Midwest's willingness to go along with the Union's war effort.

The general had a scheme which he wanted to put into operation, and he sought the president's blessing. As the Mississippi River was the key to the whole war, Vicksburg was the key to the river. There was a hairpin curve in the Mississippi below the bluffs on which the city stood, making it difficult, if not impossible, to send transports past the guns. The Rebels still held the river from Vicksburg to Baton Rouge. Through this sector ran their communications and supply lines east and west. To deprive the Confederates of this route would be a severe blow, the most decisive in the conduct of the war.

McClernand asked Lincoln's permission to raise an army in Illinois. With this force, he proposed to go down the Mississippi River, capture Vicksburg, and then head east toward Atlanta or west into Texas, whichever the president preferred.

McClernand's plan seemed plausible, especially since the Union force at New Orleans would be simultaneously moving upriver. Lincoln assented and informed Stanton and Halleck of his decision.

Secretary Stanton drew up a set of orders. General McClernand would take command of the men remaining in Indiana, Illinois, and Iowa and raise reinforcements. These forces would be sent to Memphis or to a site selected by General Halleck, before McClernand led them against Vicksburg.

Lincoln's decision created a command independent of Grant's department. Halleck argued against the whole scheme, but the president stood firm. He did, however, permit a minor concession. McClernand's army would be subject to Halleck's orders.

Distrusting the politician-turned-general, Halleck detailed plans that would cut McClernand's command from under him. As rapidly as the general corralled his men in Indiana and Illinois, Halleck dispatched them to Memphis to report to General Sherman.

At his headquarters Grant heard rumors of reorganization and queried Halleck. He did not want McClernand in his command as he was "incompetent." Halleck promptly answered: "You have command of all the troops sent to your department and have permission to fight the enemy where you please."

In early December Sherman met with Grant at Oxford, Miss., where they talked about the campaign for the Mississippi River. Grant, who had little patience with citizen-soldiers, paid no attention to McClernand and his plan and assigned Sherman the command of an expedition down the Mississippi to assault Vicksburg. A force of 40,000 on board transports, supported by Union gunboats of Adm. David Dixon Porter, was to land on the banks of the Yazoo River, which empties into the Mississippi, and strike Vicksburg from the rear. Meanwhile, at Oxford, Grant with his troops would move on Vicksburg by way of Grenada, keeping Confederate Gen. John C. Pemberton's army away from the city and its defenses. From New Orleans, Gen. Nathaniel P. Banks and his army, aided by Union gunboats, would ascend the Mississippi to Vicksburg.

The campaign was extremely hazardous. The Confederate line of defense, of which Vicksburg was the center, faced the river, the right resting on Haynes Bluff, a strongly fortified position on the Yazoo River, 12 miles from Vicksburg, while the left was on the Mississippi at Grand Gulf, 60 miles below by river, though not over 30 by land. Vicksburg itself was fortified by land and water and was within telegraphic and railroad reach of Meridian, Miss., and Mobile, Ala., and Grenada, Miss., where Pemberton commanded a large force.

When Sherman returned to Memphis there were 49 regiments

of infantry all forwarded by McClernand from Indiana and Illinois. He had his first meeting with Admiral Porter and explained the plans for the entire expedition. Listening to Sherman, Porter realized that he differed from Grant in one major respect: "Sherman attended to all the details himself, while Grant left them to others." Of Sherman, Porter later said that he seemed a "nervous, restless, active man."

At the wharves troops, horses, mules, wagons, and artillery were loaded on the transports. On December 20 Sherman went on board the *Forest Queen*, and at noon 70 steamboats were under way for Vicksburg. Four days later the force arrived at Helena, Ark., where Gen. Frederick Steele's division joined the expedition. At Milliken's Bend 7,000 soldiers landed, marched to Monroe, La., and tore up 30 miles of railroad tracks. Such actions momentarily halted communications between Vicksburg and the rich districts in Texas from which the Rebels drew most of their supplies.

Unknown to Sherman at the time, Gens. Earl Van Dorn and Nathan Bedford Forrest of the Confederate forces, were cutting off Grant and his army from all communications, forcing him to return to his initial point of departure. After Grant retired, General Pemberton fell back on Vicksburg, where he quickly concentrated 12,000 men to combat Sherman's unsupported effort. Sherman was also unaware that General Banks was confined to a New Orleans hotel room suffering from exhaustion. Sherman was now committed to "a forlorn hope venture."

On December 26 the expedition steamed up the Yazoo River and disembarked on the flat shelf beneath the steep cliffs of the Walnut Hills on which Vicksburg stood. For the next two days the troops inched forward, skirmishing with Pemberton's pickets, until they reached a broad bayou almost at the foot of Chickasaw Bluffs. Beyond this was a strip of firm ground lined with rifle pits and cannon. Batteries crowned the bluffs behind. The bluecoats drew in and trusted to a narrow frontal assault in the center.

On the riverbanks Sherman vainly waited for news from Grant. He heard only the sound of enemy troop trains steaming into the Vicksburg depot.

Delay would forfeit the bare chance that remained, so on December 29 Sherman launched the assault. At his command post he ordered the first attack to begin on the flanks and later ordered the main assault. As the morning advanced, the din of battle rose to a crescendo. One brigade sloshed across the bayou at the foot of Chickasaw Bluffs and found shelter under the bank. Another outfit crossed lower down. But the advance was not well supported. The disheartened Federals held these forward posts until dark, when they withdrew. That day Union losses numbered 175 killed, 930 wounded, and over 700 missing.

Although Union troops stood in their original positions, they had suffered a severe repulse. Dejected and exhausted, Sherman boarded Porter's flagship, *Blackhawk*. "My spirits are on Chickasaw Bayou," he said. "I was never so cut in my life. This has been a dreadful disaster to us."

Porter tried vainly to cheer him up and asked his steward to serve whiskey toddies.

Where was Grant? Where was Banks? In the combined movements, Sherman alone had been present and on time at Vicksburg. To Porter he complained of the greenness of his troops. Had they been battle-tested, they might have clawed their way to the top of the bluff. He had done all that was possible to push the attack.

On the following day Sherman assembled a fresh detachment to make one further landing effort at a greater distance from Vicksburg, but the attack never took place. On New Year's morning, 1863, a dense fog closed in and prevented any movement up or down the river. On the next day, increasing numbers of Confederates were plainly visible on the heights. Rain fell. The element of surprise had long since passed.

Sherman embarked his troops and retreated to the safety of Milliken's Bend. Extremely disheartened, he wrote Ellen: "Well, we have been to Vicksburg and it was too much for us and we have backed out." Later he told her: "It will in the end cost us at least ten thousand lives to take Vicksburg. I would have pushed the attack to the bitter end, but even had we reached the city unassisted we could not have held it if they are at liberty to reinforce it from the interior." He sent a brief report to General Halleck: "I reached Vicksburg at the appointed time, landed, assaulted, and failed, re-embarked my command unopposed."

That January gloom shrouded the entire North. Twenty months had passed since the fall of Fort Sumter, and there had been more Union defeats than victories. In Tennessee General Rosecrans' Army of the Cumberland had fought savagely with Braxton Bragg's forces. It was a drawn battle, producing on neither side a result commensurate with the cost in dead and wounded. Eastward, the soldiers of the Army of the Potomac, now commanded by Gen. Ambrose E. Burnside, sat around their campfires on Stafford Hills opposite Fredericksburg, beaten and demoralized from the repulse meted out by Gen. Robert E. Lee.

"I suppose you are now fully convinced of the stupendous energy of the South and their ability to prolong this war indefinitely," Cump wrote his brother, "but I am further satisfied that if it lasts 30 years we must fight it out, for the moment the North relaxes its energies the South will assume the offensive and it is wonderful how well-disciplined and provided they have their men."

The press descended on Sherman for his failure to take Vicksburg. The *Missouri Democrat* railed: "We came, we saw, and did not conquer." Newspapers termed the expedition "a stupid blunder," "a shame," "a national calamity." Who was responsible? the press demanded. The mismanagement, incompetence, and insanity of the commanding general, retorted the *Missouri Democrat*. "We want McClellan!" stormed the *Cincinnati Daily Commercial*. Ellen wrote her mother: "Don't let the miserable newspapers get you down. They can't effect Cump or me again. They can howl but they will in the end be compelled to admit his superiority."

The day after New Year's, 1863, General McClernand arrived at Milliken's Bend and to Sherman showed Lincoln's orders, issued the October before, to assume command of the forces on the Mississippi. McClernand reported to Sherman that Grant's advance toward Vicksburg had been halted by a Confederate drive in his rear, which had destroyed his depot at Holly Springs, Miss. Sherman was forced to agree that under such conditions a move against Vicksburg was hopeless.

Sherman rankled at having to step down to a corps command. Had the president sent a professional soldier to Vicksburg, "I would not have breathed a syllable of complaint," but to put "a damned politician" in command, who pretended "a knowledge he knew he did not possess, has but one meaning."

Sherman interpreted Lincoln's evaluation of McClernand as a direct insult to himself and the entire military profession. Controlling his urge to quit, he conceded that at times of crisis everyone had "to submit to insult and infamy of necessity." "I never dreamed of so severe a test of my patriotism as being superseded by McClernand," he told John, "and if I can keep my tamed spirit and live I will claim a virtue higher than Brutus."

Brooding over the heavy cost of the war in battle casualties, Cump wrote Ellen: "Indeed do I wish I had been killed long since. Better that than struggle with the curses and maledictions of every woman that has a son or brother to die in any army with which I chance to be associated. Of course Sherman is responsible."

The Ewing-Sherman clan was shaken by McClernand's appointment. John Sherman called Lincoln a fool and assured his brother that no one in high office blamed him for the Vicksburg defeat. Halleck, Stanton, and others were his friends. Thomas Ewing was sure that his son-in-law was mistaken in supposing that the president was malicious. He wrote Ellen: "On the whole Genl. Sherman need not desire a higher reputation than he now holds here. The Department relies on him more fully than on any other officer in the field."

During those first days of January, 1863, General McClernand had no definite plan for opening the Mississippi River and cutting his way through to the Gulf. After several conferences, he and his staff decided that nothing could be done against Vicksburg for the present. Sherman suggested that they turn around, move 50 miles up the Arkansas River and attack Arkansas Post, also known as Fort Hindman, garrisoned by 5,000 Confederates. From there the enemy had struck at the Mississippi River traffic and had captured a boat towing two barges loaded with navy coal.

McClernand consented. Soon Porter's gunboats and the army transports were maneuvering up the Mississippi toward the mouth of the Arkansas.

Early on the morning of January 8, they rendezvoused at the mouth of the White River and on the 9th turned from the Mississippi into a stream which was hardly more than a bayou. After a few miles the expedition passed into the broad Arkansas River.

In a two-day assault, Union troops overwhelmed the Rebels and captured Arkansas Post. It was not a great victory, but it was an inspiring change from the repulse at Vicksburg.

After the battle Sherman, tired from active fighting, sought out McClernand in his cabin on the transport *Tigress* and found the general, who had taken only a passive role, in high spirits. He repeated over and over, "Glorious! Glorious! I'll make a glorious report!" At the fort Union officers were thankful that McClernand had had the good sense to keep out of the way and leave the actual fighting to Sherman.

While at Arkansas Post, Sherman and McClernand received orders that the western armies under Grant had been regrouped into five corps: the Thirteenth, to be commanded by McClernand; the Fourteenth, by George H. Thomas, operating in middle Tennessee; the Fifteenth, by Sherman; the Sixteenth, by Stephen A. Hurlbut, near Memphis; and the Seventeenth, by James B. McPherson, in western Tennessee.

In late January General Grant came downriver to Young's Point on the Louisiana side of the river and assumed personal command of operations against Vicksburg. "If General Sherman had been left in command here," he wrote Halleck, "such is my confidence in him that I would not have thought my presence necessary."

It had been a winter of heavy and continuous rains. The river rose to unusual heights, and in places, levees gave way. The countryside was bathed in water. Troops could scarcely locate dry ground on which to pitch tents.

Grant faced a Herculean labor. Vicksburg, "The Gibraltar of the West," seemed even more impregnable now than it had when Sherman assaulted Chickasaw Bluffs. The city stood on a range of hills 200 feet above sea level. To the northeast, east, and south there was ample dry ground, but in the direction from which Grant must advance, there was little or no dry footing.

Grant's major problem was to secure a base on the east side of the Mississippi. Three schemes were suggested. First, to march the army down the west bank of the Mississippi, cross the river below Vicksburg, and cooperate with Banks coming up from New Orleans; second, to dig a canal across the peninsula opposite Vicksburg, through which gunboats and transports could pass safely, out of range of enemy guns; third, turn the Mississippi from its course by opening a new channel, via Lake Providence and through various bayous to the Red River.

Grant set Sherman and his men to work on the second plan, digging the canal opposite Vicksburg, but Sherman had little faith in the project. "Here we are at Vicksburg on the wrong side of the river trying to turn the Mississippi River by a ditch," he wrote Ellen, "a pure waste of human labor."

Heavy rains soaked the soldiers' camps. Sherman's corps was finally forced to seek the safety of the transports, while Mc-Clernand's command moved upriver from Young's Point to Milliken's Bend.

"Rain, rain,—water above, below and all around," Cump told Ellen. "I have been soused under water by my horse falling in a hole and got a good ducking yesterday where a horse could not go. No doubt they are chuckling over our helpless situation in Vicksburg."

Meanwhile General McPherson's corps was trying to cut the levee at Lake Providence and find a route via the lake, several rivers, and bayous into the Mississippi again below Vicksburg. Although Grant realized that this scheme was impossible, he let the work go on, believing that employment for his troops was better than idleness.

Two other efforts to reach dry land above the Confederate defenses were undertaken via the Yazoo River. The first attempt failed when Confederate infantry and artillery repelled the Union thrust. "We are no nearer to taking Vicksburg now," Sherman wrote, "than we were three months ago. A pass is made into the Yazoo by which we may introduce our Army as far back as Yazoo City, but Vicksburg is as far off as ever. Not a blow has been struck at it since I assaulted Chickasaw."

On March 15 Grant and Admiral Porter began a reconnaissance up Steele's Bayou with five gunboats and decided that there was a navigable route to the Yazoo through a labyrinth of creeks and bayous. Returning to his headquarters on the Mississippi, Grant ordered Sherman and a detachment of troops to proceed up Steele's Bayou through Black Bayou to Deer Creek and there, cooperating with the gunboats, to push on alone to the Yazoo River above the Confederate defenses.

The expedition got under way in the wooden transports, but progress was painfully slow through the crooked, sluggish swamps. Up ahead Porter had about reached the Big Sunflower River, when his ironclads became ensnarled with freshly felled trees. They were stuck while Confederate infantry and artillery advanced in the forest.

Thirty miles below, Sherman and his troops heard the naval guns booming more frequently than seemed consistent with mere guerrilla actions. On the night of March 19 the general received a message from Porter, written on tissue paper, brought through the swamps by a Negro. Porter begged Sherman to hasten to the rescue.

Preceded by a tug with a coal barge in tow, one transport got under way and crashed through the trees, sweeping away the pilot's house, smokestack, and everything above deck. As soon as it reached the first strip of dry ground, Sherman disembarked the soldiers, sent a courier back with orders to bring up more troops, and led his force through the dense canebrake. Darkness overtook them, but by dawn the command was again on the march. A major on horseback met them and explained the situation, offering the general his horse. Riding up the levee, Sherman saw the sailors streaming from the ironclads to cheer him as he trotted by. The Union troops swept forward across a cotton field in full view, driving the enemy before them. The outnumbered Confederates retreated to safety and failed to launch another offensive.

It took three days to back the fleet out of the bayous and creeks. On March 27 the ironclads and transports were back in the Mississippi after an 11-day expedition, an exercise in frustration.

That spring Sherman fought with a *New York Herald* correspondent, Thomas W. Knox, who had accompanied the forces in defiance of orders. His articles contained unauthorized information and misinformation, interspersed with some personal criticisms of General Sherman. Sherman ordered Knox to headquarters and had an aide read the newspaper columns aloud. Sherman showed him the official military reports and how they differed drastically from the *Herald's* accounts. The general demanded that Knox be tried by a military court as a spy, pointing to the Fifty-seventh Article of War: "Who shall be convicted of holding correspondence with, or giving intelligence to the enemy, either directly or indirectly, shall suffer death." Sherman planned to use this case to establish a precedent. He was convinced that the Confederates maintained many newspapermen in the North, and through them, controlled a vast intelligence system. "The newspapers are after me again . . . ." he wrote Ellen. "Do they rule or the commanding general?"

In another letter he said: "If the President has not the nerve to back the officers who are fighting his battles, but yields to the clamor of the Press, I can slide out and let the Press do his fighting. I can almost foresee the Result. . . . I cannot allow a newspaper reporter to come into my Camp, against orders, and tell me to my face that I must tell him the Truth else he will publish Falsehoods and I know the whole Press of the Country will adopt his cause and whatever sentence the court may adjudge the President by their Clamor must set aside. . . . I will never again command an army in America, if we must carry along paid spies. I will banish myself to some foreign country first."

In Ellen's reply, she said: "You cannot stand up against newspaper power, alone, as you do, without being engulfed in the abuse. Instead of resisting it, why not use it? John Sherman *uses* the newspapers and takes pains to conciliate them. Consider this Cump and act on it. . . . You must *endure* reporters."

She urged Cump not to resign. "Do not desert the good ship whilst she is in danger of sinking, you cannot do it.—If you have sent in your resignation let me beg you to recall it. God, who knows my heart, knows that in giving you up I make a *true* & a *great* sacrifice but I consider it duty & Honor & God's service and I dare not do otherwise."

Both John Sherman and Phil Ewing also advised caution. "Your resignation," wrote John, "would be injurious to your reputation which is unimpaired by recent assaults and you should not give your enemies the satisfaction of your resignation. . . . Don't I pray you . . . take a step which you may have cause to regret for a lifetime.

"We are brothers and a folly committed by one casts a shade upon the other," John added. "I have taken sincere pride in all you have done & have heartily sustained you. Do you wish to humiliate me—& not only me but Halleck, Stanton (The Sec of War who is truly your friend), Mr. Ewing. . . ."

Knox was tried, found guilty of violating War Department

orders, and sentenced to be removed beyond the lines of the army. On appeal, President Lincoln revoked the sentence in part—Knox could return and stay only if Grant consented.

Sherman was dumbfounded when he learned of Lincoln's decision. "I'll tell Lincoln to his face," he wrote John, "that even he shall not insult me. If Knox comes into my camp he'll never leave it again at liberty. I have soldiers who will obey my orders and Knox shall go down the Mississippi, floating on a log if he can find one, but he shall not come into my camp with impunity again."

"Mr. Lincoln, of course, fears to incur the enmity of the *Herald*," Sherman told Grant, "but he must rule the *Herald* or the *Herald* will rule him; he can take his choice."

Loyal to his friend, Grant refused to give permission to Knox to visit the camps.

Vicksburg

In April, 1863, Union forces were still before Vicksburg. Northerners began to believe that the western army was hopelessly bogged down and was commanded by an incompetent. Newspapers circulated the old stories concerning Grant's bouts with the bottle, criticized his troops' inactivity, and demanded that Lincoln remove him. Hundreds of suggestions poured into Grant's headquarters on what strategy should be employed to invade Vicksburg. Charles A. Dana, special commissioner for the War Department, came west to survey the situation for Lincoln and Stanton.

In an interview with Dana, Grant revealed a new plan. Admiral Porter's ironclads and a half dozen transports would run past the enemy batteries at Vicksburg, while the army would march down the Louisiana side of the Mississippi to a point opposite Grand Gulf, cross the river on the transports, storm the place, then threaten Jackson and Vicksburg from the south.

Sherman was against this plan. The line of supply would be precarious once the army was across the Mississippi. He believed that the unsuccessful December operation, if correctly executed, had a better chance of breeching the defenses. He recommended resuming the old positions and moving the army inland via Grenada in cooperation with an expeditionary force up the Yazoo River. But Grant would not agree. Sherman felt sure that his friend, "trembling at the thunder of popular criticism," was risking everything on "a damn fool" move down the Mississippi. "I say," Sherman said, "we are farther from taking Vicksburg today than when we were the day I was repulsed.

"This whole plan of attack will fail, must fail and the fault will be on us all of course," he wrote, "but Grant will be the front—his recall leaves McClernand next. I would simply get a leave and stay away."

Just before the big move downriver commenced, Cump sent a letter to Minnie:

Dear Minnie, We are on the point of moving our army south of Vicksburg, we have not yet captured the city, and I don't know that we can, but we are gradually extending beyond it. Tomorrow I move with my army up to Milliken's Bend, when we march along a road on the west of the Mississippi to a point on it at Carthage, where we again take boats and cross to the east bank. I expect we will have some hard fighting but we do not know. I am in very good health and our soldiers are generally very well, though if we pass the summer here in this swamp I expect a good deal of sickness.

The spring is about a month earlier here than where you are. The trees are all now in full leaf and the flowers in bright bloom. The rose, honeysuckle, the verbena and lilac are all in full bloom, and I wish I could send you some; but I suppose it will not be long till you have them bright & beautiful in the gardens at Notre Dame.

Your affectionate father

In mid-April Porter's fleet of ironclads and nine transports successfully ran the guns of Vicksburg. The land forces then began their march across the Louisiana countryside. On April 29 Porter's gunboats failed in their attempt to destroy the defensive works on the bluff at Grand Gulf, and the army continued to push southward to a point opposite Bruinsburg. At daylight on April 30 General McClernand's command started moving across the Mississippi on the transports.

Sherman and his corps were ready to follow Grant and the rest of the army downriver, when the orders were countermanded. Units of his corps were to make a feint against Haynes Bluff on the Yazoo to divert the enemy's attention from the actions of Grant's army to the south.

A week later, after leading an assault force up the Yazoo, Sherman and his divisions rejoined Grant's force in Mississippi. Grant was pleased with his success so far. "This army," he wrote Halleck, "is in the highest health and spirits. Since leaving Milliken's Bend they have marched as much by night as by day, through mud and rain, without tents or much other baggage and on irregular rations without a complaint and with less straggling than I have ever before witnessed."

Grant's plan was to head for Vicksburg with his army of 41,000 via Jackson, the capital of Mississippi, to the east. Opposing the Union legions were General Pemberton with 40,000 men in Vicksburg and General Johnston with 15,000 men in Jackson.

Meeting slight resistance, Grant's three corps pushed eastward under their respective generals—McClernand, McPherson, and Sherman. By May 12 McPherson's forces were in Raymond, only 18 miles west of Jackson. General Johnston and his troops quickly evacuated the capital, retiring northward, increasing the distance between his forces and those of Pemberton.

So rapid was Johnston's withdrawal from Jackson, that the looms of a Confederate factory were still turning out tent cloth marked "CSA" when the Union troops arrived.

Sherman's corps remained in Jackson only long enough to destroy the railroads, arsenals, a government foundry, a gun carriage establishment, the penitentiary, and the cotton factory. Overzealous soldiers set fire to other buildings, including the Roman Catholic church and the Confederate Hotel. The *London Times* described Sherman as "the modern Atilla."

Grant now turned west and marched back toward the Mississippi to place his troops between those of Pemberton and Johnston. On May 16 and 17 Grant met Pemberton and defeated him at Champion's Hill and Big Black River Bridge. Pemberton and his army fell back to their defenses at Vicksburg. By May 18 Grant had the city completely invested.

The Yankees assaulted Pemberton's works on May 19 and 22, but failing to penetrate the defenses, Grant's army prepared for a long siege. For over six weeks the Union and Confederate forces faced each other at a distance of 600 yards or less.

Less than a month before, Sherman had been skeptical of Grant's sudden move down the Mississippi. Yet Grant had carried it off. Now, Cump wrote: "Grant is entitled to all the merit of its conception and execution." And later he said: "I have a much quicker perception of things than he, but he balances the present and remote so evenly that results follow in natural course."

The Vicksburg campaign had not been prearranged; it "grew

out of happenings" of which Grant took prompt advantage. None of the Union armies had labored so hard and so faithfully as Grant's, and none was less affected with petty jealousies.

Observing the siege and the behavior of various Union officers, Dana was impressed by Sherman, whom he evaluated as a "brilliant man," a fine field commander, always well informed. Dana was struck by Sherman's loyalty to Grant, especially since Sherman had at first disagreed with his superior's overall plan. Despite misgivings, Sherman had supported Grant's every move with all his energies.

Union guns continued to pound Vicksburg. Early each morning Sherman supervised the fire of his artillery, and from his vantage point he could pick out the courthouse, church steeples, and other buildings. "Vicksburg at this moment must be a horrid place," he told Ellen, "yet the people have been wrought up to such a pitch of enthusiasm that I have not yet met one but would prefer all to perish rather than give up.

"Vicksburg contains many of my old pupils and friends; should they fall into our hands I will treat them with kindness," he continued, "but they have sowed the wind and must reap the whirlwind. Until they lay down their arms and submit to the rightful authority of government they must not appeal to me for mercy or favors."

Inside Vicksburg 2d Lt. Gabriel M. Killgore, Seventeenth Louisiana Infantry, jotted in his diary: "Still the attack continues —Still we have no relief from the outside but Still We Hope." General Pemberton cut the rations of his men, and like Lieutenant Killgore, wondered when General Johnston would arrive with reinforcements and break the siege.

At Union headquarters General Grant relieved McClernand of command after Sherman and McPherson complained of McClernand's injudicious order of congratulations to his own corps. In this order he had claimed credit for his men for almost everything that had happened during the campaign, and hinted that the corps would have captured Vicksburg if the rest of Grant's army had done its job properly. This order got into the newspapers in mid-June—not without some help from McClernand's headquarters.

The order was a "catalogue of nonsense," Sherman said.

"Such an effusion of vain glory and hypocrisy.... It is manifestly addressed not to an Army, but to a constituency in Illinois." McPherson agreed that it was written "to impress the public mind with the magnificent strategy, superior tactics and brilliant deeds" of General McClernand. By failing to submit his order to army headquarters before sending it to the press, McClernand had violated War Department regulations. When McClernand finally packed up and left, Sherman was elated. "Now we have a fine army, perfectly harmonious." Later he wrote Mr. Ewing: "McClernand is a mean, envious and impracticable fool that caused Grant and me more real trouble than any volunteer General we had to deal with." Major General Edward O. C. Ord, Sherman's friend of West Point days, assumed command of the Thirteenth.

During the siege, Sherman usually found time to get letters off to his children. To Minnie he wrote: "We are here on the high hills fighting daily with the garrison of Vicksburg, which are surrounded and must soon be destroyed or surrendered unless a very large southern army comes to their aid. We also have a very large army and its daily increasing by the arrival of troops from the north ....

"I have a good tent and plenty to eat and drink, and you would be surprised to see how comfortable we are. Night and day our soldiers are digging roads leading up to the enemy's forts, and I daily ride about to see how the work progresses.

"All the time the heavy roar of cannon and the sharp crash of rifles tell that we are near the enemy. A good many of our soldiers have been killed and wounded, and I suppose, before we get to Vicksburg more will be, but I hope still to escape and to see you all grow up good and happy.

"Tell Willy I will write in a day or two and that I have gathered some fishing poles, which grow here in what are called cane breaks, which I will send for him and Tom to catch fish within the reservoir. He will value them because I sent [them], and because they came from the battlefield where so many have fallen and where for months war has raged in all its fury. Write to me as often as you can, because you can now write all you feel. I can hardly realize you are so large, but time passes faster than I think."

On July 3, 1863, General Pemberton opened negotiations with Grant for the surrender of Vicksburg. The exultant Union army moved down the road toward the city on the Fourth of July. At 10:00 A.M., as bands played "Yankee Doodle" and "Hail Columbia," General Steele's division marched triumphantly into Vicksburg. The Confederate garrison moved out of their works, stacked their arms, and marched back in good order. The Stars and Stripes floated above the city buildings.

Corporal Charles E. Wilcox, A Company, Thirty-third Illinois Infantry, caught the significance of the event in his diary: "This day in American history is only second to the one which today is the eighty-seventh anniversary. The fate of the American Republic has positively been decided this day."

To his wife, Gen. William Ward Orme wrote from Vicksburg: "Oh! what a glorious 4th of July—What a proud day for those of us who are so fortunate as to have taken part in this siege. ... We have been very—very busy—marching and moving; securing the rebel arms and properly guarding and picketing our lines— This is a proud day, Nannie, and I would not have missed it for anything.—Only think of it! To March proudly over the great works of the rebels, from which have poured upon us constantly for three weeks their heavy guns, and victoriously to view what before we were combating!"

Sherman computed the Confederate losses during the six-month Vicksburg campaign—about 27,000 prisoners at Vicksburg; 5,000 at Arkansas Post; 250 at Jackson; 3,000 at Champion's Hill, besides the captured field and siege guns, ammunition, horses, and wagons.

He wrote to Ellen: "There is glory enough for all the heroes of the West, but I content myself with knowing and feeling that our enemy is weakened by so much, and more yet by failing to hold a point deemed by them as essential to their empire in the Southwest. We have ravaged the land ... so that this country is paralyzed and cannot recover its strength in twenty years."

As a result of their actions during the Vicksburg campaign, Grant recommended the promotion of both Sherman and McPherson to brigadier generals in the Regular Army. His official report was extremely laudatory of Sherman's actions from Paducah to Vicksburg.

News arrived from the east that Gen. George Meade and his

Army of the Potomac had won a glorious victory at Gettysburg. Lee's army was in full retreat. To the south, Confederate-held Port Hudson surrendered to General Banks's force, and the Mississippi River was now open to Union commerce from its source to the Gulf.

The fall of Vicksburg, the capitulation of Port Hudson, and the opening of the Mississippi, Cump wrote to his brother, "complete as pretty a page in the history of war and of our country as ever you could ask my name to be identified with. The share I have personally borne in all these events is one in which you may take pride for me."

In the heat and dust Sherman's columns crossed the Big Black River and forced General Johnston's army to take refuge behind their trenches at Jackson. On July 9 Sherman ordered the state capital besieged and the artillery to open fire. Yankee detachments meanwhile began systematically to destroy the railroads "so that the good folks of Jackson will not soon again hear their favorite locomotive whistle." Foragers stripped the countryside of corn, cattle, hogs, sheep, and poultry. Sherman tried to prevent looting and individual foraging, but officers at the company level seldom enforced his edicts.

"The wholesale destruction to which this country is now being subjected is terrible to contemplate," Sherman told Grant, "but it is the scourge of war, to which ambitious men have appealed, rather than the judgment of the learned and pure tribunals which our fore-fathers had provided for supposed wrongs and injuries. Therefore, so much of my instructions as contemplated destroying and weakening the resources of our enemy are being executed with vigor, and we have done much toward the destruction of Johnston's army."

Near Jackson, Union troops were gradually gaining the flank and rear when Johnston departed one night, crossing the Pearl River, carrying off most material and men. Before the retreat, the Confederates fired buildings and stores.

When the Federals moved in, the troops widened the circle of fire without orders to do so. They left the entire business district ablaze, burned some of the finest residences, and looted homes. Fortunately, the statehouse, governor's mansion, and some of the better dwellings remained untouched. But "Jackson, once the pride and boast of Mississippi," wrote Sherman, "is a ruined town." The *Chicago Times* reported that "such complete devastation never followed the footsteps of an army before." Charles E. Wilcox noted in his diary for July 17: "During the day some of our men—the *roughs*—after pillaging the place set fire to a great many buildings some of which were very fine. It is noteworthy that the rebel soldiers before leaving pillaged a good many houses. I never saw or heard of a city being so thoroughly sacked and burned as this place."

From Jackson Sherman wrote Grant: "We have made fine progress to-day in the work of destruction. Jackson will no longer be a point of danger. . . . The inhabitants are subjugated. They cry aloud for mercy. The land is devastated for 30 miles around." Soldiers called Jackson "Chimneyville."

Throughout his lifetime Sherman had a highly developed sense of justice, and anarchy in any form was anathema to him. Yet Sherman, kind and considerate as an individual, was committed to the practice of destroying the enemy's resources. His ruthlessness was prompted by his theory of effective warfare, his belief that laying waste to the enemy countryside would win the war in the shortest possible time, and thus would be a blessing to the South as well as to the North.

Sherman and many of his officers attempted to suppress the excessive looting of private property by dealing vigorously with such crimes, as they had in previous campaigns. To keep the troops from plundering, Sherman ordered looters tied up by their thumbs, held courts-martial, and issued stern orders, but most of the time these tactics had little effect.

At Grant's suggestion, Sherman dispatched food, clothing, and medicine to hospitals and asylums and fed army rations to 800 impoverished women and children. The actions of the Federal soldiers "have left the country destitute both of transportation and subsistence," said Grant, and "having stripped the country thereabouts we can do no less than supply them." Sherman also started to reequip the looted farms with horses and mules. No proof of loyalty to the Union was asked. Sherman told his officers: "Provisions are issued as a pure charity to prevent suffering just as we would to . . . shipwrecked people."

Never for a moment, however, did Sherman miss an opportunity to impress upon the destitute the price they were paying for the traitorous acts of the leaders of secession. To a citizens' committee of Warren County, Sherman said: "General Grant can give you now no permanent assurance or guarantees, nor can I, nor can anybody. Of necessity, in the war the commander on the spot is the judge, and may take your house, your field, your everything, and turn you all out, helpless to starve. It may be wrong, but that don't alter the case. In war you can't help yourselves, and the only possible remedy is to stop war. . . ."

He continued: "Look around you and see the wreck. Let your minds contemplate the whole South in like chaos and disorder, and what a picture! Those who die by the bullet are lucky compared to those poor fathers and wives and children who see their all taken and themselves left to perish, or linger out their few years in ruined poverty. Our duty is not to build up; it is rather to destroy both the rebel army and whatever wealth or property it has founded its boasted strength upon."

Sherman had grown sure of himself, decisive on the field of action. He had been tried by emergencies and not found wanting. In a letter to Grant, he showed that he recognized his superior's "simple faith in success." When you have completed your best preparations, he told Grant, you go into battle without hesitation, and "I tell you that it was this that made me act with confidence. I knew wherever I was that you thought of me, and that if I got into a tight place you would come—if alive."

That August Sherman received his commission as brigadier general in the Regular Army. Immediately he wrote Grant, "I know that I owe this to your favor . . . I beg to assure you of my deep personal attachment, and hope that the chances of war will leave me to serve near and under you till the dawn of that peace for which we are contending. . . ."

Sherman admired Grant's simplicity, modesty, and his encouragement and support of his junior officers. Throughout the Vicksburg campaign, Admiral Porter maintained that there was something lacking in Grant, which Sherman had always supplied and vice versa, but that the two together made "a very perfect officer." He suggested to Secretary of the Navy Gideon Welles that they ought never to be separated.

The weather was too hot, the men too exhausted to attempt a summer campaign. On July 22 Sherman issued orders for the divisions to return to their camps on the Big Black River for a needed rest.

For some time Cump had been urging Ellen and the children to come south to Vicksburg for a visit. "Grant and his wife visited me in camp [on the Big Black] yesterday," he wrote. "I have the handsomest camp I ever saw." In mid-August Ellen arrived with the four oldest children.

The camp on the Big Black had plenty of grass, water, and shade trees, and the tents the Shermans lived in were spacious. Here they were reunited with Brig. Gen. Hugh Boyle Ewing, commanding the Fourth Division, Fifteenth Corps, and Capt. Charles Ewing of the Thirteenth.

This new world into which the Sherman children were thrown unfolded itself quickly, as the vast camp with its manifold activities absorbed them.

"Willie [the oldest son] who was then nine years old, was well advanced for his years, and took the most intense interest in the affairs of the army," Cump wrote later. "He was a great favorite with the soldiers, and used to ride with me on horseback in the numerous drills and reviews of the time. He ... displayed more interest in the war than any of them. He was called a 'sergeant' in the regular battalion, learned the manual of arms, and regularly attended the parade and guard-mounting of the Thirteenth, back of my camp.

"We made frequent visits to Vicksburg, and always stopped with General McPherson, who had a large house.... General Grant [with his family] occupied another house ... during the summer.... The time passed very agreeably."

While Sherman's command lay idle in camp, the war was entering a new phase. The Army of the Cumberland, commanded by General Rosecrans, moved against the Confederate forces of General Bragg in Tennessee but was repulsed at Chickamauga Creek. Only the action of General Thomas's wing saved the Union from complete disaster.

In Chattanooga the demoralized remnants of the Yankee army girded themselves to endure Bragg's siege. The Confederates took possession of Missionary Ridge overlooking Chattanooga and occupied Lookout Mountain, west of the city. Union reinforcements were hurried from the east, while Halleck sent word to Grant to dispatch at once to Chattanooga such troops as he could spare.

Grant ordered Sherman to take the major part of his corps from the Big Black River into eastern Tennessee via Memphis. With these orders Grant sent along a personal note, which ended: "I hope you will be in time to aid in giving the rebels the worst, or best, thrashing they have [had] in this war. I have constantly had the feeling that I should lose you from this command entirely. Of course, I do not object to seeing your sphere of usefullness enlarged and think it should have been enlarged long ago, having an eye to the public good alone."

Sherman planned to accompany his family upriver as far as Memphis on their return to Ohio. En route Ellen became concerned about Willy, who did not seem well. His cheeks were flushed; his forehead seemed hot. Ellen put him to bed and summoned the surgeon, who diagnosed the illness as typhoid. Cump haunted Willy's bedside, cursing himself for ever urging his family to visit Big Black River.

When the steamboat finally docked at Memphis, Willy was carried ashore and into the Gayoso House. He was left for a moment with a priest, who told Ellen later: "He told me that he was willing to die if it was God's will, but it pained him to leave his Father and Mother. He said this with an expression of such deep earnestness that I could hardly refrain from giving way to my feelings. . . . 'Willy,' I said quietly and calmly, 'trust in God and the Blessed Virgin and all will be well with you. If God wishes to call you to Him now do not grieve, for He will carry you to Heaven and *there* you will meet your good Mother and Father again.' "

Willy died that afternoon.

Grief stricken, Ellen and Cump packed away his clothes, his sergeant's uniform, toothbrush, cap, and old straw hat, his sergeant's commission, his card of admission to the "Society of Holy Angels" at his school, his knife, and his silver money.

"We procured a metallic casket," recalled Cump, "and had a military funeral, the battalion of the Thirteenth United States

Regulars acting as escort from the Gayoso House to the steamboat *Grey Eagle,* which conveyed him and my family up [river]."

That night Cump could not sleep. "Sleeping, waking, everywhere I see poor Willy. His face and form are as deeply imprinted on my memory as were deep-seated the hopes I had in his future. Why, oh why, should that child be taken from us, leaving us full of trembling and reproaches?"

He wrote Ellen: "Oh! that poor Willy could have lived to take all that was good of me in name, character and standing, and learn to avoid all that is captious, eccentric and wrong. But I do not forget that we have other children worthy of my deepest love. I would not have one different from what they are."

Two days later he wrote her again: "I still feel out of heart to write. The moment I begin to think of you and the children poor Willy appears before me as plain as life. I can see him now stumbling over the hills on Harrison Street, San Francisco, at the table in Leavenworth, running to meet me with open arms at Black River, and last, moaning in death at his hotel.... Why was I not killed at Vicksburg, and left Willy to grow up to care for you? God knows I exhausted human foresight and human love for that boy."

There was little time for Sherman to indulge in grief. In mid-October General Thomas superseded Rosecrans as commander of the Army of the Cumberland, and Grant was sent to Chattanooga and placed in command of the Military Division of the Mississippi, comprising the Armies of the Ohio, Cumberland, and Tennessee.

On Sherman devolved the command of the Army of the Tennessee. "My desire has always been to have a distinct compact command, as a Corps," Cump confessed, "but in spite of my efforts I am pushed into complicated plans that others aspire to and which I wish they had. But with Grant I will undertake anything within reason."

On Sunday, October 11, 1863, Sherman set off on a special train for Chattanooga.

"...we went through the town like a dose of salts...."

ON NOVEMBER 15 Sherman was in Chattanooga, where with Grant and Gens. George H. Thomas and William F. Smith, he inspected the defenses of the city. Off to the east all along the western slopes of Missionary Ridge were the tents of the enemy; the lines of trenches were plainly visible, and Rebel sentinels in one continuous chain were walking their posts in plain view.

General Braxton Bragg's army faced Chattanooga in a crescent-shaped position, one point touching the Tennessee River above the city, the other touching it below. Upstream the Rebels commanded Tunnel Hill, standing a little back from the riverbank, and downstream they held Lookout Mountain; and the center of the crescent was on Missionary Ridge, rising 500 feet above the plain, running southwest to northeast, more than five miles. Bragg's forces had made their positions almost impregnable. At the base of the ridge on the plain, the Confederates had dug trenches, and on the crest they had another line bristling with cannon. Halfway up the ridge they had constructed more trenches, manned by veterans. Rebel units also held the steep sides of Lookout Mountain, running down from the foot of the palisade to the edge of the Tennessee River, a few miles below the city. The mountainside was steep, and the Confederate command believed that the troops could hold the ground against any Union onslaught. The flat country between Lookout Mountain and the southwestern tip of Missionary Ridge was a line of works controlled by enemy infantry and artillery.

To break Bragg's stranglehold on Chattanooga, Grant developed a three-pronged plan of attack. General Joseph Hooker would assault Lookout Mountain, and Sherman, moving up the

Tennessee River on the north side opposite Chattanooga, would cross over on pontoon bridges and strike the upper end of Missionary Ridge. While these forces were fighting the Confederates on their flanks, Thomas's army would hit the center.

Laboring day and night, Sherman got his divisions over to the hills on November 23, driving the enemy from the north end of Missionary Ridge on the 24th. There he discovered that a deep gap blocked his way. "I had inferred," he reported, "that Missionary Ridge was a continuous hill; but we found ourselves on two high points, with a deep depression between us and . . . my chief objective point."

The Rebels probed Sherman's left flank about 4:00 P.M., November 24, and an engagement with artillery and muskets ensued until the enemy drew off gradually.

General Hooker meanwhile had sent his command forward from Lookout Valley to seize the mountain that overlooked Chattanooga. His troops found the going surprisingly easy. Outnumbering the enemy on Lookout Mountain almost six to one, they drove the Rebels off with a minimum of effort.

During the cold night, Sherman's details worked on the hill entrenchments. Their campfires revealed to the Confederates and to the other Union forces in Chattanooga their position on Missionary Ridge. At midnight Sherman received an order from Grant directing him to attack at dawn. General Thomas was to assault in force early in the day.

Sherman was in the saddle well before sunrise, November 25, and with his staff began preparing the brigades. The wide valley lay between his forces and the next hill of the series, and the farther point of this hill was held by the enemy. The Confederates were also seen in great force on a still higher hill.

The sun had hardly risen when bugles sounded "Forward." The men of the Fortieth Illinois, the Thirteenth and Forty-sixth Ohio moved down the face of the hill and then up the slope held by the Rebels, until they seized a secondary crest at the northern end of Missionary Ridge.

Then came an assault by the Yankee battalions, the stubborn defense of the enemy. After a bloody contest, the Federals held their original position. More troops moved forward.

The enemy, massed in strength in the tunnel gorge, suddenly emerged on the right rear of the Union soldiers who, exposed as they were to a withering crossfire, fell back in disorder but quickly re-formed.

On a knoll Grant and Thomas were watching the slow progress of the battle. Sherman believed that the enemy in his front was being reinforced, and he called for more troops. Some of Thomas's regiments marched to his aid, but still Sherman could not smash the Rebels on the heights. His attack stalled.

About 3:00 P.M. Sherman noticed a white line of musket fire. Thomas was at last moving on the center, his men jumping forward in one of the most dramatic moves in the entire war—18,000 soldiers marching toward an impregnable mountain. Guns which had been firing on Sherman's forces all day swung in a different direction. The advancing line of Thomas's musket fire disappeared from Sherman's view behind a spur of the hill.

It was not until nightfall that Sherman learned that Thomas's army had swept up Missionary Ridge and broken the enemy's center. Bragg was in full retreat, and the virtual siege of Chattanooga was lifted.

The audacious way Grant had handled the Chattanooga campaign impressed Sherman. "It was magnificent in its conception, in its execution, and in its glorious results."

Sherman received a dispatch from Grant: "No doubt you witnessed the handsome manner in which Thomas's troops carried Missionary Ridge this afternoon, and can feel a just pride, too, in the part taken by the forces under your command in taking first so much of the same range of hills, and then in attracting the attention of so many of the enemy as to make Thomas's part certain of success."

Chattanooga had been of vital importance to the Confederacy. Its loss cut off the Georgia iron mills from their normal supply of ore, and instead of giving the Rebels an excellent sally port into Tennessee, Chattanooga now gave the Union a window into Georgia.

Sherman's esteem for Grant and his ability did not dim his respect for General Halleck. "He has more capacity than any man in our Army," he wrote John. "Grant has qualities that Halleck does not possess but not such as would qualify him to command the whole army. The war has not yet developed Halleck's equal as General in Chief."

Again he wrote: "Halleck is yet the best man as General in Chief. Grant has not the qualities for that place, & no man has yet made his appearance to take supreme command."

Grant ordered Sherman and his forces to march to the aid of General Burnside, besieged at Knoxville. The ease with which they rode into the city on the morning of December 6 surprised Sherman. Confederate Gen. James Longstreet had already raised the siege and started a retreat up the valley toward Virginia. Sherman was astonished at the comfortable appearance of things in Knoxville.

At Burnside's headquarters, he recalled: "We all sat down to a good dinner, embracing roast-turkey. There was a regular dining-table, with clean table-cloth, dishes, knives, forks, spoons, etc., etc. I had seen nothing of this kind in my field experience, and could not help exclaiming that I thought 'they were starving,' etc.; but Burnside explained that Longstreet had at no time completely invested the place, and that he had kept open communications with the country on the south side of the river.... Had I known this, I should not have hurried my men so fast; but until I reached Knoxville I thought our troops there were actually in danger of starvation." Supplying the general with such troops as he needed, Sherman and his command began a leisurely return to Chattanooga.

After establishing headquarters in Nashville, Grant called Sherman and his other generals to a strategy conference. At a dinner party given by a family of Union sympathizers, one woman, obviously Confederate in sympathy, denounced Sherman for his troops' looting of Mississippi. "She pecked and pounded away," remembered Gen. Grenville M. Dodge, "until finally the General turned on her." "Madam, my soldiers have to subsist even if the whole country must be ruined to maintain them. There are two armies here; one is in rebellion against the Union, the other is fighting for the Union—if either must starve to death, I suppose it shall not be the army that is loyal.

"War is cruelty," he continued. "There is no use trying to reform it; the crueler it is, the sooner it will be over."

Sherman's words, recalled Dodge, "put a cold douche on the whole dinner and no effort of any of us could relieve the strain. The lady said no more, for it was a great rebuke."

After months in the field, Sherman asked for and was granted a short leave to spend the Christmas holidays with his family in Ohio. Wherever he went in Lancaster—to a reception, to a friend's home, in the shops along Main Street—he found men and women talking of war. And Cump Sherman had become a hero. One afternoon many acquaintances and neighbors came to the Ewing mansion to see the distinguished visitor, direct from the battlefield. The house was full. People crowded around Cump, greeting him, asking more questions than he could answer. The young girls stared at him in awe.

He rather liked the fanfare. He was confident now that he stood high with the army. "Today," he said, "I can do more with Admiral Porter or the Generals than any general officer out West except Grant, and with him I am as a second self. We are personal and official friends."

He was proud to receive the joint resolution of Congress, thanking him and his officers and men for their "gallant and arduous services in marching to the relief of the Army of the Cumberland, and for their gallantry and heroism in the battle of Chattanooga, which contributed in a great degree to the success of our arms in that glorious victory."

To Grant on December 29, Sherman wrote: "Your reputation as a general is now far above that of any man living, and partisans will maneuver for your influence; but if you can escape them, as you have hitherto done, you will be more powerful for good than it is possible to measure."

He went on to advise Grant: "Presume a plain military character, and let others maneuver as they will. You will beat them not only in fame, but in doing good at the closing scenes of the war when somebody must heal and mend up the breaches made by war."

Cump and Minnie, who was returning to the school at Notre Dame in Indiana, left Lancaster on the first of January. At Cincinnati they said good-bye. "I ought to be well schooled now at parting," Cump wrote Ellen, "but I felt bad to leave Minnie."

On January 2, Sherman was on his way down the Mississippi

River. Planning to return to his army in Tennessee by February, his object in going downriver was to check on reported guerrilla attacks on unarmed boats. "For every bullet shot at a steamboat," he reported, "I would shoot a thousand [cannon] into even hapless towns on Red, Ouachita, Yazoo [Rivers], or wherever a boat can float or soldiers march." He found that the stories were greatly exaggerated and that legitimate commerce on the Mississippi was moving safely.

From on board the gunboat *Juliet*, Sherman sent Minnie the first of several letters written on his trip. "Already Willy is gone from us, and you are growing into womanhood, before I have had the time to know you, but I feel assured that you will in some way remember me and make my later years compensation for our long separation. There is nothing that I have or can obtain that you shall not have by asking, if for your own good, and in return you must tell me everything that happens to you or interests you, no matter what, tell me and you need not fear.... You may not hear from me for some weeks, but you know that I think of you always and that I will write when I can."

Several days later, he wrote her: "... I would rather a million times that you should be happy than that I should become honored and famous. I have many friends in New York, in California, in Missouri, and all over our country, as well as in Ohio, and it gives me more pleasure to think that in after years, when I am dead and almost forgotten, that some of these friends will remember my Minnie and Lizzie and other children who must live long after me.

"The war is not over yet and I do not see its end. Many of us must die by it yet, and it may be my fate; but I feel certain our cause will prevail.

"My dear Minnie will remember that before she was born I lived in South Carolina and afterwards in Louisiana, and that in every battle I am fighting some of the very families in whose houses I used to spend some happy days. Of course I must fight when the time comes, but whenever a result can be accomplished without battle I prefer it."

At Memphis in his rooms at the Gayoso House, it was difficult for Cump to blot out his memory of Willy. "Though Willy died here," he wrote Ellen, "his pure and holy spirit will hover over the Mississippi, the grand artery of America."

He wrote Minnie again: "... Time passes so fast to me and my life is such a turmoil that it is only in the quiet of the night that I can think of my dear children that seem to me dearer and dearer as they are farther away....

"I judge this year of war will be the most important of all and I must be busy. I have a most important office; more than 50,000 men are at my command.... I have escaped death thus far and maybe will again, but I always am prepared for anything.

"If I should be killed or wounded I know that my sweet Minnie will think of me always. Tell the Sisters who teach you that you are the child of one who is fighting that they may have a country and peace, and that I expect them to be to you both as father and mother."

With the Federal forces encamped at Vicksburg, Sherman decided to move on Meridian, Miss., Demopolis, Ala., and the Confederate-held railroads. "I'll break up those roads so effectively," he wrote John, "that repairs will cost more time and money than they can afford in a year. The effect of this will be to keep the force in Miss. from receiving prompt reinforcements and supplies, and will gradually alienate them from the rest of the Confederacy."

Arriving in Vicksburg, Sherman and his divisions marched on February 3, crossed the Big Black River, and passed through Jackson. The enemy retreated through Meridian without battle, the only trouble coming from the Rebel cavalry, who hung on the Union flanks. Mile after mile the Yankees ripped out railroad tracks, cutting a swath across the land that "the present generation will not forget."

Late on February 14 Sherman and his divisions entered Meridian. Immediately the troops spread out, wrecking railroad facilities, burning public property, and destroying the town. "For five days 10,000 men worked hard with axes, crowbars, sledges, and with fire, and I have no hesitation in pronouncing the work well done," he told Grant. "Meridian with its depots, store-houses, arsenal, hospitals, offices, hotels and cantonments no longer exists."

The Rebels concluded that the Federals intended to march forward to capture Mobile, but because Sherman's cavalry failed him, he did not push on. Union cavalry, led by Brig. Gen. William Sooy Smith, coming down from Corinth, had run into 2,500

Confederates near Okolona and had been severely whipped. On his way back to Vicksburg, Sherman once more turned his men loose on the towns and villages. An officer in Sherman's Signal Corps reported that at Lake Station—"we went through the town like a dose of salts and just as we were leaving I noticed a man hunting around to get someone to make an affidavit that there had been a town there."

To his assistant adjutant general, Sherman wrote: "When men take up arms to resist a rightful authority, we are compelled to use like force, because all reason cease when arms are resorted to. . . . These are well established principles of war and the people of the south having appealed to war are barred from appealing to protection [and] to our Constitution, which they have practically and publicly defied. They appealed to war and must abide [by] *its* Rules and Laws."

Sherman laid down the policy of protecting the houses of women, children, and noncombatants, as long as they remained in their dwellings and kept "to their accustomed peaceful business," but "if any of them keep up correspondence with parties in hostility they are spies and can be punished according to Law.

"To those who submit to rightful law and authority," Sherman continued, "all gentleness and forbearance; but to the petulant and persistent secessionists, why, death is mercy and the quicker he or she is disposed of the better.

"Satan and the rebellious saints of Heaven were allowed a continuous existence in hell merely to swell their just punishment. To such as would rebel against a Government so mild and just as ours was in peace, a punishment equal would not be unjust."

Evaluating the results of the expedition, he concluded that it had imparted hardihood and confidence to his command, which was now "better fitted for war." At Vicksburg Sherman wrote his official report. In part, he said, "We drove him [the enemy] out of Mississippi, destroyed the only remaining railroads in the state, the only roads by which he could maintain an army in Mississippi threatening to our forces on the main river."

Sherman had been working to immobilize the Confederacy so that the Mississippi River might remain peaceful during his ensuing campaigns. In a note to the general commanding the District of Vicksburg, he said: "I believe that our recent expedition in which we destroyed absolutely the Southern Railroad, & Mobile & Ohio as [well as] an armed Meridian will prevent the enemy from approaching the River with Infantry or heavy artillery."

During this period no personal letters in the Sherman correspondence from his civilian or military friends condemn his acts in Mississippi. Later in the war, General Halleck approved wholeheartedly of Sherman's operations. Writing from Washington, he said: "The safety of our armies and a proper regard for the lives of our soldiers, require that we apply to our inexorable foes the severe rules of war.... I have endeavored to impress these views upon our commanders for the last two years. You are almost the only one who has properly applied them."

As word of Sherman's expedition to Meridian raced up and down the Mississippi, Southerners were outraged. General Stephen D. Lee reported that Sherman had taken "300 more wagons than he started with"; burned 10,000 bales of cotton and 2,000,000 bushels of corn; and carried off 8,000 slaves, "many mounted on stolen mules." Later General Lee asked, "Was this the warfare of the civilization of the nineteenth century?"

To discuss with Gen. Nathaniel Banks an expedition up the Red River, Sherman went to New Orleans. He agreed to loan Banks 10,000 men for one month and emphasized the importance of close cooperation with Admiral Porter's gunboats. Banks, however, was late at the rendezvous with Porter, let his command be caught strung out along a single road, and suffered a stinging defeat. Sherman never saw his men again, although they eventually returned to Tennessee.

On his way back to Memphis, Sherman received a letter from Ellen saying that her mother, Maria Ewing, had died. He also heard from Grant, who had been promoted to lieutenant general and given supreme command of all Union armies, with headquarters in Washington. Halleck was stepping down to become chief of staff. The letter went on to express Grant's "thanks to you and McPherson as *the men* to whom, above all others, I feel indebted for whatever I have had of success. How far your advise and suggestions have been of assistance, you know. How far your execution of whatever has been given you to do entitles

you to the reward I am receiving, you cannot know as well as
I do."

At Nashville Sherman learned that he was to take command in
the west, from the Mississippi to the Alleghenies. He begged Grant
not to act as general-in-chief from Washington, but to establish
his headquarters in the west: "Here lies the seat of the coming
empire; and from the West when our task is done, we will make
short work of Charleston and Richmond and the impoverished
coast of the Atlantic."

He traveled with Grant as far as Cincinnati, planning the
spring offensive. In a private railroad car they pored over maps of
the country between Tennessee and Georgia. Sherman detailed his
plan for a march from Chattanooga to Atlanta. At first Grant objected to this scheme, but after more discussion, he finally consented and promised to submit the plan to the president for
approval.

Ellen and Mrs. Grant were at the Cincinnati station, and the
four adjourned to the spacious Burnet House. As always it was
crowded; a gaudy parade of correspondents, politicians, and
hangers-on. While the ladies discussed domestic affairs, their
husbands secreted themselves in an adjoining room and continued
their discussions. Grant stressed two basic objectives: destruction
of Robert E. Lee's army in Virginia and of Joseph E. Johnston's
army in Georgia.

When the strategy conference ended, Grant left for Washington. Cump told Ellen that with the spring campaign the real war
would begin. All that had gone before had been mere skirmishing.

Returning to Nashville, Sherman received a long letter from
Grant revealing the grand strategy for the spring. All armies were
to move together. General Banks's forces would concentrate on
Mobile; Gen. Benjamin F. Butler's would attack Richmond from
the south side of the James River. Grant himself would stay with
the Army of the Potomac and march against General Lee's Army
of Northern Virginia. Sherman's command would move against
Johnston's forces, break them up, and hit the heart of Georgia.

Sherman was now his own commander; on his shoulders was
the entire responsibility for success or failure, involving consequences beyond the fate of his armies. Only twice had he had
independent commands—in Kentucky where he had resigned and

in the recent Meridian expedition, which had met little opposition. But the two years of training and the tutelage of Halleck and Grant had strengthened his confidence and had taught him to cut through extraneous detail to the heart of things. "Think of me," he wrote Ellen, "with fifty thousand lives in my hand, with all the anxiety of their families. This load is heavier than even you imagine."

In preparing for the march to Atlanta, he demonstrated that he was a great engineer and a master of logistics. This campaign, more than any other military operation during the war, was to underline the close relationship between war and technology.

Sherman planned to move from Chattanooga through Georgia along the railroad lines. These lines formed a single railroad from Louisville to Atlanta. The Nashville and Northwestern road, which before the war had been built from Nashville to Kingston Springs, was now extended by Union troops to Reynoldsburg on the Tennessee River, where soldiers could swiftly transfer freight from steamboats to waiting boxcars. This concept of the continuous haul would give his marching men, hundreds of miles away, a port on the Tennessee. He made the railroad and the river as much a part of his command as the bullets for his muskets. Never did his horses and mules run out of grain.

"Locomotives don't eat corn and hay like mules," Sherman stressed, "but a single locomotive will haul 160,000 pounds. A man eats 3 pounds a day, and therefore one train will feed 50,000 men. Animals eat about 15 pounds. I estimate 65 cars a day necessary to maintain an army of 100,000 men and 30,000 animals." He later raised the figure to 120 cars a day and set to work corralling 100 locomotives and 1,000 cars, expecting to lose 2 trains a week by accident or to the enemy.

Rail service to army outfits in the rear echelon was denied, and all civilian traffic was barred. In Nashville hundreds of people descended on headquarters demanding transportation. Sherman insisted that the road was needed purely for military freight. "Show me that your presence at the front is more valuable than two hundred pounds of powder," he said. He also refused to transport food to the starving civilians in Tennessee. To Dana he wrote: "In peace there is a beautiful harmony in all departments of life —they all fit together like a Chinese puzzle; but in war all is ajar.

Nothing fits, and it is the struggle between the stronger and weaker, and the latter, however much it may appeal to the better feelings of our nature, must kick the beam. To make war we must and will harden our hearts."

At the depot at Nashville by April 20, quartermasters had piled up 24,000 army rations and enough food for 50,000 horses and mules. One day Sherman happened upon a quartermaster napping behind some crates. He exploded: "I'm going to move on Joe Johnston the day Grant telegraphs me he is going to hit Bobby Lee; and if you don't have my army supplied, and keep it supplied, we'll eat your mules up, sir—eat your mules up!"

To ensure that the railroad lines would be safe from Confederate marauders, Sherman worked out precautionary arrangements. A movable railroad base, with repair tools and crews trained to rebuild lines and bridges, would make it possible for the Yankees to advance with no serious interruption. He trained hundreds of men for railroad maintenance, and eventually came to have so many experienced construction men in his army that he was able to order 10,000 soldiers to repair an eight-mile break in the Western and Atlantic line. These men became a talented reservoir which served the nation well, not only in the war, but later in building the Union Pacific Railroad.

Sherman realized that he could not be bound too closely to the railroad, that in penetrating enemy country he would have to have freedom to strike out. So he organized a system of horse and wagon transportation, which would provide adequate supplies without sacrificing mobility. He studied the United States Census reports for Georgia and the tax rolls of the counties, and from these he learned which areas could best furnish food for his soldiers and animals. "No military expedition," he said later, "was ever based on sounder or surer data."

Each division and brigade was allotted only enough wagons to carry food and ammunition, and every man was to take only five days' rations. Apart from these supply trains, one wagon and one ambulance were assigned to each regiment, with a mule for the baggage of the officers of each company. The use of tents was forbidden except to shelter the wounded and to serve as headquarter offices.

It was an enormous task to collect, transfer, and "concentrate at one point horses and mules by the tens of thousands, corn and oats by the millions of bushels, hay by the tens of thousands of tons, subsistence stores by the hundreds of thousands of tons, and miscellaneous articles in the aggregate proportionately large."

"I will see that by May 1st I have on the Tennessee one of the best armies in the world," Cump wrote to John, and to Ellen: "The task of feeding this vast host is a more difficult one than to fight." Due to his brilliant handling of logistics he was to become master of the Georgia campaign.

Just before his departure, Cump sent letters to his family:

Nashville, Tenn. April 25, 1864

Dear Tommy,

I must go to the front in a day or two.... I cannot tell when I will come back, as we must have some hard battles. Whatever may happen to me you are old enough to remember me, and will take my place. Don't study too hard as it may make you weak and sick. Play at all sorts of games. And learn to ride a pony this summer. Also as soon as you are old enough you can learn to swim, to hunt and to fish. All these things are necessary as to read and write.

I am going to Chattanooga and from there into Georgia. I can hardly tell, and you can hardly understand the great things now transpiring, but whatever I do, is for you, and our Country. We must have peace, and that can only be by battle.

Your father

Nashville, May 1, 1864

Dear Minnie,

This is Sunday May 1st, and a beautiful day it is. I have come from a long ride over my old battlefield of November 25th, which is on a high ridge about four or five miles from Chattanooga. The leaves are now out and the young flowers have begun to bloom. I have gathered a few on the very spot where many a brave man died for you and such as you. I have made up a similar bouquet for Lizzie, which I will send her in a letter today, so that both of you will have a present to commemorate this bright opening of spring. You can keep this bouquet in some of your books and though it may fade away entirely it will in after years remind you of this year, whose history for good or evil is most important, and may either raise our country's fame to the highest standard,—or sink it to that of Mexico.

Your father.

Unfortunately for the Union cause, two of Grant's proposed moves for the spring offensive were carried out in such an indifferent manner by their commanders that the expected annihilation of the Confederacy did not materialize that summer. Butler's advance on Richmond was stopped at the battle of Drewry's Bluff, Va., while Banks, defeated in Louisiana, never started for Mobile.

Atlanta

On May 5, after the Army of the Potomac crossed the Rapidan River in Virginia and pressed on through the Wilderness, Sherman began moving his three armies—the Cumberland (under Thomas), the Tennessee (McPherson), and the Ohio (Schofield) toward their objective. In that line of march was Maj. James A. Connolly who, when the command rested on the first night, wrote to his wife: "I do dread starting out in the dust and hot sun after such a long period of ease, but the rebels must be whipped, and since we can't do it sitting in the house, I suppose we must content ourselves with going out after them. Everybody about me is bustling and hurrying, but I am trying very hard to keep cool until I get this finished."

Mile by mile, throughout the lengthening days of spring and into the sapping torment of summer, Sherman's army dragged across Georgia. On that trek from Chattanooga to Atlanta, town after town was destroyed. Five hundred women workers from the Roswell cotton and woolen mills were deported to the North, and noncombatants were seized and used as hostages to guarantee the submission of the hostile civilian population.

Control of the troops proved difficult. In certain cases, reported Major Connolly, some of the foraging parties degenerated into mobs and pillaged outrageously. "We have devoured the land and our animals eat up the wheat and corn fields close," Cump wrote Ellen. "All the people retire before us and desolation is behind. To realize what war is one should follow our tracks."

As in the Meridian Campaign, Sherman felt the deep hatred of the inhabitants. He was convinced that there were thousands who would shoot him on sight and thank their God that they had slain a monster. "Yet," he continued, "I have been more kindly disposed to the people of the South than any general officer of the whole Army."

One evening he answered a letter from a Southern lady, whom he had known in his Charleston days. "Your welcome letter of June 18th came to me amid the sound of battle, and as you say, little did I dream when I knew you, playing as a schoolgirl on Sullivan's Island beach, that I should control a vast army pointing, like the swarm of Alaric, toward the plains of the South.

"Why, oh, why is this? If I know my own heart, it beats as warmly as ever toward those kind and generous families that greeted us with such warm hospitality in days long past . . . and today . . . were any and all our cherished circle . . . to come to me as of old, the stern feelings of duty would melt as snow before a genial sun, and I believe I would strip my own children that they might be sheltered.

"And yet they call me barbarian, vandal, a monster. . . . All I pretend to say, on earth as in heaven, man must submit to some arbiter. . . . I would not subjugate the South . . . but I would make every citizen of the land obey the common law, submit to the same that we do—no more, no less—our equals and not our superiors. . . .

"God only knows how reluctantly we accepted the issue joined, like in other ages, the Northern races, though slow to anger, once aroused are more terrible than the more inflammable of the South."

Sherman went on: "Even yet my heart bleeds when I see the carnage of battle . . . but the very moment that men of the South say instead of appealing to war they should have appealed to reason, to our Congress, to our courts, to religion, and to the experience of history, then will I say, peace, peace. . . .

"Whether I shall live to see this period is problematical, but you may, and may tell your mother and sisters that I never forgot one kind look or greeting, or ever wished to efface its remembrance, but putting on the armor of war I did it that our common country should not perish in infamy and disgrace. . . .

"I hope when the clouds of anger and passion are dispersed, and truth emerges bright and clear, you and all who knew me in early years will not blush that we were once close friends. . . ."

The invasion of the South was hurrying the disintegration of the Confederacy. In Major Connolly's evaluation, "These two campaigns of Grant and Sherman are the most stupendous the world has ever seen going on at the same time, and I really consider myself fortunate to be engaged in one of them."

Lieutenant George Wise of the Forty-third Ohio also understood the historical significance. "This year," he told his brother, "our Republic has put forth the mightiest energies for the preservation of true liberty and self-government that any nation has ever put forth in any cause."

At first Sherman was held in check by the defensive skill of General Johnston with whom he had fought a series of severe battles at Resaca (May 13–16), New Hope Church (May 25–28), and Kennesaw Mountain (June 27).

Sherman was impressed with his men and, unashamedly, proud of himself—of the way he had maneuvered in the field and of the way his supply lines were holding up. He believed he had made few, if any mistakes. Nothing foreseeable had been left undone. Not a man, horse, or mule had been without food; not a musket without adequate ammunition. "I esteem this a triumph greater than any success that has attended me in battle or in strategy," he wrote to Mr. Ewing, "but it has not been the result of blind chance."

To his wife, Major Connolly wrote: "We may have neither Richmond nor Atlanta by the 4th of July, but the situation is excellent and no such thing as failure is thought of in this army. True, we are encompassed by rebels.... But all their efforts are futile, and this army to-day, is better provisioned than the Army of the Cumberland was in its last summer campaign. Flour, Fresh Beef, Salt Pork, Ham, Bacon, Beans, Sugar, Coffee, Hard Bread and everything necessary for the soldier we have in the greatest abundance; much better off in that respect than when we were in Chattanooga."

Sherman's only apprehension was that the enlistment time for the men was expiring, and each day regiments were leaving Georgia for home. His brother John sent him a letter from Schuyler Colfax, a congressman from Indiana, urging that the Indiana regiments be ordered to the rear, so that the men could vote in the fall elections. Even President Lincoln wrote Sherman, suggesting that he furlough the Indiana troops. The president, however, also told the governor of Indiana that he would not press General Sherman on this point. Sherman sent an angry reply to Colfax and told John: "I can't spare these men and if I could it would be an outrageous breach of public law, to use an Army to facilitate elections. Why Congress itself is not half as important now as this army."

As Sherman pushed deeper into Georgia, Negroes, hoping for protection, began flocking to his armies—gnarled old men in baggy trousers, women hooded in shawls, and bony horses pulling wagons that held chests, quilts, and iron kettles. There were carts pulled by dogs, and wheelbarrows pushed by little boys with grimy faces. Their helpless condition concerned Sherman, but he could not afford to devote time to caring for refugees. As they began to impede his progress, he left many behind.

Since the start of the march from Chattanooga, Sherman had been at odds with the Lincoln Administration over the refugee problem and the policy of enlisting Negroes into the army. From the beginning the general hired the able-bodied at $10 per month as manual laborers, but recruiting agents often lured them away with wages of $14. On June 3 Sherman ordered all recruiters arrested. Gen. Lorenzo Thomas, enlisting Negro troops in the west, bitterly complained to Secretary of War Stanton that Sherman's order was too harsh and would virtually cancel out the entire Negro recruitment program.

On July 4 Congress passed legislation authorizing the state governors to dispatch agents into the South to recruit Negroes for the army. To Halleck, Sherman wrote: "I must express my opinion that [this] is the height of folly. I cannot permit it here, and will not have a set of fellows hanging around on any such pretenses."

"State agents are gathering negroes and vagabonds by high bounties to fill our armies," Cump wrote Ellen, "and as this kind of trash mainly fill our Hospitals and keep well to the Rear I suppose I have to fight till this army is used and wait for a new Revolution. Agents are coming to me from Massachusetts, Rhode Island and Ohio to recruit negroes as fast as we catch them to count as soldiers.

"I remonstrated to Mr. Lincoln in the strongest possible

terms," he continued, "but he answered it was the Law and I have got [to] submit."

The president had written Sherman on July 18 asking his cooperation, but the general refused to change his policy. He told Halleck that he did not wish to be "construed as unfriendly to Mr. Lincoln," but that "it is not fair to our men to count negroes as equals." Then he added: "We want the best men of the land [for our armies], and they should be inspired with the pride of freemen to fight for their country. If Mr. Lincoln or Stanton could walk through the camps and hear the soldiers talk they would hear new ideas. I have had the question put to me often: 'Is not a negro as good as a white man to stop a bullet?' Yes; and a sand-bag is better; but can a negro do our skirmishing and picket duty?.... Can they improvise roads, bridges, sorties, flank movements, etc., like the white man? I say no."

Later Sherman sent a telegram to Lincoln apologizing, claiming that the only reason he had questioned the law was because he had never seen a copy of it. He promised to obey orders, even though they were contrary to his wishes. As the president was exceedingly loath to permit political questions to hamper successful campaigns, Sherman escaped reprimand from higher authorities. His half-hearted measures at cooperating with the state agents was given by General Thomas's investigators as the principal reason for the collapse of the Negro recruiting experiment in Georgia.

At the outbreak of the war Sherman had been against using untested, untrained volunteers. He responded the same way to the suggestion that he must enlist Negroes. Throughout the war he stoutly maintained that he was the friend of the black man and that he had sent more Negroes back into Federal lines than had any other commander. But he wanted the blacks kept in menial positions as laborers and servants.

When it was apparent that the Radical Republicans' views favoring the Negroes were making headway in the North, Sherman advised moderation. He pleaded with General Thomas: "For God's sake, let the negro question develop itself slowly and naturally.... I think I understand the negro as well as anybody ... he ... must pass through a probationary state before he is qualified for utter and complete freedom."

One general recalled: "Sherman was right when he said ... 'If you admit the negro to this struggle for any purpose, he has a right to stay in for all; and, when the fight is over, the hand that drops the musket cannot be denied the ballot.' "

Sherman was expressing the attitude of the men in the ranks. Letters and diaries of the troops disclose that the overwhelming majority were against the blacks serving in the armies, as they saw in them a threat to white supremacy. Others objected to Negroes enlisting, as they considered them deficient in soldierly qualities.

On the march toward Atlanta, Lt. Col. Samuel Merrill wanted his wife to know that if she heard anyone wondering why Sherman's armies were moving so slowly, she could tell them that the soldiers had not been beyond the sound of battle for a day since May 8, and that his regiment had already lost one-third of its original number. "The whole country," he wrote, "is traversed by breastworks of the most formidable character . . . you can have no idea of how terrible a thing it is to advance upon a foe who is pouring death into the ranks without in the least exposing itself. War is simply assassination."

On July 17 Sherman's legions crossed the Chattahoochee River and began their move directly against Atlanta. At this stage the Confederate government in Richmond gave valuable assistance to the Federals by removing General Johnston. Mindful only that Sherman had been allowed to approach Atlanta instead of being thrust back into Tennessee and Johnston had expressed "no confidence" that he "could defeat or repel" his antagonist, the Confederate War Department requested the general to hand his command over to John B. Hood, a brave but less skillful officer. Such a change was a "God send" to Sherman. He knew that ultimately he could have outmaneuvered Johnston, but it would have required time and cost many lives.

Hood left his entrenchments to fight a losing battle at Peach Tree Creek, July 20. He then withdrew to the defensive lines outside Atlanta. Almost immediately, on July 22, the armies were again at grips, in the battle of Atlanta, with the Army of the Tennessee winning the advantage.

The Northerners paid dearly. General McPherson was killed by Rebel skirmishers. As Sherman looked at the body of his friend, he said sadly, "Have the body carried to Marietta, and I will see that it is taken back to his home in Ohio." As he covered the coffin with his country's flag, in a voice scarcely audible, he said, "Better start at once and drive carefully."

McPherson's death shook the Army of the Tennessee. General John A. Logan, a politician from southern Illinois, viewed the tragedy as a chance for his own advancement. Now that he was the army's senior officer, he believed he should be its new commander. Sherman, however, considered Logan an opportunist. Shortly after the Battle of Atlanta, Sherman assigned Gen. Oliver Otis Howard, who was serving with the Army of the Cumberland, to replace McPherson. A West Point graduate, Howard had a distinguished record, and Sherman had praised him several months before as a "prompt, zealous and gallant soldier."

General Joseph Hooker, commanding the Twentieth Corps in the Army of the Cumberland, was aggrieved that he himself had not been selected to succeed McPherson. He was bitter, calling Sherman "crazy" and "an utter fool."

In mid-July Cump learned that he was again the father of a baby boy. Ellen's letters were full of worries about her health, the high cost of living, and the children's schooling.

As the weeks passed, the Yankees extended their lines around Atlanta and succeeded in cutting off all rail communication. The digging of, and constant service in, the trenches had injured Confederate morale. Desertions increased. Under these circumstances, Hood evacuated Atlanta.

On September 1 the long roll was sounded, and with the first break of day Sherman's legions moved toward the city. As the army approached the town, a group of men in civilian dress rode out waving white flags, asking protection of private property.

"For us it was a glorious morning," wrote Maj. Stephen Pierson: ". . . . It meant the end of a campaign of more than a hundred days of almost continuous fighting, upon each of which, somewhere along those lines, could have been heard the sounds of war, the sharp crack of the rifle of the outpost, the rattle of the skirmish, or the roar of a full line of battle; the end of a campaign of more than a hundred miles of marching, manoeuvring, struggling, scarcely one of which was made unopposed; the end of a campaign crowned with victory and honor for the one, closed by defeat, without dishonor, for the other. . . .

"As I neared the city I turned in my saddle to look back at the Regiment. A fine and hardy lot of men they were.... How few there are of them! Of the more than 500 who marched out of Chattanooga, but few over a hundred were left to follow the flag into Atlanta."

Union surgeon J. C. Patten noted in his diary: "The City is about the size of Evansville [Indiana] and is terribly shattered. I had often heard of the terrors of bombardment of a crowded city but I never realized it before. Houses were shattered and torn in every shape that can be imagined, some utterly destroyed and some but little injured. Some had shells through the doors, some places the shell had burst inside of a house and torn it all to pieces. After seeing the destruction I no longer wondered at the insane fury with which they charged our works, rushing on as they often did with their hats pulled down over their eyes so that they could not see the certain destruction that awaited them. I am glad that I have taken part in this campaign. I would not for a great deal have missed that ride through Atlanta. It almost paid me for the whole campaign."

Union soldiers found it strange to march past hostile works through the city unopposed. The first night, one general related how he rode along "full of queer sensations and exciting emotions. It was too dark to see much, but there was the principal battlement which had caused so much trouble and injury and not a sound came from it...."

To the average Northerner, weary with hope deferred after three years of fearful loss, the victory at Atlanta seemed the most important achievement of Federal arms in the year 1864. To President Lincoln and the Republican party, it seemed providential. Lincoln had passed an anxious summer, fearful that Grant was checkmated at Richmond and Petersburg and afraid that Sherman had "run up against an impassable barrier."

The entire North was jubilant. "The fall of Atlanta," wrote Horace Greeley in the *New York Tribune*, "is truly, and in full military sense, the loss of Georgia; and it is not too much to say that this crowning triumph of General Sherman's campaign does, in effect, enclose the Rebellion within the narrow limits of the Carolinas and of southern Virginia. It destroys beyond all hope of recovery the unity of the Confederacy, and all probability of its retaining a permanent hold on the continent."

Simultaneously with news from Atlanta, came dispatches from Adm. David Farragut, whose gunboats had entered Mobile Bay. On September 3 the president issued a proclamation asking the people when they gathered in their churches the following Sunday to "make a devout acknowledgement to the Supreme Being for the success of the fleet in Mobile and the glorious achievements of the army in the State of Georgia."

In this moment of victory Sherman acknowledged to Halleck: "I owe you all I now enjoy of fame, for I had allowed myself in 1861 to sink into a perfect slough of despond, and so believe I would have run away and hid from dangers and complications that surround us."

Halleck replied: ". . . your campaign has been the most brillant of the war." Near Berryville, Va., Gen. Rutherford B. Hayes wrote on September 6: "What a glorious career Sherman's army has had! That is the best army in the world. Lee's army is next. . . ."

In Chattanooga Gen. Robert Allen, the quartermaster, summed up the nature of Sherman's logistics: "I must be permitted to remark that history furnished few, if any, examples of armies . . . traversing territories so wide and having their want at every step supplied. It demonstrated how vital to the success of military operations is an efficient quartermaster's department." Through the Nashville railroad depot from November 1, 1863, to September 1, 1864, the time of preparation and follow-through, there had passed: 41,122 horses, 38,724 mules, 3,795 wagons, 445,355 pairs of shoes, 182,000 woolen blankets, and 107,715 waterproof blankets.

In Atlanta, General Sherman planned stern military measures. He demanded that all civilians leave the city temporarily, with the option of going either north or south "as their interests or feelings dictated." Their continued residence would compel the army to feed and clothe them.

"I was resolved," said Sherman later, "to make Atlanta a pure military garrison or depot, with no civil population to influence military measures. I had seen Memphis, Vicksburg, Natchez and New Orleans, all captured from the enemy, and each at once was garrisoned by a full division of troops, if not more; so that success was actually crippling our armies in the field by detachments to guard and protect the interests of a hostile population."

He realized that these orders would bring a storm of invective from the enemy. Just two days after Hood's evacuation of Atlanta, Sherman told Halleck that "if the people raise a howl against my barbarity and cruelty, I will answer that war is war, and not popularity seeking. If they want peace, they and their relatives must stop the war."

While Sherman computed the losses of the campaign, he engaged in an angry correspondence with General Hood, who protested the order for depopulating Atlanta. "Permit me to say," Hood wrote, "that the unprecedented measure you propose, transcends, in studied and ingenious cruelty, all acts ever before brought to my attention in the dark history of war. In the name of God, and humanity, I protest, believing that you will find you are expelling from their homes and firesides the wives and children of brave people."

"It is not unprecedented," Sherman answered, "for General Johnston himself very wisely and properly removed the families all the way from Dalton down, and I see no reason why Atlanta should be excepted." Sherman pointed out that Hood himself had destroyed houses all along his parapet and had rendered uninhabitable 50 dwellings in Atlanta, as they stood in the way of his forts and men. "You defended Atlanta on a line so close to town that every cannon-shot, and many musket-shots from our line of investment, that overshot their mark, went into the habitations of women and children. I say that it is kindness to these families of Atlanta to remove them now, at once, from a scene that women and children should not be exposed to.

"If we must be enemies," he continued, "let us be men, and fight it out as we propose to do, and not deal in such hypocritical appeals to God and humanity. God will judge us in due time, and He will pronounce whether it be more humane to fight with a town full of women and the families of a 'brave people' at our back, or to remove them in time to places of safety."

His aim was "to whip the rebels, to humble their pride, to follow them to their inmost recesses, and make them fear and dread us. 'Fear of the Lord is the beginning of wisdom.' "

Meanwhile the mayor of Atlanta and members of the city council were writing Sherman, picturing to him the heartrending loss and suffering which the removal order was entailing. In answering, Sherman used one of his famous expressions, "War is cruelty." "You cannot," he declared, "qualify war in harsher terms than I will. War is cruelty, and you cannot refine it; and those who brought war into our country deserve all the curses and maledictions a people can pour out. I know I had no hand in making this war, and I know I will make more sacrifices than any of you to-day to secure peace. . . ."

Sherman's troops approved wholeheartedly their general's controversial order. In a letter home, one officer wrote: "Have you seen Genl Shermans letter [in the newspapers] in reply to the Mayor & others asking him to revoke his order sending citizens out of the city? It is a capital thing, a little the best of the kind I have seen yet. In short we begin to think Genl Sherman is a little ahead of any body in the U S not excepting Grant now."

That September Rt. Rev. Henry C. Lay, bishop of Arkansas, traveled through Atlanta under cover of a pass to see friends in Huntsville, Ala. While in the city, he wanted to meet the famous general. He found Sherman comfortably settled in a fine house near City Hall. Sherman greeted the bishop warmly and invited him to stay for dinner. General Lovell H. Rousseau's wife and daughter and a number of the staff officers were at the table, dining on pea soup in tin plates, roast beef, and vegetables. They talked of McPherson's death, of Sherman's stay in Vicksburg, and of guerrilla warfare.

Once dinner was over, Sherman showed the bishop to the piazza and offered him a cigar. They sat there for an hour, talking. Sherman complained that General Hood had treated him ungenerously in their correspondence. "To be sure," he said, "I have made war vindictively; war is war, and you can make nothing else of it; but Hood knows as well as anyone I am not brutal or inhuman."

When they spoke of the war in general, Bishop Lay expressed the belief that there was now a deep-seated alienation which would make it impossible for the two nations to live together on intimate terms. Sherman, however, said he believed that once the war was over, the past would be quickly forgotten.

He added: "Your people had much the advantage in the beginning of this war. You were a military people, respected the profession of arms and cultivated military education. If I went to

New York and was introduced as Captain or Major Sherman, U.S.A., the people passed me by as a useless man; but if I went to Charleston, my profession was a passport into society and caused my acquaintance to be sought. You took to arms naturally and easily; we had to acquire the military profession against our tastes.

"But you made a great mistake in organizing a Confederacy. Had you clung to the Union and claimed to be legitimate exponents of the American ideas, the true representatives of the American Constitution, you would have had better success.

"This war," he continued, "ought to be arrested. It is intensifying the greatest fault and danger in our social system. It daily increases the influences of the masses, already too great for safety. The man of intelligence and education is depressed in value far below the man of mere physical strength. These common soldiers will feel their value and seek to control affairs hereafter to the prejudice of the intelligent classes."

That night Cump wrote a note to Minnie: "You will hear so much about Atlanta and the battles that I need not speak of them to you, but I hope someday we will all sit round the fire when I can tell you all my stories about battles. Atlanta is a town which once had 20,000 people, with large foundries and workshops, but these are all gone and nothing remains but the dwelling houses, which are empty."

Captain Charles Ewing came into the parlor where Cump was writing and showed him a letter from his brother Tom, dated August 30, asking Cump whether he would be willing to run against Lincoln or General McClellan, the Democratic candidate, in the upcoming presidential election. Cump told Charles: "I am no fit subject for a Democratic, Republican Candidate for any office. The people of the United States have too much sense to make me their President."

Sherman well remembered how years ago a committee in San Francisco had tendered him the Democratic nomination for treasurer. "If a similar committee should be rash enough to venture the other nomination," he wrote Ellen, "I fear I should proceed to personal violence, for I would receive a sentence to be hung and damned with infinitely more composure than to be executive of this nation."

In the forthcoming presidential election Sherman preferred

Sherman's sketch for his children of a Civil War scene (presumably the
siege of Vicksburg, Mississippi)

Sherman's sketch for his children of the mess tent at the camp near the Big
Black River, September 1863

General Sherman (leaning on the breach of the gun) and his staff during the campaign in Atlanta

Sherman's Grand Army on Pennsylvania Avenue, Washington, D.C. Major
General Slocum and staff and Army of Georgia passing in review

Lincoln over McClellan. However, he felt that the ideal choice for the position would be someone like Jefferson Davis, for such a man would prosecute the war more forcefully than the other two.

When Sherman arrived in Atlanta, he had accomplished all of his assigned task except destroying the Confederate army. After evacuating Atlanta, Hood had marched southward. Sherman's forces had pursued him for 30 miles and then had returned to the city.

Now free to move as he wanted, Hood proceeded to strike the Union line of railroad communications running to Chattanooga. Although Sherman worked to protect these lines with troops, he made no real attempt to engage Hood. He argued that he could never bring the Confederates to battle or run them down, and he did not propose to scramble all over the state in a wild-goose chase. He was not interested in John B. Hood. He was working out a brilliant plan of operations. In war, Sherman had learned long ago, whoever acted with speed, surprise, and resolution got the advantage.

Speculation and rumor mounted in Atlanta about Sherman's next move. "But what it is, or where he is going to take us is more than we can guess," Dr. Patten wrote in his journal. "We may go to Mobile or Charleston or Richmond. We would like to know, and I doubt not that Gen. Hood would like it better than we would."

In a letter home, one soldier said: "I hope sometimes it is to Augusta & then to Savannah, but I will try to content myself till we go. I will try & write again but you need not worry if you don't hear from me in a month."

On October 1, 1864, Sherman telegraphed Grant, proposing that General Thomas and his force be sent to deal with Hood, who, he believed, would march for Tennessee. Meanwhile Sherman would take the rest of his army "across Georgia to Savannah or Charleston, breaking the [rail]roads and doing irreparable damage. We cannot remain on the defensive."

Grant wired approval of Sherman's plan to march to the sea. To Halleck, Sherman wrote: "I now consider myself authorised to execute my plan ... strike out into the heart of Georgia, and make for Charleston, Savannah, or the mouth of the Appalachicola [on the Gulf]. . . . I must have alternates, else, being confined to one route, the enemy might so oppose that delay and want would trouble me, but, having alternates, I can take so eccentric a course that no general can guess my objective.

"Therefore when you hear I am off have look-outs at Morris Island, S. C., Ossabaw Sound, Ga., Pensacola and Mobile Bays. I will turn up somewhere, and believe I can take Macon and Milledgeville, Augusta and Savannah, Ga., and wind up with closing the neck back of Charleston so that they will starve out."

"I propose to demonstrate the vulnerability of the South," he wrote General Thomas, "and make its inhabitants feel that war and individual ruin are synonymous terms." Sherman wanted to show the world that the Confederacy was a hollow shell. Watching his army move through Georgia unhampered would create a sense of helplessness not only for Georgians, but for troops in Hood's and Lee's armies and plantation owners in the Carolinas. They must realize that there was no hope for the Confederacy. "This war," he wrote Halleck, "differs from European wars in this particular; we are not only fighting hostile armies, but a hostile people, and must make old and young, rich and poor, feel the hard hand of war."

Sherman was positive that Lee could not get away from the defense of Richmond without Grant's knowledge or without serious loss to his command. The officers to whom Sherman confided his strategy gazed at the map on the wall and measured the hundreds of miles through hostile country. To one officer, "the whole scheme, in the hands of any man but he who conceived it, seemed weird, fatal, impossible."

To his friend Maj. Henry Hitchcock, Sherman confided: "It's a big game, but I can do it—I *know* I can do it." In his diary, Hitchcock added: "And you may be sure of one thing—that what he says he can do, he *can*."

Sherman hurried forward preparations for the 300-mile march. The army, thoroughly equipped and organized, now numbering 60,000 men, was divided into a right wing, commanded by Maj. Gen. Oliver O. Howard, and a left wing, by Maj. Gen. Henry W. Slocum.

Without divulging to the troops their ultimate destination, Sherman issued a special field order indicating the requisites of the campaign. There was to be no general supply train, but each corps was to have its own ammunition and provision trains. The army was to forage liberally on the country. Soldiers were not to enter the dwellings of the inhabitants or commit any trespass, but during the halts they might collect potatoes and other vegetables and drive in livestock. Horses, mules, and wagons were to be appropriated freely. The country to the rear of the army was to be rendered as useless as possible by destroying railroad tracks, mills, and factories, thus enforcing a "devastation more or less relentless."

As the days passed, excitement grew. Major Connolly knew that the army was on the eve of something big. He wrote his wife: "There is something romantic in the conception of this campaign and I am really charged with it. Nothing in military history compares with it except the invasion of Mexico by Cortes, the Spaniard, who, landing on its hostile shore, burned his ships, destroyed all his means of retreat, and then turning to his army, told them they must rely on God and their own right arms; that they must conquer or die. So with Sherman." The major added, "I want to ride my fine grey—Frank—entirely through the Confederacy and let him drink out of the Atlantic—if he wants to—I shall then be content."

On November 14 Sherman's Engineer Corps began the special task of destruction. They demolished the railroad depot, roundhouse, machine shops, and all facilities that might aid the Confederates. During the night the heart of Atlanta became an inferno, as one explosion followed another. Torrents of sparks shot skyward. "The heaven is one expanse of lurid fire," exclaimed an officer. "The air is filled with flying, burning cinders; buildings covering two hundred acres are in ruins or in flames; every instant there is the sharp detonation or the smothered boom sound of exploding shells and powder concealed in the buildings, and then sparks and flame shoot away up in the black and red roof, scattering cinders far and wide.... The city, which next to Richmond, has furnished more material for prosecuting the war than any other in the South, exists no more as a means of injury to be used by the enemies of the Union."

"All the pictures and verbal descriptions of hell I have ever seen," reported Major Connolly, "never gave me half so vivid an idea of it, as did this flame wrapped city to-night. Gate City of the South, farewell!"

One evening just before he was due to leave, Sherman wrote

to Minnie and Lizzie: ".... I am going to make another campaign that I hope will prove as successful as that of Atlanta, and after it is over I will try and come to see you. I want to see you very much—indeed, I cannot say how much—and then I can tell you all about the things of which you hear so much but know so little.

"War is something about which you should not concern yourself, and I am fighting now that you may live in peace. I am not fighting for myself, but for you and the little children, who have more to live for than we older people.

"But if I do lose my life, I know there will be some people still living who will take care of you. Mama tells me the baby is quite sick, and she is afraid he will not get well. I hope that he will live long and take poor Willy's place in our love. . . .

"Believe me always thinking of you, no matter how great the danger."

That same evening he wrote also to Tommy: "People write to me that I am now a Great General, and if I were to come home they would gather round me in crowds & play music and all such things. That is what people call fame & Glory, but I tell you that I would rather come down quietly and have you and Willy meet me at the car than to have the shouts of the People.

"Willy will never meet us again in this world and you and I must take care of the family as long as I live and then will be your turn. So you see you have a good deal to do. You have much to learn, but while your body is growing up strong as a man you will have time to learn all I know & more too. . . ."

The March

SHERMAN and his army of just over 60,000 men moved out of Atlanta on November 16. The weather was superb. An enlisted man called out to Sherman, "Uncle Billy, I guess Grant is waiting for us in Richmond!" Dr. James Zearing wrote: "We then started for unknown country and unknown destination with apprehensions of having to meet with many difficulties."

"The eventful day has come," wrote an officer in his diary. "We turn our backs upon Atlanta, and our faces seaward.... We must succeed. Not a man in this army doubts it. We'll march straight through and shake the rebellious old State from center to circumference."

Once the city of Atlanta was lost to sight, the work of destruction began. Major Connolly depicted the soldiers as determined to burn, plunder, and destroy everything in their way. "If we are to continue our devastation as we began today," said the major, "I don't want to be captured on this trip, for I expect every man of us the rebels capture will get a 'stout rope.'"

One young Southern girl had vivid memories. "Heaven grant that I may *never* pass another such day," recalled Martha Quillin. "Sherman's troops were then passing us on their way...." All day one continuous stream of wagons and guards poured past her house, and as darkness came on, the burning commenced. "No one I hope will ever expect me to love Yankees," she said. "The shadow of a great sorrow lies dark over our land."

The divisions advanced through the Georgia countryside without seeing or hearing armed Rebels. Bridges were destroyed, railroad cars burned, wheels broken, axles bent, boilers punctured, and cylinder heads cracked and dumped into deep water. "Columns of smoke by day and pillars of fire by night, for miles and miles on our right and left indicate to us daily and nightly the route and location of the other columns of our army," commented Major Connolly. "Every 'Gin House' we pass is burned; every stack of fodder we can't carry along is burned; every barn filled with grain is destroyed; in fact everything that can be of use to the Rebels is either carried off by our foragers or set on fire and burned."

Foraging was carried out with military precision. Each brigade sent out a party of 50 men on foot who would return mounted, driving cattle, mules, and horses, and hauling wagons or family carriages loaded with smoked bacon, turkeys, chickens, ducks, cornmeal, jugs of molasses, and sweet potatoes. "The boys," one soldier wrote home, "wasted as much as they used, but no complaint was made, in fact I think Genl Sherman didn't intend to leave anything for the Rebs."

The march became a wild excursion of an army in a holiday spirit. Wrote a soldier of the 100th Indiana: "Such an Army as we have I doubt if ever was got together before; all are in the finest condition. We have weeded out all the sick, feeble ones and all the faint hearted ones and all the boys are ready for a meal or a fight and dont seem to care which it is."

There was a wide discrepancy between Sherman's orders concerning looting and the performance of his men. A shocking amount of plundering and vandalism took place. Dwellings were needlessly burned; family silver seized; wine cellars raided.

Sherman and many of his officers unquestionably tried to prevent such abuses. "Foraging," the general insisted, "must be limited to the regular parties properly detailed." But the suppression of plundering was impossible because of the width of the army's front. The only effective deterrent—death, to men who were caught—could not be applied without Washington's sanction. But Sherman's armies were too remote to secure consent from the higher authorities in the War Department. In fact, rumor spread throughout the ranks that Sherman himself favored all-out plundering.

When, after the war, a full record was made, one of the most striking features it revealed about the march was that the destruction of property was accompanied by so little personal violence. Murder and rape were almost unknown.

As on the march from Chattanooga to Atlanta, Negro refugees poured out across the fields to the marching columns. As many as 25,000 people flocked to the Yankees at one time or another. Men in the ranks saw them clinging to "Massa Sherman's" stirrups, hailing him as an angel of the Lord, shouting "De day ob Jubilo hab arrived!" One Negro, who seemed to be the spokesman for a number of fellow slaves, told an aide of Sherman's: "Ise hope de Lord will prosper you Yankees and Mr. Sherman, because I tinks and we all tinks dat you'se down here in our interests."

Sherman forbade his legions to encumber themselves with these refugees. Only the able-bodied, enrolled as laborers, were welcome to join the regiments. To Negro leaders, Sherman explained why he was refusing escape to blacks. He could not care for them; he could barely feed his own men; he felt that the thousands of blacks would hamper his movements. "At some future time," he said, "we will be enabled to provide for the poor whites and blacks who seek to escape from bondage."

"The Darkies come to us from every direction," wrote one soldier, "despite all discouragements. We have a large following though General Sherman has tried every way to explain we do not want them."

In his diary, Major Connolly noted: "Negroes stare at us with open eyes and mouths, but generally, before the whole column has passed they pack up their bundles and march along, going [where], they know not, but apparently satisfied they are going somewhere toward freedom.

"But these wretched creatures, or a majority of them," he added, "don't know what freedom is. Ask them where they are going as they trudge along with their bundles on their heads, and the almost invariable reply is 'Don't know Massa; gwine along wid you all.' "

On November 23 advanced units of the army marched through Milledgeville, Ga., the state capital, with bands blaring "John Brown's Body," and set up camp on the east side of the Oconee River. Already Gov. Joseph Brown and members of the legislature had fled their homes, trailed by many of the town's citizens. Soon the main body of the Fourteenth and Twentieth Corps occupied this "miserable, dirty, God-forsaken city." Officers were besieged with petitions from the local citizenry seeking protection from vandals. The burning of private dwellings was rare in Milledgeville, in marked contrast to the army's previous destruction. However, the comptroller general estimated the damage to his own house on Columbia Street at $20,000—the silver was stolen and the furniture either destroyed or given to the Negroes.

Sherman spared the warehouses of two of the richest cotton merchants, who held no sympathy with the South, and the large flour mill on the Oconee River, when the owner produced evidence of having been born in Ireland. Two textile mills and an iron and brass foundry, whose managers were either New Englanders or of foreign birth, also went unmolested. These favorable circumstances of ownership failed to apply to the Central of Georgia Railroad Station and the toll bridge, both of which were burned.

Despite the rumors that all public buildings in Milledgeville would be leveled, only two were actually demolished—the arsenal and the magazine. But explosions from the magazine damaged some church buildings, and residents were outraged by what they considered the soldiers' desecration.

The most excessive act of vandalism occurred when some of the younger officers staged a mock session of the Georgia legislature, which turned into bedlam. They ransacked the entire building, including the state library. Books were tossed out windows to the muddy ground below, where troops trampled all over them.

"Our soldiers and even some officers," wrote Major Connolly, "have been plundering the State library today and carrying off law and miscellaneous works in armfuls. It is a downright shame. Public libraries should be sacredly respected by all belligerents, and I am sure General Sherman will, some day, regret that he permitted this library to be destroyed and plundered. . . . I don't object to stealing horses, mules, niggers and all such *little things*, but I will not engage in plundering and destroying public libraries."

Sherman's army departed from Milledgeville on November 24,

Thanksgiving Day. By Friday the last of the troops had vanished. "A stillness almost Sabbath like pervades our business streets," reported the *Milledgeville Confederate Union*, "and the blackened sightless walls of the Arsenal, Magazine and Depot remind us constantly of the presence of the vandal hordes of Sherman."

Sherman's advance through the heart of the state so alarmed the Confederates, lest Macon or Augusta or both be attacked, that they divided their forces. When it finally became manifest that Savannah was his objective, they found it impossible to concentrate large numbers of troops for its defense. By December 10 Sherman's forces had driven the enemy toward Savannah. On December 13 Sherman opened communications with the Union fleet, and two nights later the Confederates evacuated the city.

Sherman's march had ended. His troops had destroyed the resources of one of the most productive sections of the Confederacy and had erased Georgia as a possible source of supply for General Lee's army in Virginia. The march had instilled in the civilians of Georgia the same sense of hopelessness that had been felt earlier in Mississippi. The ease with which such devastation and demoralization had been wrought had demonstrated the weakness of the Confederacy and indicated to both sides that the end of the war was approaching.

To Ellen, Cump wrote: "After having participated in driving the Confederacy down the Mississippi I have again cut it in twain, and have planned and executed a Campaign which Judges pronounce will be famous among the Grand deeds of the World. I can hardly realize it for really it was easy, but like one who has walked a narrow plank I look back and wonder if I really did it, but here I am in the proud city of Savannah . . . . still I do more than ever crave for peace and quiet and would gladly drop all these and gather you and my little ones in some quiet place where I could be at ease. People here talk as though the war was drawing to a close, but I know better."

"I don't know if you can understand the merit of all this," he wrote Ellen again, "but it will stamp me in years to come, and will be more appreciated in Europe than in America. . . . For your father's sake I am glad of the successes that have attended me, and I know he will feel pride in my success more than you or I do. Oh that Willy were living! How his eyes would brighten and his bosom swell with honest pride if he could hear and understand these things."

Amid hurrahing and the crashing of bands, Gen. John White Geary's division of the Twentieth Corps marched into Savannah and took peaceable possession. Sherman occupied the spacious house of Charles Green, a rich cotton merchant and a British subject. He sent a dispatch to President Lincoln which arrived, opportunely, on Christmas night: "I beg to present you as a Christmas gift the city of Savannah with 150 heavy guns and plenty of ammunition and also about 25,000 bales of cotton."

That Christmas Day Cump wrote greetings to Ellen and the children. "A happy Christmas I hope this will prove to you and Lizzie and all," he told Minnie, "for you will probably know by this time that we have captured Savannah, and that we are all well. We are enjoying ourselves in an elegant house, and will have a real Christmas dinner, turkey and all. . . ."

To Tommy he wrote: "I expect soon to march again to danger and battle but hope the good luck of the past will stick by me, and that one of these days we will all have a home where we can live together and then I will tell you all about my travels and battles. . . .

"You can take your own time learning as fast as you please, and when you get old enough can choose for yourself whether to be a soldier, a Lawyer, a Doctor or Farmer. . . ."

"I may be mistaken but I don't think Tommy so entirely identifies himself in my fortunes," Cump wrote Ellen. "He is a fine manly boy and it may be as he doubtless will realize our fondest expectations, but I cannot but think that he takes less interest in me than Willy showed from the time of his birth. It may be I gave the latter more of my personal attention at the time when the mind began to develop."

By this time Ellen and the children had moved from Ohio, because of the high cost of living and the crowded conditions in the Ewing household, to South Bend, Ind., into a rented house near the schools at Notre Dame. The new baby, who was ailing with lung fever, died that December. Cump had been worried about his health ever since leaving Atlanta. When the letter came from Ellen about the baby's death, the baby Cump had never seen, he was deeply touched. To Tommy, he wrote: "We are all very sorry poor little Charley is lost to us. But we must submit, for death does not consult our wishes."

The excitement of entering Savannah soon waned, and the troops settled into the military routine. The atmosphere in Savannah was much different from that of Atlanta. "The people here," Sherman told Grant, "seem to be well content, as they have reason to be, for our troops have behaved magnificently; you would think it Sunday, so quiet is everything in the city day and night."

The Yankee occupation of Savannah, unlike that of Atlanta, was marked by cooperation between the Federals and city officials, and no overt clashes erupted between Sherman's troops and the inhabitants. "The citizens of Savannah seemed well pleased with their change of rulers," remarked one soldier. "They . . . displayed sociability that we didn't usually get in the South. In return Sherman showed them every possible consideration.

"I was never in a captured place," he added, "where private property was respected and protected as it was here, or where citizens were allowed so many privileges. Employment was furnished to those who wanted it."

The majority of Savannah's citizens treated the Northerners with courtesy and respect, but understandably, there were segments of the population that were hostile. Some of the people would leave the sidewalks and make detours to avoid walking beneath the Stars and Stripes. Others refused to attend any function where Union officers were present.

There were numerous administrative problems to solve—the handling of Confederate property, the organizing of a civil government, the billeting of troops, and most important, the feeding of the population. The last problem was complicated by the fact that thousands of refugees had stampeded into the city as Sherman's forces had advanced. "The people of Savannah are, in a measure, destitute," wrote Gen. John G. Foster, "and will have to be supported to a certain extent, until such time as the ordinary course of labor and supplies is resumed in the city."

Although Sherman had advised a Confederate general in the field that "no provision has been made for families in Savannah, and many of them will suffer from want—and I will not undertake to feed them," after the occupation he changed his mind. He ordered Col. Amos Beckwith to seize all subsistence stores and charged him with the responsibility of supplying them to starving families. During the course of the same day, Sherman further liberalized his policy. "Citizens destitute of provisions," General Order No. 2 stated, "can make application at the city store, where they will be supplied upon the order of . . . the mayor of the city."

Mayor Richard D. Arnold told Sherman privately that he was ready to see Georgia return to the Union. "Where resistance is hopeless," he said, "it is criminal to make it." A large meeting of prominent citizens adopted resolutions paving the way for Savannah's pulling out of the war. One article stipulated: "That we accept the position and language of the President of the United States, seek to have peace by laying down our arms and submitting to the national authority under the constitution, leaving all questions which remain to be adjusted by the peaceful means of legislation."

After the adoption of these measures, Sherman authorized the mayor and city council to remain in office and to cooperate with General Geary, who was in command of the city. To the city council, Sherman reported that he would turn over to it all the food his army had captured when it occupied the city. Fifty thousand bushels of rice, worth about $265,000, would be sold in New York and Boston, and the proceeds used to purchase other foods. Shortly after these sales and with the help of money from Northern philanthropists, cargo ships were discharging barrels of flour, pork, and other staples on Savannah wharves.

"Whilst almost everyone is praising your great march through Georgia and the capture of Savannah," General Halleck wrote to Sherman, "there is a certain class, having now great influence with the President and very probably anticipating still more on a change of cabinet, who are decidedly disposed to make a point against you. I mean in regard to 'inevitable Sambo.' They say you have manifested an almost *criminal* dislike to the Negro, and that you are not willing to carry out the wishes of the Government in this regard to him, but repulse him in contempt."

Sherman replied: "If it be insisted that I shall so conduct my operations that the negro alone is consulted, of course I shall be defeated, and then where will be Sambo? Don't military suc-

cess imply the safety of Sambo, and *vice versa?* They gather round
me in crowds, and I can't find out whether I am Moses or
Aaron or which of the prophets. The South deserves all she has
got for her injustice to the negro, but that is no reason why we
should go to the other extreme. I do and will do the best I can for
the negroes, and feel sure that the problem is solving itself slowly
and naturally. It needs nothing more than our fostering care."

Despite Secretary of War Stanton's appreciation of Sherman's
military accomplishments, he distrusted the general. Sherman had
disapproved of the government's policy toward the blacks, opposing vehemently the enlistment of Negroes in the United States
Army. Stanton urged Grant to impress on Sherman the difficulty
of recruiting white replacements and the advisability of forming
colored regiments. Grant answered that he had already done so,
and he asked Stanton to explain to Sherman in person that the employment of Negro soldiers for garrison duty would free white
soldiers for the battlefield.

On January 11, 1865, a revenue cutter brought Secretary
Stanton, Quartermaster General Meigs, and other Washington
officials to Savannah. Stanton explained the overall situation to
Sherman. He proposed that the general arrange a meeting with
the leaders of the Negro community to ask what they wanted for
their people. That same day Sherman invited 20 freedmen to come
to the Green house the following evening.

The elderly Garrison Frazier, an ordained minister of the
Baptist church, acted as their spokesman. While they stood around
the room, Stanton sat at the table, questioning, taking notes.
Sherman sat by the fireplace and frequently made suggestions.

STANTON: State in what manner you think you can take care of
yourselves and how you can best aid the government in maintaining your freedom?

FRAZIER: The best way is to have land, and turn it and till
it by our own labor—we can soon maintain ourselves and having
something to spare. To assist the government, the young men
should enlist in the service of the government to serve in such a
manner as they may be wanted.

STANTON: What is the feeling of the black population toward
the Government of the United States, and what is the understanding in respect to the present war?

FRAZIER: I think you will find there are thousands that are willing to make any sacrifice to assist the Government, while there are also many that are not willing to take up arms. I do not suppose there are a dozen men that are opposed to the Government.

Then, displaying remarkable insight into the basic causes of the Civil War, Frazier continued: "I understand, as to the war, that the South is the aggressor. The object of the war was not at first to give the slaves their freedom, but the sole object . . . was at first to bring the rebellious states back into the Union. Afterward, knowing the value set on slaves by the Rebels, the President thought that this proclamation would stimulate them to lay down their arms. Their not doing so has now made the freedom of the slaves part of the war."

At one point in the meeting Stanton asked Sherman to leave the room for a moment, then he turned to Frazier and asked: "What is the feeling of the colored people in regard to General Sherman and how far do they regard his sentiments and actions as friendly to their rights and interests, or otherwise?"

Without hesitating, Frazier replied: "We looked upon General Sherman, prior to his arrival, as a man in the Providence of God especially set apart to accomplish this work, and we unanimously feel inexpressible gratitude to him, looking upon him as a man that should be honored for the faithful performance of his duty. Some of us called upon him immediately upon his arrival and it is probable that he would not meet the Secretary of War with more courtesy than he met us. His conduct and deportment toward us characterized him as a friend and gentleman. We have confidence in General Sherman, and think that what concerns us could not be under better hands."

The meeting broke up at midnight. Stanton came away pleased. This was the first time in the history of the nation that representatives of the government had gone to these "poor debased people to ask them what they wanted for themselves."

Stanton invited Sherman and his staff, together with the naval commanders, to dine with him on board the cutter. He pressed the general to give his thoughts on how best to handle the Negro question. Sherman suggested that they should colonize the lands abandoned by the Confederates on the offshore islands, and isolated from exploitive whites, bridge the gap between slavery and responsibility.

Stanton was impressed with Sherman's grasp of the situation. Together they lingered over dinner, developing and refining the idea. The result was Special Field Order No. 15, which set apart and reserved for the settlement of Negroes the islands from Charleston south, the abandoned rice fields along the rivers for 30 miles back from the sea, and the region bordering on the Saint Johns River in Florida. The freedmen were to be the only settlers and were to manage their own affairs. Sherman's order was based on the Confiscation Act of 1862, which provided for the confiscation of property of certain classes of Rebels. However, this act was never put into effect, and thus, neither was Sherman's order.

After his four-day visit, Stanton felt easier about Sherman's attitude toward the ex-slaves. Yet after Stanton had gone, Cump wrote Ellen that now the secretary was "cured of that Negro nonsense.

"Mr. Chase and others have written to me," he continued, "to modify my opinions, but you know I cannot, for if I attempt the part of a hypocrite it would break out at each sentence. I want soldiers made of the best bone and muscle in the land, and won't attempt military feats with doubtful materials. I have said that slavery is dead and the Negro free, and want him treated as free, and not hunted and badgered to make a soldier of, when his family is left back on the plantations. I am right and won't change."

During January Sherman and his staff were busy formulating plans for their next move. "With Savannah in our possession," Sherman told Grant, "we can punish South Carolina as she deserves, and as thousands of people in Georgia hoped we would do."

Halleck was enthusiastic over advancing into South Carolina: "Should you capture Charleston, I hope that by some accident the place may be destroyed, and if a little salt should be sown upon its site, it may prevent the growth of future crops of . . . secession."

Replying, Sherman wrote: "The truth is, the whole army is burning with an insatiable desire to work vengeance upon South Carolina. I almost tremble for her, but feel she deserves all that seems in store for her."

Sherman felt that a march northward from Savannah through the Carolinas would be as much an attack on Lee's army as if his forces were maneuvering within sound of the guns of Richmond. Total war in the Carolinas would directly affect the outcome of Grant's push in Virginia. Sherman's persistence and the news of General Thomas's victory over Hood at Nashville pressed Grant to authorize the advance north from Savannah. Once again Sherman planned to cut himself off from his base of supplies: his 60,-000 men would again live off the land.

Before leaving Savannah, Cump wrote Ellen: "I have hitherto attempted so much and have been rewarded with success that it would be [a] pity if my good fortune should now fail me, but, I will not count on it but rather count on success and if again success crown my efforts I will feel I have done my full share in this war.

"Step by step have I been led deeper and deeper in the game till I find myself a Leader to whom not only my soldiers look to but the President and the People, not only our own, but Foreigners and the South now account me one of the Great Leaders of Armies endowed with extraordinary qualities that make me more distrustful than if I were nobody. I cannot now help it and must go on to the end."

With the Seventeenth and Fifteenth Corps in the advance, the troops marched out of Savannah on a drive about which Sherman's son would write: "My father always rated this campaign as his greatest military achievement, and believed that it settled the fate of the Confederacy."

The rank and file in the army, and most of the officers, believed that South Carolina, the first state to secede, had triggered the Civil War by firing on Fort Sumter and was responsible for all the bloodshed. No punishment for her could be too severe. In his journal Dr. Patten wrote: "I think that they will be able to see our track for a generation to come. We have laid a heavy hand on Georgia, but that is light compared to what S. C. will catch. . . . We shall make it a desert."

The major part of Sherman's force moved without difficulty well into South Carolina, laid waste to the countryside, and by February 7, was camped along the Charleston-Augusta Railroad. As Sherman marched deeper into enemy country, foraging became more vital to success. Although the general issued orders that officers command all foraging parties, plunderers roamed about without restriction.

"The actual invasion of South Carolina has begun," wrote one officer. "The well-known sight of columns of black smoke meets our gaze again; this time houses are burning, and South Carolina has commenced to pay an instalment, long overdue on her debt to justice and humanity."

"The Army burned everything it came near in the State of South Carolina," wrote Major Connolly to his wife, "not under orders, but in spite of orders. The men 'had it in' for the State and they took it out in their own way. Our track through the State is a desert waste."

South Carolina despaired. "There is a great alarm through the country," a Confederate general wrote his wife, "and a strong disposition to give up, among the old residents even, and with the females especially."

At Columbia Gov. Andrew G. Magrath pleaded with little avail for the people of South Carolina to rise up to a man and halt the invader. Of Sherman's advancing legions, a Confederate enlisted man wrote home: "deer sister Lizzy: i hev conkludid that the dam fulishness uv trying to lick sherman had better be stoped. we have ben getting nuthing, but hell & lots uv it ever since we saw the dam yanks and i am tirde uv it. shurmin has lots of pimps that dont car a dam what they doo. and its no use tryin to whip em."

Letters and diaries of Union soldiers on the march northward reveal that, despite the destruction, there was a considerable amount of good-natured social intercourse between the army and South Carolinians. Officers doled out welcome food, coffee, sugar, and bread to many people. "Although pretty clean work is done [to the countryside] by our Army," wrote one, "yet the people are generally allowed to carry to their houses a sufficient supply of corn, potatoes to keep from starving."

The diary of Capt. Dexter Horton suggests that the traditional Southern concept of the Yankees' ruthlessness developed during the embittered Reconstruction period. Southerners, especially women, have written often exaggerated accounts of the destruction perpetrated by Sherman's army.

By February 12 Orangeburg was in Union hands, and from there the army marched on in the direction of Columbia.

The state capital was in an uproar. Columbians began moving out of the city. The governor declared martial law, but this failed to halt rioters. Shops were broken into and robbed. The South Carolina Railroad Depot caught fire through the reckless actions of a band of vagabonds. One Confederate major, trying to secure transportation for his ordnance supplies, wrote: "The straggling [Confederate] cavalry and rabble were stripping the warehouses and railroad depots. The city was in the wildest terror."

On February 17 Columbia fell, and before noon Sherman and his staff were cantering through the streets. "The welcome given to Sherman by the Negroes," one officer wrote, "was touching. They greet his arrival with exclamations of unbounded joy. 'Tank de Almighty God, Mister Sherman has come at last. We knew it; we prayed for de day, and de Lord Jesus heard our prayers. Mr. Sherman has come wid his company.'"

That evening Sherman and his staff were at dinner, when suddenly the fire bells clanged. A fire of unknown origin was raging out of control in the business district. The high wind intensified the flames. The smoke changed from blue to black, dense, coiling billows. The air was full of wisps of burning cotton, blowing like autumn leaves.

"In some of the buildings the rebels had stored shot, shell and ammunition," wrote an officer, "and when flames reached these magazines we had the Atlanta experience all over again—the smothered boom, the huge columns of fire shooting heavenward, the red-hot iron flying here and there. . . ."

The testimony of Sherman and his generals and several of Columbia's leading citizens indicates that there is little truth in the traditional belief that hordes of Federal soldiers swarmed through the city starting fires. General Logan, who directed the fire fighters that night and did not leave until the fire was under control, related that he did not see a single soldier set a building ablaze. Nevertheless, during the night small bands of intoxicated Yankee soldiers and deserters from the Rebel army did force their way into private homes, pillaging property, and at times, setting houses on fire. Lieutenant Wise, Forty-third Ohio, watched in horror as soldiers, firebrands in hands, rushed from house to house. "Sober men too were engaged in the same work, 'Here is the place where it all begun, and we will burn it,' " wrote Wise. ". . . . Women & aged men pleaded and begged for protection; Sherman, standing on a corner, answered all alike, 'it is your own fault & I can do nothing for you.' It was plain that the city was given up to pillage and destruction. And it *was pillaged. . . .*"

Another soldier recalled seeing Sherman and his officers working with their "own hands until long after midnight, trying to save life and property." Sergeant Theodore Upson, 100th Indiana, remembered: "We soon began to help women and children. They did not know what to do. All we could do was to hustle them out and if they had any little valuables help them get them to safety. . . . Our men, although they realized the danger and the need of haste, were kind and careful, and I don't believe there was a man among them who had any thought except to do all in their power for these helpless people. . . . We could hardly get some to leave their homes; in fact we had to carry some out."

"February 18, at 4 A. M. the Third Brigade was called out to suppress riot; did so," Gen. John M. Oliver reported, "killing 2 men, wounding 30, and arresting 370."

By the efforts of Regular units of the Union army and with a sudden shift in the wind, the fire was controlled in the early morning hours of February 18. Sherman entered in his diary: "Columbia burned from high wind, cotton in the streets, fired by the enemy, and the general animosity of our own men—great distress of people."

When the smoke lifted, officers discovered that fewer houses had been destroyed than had been at first supposed. The devastation was confined chiefly to the business district. But to Sherman, the burning of private homes, although not designed by him, was a trifling matter "when compared with the manifold results that soon followed.

"Though I never ordered it and never wished it," he added, "I have never shed many tears over the event, because I believe it hastened what we all fought for, the end of the war."

The army remained in Columbia for two more days, destroying public and railroad property. Sherman ordered his staff to provide shelter for Columbia's homeless and to see that the new capitol was saved from the torch. "I think," said a Federal officer, "the general saves this building more because it is such a beautiful work of art than for any other reason."

On February 21 the soldiers moved out of Columbia. In the ranks, one private predicted: "Columbia will have bitter cause to remember the visit of Sherman's army. Even if peace and prosperity soon return to the land, not in this generation nor the next —no, not for a century—can this city or the state recover from the deadly blow which has taken its life."

Winnsboro, Camden, and Cheraw were the next towns to suffer at the hands of the Union army. At the border of North Carolina, Sherman learned that General Johnston had assumed command of the Rebel forces in the Carolinas. He decided that his opponent was uniting the widely scattered Confederate units and would soon hit the Union columns moving northward.

While the army rested at Cheraw, Lieutenant Wise overheard a conversation between Sherman and several of his generals. He recalled Sherman saying: "When the rebels took Sumter an army ought to have been sent against Charleston and every building burned & leveled to the ground, more than this I would have killed every man, woman and child found in it."

The general also said: "This people are possessed with devils and when we fight the devil we must fight him with fire. . . . Let South Carolina take warning for if it ever becomes necessary to come here again to put down the rebellion of her people they will see war such as they never dreamed of before."

In a letter to his brother, Wise wrote: "I know, that the course of this army in South Carolina will be severely condemned by many in the North. If you hear any condemning us for what we have done, tell them for me and for Sherman's Army that *'we found here the authors of all the calamities that have befallen this nation & the men & women whose hands are red with all the innocent blood that has been shed in this war, and that their punishment is light when compared with what justice demanded.'* "

After the army entered North Carolina, Major Connolly noticed that the general conduct of the soldiers changed dramatically. The orgy of destruction had ended. "I have seen no evidence of plundering," noted an officer. "The men keep their ranks closely; and, more remarkable yet, not a single column of the fire or smoke which a few days ago marked the positions of the heads of column, can be seen upon the horizon."

The troops seemed to understand that they were marching into a state where the people had been more reluctant to leave the Union than had those of South Carolina.

On March 11 Fayetteville surrendered, and now Sherman was in communication, via the Cape Fear River, with Federal-held Wilmington and the armies of Gens. John M. Schofield and Alfred H. Terry.

News came of the fall of Charleston and its occupation by Union forces that had been on board transports in the harbor. "I took Charleston, fortified with over 400 guns, without fighting at all," Sherman told Minnie. "You may not understand how we took Charleston . . . without going near, but [the city] . . . is on the seashore, where the country is poor and all the people had to eat came from the interior by railroad. Now when my army was in the interior we broke up the railroads and ate the provisions so the rebel army have to leave [Charleston] or starve. I knew this before and had small armies on ships ready to take possession when they left."

Overjoyed with the results of the campaign, Sherman wrote a long letter to Thomas Ewing, which ended with the remark: "By this time the country will have plenty of officers who could fill my shoes, though none seem willing or anxious to play the bold strokes I have been forced to make."

The army moved out of Fayetteville toward Goldsboro, but Sherman permitted his force to become strung out. At Bentonville, a small town west of Goldsboro, General Johnston and his troops came close to overwhelming the Federal Fourteenth Corps. Although the Yankees were victorious in the battle of Bentonville, March 19–21, they failed to pursue the enemy and instead advanced into Goldsboro. Here Sherman was joined by the forces of Generals Schofield and Terry, that had marched from New Bern and Wilmington.

The drive through the Carolinas was an imaginative stroke masterfully executed. Yet the destructiveness of that march was to have little bearing on General Lee's eventual decision to surrender. Although Sherman's columns had destroyed railroad communications in South and North Carolina and razed quantities of supplies, Lee's forces were not short of rations by reason of these actions. Their plight was primarily due to the breakdown of the Virginia transportation system. However, Lee's army was thinned by deserters hurrying south to protect their home states from the invader. In this respect the march through North and South Carolina had indirectly affected the campaign in Virginia.

Lee was pinned down at Petersburg by Grant. Union cavalry raids to Lee's rear had smashed railroad installations. If most of the railroads had been operating during the last months of the war, the Confederate army in Virginia, now reduced to 25,000 men, might have had adequate provisions.

As a military strategist, Sherman was ahead of his time. He had thrown away the orthodox methods and traditions, which called for the defeat of the enemy's main army before invading enemy territory. His grasp of this principle places Sherman among the top-ranking generals in the annals of military history.

The Civil War was the first conflict fought between modern democracies. One noted present-day military historian, Basil H. Liddell Hart, stresses that Sherman clearly saw that the resisting power of a democracy depends even more on the strength of the people's will than on the strength of its armies. Liddell Hart discerns similarities between Sherman's operations and the paralyzing and demoralizing shock effect upon the opposing armies and peoples by the German blitzkriegs of 1939–41, which combined deep-thrusting armored penetration with air attack.

Sherman's concept of collective responsibility, his belief in the use of armed might against the enemy's civilian population, violated the accepted rules of mid-nineteenth century civilized warfare, rules in which there was a certain regard for human dignity. His thrusts into Mississippi, Georgia, and the Carolinas hastened the downfall of the Confederacy. By destroying the enemy's ability to supply its armies and by terrorizing civilians, Sherman sapped Confederate morale.

The actions of Sherman's troops on their expeditions deep into enemy country were at variance with the official pronouncements of the War Department, especially General Order No. 11, issued in April, 1863, which contained provisions concerning the treatment of civilians in the war zones. Article 44 read: "All wanton violence committed against persons in the invaded country, all destruction of property not commanded by the authorized officer, all robbery, all pillage or sacking, even after the taking of a place by main force ... are prohibited ... under penalty of ... severe punishment."

Sherman at times was disturbed over the violation of these rules, especially those regarding private property rights, and once said he hoped that "a common sense of decency may be inspired into the minds of the soldiery in respect to life and property." Officially, Halleck approved of Sherman's methods. Lincoln congratulated him after the capture of Savannah, and Secretary of the Navy Gideon Welles noted in his diary: "General Sherman is proving himself a great general, and his movements from Chatanooga to the present [February 1865] demonstrate his ability as an officer. He has undoubtedly greater resourses, a more prolific mind, than Grant, and perhaps as much tenacity if less cunning and selfishness."

Much later, after the war, Sherman said in a speech at West Point that he had often been asked which books had taught him the secret of leading vast armies. "They seemed surprised when I answered that I was not aware that I had been influenced by any of them," he declared. "I told them ... that, when I was a young lieutenant of artillery, I had often hunted deer in the swamps of the Edisto, the Cooper, and the Santee [in South Carolina], and had seen with my own eyes that they could be passed with wagons. ... I had ridden on horseback from Marietta, Georgia, to the valley of the Tennessee and back to Augusta, passing in my course over the very fields of Altoona, Kenesaw and Atlanta, when afterwards it fell to my share to command armies and to utilize the knowledge thus gained."

Sherman continued: "Again ... I was in California, and saw arrive across that wild belt of two thousand miles of uninhabitable country the caravans of emigrants, composed of men, women and children, who reached their destination in health and strength; and when we used to start on a journey of a thousand miles, with a single blanket as a covering, and a coil of dried meat and a sack of parched corn as food—with this knowledge fairly acquired in actual experience, was there any need for me to look back to Alexander the Great [and other strategists] ... for examples?"

At Goldsboro Sherman had a chance to go to Washington, but he preferred to stay with his troops. There was a mutual respect between him and his men. On the march they enjoyed seeing Sherman pacing before his campfire, haphazardly dressed, more concerned for their welfare than his own. Somehow they felt he "had his eye" on each of them. He slept among them, and unlike many generals, he seemed to experience the hardships of war as they did.

"Many had seen him in a slouch hat and ulster by a river at an early morning crossing; some had seen him prowling about a campfire in red flannel drawers and a worn dressing gown. . . . [They] had seen him naked, swimming in the river like any of his soldiers. That was Uncle Billy—a great man, a brilliant general, but still one of them."

Sherman's men showed their admiration and affection: " 'Don't ride too fast, General,' they would cry out, seeing his horse plunging along in the mire at the roadside, as he tried to pass some division. 'Pretty slippery going, Uncle Billy; pretty slippery going.' Or 'Say, General kin you tell us is this the road to Richmond?' "

Some of their songs expressed their confidence in their general.

> Sherman, hurrah, we'll go with him
> Wherever it may be
> Through Carolina's cotton fields
> Or Georgia to the Sea.

"Soldiers have a wonderful idea of my knowledge and attach much of continued success to it," Cump told Ellen. "And I really do think they would miss me, if I were to go away even for a week."

He was forced, however, to leave Goldsboro and his men when he received orders to proceed to City Point, Va., to consult with President Lincoln, General Grant, and Admiral Porter about the course of the war. On board the *River Queen*, the four held two conferences, on March 27 and 28. They discussed in detail past operations and the approaching end of the war. Sherman hoped to join his forces with Grant's around Richmond and to share in the glory of capturing the Confederate capital, but Grant was not disposed to delay his own offensive against Lee until Sherman arrived.

The talks turned to the eventual peace terms. The president was not looking for a vindictive peace but hoped to reunite the nation with as little bitterness and as rapidly as possible. Sherman was to get General Johnston to surrender on whatever terms possible. He was also to tell Gov. Zebulon B. Vance of North Carolina that as soon as the Confederate armies ceased fighting, Southerners would be protected in their civil pursuits. State governments were to stay in existence and be recognized as de facto governments until Congress acted.

After the conferences ended, a colonel watched as Sherman prepared to return to Goldsboro. "He was," he said, "a very remarkable looking man, such as could not be grown out of America—the concentrated quintessance of Yankeedom. He is tall, spar, and sinewy. . . . He is a very homely man, with a regular nest of wrinkles but his expression is pleasant and kindly.

"He believes in hard war. I heard him say, 'Columbia!—pretty much all burned; and burned *good!*' "

On April 2 Richmond and Petersburg fell to Union arms, and Lee and his army fled westward. Eight days later Sherman's columns broke camp near Goldsboro and moved toward Raleigh, sure that Johnston's army was somewhere between those two points. During the night of April 11 Sherman learned of Lee's surrender to Grant at Appomattox Court House. In his makeshift headquarters he reread dispatches from Virginia, then issued a jubilant field order: "Glory to God and our country, and all honor to our comrades in arms, toward whom we are marching. A little more labor, a little more toil on our part, the great race is won, and our government stands regenerated after four long years."

Peace commissioners from Raleigh arrived that night, but after listening to their petitions, Sherman refused to suspend hostilities. He did, however, assure them that the lives and property of the citizens would be protected. Meanwhile, Rebel forces evacuated Raleigh.

On the morning of April 13 the first units of Sherman's army marched into the state capital. A young Texan from Gen. Wade Hampton's rear guard, the only Rebel soldier remaining, emptied his pistols at an approaching Federal patrol. He was caught and hanged. Aside from this action, there was little violence in Raleigh.

Federal soldiers razed the newspaper offices of the *Confederate* and sacked a few buildings but did not destroy them.

Sherman received a communication from General Johnston asking for a suspension of hostilities. A meeting was set up at Bennett's farmhouse a few miles from Durhams Station to work out details. Just as he was about to depart for the conference, news came of President Lincoln's assassination. Sherman had received no specific instructions on peace terms from Lincoln. He was neither lawyer nor statesman and was unaware that the concessions he was about to make to Johnston carried with them vast legal and political implications. Once, when Sherman was in Savannah, he had an opportunity to voice his opinions on Reconstruction. A number of Georgians had asked how their state could once again become a member of the Union. Sherman had replied by sending a letter to a prominent Georgian. "Georgia is not out of the Union, and therefore the talk of 'reconstruction' appears to me inappropriate." Sherman felt that when the last of the Rebels had returned to their homes, they would "be dealt with by the civil courts. My opinion is that no negotiations are necessary, nor Commissioners, nor Conventions, nor anything of the kind. Whenever the people of Georgia quit rebelling against their Government, and elect members of Congress and Senators, and these go and take their seats, then the State of Georgia will have resumed her functions in the Union."

For several hours on April 17 Sherman and Johnston discussed the peace. Both respected each other as soldiers, although they had never met before. Johnston reported that his military situation was hopeless, and he startled Sherman by offering to surrender not only his own command, but all the Confederate armies everywhere. Sherman replied that Johnston had no authority over any armed forces other than his own, but the Southerner said that could be arranged. Not far away from the farmhouse was the new Confederate secretary of war, Gen. John C. Breckinridge, who had the power over all Southern armies.

The conversation turned to what form of government the South was to have. Johnston asked many questions. Were the states to be severed from the Union? Were the people to be denied representation in Congress? Were Southerners to be "the slaves of the people of the North?"

"No," Sherman replied, "we desire that you shall regain your position as citizens of the United States, free and equal to us in all respects, and with representation, upon the condition of submission to the lawful authority of the United States as defined by the Constitution, the United States courts, and the authorities of the United States supported by the courts."

Detailing his peace terms, Sherman leaned strongly toward Southern interests and went far beyond anything Lincoln had ever been prepared to offer, even when the bargaining position of the South had been stronger. Unlike Lincoln's terms, Sherman's contained no mention of the Negro or slavery.

Both generals realized that slavery was dead as a result of the war, but Sherman believed that if there were to be new relationships between the races in the South, it was the responsibility of the Southern whites, not the Union military commanders or Northern statesmen.

On Tuesday, April 18, Sherman and Johnston met again. This time Breckinridge was present. Sherman offered terms that restored to the South a large measure of the status quo of the prewar days. This clearly demonstrated that his total-war concept was purely strategic, not vindictive. In effect Sherman's terms recognized insurgent state governments, once their officials had sworn allegiance to the United States; guaranteed peaceful Southerners "their political rights and franchises, as well as their rights of person and property, as defined by the Constitution of the United States and of the states respectively"; provided for an amnesty for everyone; and reestablished the Federal courts.

Johnston and Breckinridge agreed that all Confederate armies would return to their state capitals, disband, turn in their arms to state arsenals, consent to cease all acts of war, and submit to Union authority. Until the United States Congress acted, the deposited weapons could be used to maintain the peace and quash guerrilla uprisings within the states' borders.

As Sherman left the conference that day, he was confident that his peace proposals would be acceptable to President Andrew Johnson and his administration. "I believed [the terms] contained what would ultimately result if the people of the South accepted and acted in prompt and willing acquiescence," Sherman wrote later, "and that it would produce instantaneously a condition of reason and lawful fidelity consistent with the Constitution . . . and the laws then in existence. . . . The only thing in April, 1865, left for us to combat was prejudice and habits of thought. This can never be controlled by force of arms, but must be left to time's influence."

General Sherman had tried to arrange a settlement so that North and South could live side by side in peace. The mass of Southerners had suffered terribly during the war, and he felt disposed to befriend the men in the ranks, who had fought valiantly for a lost cause. Although well intentioned, Sherman had blundered as a statesman. He had agreed to a policy that virtually recognized the Confederacy; he had left the South armed; he had taken Reconstruction out of the hands of the president and the Congress. Sherman, in fact, had attempted to deny any meaning, except the preservation of the Union, to the war. Throughout the entire North, men were now demanding that the South be punished for its sins, while a vast segment of the population wanted safeguards for the newly won rights of the Negroes.

Sherman justified his stand in a letter to a friend. "We cannot," he said, "combat existing ideas with force." He was positive that if the government tried to put both races on an equal footing in the South, it would produce a new war, "more bloody and destructive than the last.

"Our own armed soldiers have prejudices that, right or wrong, should be consulted. . . . I say that to give *all* negroes the same political status as white 'voters' will revive the war and spread its field of operations. Why not therefore trust to the slower and not less sure means of statesmanship? Why not initiate the example of England in allowing causes to work out their gradual solution instead of imitating the French whose Political Revolutions have been bloody and have actually retarded the development of political freedom.

"I think the changes necessary in the Future can be made faster and more certain by means of our Constitution, than by any plan outside it. If now we go outside the Constitution, for a means of change, we rather justify the Rebels in their late attempt whereas now . . . the people of the South are ready and willing to make the necessary changes without shock or violence.

"I, who have felt the past war as bitterly and keenly as any man could," he continued, "confess myself, 'afraid,' of a New War, and a new war is bound to result from the action . . . of giving to the enfranchised negroes so large a share in the delicate task of 'putting the Southern States in practical working relations with the General Government.' "

"Our favored country is so grand, so expansive...."

ON APRIL 21 dispatches concerning Sherman's peace terms reached Washington. Far from being a mere promise to terminate hostilities, the Sherman-Johnston pact was a virtual treaty of peace. Officialdom erupted in anger. Immediately and unanimously President Andrew Johnson and his cabinet rejected Sherman's peace proposals that same day, because, as Stanton declared, "we gave up all for which we had been fighting, and threw away all the advantages we had gained from the war." No general on any battlefield had the authority to settle legal and political questions. "Grant, I was pleased to see," Gideon Welles wrote in his diary, "while disapproving of what Sherman had done, and decidedly opposed to it, was tender to the sensitiveness of his brother officer and abstained from censure."

Sherman was wildly denounced in the North for negotiating such a mild peace; his good faith, his loyalty, his sanity were questioned by an angry radical press. He had practically recognized the Rebel government; he had made it possible to reestablish Negro slavery; he had permitted the Rebels to keep their weapons "which might be used as soon as possible as the armies of the United States are disbanded . . . to conquer and subdue the loyal States." The *New York Herald* declared: "Sherman's splendid military career is ended, he will retire under a cloud. . . . Was he caught napping or was he too eager for laurels of the peacemaker? . . . Sherman has fatally blundered, for, with a few unlucky strokes of his pen, he has blurred all the triumphs of his sword."

Largely responsible for this outcry against Sherman were the press releases of Secretary Stanton, which were carefully worded to put Sherman in the worst possible light. "Stanton," recalled

John Sherman, "issued a bulletin in which he intimated that [Jefferson] Davis and his partisans were on their way to escape to Mexico or Europe with a large amount of gold plundered from the Richmond banks and from other sources, and that they hoped to make terms with General Sherman by which they would be permitted with their effects, including their gold plunder, to go to Mexico or Europe.

"The most violent and insulting paragraphs were published in the newspapers, substantially arraigning General Sherman as a traitor and imputing to him corrupt motives.... I believed then and still believe that he [Stanton] was under the influence of perhaps a well-grounded fear that his life was in danger. The atmosphere of Washington seemed to be charged with terror, caused by the assassination of Lincoln . . . and threats against all who were conspicuous in political or military life in the Union cause."

To Secretary Welles, Stanton's actions against Sherman were "not particularly commendable, judicious, or correct.... Stanton . . . seems to have a mortal fear of generals and armies."

Although Sherman had frequently denounced politicians and had denied any interest in politics, next to Grant he was the most popular commander in the eyes of the general public. Stanton was sure that the Democratic party wanted the general to run for high political office. If he had delayed censuring Sherman in the press, Stanton was afraid there would have been a popular movement to support the peace terms with General Johnston.

President Johnson told Stanton to inform Sherman that his course was repudiated and that hostilities against Johnston should be resumed immediately. Grant carried Stanton's order to Raleigh, where on April 24, he told Sherman of the administration's disapproval of the peace terms and instructed him to resume the war against Johnston. He said nothing about the wild charges Stanton had issued to the press.

Sherman received the news with a calmness that was surprising, undoubtedly a result of Grant's steadying influence. He obeyed orders, but he staunchly maintained that his original plan had been right, honest, and good, and later said: "I want no apology for those terms." As soon as Sherman and Johnston met on April 26 and signed a new set of terms—as simple and brief as those which Lee accepted at Appomattox—Grant returned to Washington.

On April 28 Sherman picked up some five-day-old newspapers and read Stanton's merciless attack. One officer recalled Sherman pacing the floor "like a caged lion, talking to the whole room with a furious invective which made us all stare. He lashed Stanton as a mean, scheming, vindictive politician who made it his business to rob military men of their credit earned by exposing their lives. . . . He berated the people, who blamed him for what he had done, as a mass of fools, not worth fighting for. . . . He railed at the press which had become the engine of vilification."

Sherman was infuriated at the charge of insubordination made against him by the *New York Times*. To Grant, he wrote: "I have never in my life questioned or disobeyed an order though many and many a time I have risked my life, health and reputation in obeying orders or even hints to execute plans and purposes not to my liking. . . .

"It is true that non-combatants, men who sleep in comfort and security while we watch on the distant lines, are better able to judge than we poor soldiers, who rarely see a newspaper, hardly can hear from our families, or stop long enough to draw our pay. I envy not the task of reconstruction, and am delighted that the Secretary of War has relieved me of it."

Sherman's friendship with General Halleck was fast deteriorating. During the chaos immediately following Lincoln's assassination, Stanton had virtually taken control of the government. He had ordered Halleck to go to war-torn Richmond and restore order there. Halleck's directives from Virginia seemed to have been prompted largely by his desire to gain favor with Stanton. He had directed Gens. George H. Thomas and James Harrison Wilson to disregard the Sherman-Johnston truce while negotiations were under way; he had dispatched units of the Army of the Potomac into parts of North Carolina, occupied by Sherman's troops, to cut off Johnston's retreat; he had sent a telegram to Sherman's subordinates "to obey no orders of General Sherman. . . ."

Sherman considered these actions direct insults. It was obvious that the man who had rescued him from obscurity in 1862 had joined forces with Secretary Stanton. "How terribly energetic all at once Halleck became, to break my truce, cut off 'Johnston's Retreat' when he knew Johnston was halted anxious to surrender," Cump wrote Ellen, "but worst of all, [was] his advice that my sub-ordinates . . . should not obey my orders. Under my orders, those Generals have done all they ever did in their lives, and it sounds funny to us to have Halleck *better* my plans and orders."

When the men in the ranks learned that Sherman was being labeled a dangerous man and a traitor, they flared in anger. Sergeant Theodore Upson of the 100th Indiana exclaimed: "They had better look a little out or they will have General Sherman's Army to reckon with the first thing they know. We don't propose to have our General called such names, 'Sherman a Traitor!' The idea!"

Sherman's own family had varying opinions. John Sherman wrote his brother to accept the administration's rebuke as penalty for overstepping the limits of military duties. Ellen had been upset by the generosity of the original peace terms with "those traitors," but she earnestly believed that President Johnson and Secretary Stanton, aided by Halleck, were seeking to crush her husband. Charles Sherman advised his brother that a strong feeling of condemnation against Stanton was fast developing and counseled him to remain quiet, bide his time, and "act prudently." Such a course would lead Sherman to an even higher standing with the American people.

Sherman's columns began to move out of North Carolina toward Washington. When they neared Richmond in early May, General Halleck invited Sherman to stay at his headquarters, but Sherman flatly refused. Later, when Halleck realized that his friendship with Sherman meant more to him than Stanton's approval, he wanted to apologize and wrote: "You have not had during this war nor have you now a warmer . . . admirer than myself. If in carrying out what I knew to be the wishes of the War Department in regard to your armistice I used language which has given you offense it was unintentional, and I deeply regret it. . . . It is my wish to continue to regard and receive you as a personal friend." Sherman was too angry to forgive him, and Halleck and Sherman never again wrote to each other.

Informing Grant of his rejection of Halleck's note, Sherman advised: "I will treat Mr. Stanton with like scorn & contempt. . . . No amount of retraction or pusillanimous excusing will do. Mr.

Stanton must publically confess himself a common libeller or—but I won't threaten. . . . He wants . . . the votes of [the] negroes . . . for political capital, and whoever stands in his way must die.

"Keep above such influences, or you will also be a victim. See it in my case how soon all past services are ignored or forgotten."

By May 20 Sherman's forces were camped at Alexandria, Va. Still smarting under what he called the disgrace put upon him by Secretary Stanton, Sherman went on to Washington. He refused to visit the War Department and denounced Stanton to fellow officers. One night was spent at the house of his friend on Capitol Hill, Orville Browning, the moderate Republican senator from Illinois. Although a friend of the late President Lincoln's who had helped write his first inaugural address, Browning had vigorously disapproved of the Emancipation Proclamation and doubted its constitutionality.

To Browning, Sherman confided that he was worried about reconstructing the war-torn South. A general amnesty and restoration of citizenship, he predicted, would make Southerners quiet and law-abiding, but harsh measures would only continue them in rebellion and compel the North to maintain a vast army to hold them in subjection. The Rebels had been fine soldiers and had fought gallantly. Those who had borne arms were the best and most earnest men in the South. Generally, those who professed loyalty to the Union cause were of no account, and the states could not be reconstructed by them and the Negro.

Sherman confessed that he had waged war ruthlessly, but now that the Confederate armies were crushed and resistance to authority had ceased, he wanted to see everyone reinstated who was willing to obey the law.

The glory of war, he said, "is all moonshine." Success, the most brilliant victory, had been bought by dead and mutilated bodies and the anguish of families, "appealing to me for missing sons, husbands and fathers." All he wanted now was peace, glorious peace. It was only those who had not heard the cannon roar or heard the shrieks and groans of the wounded who now cried for more blood and vengeance, more desolation, and "so help me God as man and soldier I will not strike a foe who stands unarmed and submissive before me but will say 'Go sin no more.' "

The Congressional Committee on the Conduct of the War, an

extremely powerful agency established to secure for Congress a voice in formulating war policies, ordered General Sherman to appear before it along with General Grant. The Radical Republican senator from Ohio, Benjamin Wade, wanted to learn whether Sherman had offered his mild terms under some previous orders from President Lincoln. Curtly and defiantly, Sherman answered the questions. The terms, he retorted, complied with Lincoln's well-known wishes for a speedy and lenient peace, and though not specifically sanctioned by Lincoln, would, in the general's opinion, have been sustained by him had he lived.

When questioned on why nothing about slavery was mentioned in his peace terms, Sherman declared: "There was nothing said about slavery, because it did not fall within the category of military questions, and we could not make it so. It was a legal question which the President had disposed of, overriding all our action. We had to treat the slave as *free*, because the President, our commander-in-chief, said he was free. For me to have renewed the question when that decision was made would have involved the absurdity of an inferior undertaking to qualify the work of his superior."

The rains of the previous days had settled the dust in the streets of Washington, when, on May 23, Gen. George Gordon Meade and his Army of the Potomac paraded down Pennsylvania Avenue. Sherman, along with Ellen, Mr. Ewing, Tommy, and John Sherman, sat in a wooden stand before the White House receiving the congratulations of hundreds of well-wishers. Close by sat President Johnson, his cabinet, governors, senators, other notables, and their ladies. Crowds jammed the avenue to see the troops pass in review. As the march progressed past the stand, Cump pointed out the differences between the eastern and western armies. Tomorrow would be the west's day, Sherman's day.

On the next morning, at 9:00 A.M. his proud army swung into the line of parade. Ahead rode General Sherman on his shining bay, his beard grizzled, his hair shorter than usual. When they started down Pennsylvania Avenue, the rank and file fell into a long swinging step, every man in perfect time, their guns at a right shoulder shift. From every window and housetop along the route, flags and banners waved in the breeze.

No one appreciated the significance of this review more than Sherman. When he reached the Treasury Building and looked behind him at the columns and columns of men marching, he was struck by the magnificence of that sight—the compactness of the lines, the array of glittering muskets, which looked like a mass of steel "moving with the regularity of a pendulum." Sergeant Theodore Upson remembered glancing down the line of his platoon and noting that every man had his eyes front, every step was perfect and "on the faces of the men was what one might call a *glory look*.

"The sidewalks were packed with people, and my! how they cheered!" Upson said. "It was one constant roar, our tattered flags bearing the names of the Regiments and of the principal battles in which they had fought were proudly carried by the Color Bearers. . . .

"When we passed the Reviewing Stand in which were President Johnson, General Grant, foriegn officers, and nearly all the great men of the nation and many from other nations, they all rose to thier [*sic*] feet and with bared heads cheered and cheered. . . . My, but I was proud of our boys."

Just past the reviewing stand, Sherman moved out of the line of march, slid from his saddle, and walked up the steps. He saluted and then shook hands with the president. Next in line was Stanton who started to extend his hand to the general, but realizing that Sherman intended to ignore it, allowed his hand to fall. Flushing deeply, Sherman deliberately snubbed Stanton, turned, and shook hands with Grant.

For five hours the Army of the West marched through the city of Washington, finally disbanding and encamping at Crystal Springs, some two miles beyond the city limits.

As the politicians and generals left the reviewing stand, Sherman nudged his way toward Johnson. He told the president that he had done all he intended to do in the Stanton affair, and he wished to avoid any further controversy that might embarrass the president.

That night there was a reunion of the Sherman-Ewing clan at John Sherman's house. The tall, spare, impressive-looking senator had risen rapidly in politics during the past four years. His industry and perseverance had gained him a reputation as one of the

Senate's authorities on finance. Devoted to capitalism and to industrial prosperity, he was linked to financial legislation and to the policies of the Republican party. As a member of the Senate's finance committee, he had planned the national banking system with Secretary of the Treasury Chase; urged government economies; and sought a plan of taxation to aid in financing the war.

An examination of Senate debates clearly indicates that John Sherman yielded to the Lincoln Administration, often abandoning his own judgment on executive recommendations, because of his reluctance to embarrass those prosecuting the war. Once he had written Cump: "I cannot respect some of the constituted authorities, yet I will cordially support and aid them while they are authorized to administer the government."

John Sherman's feelings on questions of Reconstruction were, like his brother's, those of moderation, favoring conciliation and restoration; and they were sufficiently well known that many Southerners were already writing him concerning tolerance. In Congress, as a warm defender of President Johnson, he spoke out against the Radical program. Yet John Sherman was also a party man, and he failed to push his efforts so far from the Radical path as to stray outside the confines of Republicanism. Although he was not by nature a Radical, his votes and his actions supported measures of the Radical senators.

While his steady party regularity would eventually make him a possibility for the presidency, John Sherman was never to arouse any great popular enthusiasm or to enjoy a large personal following. His sober, colorless personality and the presence of strong rivals in his home state of Ohio were serious obstacles in his path.

John and Cump were as affectionate toward one another now in 1865 as they had been in their younger days. In fact, said a close friend, "there seemed to exist between [them] . . . a stronger love than between the other brothers." When Cump was away, his correspondence with John was voluminous, and there was often a good-natured argument between members of the family as to whether Cump wrote more to his brother than he did to his wife. To John Sherman, his brother "was the most unselfish man I ever knew. He did not seek high rank, and often expressed doubts of his fitness for high command. . . . He never asked for promotion, but accepted it when given. His letters to me are full of urgent requests for promotion of officers who rendered distinguished service, but never his own."

Tom Ewing, who had resigned his army commission earlier in the year, was also in Washington. His reputation among the Radicals was, at the moment, worse than his brother-in-law's. Since early May he had been defending in a military court Dr. Samuel A. Mudd, Samuel Arnold, and Edward Spangler—three of the eight persons accused of complicity in the Lincoln assassination. He was bitterly castigated by the Radicals, who had planned a quick verdict of guilty against all the prisoners. It was through Tom Ewing's efforts that these three escaped the scaffold that claimed four of the remaining five.

The morning after the Sherman-Ewing reunion, Ellen Sherman sent flowers to Mrs. Stanton as a "mute appeal for forgiveness" for her husband's discourtesy. Ellen told Orville Browning that she wished to call on the Stantons but was concerned about the propriety of such an action. Browning suggested that he serve as mediator, and later that day, at the Stanton's, he told the secretary that he regretted the situation which had arisen. When Stanton replied that there was no bitterness toward the general as far as he was concerned, Browning asked if Mrs. Sherman could pay her respects. Stanton agreed wholeheartedly. A few evenings later, Ellen and Browning arrived at the Stanton home and visited with Secretary and Mrs. Stanton for a half hour.

On May 30 Sherman wrote his farewell to his men. "Our work is done," he said. His words recounted the army's triumphs and emphasized that victory in the past had been due to hard work and discipline and that hard work and discipline were equally important in the future.

"Our favored country is so grand, so expansive, so diversified in climate and productions," he said, "that every man may find a home and occupation suited to his taste ... none should yield to the natural impatience sure to result from our past life of excitement and adventure. You will be invited to seek new adventures abroad; do not yield to the temptation, for it will lead only to death and disappointment .... farewell ... you have been good soldiers ... you will make good citizens."

On May 31 Cump, Ellen, Tommy, and Mr. Ewing boarded the train for New York. Cump was only 45, but he had reached the height of military fame. He had achieved glory at the exact age that Napoleon Bonaparte had prophetically fixed as the zenith from which the power of generalship declined.

The immediate aftermath of the Civil War held out the deceptive promise of tranquility. Released from the rigors of war, Cump enjoyed his prestige as a national figure. He desperately wanted to establish a close relationship with his family after four years of separation, yet his restless spirit was to allow him little time for that.

The old home in Lancaster seemed to fit the Sherman family perfectly, but Cump had no time to linger there. He went almost immediately to Chicago to meet General Grant and to learn his new assignment. The nation was to be divided into military divisions, departments, and districts commanded by lieutenant, major, and brigadier generals. Sherman was to command the military division of the Missouri, which encompassed the whole of the Great Plains, with headquarters in Saint Louis.

Cump was elated at the prospect of returning to old friends and familiar surroundings in Missouri. Journeying through Toledo, Mansfield, and Newark on his way back to Lancaster, he was overwhelmed by crowds, who surged around him "as a natural curiosity." A quiet week with the family was followed by a trip to Louisville to attend a Fourth of July barbecue. On this swing he developed an extreme dislike for the war song "Marching Through Georgia," which greeted his appearance in every town.

Later that summer, he went alone to Saint Louis to set up headquarters and to find suitable housing. Ellen wanted a double house so that Mr. Ewing could have a room on the first floor when he visited, because she swore she would not go back to Lancaster as often as she had done before. In fact Ellen said: "I want rest & comfort and feel that we ought to look to our individual & present wants rather than . . . to the prospective interests of the children . . . what we want is to be properly settled & now."

By the time Ellen and the children arrived in Saint Louis, Cump had taken the new Nicholson house, a pretentious red-brick dwelling on Garrison Avenue. Here the Shermans settled down with bright hopes of happiness.

Letters, invitations, and notes of thanks from all parts of the country poured into Sherman's office. He was beset by people. They swarmed about him, wanting his advice, money, and support.

Among those who wrote was David French Boyd, Cump's old friend from seminary days in Louisiana, who was now superintendent of the academy. "For you, the great Federal Commander," Boyd declared, "I feel as do all good Southerners, not *amiably*, nor yet unkindly; for the noble and brillant manner in which you did your duty commands our admiration. . . .

"I have not a particle of ill feeling towards any man in the Federal Army. On the contrary, I have few friends whom I value none the less for whipping men.

"Understand me rightly. I speak with no cringing spirit. Though beaten and so poor that none do me reverence, I am *patient* and *proud*. The end of matters has decided that the rights I battled for were in vain."

The academy, Boyd said, was in desperate need of a library, and he pressed Sherman to send him patent office reports, military books, maps—materials which had been showered on the general and which he no longer wanted. "I would also like," he continued, "to have a large picture of you in *citizen's* dress (unless you prefer your uniform) to be part of our library as our first superintendant." Immediately after reading the letter, Sherman made arrangements to send the books and portrait.

Requests that the general use his influence were received; even Tom Ewing urged him to secure for a friend a high position in Washington. Cump refused. "I will not be recommending persons for high office by reason of personal acquaintance," he wrote. "I may be wrong not to assist my friends all I can, but this habit of asking for several letters is so common . . . that for one I want to stop. I will not bore the President and Cabinet with such letters."

To a mother, who had also written the secretaries of state and war to use their influence with the academic board at West Point in behalf of her son, Sherman explained: "The Cabinet Ministers have as little influence with the Academic Board . . . as the Emperor of China. West Point is governed by *Law*, above secretaries and Presidents, and the branch of service to which . . . your son may fall on graduation depends on the Academic Board and himself. . . . If your son wants to go into artillery he must graduate above the number determined by the Academic Board. The President and Cabinet cannot change this Rule if they wanted to, and they have never wanted to. Every mother thinks her boy a paragon, but Uncle Sam don't allow even a mother to reverse the Laws of Congress."

In the immediate postwar period, the South lay stunned and prostrate. The Southern armies had disbanded; the Southern leaders sat back in exhaustion. The men who had engineered the war, and lost it, had seen great empires of cotton, rice, sugar, and tobacco collapse. Millions of slaves were emancipated, and millions and millions in capital had vanished into thin air.

A whole class of people, a ruling class, had been stunningly and quickly deprived of its property. The first reaction of the planters was silence, a sick and bewildered silence, during which they contemplated the ruin that had been accomplished. Great plantations stood empty and abandoned or were worked in a desultory way; other plantations were put up to auction, sold for debts and taxes. Fields lay fallow; cotton planting dwindled, and in many sections it was discontinued completely.

When the first paralyzing shock passed, Southerners realized that the farce of Emancipation would not be played through to its conclusion. They intended to inaugurate laws that would legally return the Negro to precisely the same position he had filled before the war.

In Washington a bitter and wrathful Congress that had just fought and won a most terrible war decided that the blood spilt should not be in vain. Radical congressmen were intent upon creating a new democracy in the South, one in which the black man and white man would stand side by side, equal, building together. Most Northerners, although not vindictive, were suspicious of the South and desirous of moving slowly toward granting full political rights to the ex-Confederates.

For these and other reasons the Republicans in Congress strenuously opposed the mild Reconstruction policies of President Johnson, which left political control in the hands of the Southern whites. Former Rebels were pardoned when they took the loyalty oath and were permitted to reestablish civil government. Johnson's program was so mild that it encouraged Southerners to return to views hardly changed from those that led to war. There was a burgeoning of Southern arrogance not only toward the freed Negro but toward Union troops as well. The Black Codes of the restored state legislatures expressed a determination to place the ex-slave in a thoroughly subservient status.

Sherman endorsed the President's Reconstruction policies and was an open and relentless foe of the Radicals in Congress. To Mr. Ewing, Sherman wrote: "Civil Government must resume its course somehow, and I think the less changes in the fundamental system which has stood such a test the better. The peculiar faction of the South that made the war, is so far crushed, and each year will be more & more so, that to manifest a fear of them is irrational, and cowardly. The Republican party was drifting so headlong to the opposite extreme that Mr. Johnson had no alternative but to assent to a new Revolution, or to separate himself from them."

"There is not a particle of national hostility left in the South," he wrote Thomas Ewing again. "The mind of the people are absorbed in preparation for next years crop, while the busy politicians are watching their chances to recover their lost power and offices." Then he added: "I saw and mingled freely with the worst Rebels, and they seem to regard Grant and myself as their best friends."

"We cannot," he explained to John, "keep the South out [of the Union] for long, and it is a physical impossibility for us to guard the entire South by armies; nor can we change opinions by force. . . . The poor whites and negroes of the South have not the intelligence to fill the offices of governors, clerks, judges, etc. etc., and for some time the making of state governments must be controlled by the same class of whites as went into the Rebellion against us."

Never would Sherman accept the Negro as an equal, politically or socially, and throughout the postwar years he clung to many of the same notions which he had expressed as a young lieutenant. Giving the Negro the right to vote was pushing beyond the "Role of Right." Everyone was entitled to the protection of the law, even infants not born, but such a natural right did not mean the right to vote.

The major problem facing Sherman at his Saint Louis headquarters was protecting the frontiersmen from the hostile Indians.

To aid the settlers' advance westward, Sherman decided to build a line of defense for 600 miles along the entire length of the southern plains, beginning with Fort Duncan on the Rio Grande, and running across Texas via Forts Clark, McKavett, Concho, and Griffin to Fort Richardson in Jack County. Forts Arbuckle and Cobb in Indian Territory connected the posts in Kansas with Fort Richardson. Other forts along the line of the Arkansas River guarded the Santa Fe Trail, while those to the north protected the Smoky Hill route to Denver. Such a defense meant the maintenance of garrisons in the old forts and the construction of new posts. Sherman had no illusions about the effectiveness of this slender barricade against the red man. To satisfy the demands of all the frontiersmen, he calculated he needed over 100,000 men, mostly cavalry.

Sherman watched with mounting interest the construction of the Union Pacific Railroad. From the start, he fully recognized the importance of rail transportation in the vast section of the country which embraced the military division of the Missouri. He estimated how many miles of marching and supply hauling would be erased when the railroad was finally completed. At every opportunity, he went west to survey the construction. Each month Gen. Grenville M. Dodge, in charge of building the line, reported to Sherman in detail concerning the road's progress. Guarding the Union Pacific was "a Herculean task." It was impossible for Sherman's command to hunt down every robber or drive off every Indian attacking a way station. "To expect infantry to chase Indians is an absurdity," said Sherman, "and to scatter our cavalry, as of now, in single companies, simply tires them down." But now, at least, the railroad would give the army in the west rapid communication, and it could "not be stolen like cavalry horses and mule trains of old."

When Congress in 1866 revived the rank of "General of the Army" for Grant, Sherman was elevated to lieutenant general, but fortunately, the promotion changed neither his headquarters nor his duties. His pay was nearly doubled, which, he confided to Tom, "would be a God send to Ellen and the children. My wants are so simple, that I will not alter my style of living."

The Shermans were happy in Saint Louis that winter and spring, living as a family for the first time in years. Minnie was now 15, much taller and fairer than her mother, while Lizzie, 13, was like Cump in appearance and disposition. Tommy was 9, and the two younger girls, Ellie, 7, and Rachel, 5, were the life of the house.

"The remembrance of the chats I had with you in St. Louis," Tommy Sherman wrote to his father later, "will be one of my most cherished recollections through life, though I suppose all of your children will be inclined to dwell on the thought of their father as he came back to the fireside in 1865 with a nation's blessing and unsullied hours thick upon him, when he read to them from Dickens, Scott and Irving with simplicity and tenderness of one of those old Roman heroes—a Fabius, a Cincinnatus, or Scipio.

"But the years that bring tenderness are more precious to both generations I take it than those that win glory. On the field you are the world's, at the fireside you are ours and will have our deepest love and most sincere devotion always."

In the summer Ellen and the children went back to Lancaster for a long visit with the aging Thomas Ewing. Sherman celebrated the Fourth of July at Salem, Ill., with many of his former comrades-in-arms, and then took off on an inspection tour of western military installations.

Many of the Indian tribes—the Wyandot, Shawnee, Potawatomi, Pawnee, Cherokee, Choctaw, and Creek—were already located on reservations and had given little trouble to white settlers. "But the wandering Sioux, who rove from Minnesota to Montana and as far as the Arkansas," wrote Sherman, "have done acts of predatory hostility almost impossible to foresee or to prevent." The Arapaho, Cheyenne, Kiowa, Comanche, Apache, Navaho, and Ute, although restricted to reservations, "will not settle down, but they roam, according to their habits, over the vast plains and they too have done acts of hostility."

Sherman wanted the frontier states to be prepared to organize volunteer companies to help the Regular Army, when and if an all-out Indian war erupted. He also was aware of the universal feeling of mistrust on both sides. "The whites who are looking for gold kill Indians," Sherman wrote the War Department, "just as they would kill beasts, and they also pay no regard for treaties so long as the Indians themselves do not profess to be bound by them further than they are to their individual interest. We must go on as now, until by law all the Indians are put in our control—a thing that must be done sooner or later."

On September 11 the general and his escort rode into Fort Garland, Colo. That evening Sherman wrote: "I think next spring I can dispose matters so as to make Indian wars of any magnitude an impossibility ... and I apprehend none *now*. It is very important that I and the generals of the department should come out to extreme parts, for otherwise every little drunken quarrel or horse-thieving is exaggerated into a big bug-bear."

The Indians in the Colorado countryside proved tame. Cattle and horses grazed loose, far from their owners, and were most tempting to starving red men. Although the hostiles could easily descend on the scattered ranches, yet they had not done so. "I see no external sights of a fear of such an event," Sherman wrote, "though all the people are clamorous for military protection." At Puebla the general received a petition signed by over 100 citizens insisting on military support. Sherman could not refrain from answering that the names to the petition exceeded in number the strength of any of his smaller garrisons.

In Sherman's opinion, the mountain territories presented the most interesting feature in the nation's future development and were worthy of the fostering care of the government in Washington. The plains could never be cultivated as could Illinois or Iowa, nor could they ever be filled with enough inhabitants to defend themselves against the Indian, but they could become a vast pastureland, open and free to all, for rearing herds of horses, mules, cattle, and sheep.

"The Mountain Territories," Sherman wrote the War Department, "seem to be more rapidly improving and assuming a condition of self protection and defence because the people can acquire fixed habitations and their property is generally grouped in valleys of some extent, or in localities of mines capable of sustaining a people strong enough to guard themselves against predatory bands of nomadic Indians.

"Still they occupy at this time an isolated position, presenting a thinly settled frontier in every direction, with a restless people branching out in search of a better place. ... To defend them is an utter impossibility, and all we can do is to aid the people in self-defence, until in time they can take care of themselves, and to make the roads by which they travel or bring their stores from the older parts of our country as safe as the case admits of."

For the Indians themselves, Sherman continued, "I propose . . . to restrict the Sioux north of the Platte, and east of the new road to Montana. . . . All Sioux found outside of these limits without a written pass from some military commander . . . should be dealt with summarily.

"In like manner I would restrict the Arapahoes, Cheyennes, Commanches, Kiowas, Apaches, and Navajoes south of the Arkansas and east of Fort Union. This would leave our people exclusively the use of the wide belt, east and west, between the Platte and Arkansas . . . over which passes the bulk of travel to the mountain territories.

"It is our duty . . . to make . . . this belt as safe as possible," Sherman added, "as also to protect the stage and telegraph lines against any hostile bands, but they are so long that to guard them perfectly is an impossibility, unless we can restrict the Indians as herein stated."

Sherman, like the other generals, strongly believed that the entire management of the red man should be controlled by military authorities, not by the civilian agents of the Indian Bureau. Commanding officers of troops should not only have surveillance duty but should supervise the disbursement of money and presents to the tribes under past and future treaties. "Indians do not read," Sherman said, "and only know our power and strength by what they see, and they always look to the man who commands soldiers as the representative of our government."

"For eleven years I have been tossed about...."

THE RIFT between President Johnson and Congress over Reconstruction policies was widening daily. General-in-Chief of the Army Ulysses S. Grant continued to make noncommittal public utterances, which led Democratic newspapers to characterize him as impartial, "above parties and politics." An inner circle of Republicans, however, felt sure his real opinions ran counter to those of the president. They knew that the general, as well as a majority of the army's other senior officers, sympathized with Republican goals for the Southern states. Grant, in fact, was secretly nursing ambitions for high political office.

To Johnson, Grant's equivocal position was a matter of deep concern, and he sought to avoid giving the general any cause to declare himself openly. He therefore listened to Secretary of State Seward's scheme for dispatching Grant to Mexico on a trumped-up mission. Grant would be asked to escort to Mexico, Lewis Campbell, the new minister. The general-in-chief's prestige would be helpful in establishing Campbell with Don Benito Pablo Juárez, the president elected by the people of Mexico. He was trying to rid the country of the hated European Maximilian, whose Mexican empire was supported by French troops. Juárez was hiding in the mountains, fighting the French guerrilla-fashion.

Seward and the president decided that Grant's known interest in Mexico would seem a valid reason for his accompanying Campbell as a military adviser. Already Johnson was prepared to oust Secretary of War Stanton, the staunch Radical, who by nature let no opportunity pass to embarrass his chief. General Sherman, who was known to be in sympathy with President Johnson, could be brought to Washington when Grant left for Mexico and made the new secretary in the War Department. Johnson wanted to ease Sherman's way by enticing Grant to lay aside his uniform for a diplomatic mission.

In mid-October the president asked Grant whether he would object to Sherman's coming to Washington for a few days. In the course of the conversation Grant learned of his role in the Mexican venture and flatly refused to go. To Sherman, Grant wrote: "I am rather of the opinion that it is the desire to have you in Washington either as Acting Secretary of War, or in some other way. I will not venture in a letter to say all I think about the matter, or that I would say to you in person."

At a cabinet meeting, which Grant attended, Campbell's instructions were read. They contained a paragraph stating that Grant would go along as a military adviser. Angered, Grant objected in strong terms. He exclaimed that it would not be expedient for him to leave the country, as he was in the process of reorganizing the army.

Several days later the general sat in on another cabinet meeting, where the matter was again debated. This time instructions for Grant were read. The general was again aroused and once more declared his unwillingness to undertake such an assignment.

The president also became angry. Turning to the attorney general, he inquired: "Mr. Attorney-General, is there any reason why General Grant should not obey my orders? Is he in any way ineligible to his position?"

Quickly, Grant exclaimed: "I can answer that question, Mr. President, without referring to the Attorney-General.

"I am an American and eligible to any office to which any American is eligible," he said. "I am an officer of the Army, and bound to obey your military orders. But this is a civil office, and purely diplomatic duty that you offer me, and I cannot be compelled to undertake it. Any legal military order you give me I will obey; but this is civil not military, and I decline the duty. No power on earth can compel me to take it."

As he listened to Grant, Secretary of the Navy Gideon Welles thought at first it was anger speaking, along with disappointment and hurt pride, but the coldness on Grant's face made it plain he meant every word. No one replied, and Grant left the cabinet chamber. That night Welles wrote in his diary: "General Sherman has ... been sent for and it was rumored that Stanton was to leave the War Department and Sherman would be assigned to that duty. Whether there was any truth in this, or whether Stanton apprehended it, I never inquired. If there was anything in it, at any time, it was frustrated by Grant, who declined to go with Campbell. He could not be willing to receive orders from his subordinate, General Sherman, of whom he is jealous, though intimately friendly. His suspicion has been excited."

In his diary Orville Browning noted later that General Rawlins, Grant's chief of staff, was "annoyed and provoked at Grant's reticence—says Grant is thoroughly conservative, but that he's not a politician or statesman—he knows how to do nothing but fight—and would fail in other positions, but the radicals are anxious to use him as a candidate for the Presidency to promote their own ends. He is not a man of ability outside the profession of arms.... That Sherman has more influence with him than any body else, and that he [Rawlins] thought it important that Sherman should be here. In his opinion Stanton ought to go out and Sherman be made Sec War."

When Sherman arrived in Washington, he immediately sought out Grant. After their discussion, Sherman wrote Thomas Ewing that Grant "does not want to be President. He told me," Sherman continued, "that 50 millions of dollars would not compensate him therefor, but that events might force him in spite of inclination. ... If the Republicans can find a good nominee he will be content. He is not an [Radical] extremist at all, but many of his good officers at the South force him to the conclusion that there is necessary some strong power to protect the negroes and Union men against legal oppression or acts of badly disposed ex-Rebels. He is frank and friendly to all well disposed men of the South."

Grant professed himself willing to see his friend become secretary of war, but Sherman would not hear of it. After talking with Grant, Sherman was convinced that Grant, like himself, desired to keep strictly to his duty in the army and out of partisan politics. "Neither the President nor Congress," Sherman said, "ought to ask us of the Army to manifest any favor or disfavor to any political measures." Later, writing to Tom Ewing, Sherman emphasized: "I will do nothing intentionally to ally myself to party, and shall try and get some business so that if I can by my very position be driven or drawn into partisan complications I'll be able to resign. I could not afford to do it now, but hope to be able before the alternative is forced upon me."

At a conference in the White House, President Johnson broached his hope of making Sherman secretary of war. Sherman countered with a proposal that he be sent with Lewis Campbell to Mexico. The president, realizing that his plan for removing Grant from Washington could not succeed, quickly accepted this suggestion.

By mid-November Sherman was on board the *Susquehanna*. He had undertaken the assignment to escape a worse duty and to save Grant from "a complication that should have been avoided." Sherman, however, regarded the mission as "inconsequential," and told Tom Ewing that he had about "as much chance of doing good or harm as a stuffed dummy." As it turned out, he was correct in his appraisal of the mission.

At Matamoros, Mexico, he and Campbell met with Gen. Mariano Escobedo, commanding the Republican army in the north. They were told that Juárez would be in Monterrey on December 20. General Escobedo then discussed with them the Mexican military and political situation in detail. The spirit of the national forces, he said, was excellent, but their progress was slow in driving Maximilian out. They lacked sufficient guns, ammunition, and supplies. Impressed by Escobedo's presentation and the worth of the cause of the Mexican Republic, Sherman expressed sympathy, but privately he remained strongly opposed to the United States' meddling with Mexican affairs.

Deciding that his part of the mission was now completed, Sherman traveled to New Orleans and reported the facts to Washington. On his way to Saint Louis, he went straight through the part of Mississippi that his army had razed years before. "I did not know but I should hear some things that would not be pleasant," Cump wrote John, "but, on the contrary, many people met me along the road in the most friendly spirit. I spent a whole day at Jackson, where chimney stacks and broken railroads marked the presence of Sherman's army. But all sorts of people pressed to see me, and evinced their natural curiosity, nothing more. . . ."

"Cump says the entire people of the South," Ellen wrote her father, "treated him with marked respect and attention. All classes

& sorts flocked to see him where he was detained on the road offering civilities & hospitalities."

When Sherman reached Saint Louis, he vowed never again to
become involved in Washington politics. Early in January, 1867,
he received orders to come to the White House, but he asked to
be excused because Ellen was awaiting the birth of another baby.

At Omaha General Dodge was urging Sherman to dispatch
10,000 more troops to the west to guard the Union Pacific's rails.
"You should hunt down the marauders," advised Dodge, "with
good officers who never give up but follow them day and night,
until dooms day if necessary—until they are severely punished
for their past wrongs and feel our power, so that they will in the
future respect us. They look upon us now as a lot of old men, who
do not know whether we are for war, or peace, or both."

Although Sherman regarded the safety of the railroad as important, he refused to send more soldiers. He believed that Gen. Christopher C. Augur, who was then guarding the rails, could handle
the Indian emergencies. But General Dodge was not alone in begging for more troops. "Every state, territory and settlement is
constantly imparting for more troops," Sherman wrote his father-
in-law, "and if these requests and demands were aggregated they
would require ten times the whole army of the U.S. Each party
exaggerates their own danger, and thus belittles that of our distant people, and all look to the Army for help, though they ought
to know that the common law of the country has withdrawn the
Indians from our control [and placed it with civilian agents].
We made desperate efforts to change this but have failed, and
must continue to grope our way as we best can."

Another problem which troubled Sherman was the sale of
arms and ammunition to the hostiles by certain traders and Indian agents. As he wrote Gen. Winfield S. Hancock, commanding
the Department of the Missouri, "We, the military, are held responsible for the peace of the frontier, and it is an absurdity to
attempt it if Indian agents and traders can legalize and encourage
so dangerous a traffic.... I now authorize you to ... at once stop
the practice.... If the Indian agents may, without limit, supply the
Indians with arms, I would not expose our troops and trains to
them at all, but would withdraw our soldiers, who already have a
herculean task on their hands."

General Grant forwarded a copy of this letter to Secretary of

War Stanton and seconded Sherman's demand for the withdrawal
of the troops if the practice of selling arms continued.

In January Ellen gave birth to a boy, Philemon Tecumseh
("Cumpy, Jr."). "I think there is no doubt we can raise the
young chap," Cump said, "and I hope this completes the family...." In March Cump traveled to Lancaster to transfer the
body of Willy to a new grave in Saint Louis and sent a friend to
South Bend for the remains of baby Charles.

Early in the spring, as a gift for good school grades, Cump
took Lizzie and some of her friends out for a 250-mile ride on the
Union Pacific Railroad. No sooner had he returned to Saint Louis
than the Indians struck the railroad near Fort Sedgwick in northern Colorado and robbed two Union Pacific subcontractors. General Dodge insisted that the assault "scared the workmen out of
their boots so they abandoned work and we cannot get them
back." On the Laramie plains a band of Indians attacked a surveying party and killed an engineer. Stagecoach way stations
were leveled. As the situation became worse, Sherman wired
Washington for additional troops and went out along the Union
Pacific tracks to survey defensive measures. He quickly concluded
that a full-fledged war against the Indian was out of the question.
Only when the railroad was completed and sufficient supplies were
moving westward could the army mount a full-scale offensive.

The Indian was an incredibly tough opponent, wily and capable of existing on the land. Lean, hardened, needing only a few
supplies, mounted on fine horses, he played hide-and-seek with
the cavalry detachments. He possessed outstanding ability to cam-
ouflage his presence, to ride extraordinary distances, to turn and
fight at places of his own selection. His hit-and-run attacks were
so unpredictable, they seemed to "materialize out of the ground."

"No amount of men," Sherman told Thomas Ewing, can
"guard the long lines of frontier," but "the Secretary of War
has given me the discretion to call out local volunteers. Of course
every gunman of the frontier is clamoring for arming and destroying but the laws of the country and the necessities of government
do not warrant this and I have to stand the pressure.

"Of course this Indian question cannot be settled in a day or
year," Sherman went on, "not until we can make settlements that
can in their own interest protect themselves, & this is hardly pos-

sible in the wide extent from the borders of Kansas & Nebraska to the mountains. I've good officers up there, but our forces are so limited that if we go to one quarter the Indians turn in another. I hardly know what legislation is called for, but some is...."

Several weeks later Sherman wrote again to Ewing: "Our Indian affairs are mixed up in the most perfect confusion. Through an unsettled country of 2000 miles long and 600 broad they are substantially at war, but so scattered that no army can be brought to bear against them. We have to scatter our forces, and they are swallowed up in the vast sea of prairie.... Nothing will solve this problem but settlement in the usual way."

Sherman was aware that the Indian problem was not all one-sided. Treaties were broken by the white man as well as by the Indian. Politicians in Washington made promises and did not keep them. But Sherman's basic feeling toward the Indians was that they, like the Negroes, were inferior beings and that the armed might of the United States should severely punish those hostiles who robbed and killed.

"I don't care about interesting myself too far in the fate of the poor devils of Indians, who are doomed from the causes inherent in their nature or from the natural and persistent hostility of the White Race," Cump wrote Ellen.

"At best," Sherman told Sheridan, "it is an inglorious war, not apt to add much to our fame or personal comfort, and for our soldiers, to whom we owe our first thoughts, it is all danger and extreme labor, without one single compensating advantage."

During the summer of 1867, Congress, concerned over conditions on the plains, decided to extend the olive branch, not the sword, and created an Indian Peace Commission. It was composed of three generals—William T. Sherman, William S. Harney, and Alfred H. Terry—and four civilians. Pending the outcome of negotiations, Sherman notified the field commands that military operations would be purely defensive.

His tenure on the commission, however, was short-lived, as President Johnson called him to Washington that October.

In the national capital, the political situation was tense. President Johnson was still engaged in a power struggle with Secretary of War Stanton and with Congress over Reconstruction policies. Throughout the crisis one of Johnson's staunchest supporters and advisers was Thomas Ewing, whose great desire was to heal the wounds of war and restore the Union. When Ewing was in Washington, he was with the president constantly. In pamphlets and open letters to newspapers and in meetings with members of Congress, he argued that the Radicals' actions in Congress were jeopardizing the Constitution and urged conciliatory measures.

The president's stubbornness, however, was influencing the mood of the House and Senate, and many Republican leaders were obsessed with the desire to defeat him. The unsettled times and the large Republican majorities, which were threatened by the possibility of a Democratic resurgence if "unreconstructed" Southern states were readmitted to the Union, also sustained the Radical determination.

Since the president had issued his lenient Reconstruction program, conservative congressmen had joined the Radicals in defense of congressional prerogatives, and Congress gradually gained the upper hand by placing progressively stricter controls on the South. "The whole fabric of southern society *must* be changed," declared one Radical congressman. Surely the crimes of the South, he added, "are sufficient to justify the exercise of the extreme rights of war—'to execute, to imprison, to confiscate.' " "If all whites vote, then must all blacks," said a senator. "Without them the old enemy will reappear."

Congress legally nullified the rebellious states and divided the South into five military districts, each under the command of a Federal general. As the price for readmission to the Union, Southern states were required to call constitutional conventions for the purpose of drawing up new constitutions and organizing state governments guaranteeing the vote and officeholding privileges to the Negro. Each Southern state also had to ratify the proposed Fourteenth Amendment, which declared Negroes citizens. The amendment further stated that no state could pass laws which would abridge the privileges of citizens, nor could states deprive any person of life, liberty, or property, without due process of law. While the amendment did not specifically grant the Negro the vote, its second section provided that in case a state denied the franchise to the blacks, its representation in Congress and the Electoral College was to be reduced proportionately.

Once a state ratified the Fourteenth Amendment, a state government could apply for readmission to the Union. Congress was the sole authority for ending military rule, withdrawing Federal troops, and seating senators and representatives from these states.

When Congress enacted laws taking away powers granted to the president by the Constitution, Johnson refused to submit. Finally in a showdown, caused more by emotional conflict than practical consideration, the Radicals tried to remove the president from office. The chief issue was the Tenure of Office Act of March, 1867, which prohibited the president from removing officials who had been appointed with the consent of the Senate without first obtaining senatorial approval.

On August 12, 1867, during a congressional recess, Johnson suspended Stanton from office and authorized General Grant to act as secretary of war *ad interim*. Grant accepted, and although Johnson realized that the general had sided with the Radicals on Reconstruction measures, he now felt assured that Grant's acceptance of a cabinet post meant he could count on the general's full cooperation. "I can perceive that Grant is not at all displeased with his new position," noted Gideon Welles, "but I doubt his sincerity to the President." However, Welles was sure that Grant had sense enough not to foment Radical intrigues.

Rumors were current that General Sherman had been ordered east to use his influence with the new secretary of war. "Colonel Edmund Cooper," Welles wrote in his diary, "says General Sherman has been called to Washington by the President and will be here by Sunday next. Both the President and he think Sherman may influence Grant by reason of their intimacy. There is no doubt that Sherman has more general intelligence and knowledge of government than Grant, but he is sometimes erratic and uncertain, whilst Grant is prejudiced, aspiring, reticent, cunning, and stolidly obstinate in his ignorance. The two men will work well and advantageously together when they agree, but when they differ, the stubborn will and selfishness of Grant will overpower the yielding genius and generous impulses of Sherman.

"That Sherman has a mortal antipathy to Stanton and is

really in sympathy with the President I can well suppose," Welles continued, "but when he associates with Grant, I apprehend from what I have seen and understood he will be powerless. Had he been here for the last fifteen months, his influence upon Grant, who is subordinated by Stanton, whom he dislikes, might have been salutary. He can now do but little."

When Sherman arrived in Washington, the first person he saw was Grant. Together they discussed the political situation for well over an hour. Grant regretted having been made secretary of war and insisted that he wished to be rid of the job. Sherman urged him to keep himself and the War Department clear of political machinations.

Sherman then called on President Johnson, but during their conversation, the president never once brought up the reason for his sudden orders to Sherman to report to Washington. Sherman thought it strange that Johnson and not Grant had telegraphed him to come to Washington, when by military law, his orders should have been sent by the president through Grant. He was sure now that no cordial understanding existed between Grant and the president.

The next day Sherman again called at the White House. He was exceedingly frank with Johnson and urged him to make overtures to certain key members of the House and Senate for support.

The president was anxious for Sherman to remain in Washington, and during a lull in the conversation, he suddenly offered the general a place in the cabinet as secretary of war. Sherman quickly replied that under no circumstances would he climb over Grant's shoulders. He suggested that the president meet with Grant and attempt to come to some mutual understanding. Johnson assented.

During a later conversation with the president, Grant did convince Johnson that he was a moderate in political views, that he had no ambitions for the presidency, and that he held the War Office only to keep the army out of politics.

Orville Browning, now the secretary of the interior, urged Sherman to remain in the capital and to exert himself to reverse what he called the dangerous drift in political affairs. He said the country was in peril and "that the extreme measures of the radicals if persisted in would eventuate in revolution and Civil War." He predicted that Congress would arrest and dispose of Johnson and inaugurate arch-Radical Benjamin Wade of Ohio as president of the United States. Johnson must be prepared to resist and should be surrounded with people whom he could trust. Browning and others did not think that Grant could be trusted in an emergency, as he was in full sympathy with the Radicals. They felt Sherman was needed in Washington, as he was a conservative, "a soldier and a statesman."

The general, however, was averse to any such scheme, believing he was more valuable out on the plains. He rejected this talk of machinations as poppycock. The president would never be impeached. Wade would never be inaugurated president. He was confident that Grant, "honest, patriotic Grant," would as a soldier obey the orders of the president.

Back in Saint Louis, Sherman tried to forget politics in order to concentrate upon military matters. Already the general was finding inaction harder to endure with each passing month. The endless papers coming to his desk, to read, to sign, to reject, to answer—the minutiae, as well as the important details of the army in the west, which only he could take care of—oppressed him.

The peace commissioners had met with the Kiowa, Comanche, Apache, Cheyenne, and Arapaho at Medicine Lodge Creek, 80 miles south of the Arkansas River, and reached an agreement with them. In exchange for food, clothing, and equipment, and the promise of schools, the Indians promised to keep the peace, to stay away from the whites, to drop all opposition to the construction of the railroads across the plains, and to live on specific reservations.

In December Sherman was again called east. On this trip he took Tommy along for company and to place him in the Roman Catholic school at Georgetown. That winter President Johnson, in accordance with the Tenure of Office Act, submitted to Congress a written report, explaining why he had dismissed Stanton. On January 11, a Saturday, before the Senate acted, Grant suddenly realized that if the senators upheld Stanton and if he refused to return the War Office to the former secretary, he would face a $10,000 fine and five years in prison. He met with President

Johnson the same morning and explained that he would not risk it. If the Senate voted in Stanton's favor, he would hand over the War Office immediately.

The president pleaded, even promising to pay the $10,000 and serve the jail sentence himself. Grant refused to give in. When the interview ended, Johnson asked the general to return on Monday to continue their talks. Later Johnson insisted that Grant had agreed to talk again, and that he had said he would not resign as secretary of war without giving the president sufficient warning.

Grant went directly to John Sherman's house, where Cump was staying. The two generals, deeply worried about the turn of events, decided to suggest to the president that he select Gov. Jacob Cox of Ohio for the War Office before the Senate considered Stanton's dismissal. The governor, a moderate Republican, could easily gain bipartisan confirmation before the senators decided on Stanton. If Cox won the post, Grant could then resign his temporary office and retain his commission as General of the Army.

Sherman hastened to the White House with the plan and explained it in detail to President Johnson. He was startled at Johnson's complete lack of interest, being unaware that the president was extremely confident Grant would not give up his portfolio to Stanton however Congress voted.

On Monday General Grant failed to appear at the White House to resume his discussions with the president. In the evening the Senate demanded that Stanton be returned to the War Department. Sherman sought out Orville Browning, spoke "bitterly of Stanton's restoration," and said that Johnson, by rejecting the plan to appoint Governor Cox, was "blameable" for the Senate's action in reinstating Stanton.

Early on January 14, Grant went to the War Department, locked the door, handed the key to the assistant adjutant general, went back to his own office, and wrote President Johnson a note to the effect that the Senate's actions had terminated his functions as secretary *ad interim*. Stanton promptly took over the War Department.

Outraged at Grant's performance, Johnson ordered him to a cabinet meeting and forced him to admit that he had violated their understanding of the previous Saturday.

When the president fully realized at last that Grant had switched completely to the Radicals, he became determined to appoint Sherman secretary of war *ad interim.* On January 24 Johnson asked Sherman whether he would accept the appointment. Although the general believed that Stanton should be out of the War Office, he himself did not wish to be the agent of his removal. Sherman promised the president to think it over and to consult with Thomas Ewing.

"The President constantly sends for me and asks opinions and assistance," Cump wrote his father-in-law. "I've shown great personal respect, and think all of us in service should respect the office. But further than that I don't want to be involved in political combinations. Yesterday he suggested and offered to remove Stanton and appoint me ad interim under some law, for six months.... I don't want the place.... It is not to my interest to replace Stanton.... To remove Stanton by force or a show of force would be the very thing the enemies of the president want."

Thomas Ewing answered that it was inexpedient for the president to take any further action against Stanton as "things are in the best possible condition. Stanton is in the department, not *his* secretary, but the secretary of the Senate, who have taken upon themselves his sins, and who place him there under a large salary to annoy and obstruct the operations of the Executive.

"Now," Ewing continued, "the dislodging of Stanton and filling the office even temporarily, without the consent of the Senate, would raise a question as to the legality of the President's act, and *he* would belong to the attacked instead of the attacking party. If the war between the President and Congress is to go on, as I suppose it is, Stanton should be ignored by the President, left to perform the clerical duties which the law requires him to perform, and let the party bear the odium which is already upon them for placing him where he is."

As for Cump himself, Ewing warned him to steer clear of the political jungle of Washington. Two days later Sherman transmitted this letter to Johnson.

Johnson, however, had not given up hopes of enlisting Sherman's help. He summoned the general to the White House and told him that he could not, under any circumstances, execute the office of the president with Stanton as secretary of war. "For the purpose of having the office administered properly in the interest of the Army, and of the whole country," he again tendered Sherman the position.

Sherman still hesitated, saying he wanted to discuss it with his father-in-law again. On January 29 Thomas Ewing wrote the president: "It will not do to adopt rash measures. It is better to let Stanton alone. Public opinion is against him and his backers, and by an imprudent act you may turn it in his favor. I cannot advise Sherman to take his place, and he is not willing to do it. There is indeed no object to be gained by it. Reconstruction will dispose of itself in spite of the act of any persons you may place in the department."

Johnson would not be swerved by Ewing's letter, and he once more urged Sherman to accept the appointment. Strangely, this time the general replied that although it was against his personal wishes, he might be willing for the good of the army to assume the war portfolio. For a moment, the president believed that Sherman had accepted.

Then Sherman asked, "Suppose Mr. Stanton does not yield?"

"Oh! he will make no objection," the president said. "You present the order, and he will retire."

When Sherman expressed doubt about this, Johnson said, "I know him better than you do; he is cowardly."

Sherman asked time to think it over. Finally, heeding Ewing's advice, he turned the offer down. The president, however, still hoped to keep the general in Washington by promoting him in rank and by creating an entirely new military department with headquarters in the capital.

"Saw the President . . . [and] took occasion to express my apprehension of public affairs, and of threatening impending calamities which were to be met," Gideon Welles wrote in his diary. "I reminded him that it was a duty for us all, particularly for him, to be prepared for approaching extraordinary emergencies; for reckless, unprincipled men in Congress had control of the Government, were usurping executive authority, and would exercise their powers to extreme, and evidently beyond constitutional limits."

Welles continued: "The President became somewhat excited. . . . He spoke of Sherman . . . and suggested that Washington might be made a military department and Sherman ordered to it. Sherman, he knew, would take it.

"I expressed misgivings as to Sherman if Grant were to be his antagonist. He is friendly disposed, but would yield, I feared, and follow Grant rather than the President. I admitted that he was in my opinion a man of superior intellect and of a higher sense of honor than Grant, but their military association and the ties and obligations of military fellowship and long personal intimacy and friendship would attach him to Grant, though I hoped not overthrow the government."

Sherman pleaded with Johnson not to order him to Washington. He did not want to become enmeshed in politics, he did not want to leave Missouri, and he could not afford to live in the capital. "For eleven years I have been tossed about so much," he told the president, "that I do really want to rest, study and make the acquaintance of my family. I do not think since 1857 I have arranged 30 days out of 365 at home."

"After I thought the danger which I have dreaded so long had passed," Sherman wrote Thomas Ewing, "it has come upon me like an avalanche.

"To create a new military department," he went on, is "a notorious . . . devise to have me . . . [in Washington]. I don't think the president means it in unkindness to me, but not with shut eyes can I fail to see the inevitable consequence. There are no military duties for me . . . [in Washington], there is no room for so many captains and the inevitable result is collision of authority, quarelling and conflict.

"Stanton is evidently resolved to stay in his office. Grant too has extraordinary powers, which he will not moderate or surrender. The President is constitutional commander in chief, with a brief period of power left to him and a Congress that deals with him as a common enemy. What good can I do in such an embroglio? Moderation is lost, conciliation out of the question, and a conflict would arouse new passions, create new parties and would end no one can say when.

"I've befriended the . . . [President] whenever I could and have advised him," Sherman continued, and "had he heeded it he would have avoided much of the trouble that now afflicts us all and he infers I suppose that because I gave him full credit for his first efforts to reconstruct the South on principles nearer right than have since been attempted, that I'll go with him to the death, but I am not bound to do it.

"He never heeds any advise. He attempts to govern after he has lost the means to govern. He is like a General fighting without an army, he is like Lear raving at the wild storm, bareheaded and helpless. And now he wants me to go with him into the wilderness. I do want Peace, and do say if all hands would stop talking, and writing, and let the sun shine, and the rains fall for two or three years, we would be nearer Reconstruction than we are likely to be with the three & four hundred statesmen trying to legislate amid the prejudices... [of] four centuries.... The President with two thirds Congress against him is not a power in the Land and we have no alternative [but to] wait till the natural change comes. Ellen doesn't appreciate my strong feelings on this point ... but she doesn't comprehend the danger."

He concluded: "If Grant does become President then I am willing to try to succeed him as Commander-in-Chief, but if he remains as now, which he gives me an official right to infer, then I am rightfully out... [of Washington].... A mere residence stript of one's self respect is a hell, which I will avoid if possible."

Several days later, after Sherman threatened to resign his commission, Johnson abandoned his plans and ordered the general to remain at his present post. Throughout that stormy January and February, despite Sherman's negative responses, President Johnson maintained extremely cordial relations with him.

The president decided to replace Stanton with Adj. Gen. Lorenzo Thomas, then 63 years old. There followed a seriocomic scene between Thomas, who demanded the war post, and Stanton, who refused to surrender it, after which the general withdrew and the secretary barricaded his office.

While the military affairs of the country were suspended amid these actions, the House was voting impeachment charges against Johnson for high crimes and misdemeanors. Stanton kept the War Office and the bulk of the functions, while General Thomas continued to attend cabinet meetings.

"I must say," Sherman wrote Thomas Ewing, "I am glad I am out of it."

Later, when on a business trip, Cump wrote Ellen: "There are plenty of people who would sow dissension between me and Grant.... I think he is as much under obligations to me as I am to him and if he allows these persons who would destroy either of us to sow coolness between us, he can do so. I'll not, but will bear a good deal, as the blow is meant for the Military Profession and not for us as individuals."

General of the Army

From his office in Saint Louis that spring, Sherman kept current on the progress of the Union Pacific's construction and wrestled with other western problems. Small forts were being abandoned. As the railroad advanced across the plains, troops could be easily shuttled back and forth to trouble zones. Instead of maintaining small contingents at distant, isolated forts, it was preferable to garrison large numbers of troops at Omaha and other cities and transport them by train when danger threatened.

By mid-May Sherman was at Denver. From there he and Samuel F. Tappan, one of the peace commissioners, rode to eastern New Mexico to talk with the Navaho on their reservation.

Sherman reviewed past events and treaties, pointed out that the government had provided tools and seeds, and asked why the Indians had not cultivated the land. The chief countered that they had done their best, but worms had eaten the corn, and one year hail had demolished the crop. They had given up.

"I have listened to all you have said of your people and believe you have told us the truth," Sherman declared. "You are right, the world is big enough for all the people it contains and all should live at peace with their neighbors. All people love the country where they were born and raised, but the Navajos are very few indeed compared with all the people of the world, they are not more than seven leaves to all the leaves you have ever seen. Still we want to do to you what is right—right to you—and right to us as people. If you will live in peace with your neighbors, we will see that your neighbors will be at peace with you."

The Navaho chief argued bitterly. The reservation had been described to him as a good place, but it was not. Sherman pledged that the Navaho could go back to their old haunts in northwestern New Mexico and settle on a 100-square-mile reservation.

"The poor Indians are starving," Cump wrote Ellen. "We kill them if they attempt to hunt [on the settlers' lands], and if they keep within the Reservations they starve. Of course we recommended they should receive certain food, for a time, during which they could try their hand at raising corn, stock, etc. Congress makes no provision, and of course, nothing is done. I wish Congress could be impeached."

Through a letter from Ellen, Sherman learned that the Senate had failed to convict President Johnson in the impeachment trials. Ellen was anxious to have Cump home. "I am getting tired out of this way of being a wife and widow at the same time," she said. "It is too lonely here when you are gone & outside visitors cannot fill the gap."

The news about General Grant's nomination for the presidency by the Republican party came as no surprise to Sherman. From Santa Fe, N. Mex., he wrote Ellen: "Considering the state of the country Grant will make the best President we can get. What we want in National Politics is quiet, harmony & stability and these are more likely with Grant than any politician I know of. His election will mean my promotion and our move to Washington.

"The moment a person is established in Washington," he went on, "friends begin to cool off and fall away. Slander is let loose and is paraded in Capital letters and underhand meanness is set to work to effect change. I saw these influences at work in ... General Scott's and General Grant's [time]. We may suppose this will not be the case in future but it will always be as long as human nature remains as now. You have realized some of the annoyances even in Saint Louis, but when you are to have newspapers publishing everytime you go to Church, every slander that may be started, every neglect to entertain to suit the demand of an exacting public you will regret the day you ever got to Washington .... the people, collectively ... simply consider every public officer their servant. There can be no privacy, no satisfaction. Yet this station may be forced on us."

During the spring Sherman's letters about the West so impressed General Grant that the candidate decided to go west himself. His campaign lieutenants approved wholeheartedly—they wanted to publicize a legend and wanted Grant conveniently out of the way. In mid-July Sherman, Grant, and Sheridan toured the plains and mountain regions, making major campaign speeches at Cheyenne, Laramie, Denver, and Omaha.

By the time Sherman was back in Saint Louis, news came that some Cheyenne and Arapaho braves had attacked settlers between the Solomon and Saline rivers in northwestern Kansas, breaking the Medicine Lodge Treaty. The atrocities were more vicious than the newspaper reports indicated.

Quickly, he ordered General Sheridan to employ his forces in pursuing the Cheyenne, and "I hope he may get hold of them and obliterate them. This amounts to war," Sherman wrote the War Department. "If the President does not approve, notify me promptly, for I deem further forbearance with these Indians impossible. In this case they are purely the aggressors." After two years of waiting, Sherman was ready to strike. The Indians had sought war, he explained, "and I propose to give them enough of it to satisfy them to their hearts' content."

After a hasty inspection tour, and consulting with Generals Sheridan and Augur, he detailed the situation to Grant in Washington. "No better time could possibly be chosen than the present for destroying or humbling those bands that have so outrageously violated our treaties."

Sherman issued orders to Gen. William B. Hazen to ride for Fort Cobb, Indian Territory. He was to round up any red man who wanted to come in and avoid war. "I propose," Sherman warned, "that Sheridan shall prosecute the war with vindictive earnestness against all hostile Indians, till they are obliterated or beg for mercy; and therefore all who want peace must get out of the theatre of war."

"Cump is very much harassed by Indian affairs," Ellen wrote her father. "He cannot get money from the Treasury that Congress gave him orders to disburse [to the Indians]. The western people are telegraphing fearful accounts of Indian outrages & imploring help, whilst the Radical hounds [in Congress] are denouncing him for his aggressive movements."

While the army girded itself for war, the nation's attention was riveted on the upcoming presidential election, in which General Grant would win a smashing victory over the Democrats.

Sherman went to Chicago to consult with the president-elect and speak before a huge reunion of ex-soldiers of the western armies. In the privacy of his hotel room, Grant outlined to Sherman his plan to reorganize the army. He then informed Sherman that he would be called to Washington to become General of the Army, and that Sheridan would step up to lieutenant general and command the Division of the Missouri.

While Sherman prepared to take over his new post, his subordinates planned what they hoped would be the final campaign against the Cheyenne. Sheridan's forces were determined to punish those who had continued to plunder frontier commerce. On November 27 Col. George Armstrong Custer's Seventh Cavalry successfully assaulted Black Kettle's camp in Indian Territory. When Sherman heard the news, he wired Sheridan: "I congratulate all the parties for their great success which I regard as decisive and conclusive."

Custer's troopers had dealt the Cheyenne a severe blow, killing 103 warriors, including Black Kettle, capturing 53 women and children, burning 51 lodges with all their contents, and destroying nearly 900 animals. This battle, together with Sheridan's sweep southward from Camp Supply to Fort Cobb, Indian Territory, resulted in the permanent settlement of nearly all the Kiowa, Comanche, and Kiowa-Apache upon a reservation set aside for them. But the Cheyenne and Arapaho, the primary objectives of the campaign, escaped toward the headwaters of the Red River. It remained for Sheridan's troopers to seek them out, secure their surrender, and drive them onto reservations.

By early March Ellen and Cump were in Washington. Grant's inauguration day was cold and rainy. Washington streets were lakes of mud. But the drizzle and mud failed to dampen the enthusiasm of the cheering crowd assembled to witness the inauguration of the soldier-president.

On March 6 Grant nominated Sherman to be General of the Army and Sheridan as lieutenant general, and these names were sent to the Senate for confirmation. Sheridan replaced Sherman in command of the Division of the Missouri and moved his headquarters from Saint Louis to Chicago. He reported that as a result of the recent campaign, most of the Arapaho and Cheyenne were slowly coming into the reservations, and the "good work of civilization, education, and religious instruction" would soon be available to them.

Ellen and the children returned home to Saint Louis, and Cump remained in Washington. Once the Grants took possession of the White House, after making some alterations, Sherman moved into the Grant house, 207 I Street, which a group of New York friends had purchased for him. The house was a heavy red-brick and brownstone edifice in what would soon be the fashionable West End.

The city was now a pleasant place in which to live, with many cultural opportunities. For official and semiofficial Washington there were endless rounds of receptions, dinners, and parties. On Sunday afternoons Cump liked to ride to the Soldiers' Home, with its long roads, groves of tall trees, and bridges overgrown with luxuriant vines.

Daily Sherman boarded the one-horse streetcar that passed near his house and went to the War Department office. To residents of Washington, he was a hero from the West, a living legend. His dress contrasted sharply with the spick-and-span uniforms worn by those who clustered about him.

A presidential order of March 5 granted the General of the Army much power in military affairs. "The chiefs of staff corps, departments and bureaus will report to and act under the immediate orders of the general commanding the Army," the order read. "All official business, which by law or regulations requires the action of the President or Secretary of War, will be submitted by the General of the Army to the Secretary of War, and in general, all orders from the President or Secretary of War to any portion of the Army, line or staff, will be transmitted through the General of the Army."

Unfortunately for Sherman, this order was very short-lived. On March 11 Grant appointed his wartime aide and devoted friend, John A. Rawlins, as secretary of war, who promptly demanded that this order be rescinded.

Sherman argued bitterly. Grant was obliged to choose between two friends, and his sympathy leaned toward Rawlins, whose health was poor. After one heated interview at the White House,

Sherman rose, bowed stiffly, and snapped: "Mr. President, you have the power to revoke your own order; you shall be obeyed. Good morning, sir." On March 26 the original orders were revoked, and now the War Department reverted to its previous status—the General of the Army was again subordinate to the secretary. To General Sheridan, Sherman wrote: "You must have noticed that the President went back on me in the matter of the Secretary of War. I did not like it at all, but could not help myself."

Ellen Sherman had doubts about moving permanently to Washington. She had always detested the limelight, the official entertaining, the returns of social calls; but now in the nation's capital, with her husband General of the Army, these activities would be multiplied. "I have serious doubts of being able to live there with Cump," she told her father, "but I shall try it provided he seems to agree to the terms on which I go, namely as the honorable faithful wife of the man, and not the subordinate of the General."

From Saint Louis Ellen dispatched the "advance guard" to Washington, Tecumseh and Ellie, and the main contingent of Shermans left on April 20. When Ellen inspected her new home she decided it was much too big, and she at once told Cump that they should seek a tenant for the entire rear section. Lizzie, Ellie, and Rachel were enrolled at the Visitation Convent School and Tom at the Jesuit school in Georgetown.

Ellen was still trying without success to convert her husband to Catholicism. Yet Cump had never vigorously argued against sending the children to parochial schools, and his tolerance toward the Roman Catholic church was apparent in his relations with the children. When Ellen was out of the city, Cump always saw to it that the children attended Roman Catholic services, and he reported to his wife the daily fulfillment of their religious obligations. Never once did he place an obstacle in the way of his children's practice of their mother's religion, and throughout these years, he displayed only friendliness toward the church. He had a deep interest in the work of the Sisters of the Holy Cross, and his support of the church was demonstrated by his responses to overtures of friendship from the priests at Notre Dame, his visits to churches during his travels, and his financial help when his wife requested it.

Minnie Sherman, now 18 years old, was one of the belles of Washington society. The Sherman house was a gathering point for distinguished visitors, and increasingly, she was becoming co-hostess with her mother. Generals Sheridan, Meade, and Thomas and Admirals Porter and John A. B. Dahlgren were frequent visitors at the Shermans. Cabinet members, Supreme Court justices, foreign diplomats, congressmen were all familiar figures in the reception room. But of all those who came to the general's door, Sheridan was the children's favorite, as he always joined them in their games. Periodically, the Sherman brood dined with the Grants at the White House. These were private, intimate affairs, with little Tecumseh always seated at the president's table in a high chair.

As the months passed Ellen Sherman was seen less and less in Washington social circles. "Mother from the first," remembered Minnie, "avoided society as much as she could possibly, accepting invitations from the White House which she could not decline."

"Washington is a great place for visiting," Ellen wrote her aunt, "and we are kept constantly occupied in entertaining company. My eldest daughter being . . . fond of society relieves me of much of the labor of receiving such returning visits. I much prefer the quiet domestic life, with time to read and chat with my children."

"Your mother," Cump told one of the children, "will never adapt her habits to the requirements of official life in Washington."

On May 10, 1869, Sherman, together with Adj. Gen. Edward Davis Townsend and Secretary of War Rawlins, sat in the offices of the War Department and listened to the news tapped out from Promontory Summit, Utah, 2,400 miles away, reporting the completion of the transcontinental railroad. The Union Pacific and the Central Pacific had been joined, Dodge wired Sherman, and "you can visit your old friends in California overland, all the way by rail."

At once Sherman replied: "In common with millions, I heard the mystic taps of the telegraph battery announce the nailing of the last spike in the great Pacific road. Indeed, am I its friend? Yea."

Now attention was focused on the construction of the Northern Pacific, and to Sherman, this spelled trouble with the Indian that spring. But, he wrote Sheridan: "I expect to stand back and do the hallooing whilst you or younger men go in." He urged the general to protect the road, "as it will help bring the Indian problem to a final solution."

The creation of new state constitutions and state governments under Radical Reconstruction had been completed the year before, in June, 1868, in all the Southern states except Virginia, Mississippi, and Texas, which were not restored to the Union until 1870. Georgia, whose legislature expelled Negroes after Federal troops were withdrawn, was returned to military rule and was also to be readmitted to the Union in 1870. In some parts of the South, army units were kept on until 1877, in order to prop up shaky Radical regimes.

Sherman had grave doubts concerning the army's occupation of the Southern states and feared the consequences of assigning army officers to control the lives of other Americans. "No matter what change we may desire in the feelings and thoughts of the people South," he wrote John, "we cannot accomplish it by force. Nor can we afford to maintain an army large enough to hold them in subjugation."

"The South is broken and ruined and appeals to our pity," he wrote again. "To ride the people down with persecution and military exactions would be like slashing away at the crew of a sinking ship."

Sherman believed that the reputation of the army would be tarnished as a result of political controversy. The war had markedly increased the prestige of the military and naval officer, but Sherman thought that the politics of Reconstruction threatened to undermine this new status.

He resented the slash in pay of all army officers. Since the war, officers had been required to perform at great personal risk the duties of Indian agent, governor, sheriff, judge, inspector of elections in the South—duties foreign to their military training. Most of them served at distant posts, garrisoned there with poor facilities, cut off from civilized life. Many had families which they could scarcely provide for. "In my whole army experience," Sherman wrote the secretary of war, "I have never known army officers so poor and yet I believe they will continue cheerfully to endure this state of facts if they can see in the future any hope of improvement. I do not understand they want more pay, but. . . any diminution of pay would turn the thoughts of every good officer to a change of profession, that would be extremely damaging to the army itself."

Sherman searched for ways to encourage the professional advancement of his officers. He was more active in military education than any previous General of the Army. Consistently, he urged his colleagues to realize the significance of training in the methods and techniques of warfare. While other officers formulated more effective specific proposals, Sherman fostered a standard of concern for education that enabled the military to endure the growing isolation it felt in the postwar years.

To him West Point was the key to all military instruction: "I do not think we claim that West Point can in four years . . . utterly remold its pupils, but it has in the past and will make in the future, men useful in the details of life, more reliable and faithful in their trusts whether private or public, and more national in their attributes and aspirations than any other system of education heretofore tried."

Sherman fathered a system of postgraduate schools beyond the military academy, thinking in terms of a pyramid of institutions through which officers could learn the special skills of their own branches of service and the principles of higher command. He also promoted the publication of professional military journals, which offered outlets for ideas and studies nurtured at the schools.

In September, 1869, Secretary John A. Rawlins died, after only six months in office. President Grant temporarily commissioned Sherman as secretary of war. But Sherman had no desire to serve permanently in that capacity. "I sit with the cabinet," he told Thomas Ewing, "but take pains not to mix in anything not purely my own. . . . I can actually perform both its [the Secretary of War's] and my own appropriate functions in complete harmony . . . [and] with more ease than the separate duties of either. There is an undefined limit between them that is calculated to produce conflict, but I'm always willing to surrender any particular branch of business involving patronage, which a Secretary naturally covets.

"Grant promises to make an appointment as soon as he can think of a man," Sherman wrote. "All I ask is a man of sense, who saw some actual swim in the late war and he agrees."

Sherman considered service in the armies of the United States the highest recommendation for a man. At his suggestion, President Grant finally appointed as secretary of war, Gen. William W. Belknap, a distinguished officer, who had commanded a brigade in the Army of the Tennessee.

The elderly Thomas Ewing had arrived in Washington in October to argue a case before the Supreme Court. On the 22nd while addressing the justices he slipped from a chair, hit his head, and sprawled unconscious on the floor. Doctors and Ewing's children were quickly summoned. After a few days, when he grew strong enough, he was taken home to Lancaster.

On Capitol Hill, Congress debated military economy and the need for peace on the plains. During February, 1870, Rep. John A. Logan sponsored a bill to reduce the number of officers in the army, to cut the salaries of high-ranking officers, and also to abolish the rank of both general and lieutenant general when vacancies occurred. Sherman denounced the bill, which he suspected was prompted by a personal feud against him and the army. He believed that Logan had never forgiven him for not naming him to the command of the Army of the Tennessee after General McPherson had been killed before Atlanta. Logan's resentment increased when he failed in his bid to become a general in the Regular Army at the end of the Civil War.

Despite vehement opposition from the War Office, Congress passed the army bill. "This is d——d mean treatment," Sherman complained to Sheridan.

Before July 1, 1871, the Regular Army was to be reduced from over 50,000 men to not more than 30,000. "As a matter of course," Sherman wrote Secretary Belknap, "I desire that the reduction should fall as lightly as possible on troops of the line, for if the

companies of cavalry and infantry which occupy the remote posts
are too small, department commanders will be forced to break up
many of the smaller posts, and to use two companies where one
now suffices. . . . The universal experience is that the constant loss
by death, discharge, and desertion, especially in more remote and
dangerous districts, will reduce the actual number present for duty
to about two thirds of the prescribed limit. . . ."

To his brother John, Cump confided that he wished now he
could dispose of his Washington house and return to Saint Louis.
His loyalty to President Grant was all that stood between him and
a hasty departure for Missouri.

Reports from the West in the fall indicated that keeping the
Indian within the narrow confines of reserves was almost impossible. Bands of braves were again roaming the Texas Panhandle,
stealing cattle, raiding isolated homesteads, and attacking overland
freighters. The entire Southwest was clamoring for relief.

Sherman decided to make a personal tour of inspection in the
spring. On his way to Texas, he stopped in New Orleans, where
he delivered a short speech to a group of businessmen on Reconstruction policies, particularly the Ku Klux Act. This legislation,
pushed through Congress by the Radicals, gave the federal courts
original jurisdiction in all cases arising out of terrorism against the
Negro and empowered the president to send Federal troops into
any terrorized zone. Sherman remarked that he thought the statements made in the North about the outrages perpetrated by the
Ku Klux Klan were exaggerated and that the troubles in the South
could best be settled by Southerners without the employment of
Federal troops.

Sherman's speech so impressed Southern newspaper editors,
that they immediately suggested he run against Grant for the
presidency on the Democratic ticket. The *New Orleans Bulletin*
published an article about Sherman and the presidency and concluded: "It will be one of the grandest exploits of the American
people ever attempted if they elevate 'Old Tecumseh' to the
Presidency."

The *Knoxville* (Tenn.) *Press and Herald* declared: "The
friends of the administration may open their batteries upon Sherman and charge him with such motives as their fertile brains may
suggest, but they will not remove from the public mind the con-

viction that he spoke but the solemn truth, and that his remarks are a direct and pointed arraignment of the administration and its reckless doings."

The *Goldsboro* (N.C.) *Messenger* said: "Were we in a position prudently to do so we would not hesitate to express our willingness to accept General Sherman as the candidate at the hands of the national democracy ... although not a partisan, General Sherman has always and constantly favored those broad and liberal views of national policy which so eminently distinguish the democrats. ... We can see no reason why General Sherman, on his New Orleans platform, should not be their choice."

"If General Sherman comes with the olive branch instead of the sword," remarked the *Montgomery* (Ala.) *Mail*, "the South will gladly meet him on half-way ground. For our own part, dropping the veil over his bygone deeds, we can see in him and his well developed character a moral force that having once gained due momentum in the proper direction, will bear down all opposition and rescue the people from the untold difficulties and dangers that surround them."

One Northern editorial stated: "It will be seen that a number of influential Southern organs believe that General Sherman is just the man to check the strides now being made by the radicals to keep the South in a continued state of humiliation, and they are ready to drop the veil over his devastating 'march to the sea,' if they are satisfied that General Sherman is sincere in his recently avowed sentiments ... about the Southern people."

With all the Southern newspaper notoriety accorded Sherman, it is strange that his speech is not referred to in his letters home or to his friends, nor could mention of it be found in the numerous biographies of Ulysses S. Grant or in published memoirs.

On April 28 Sherman and his party reached San Antonio, and a few days later, escorted by 17 troopers of the Tenth Cavalry, they headed for the outposts. Traveling in a vast semicircle, via Forts Concho and Griffin, they rode into Fort Richardson on May 17. Although there had been constant reports of Indian attacks, they had seen no hostiles.

At headquarters in Fort Richardson, Sherman discussed the military situation with the post commander, Col. Ranald S. Mac-

kenzie, Fourth Cavalry, and politely listened to a delegation of
Jacksboro citizens recite a long list of Indian outrages. But since
his trip through Texas had been so uneventful, he was disinclined
to believe such stories.

That evening, however, a wounded man struggled into the
post hospital, identifying himself as Thomas Brazeale, and reported
an attack on his wagon train. The Indians had killed five of his
men.

Sherman immediately sent Mackenzie in pursuit of the hostiles
and dispatched a courier to Fort Griffin ordering a detachment to
search the headwaters of the Little Wichita. Meanwhile Sherman
and his party rode to Fort Sill, Indian Territory, to await results.

On May 23 they arrived at the fort, and Sherman discussed the
recent assault with Indian agent Lawrie Tatum. On the following
Saturday, May 27, Satanta, Satank, Big Tree, and several other
Kiowa chiefs with their women and children rode into the fort for
food. Readily Satanta admitted assaulting the wagon train. Sherman arrested the chiefs for murder and told the other Kiowa that
he intended to send them to Texas for trial.

The prisoners—Satanta, Satank, and Big Tree—were clamped
in irons and loaded into wagons, and under heavy escort, moved
out from the fort. Two days later Satank was killed trying to
escape.

Sherman wrote to his son Tom: "We may have war with
them, but that is better than to permit them to raid on the Fron-
tiers of Texas, and find Refuge here on this Reservation. Of course
the newspapers and those who believe the Indians are always
wronged will raise a howl against me personally, but I know
Indians well enough to believe that they must be made to feel the
power of the United States before they will cease their murders
and Robbery. If the Kioways want to fight it is better for the
soldiers to fight them, than to allow them to attack with impunity
unguarded trains on the Roads leading to the Forts in Texas."

When Sherman returned to the capital, he learned that a Texas
jury, after a dramatic trial which aroused national interest, had
found Satanta and Big Tree guilty of murder, and the judge had
sentenced them to hang. The judge was inundated with letters,
mostly from Quakers, pleading for the Indians' lives. Under
mounting criticism, the governor of Texas issued a proclamation
commuting the sentences to life imprisonment.

This action was damned throughout the state. Many men believed that commuting the sentences would mean the eventual release of the chiefs and that the frontier would then suffer as never before. And from Washington Sherman warned that if the Indians went free, "no life from Kansas to the Rio Grande will be safe, and no soldier will ever again take a live prisoner."

Rumors were current that Sherman and Secretary of War Belknap were at odds and that the secretary was trying to usurp the general's functions and power. Sherman was deeply troubled over the increasing strength of the secretary. The old method of ignoring the General of the Army and consulting only with bureau subordinates was reinstituted. Sherman discovered himself in the embarrassing position of learning from newspapers and friends of orders and decisions relating to the regulation and discipline of the army. These were issued without his knowledge though sometimes in his name.

Sherman's respect for President Grant was eroding. "I have observed with great concern," Cump wrote John, "that General Grant is moved by the urgent demands of remonstrances of men who care no more for him, and who would gladly sacrifice him .... [like] Logan and men of that stripe."

"I feel every day the growing jealousy of Grant and his Cabinet, who think I do not blow their trumpet loud enough," Sherman wrote Thomas Ewing. "This is not my task or my office, and I'm resolved not to have my latter tour of life poisoned by political factions. I will not be used by either party, and will consequently be kicked by both. Little by little the fame acquired by war will sink, and I can quietly withdraw to St. Louis, and from that point do such duties as may be specially assigned me, leaving the War Department to control the Army in all its details, which is now done in offensive obtrustion [*sic*] upon my real office."

Then, he added: "Ellen may have conveyed her impression that the President and Secretary are disposed to go back on me. ... This is partially true, but the motive is general and not special or personal."

To John, Cump wrote: "My office has been by law stripped of all the influence and prestige it possessed under Grant, even in matters of discipline and army control I am neglected, overlooked, and snubbed." Later, he told a friend: "There is, in fact, no use for a general now, provided that the law and custom sanction the issuance of orders direct by the adjutant general in the name of the Secretary of War, and, should a fair opportunity offer, I would save Congress the trouble of abolishing my office."

That fall he received a direct rebuke from the president. Grant and Secretary Belknap, over the protests of Sherman, eliminated one military department in the West. The area's settlers, assuming that Sherman was responsible, vehemently denounced him. Outraged and embittered, Sherman wrote Sheridan that it was "one of the meanest acts ever done by persons professing friendship."

"It was the sole act of the President after he knew the full outcry the knowledge [of] it would cause," Cump told John. "Grant has simply let down his pressure and now allows his understoppers to throw off on me. This is eminently mean—but he has done it more than once, merely saying that he cannot prevent the misconstructions of newspaper reporters."

Yet these grievances and irritations failed to shake the bonds between Sherman and Grant that had been forged by the war. "I saw him yesterday," Sherman wrote his brother, "and he seems to be unconscious that he is losing the confidence of some of the best men of the country. Still, I want to stand by him, for as his term draws to a close he will have a hard time, and I don't want you to abandon him, unless self-respect compels you. . . ."

The Grand Tour

ONE EVENING at the Arlington Hotel in Washington, Sherman dined with Adm. James Alden and Secretary of War Belknap. During the dessert Alden casually announced that he was soon to take command of the United States Navy squadron operating in Mediterranean waters and that in late November he was leaving New York for Gibraltar in the steam frigate *Wabash*. Half jokingly, he invited Sherman to go along as far as Gibraltar and then suggested he tour the Continent and parts of Africa and Asia on his own. Later that night Cump talked the matter over with Ellen, who was enthusiastic. The chance to escape the rigors of War Department politics had come at the opportune time.

Sherman immediately plunged into plans for the trip, poring over travel books and losing himself in their pictures. He would be accompanied by his friend and aide, Col. J. C. Audenried, and by the president's son, Lt. Fred Grant, Fourth Cavalry.

Amid the excitement of planning and packing, tragedy struck the Sherman family. Thomas Ewing died at Lancaster on October 26, within two months of his 82nd birthday. It was a sorrowful trip back to Ohio. All during the funeral it rained. The person Mr. Ewing's death affected most was Ellen. Still terribly shaken, she wrote her aunt, Mrs. Jane Ewing Latimer, answering the letter of condolances: "I cannot tell you my dear Aunt, the grief I feel at losing so grand and good a Parent. Such a Sense of utter desolation it has never been my lot to experience.

"I feel that Earth has no longer any charms for me. The brightness has gone out of everything and the best of all earthly goodness has passed away.

"He was so ... tender, true and just. So sympathetic and

343

patient, so wise and so discreet, so brave & so forebearing. In short, he exemplified all the virtues, in his long and useful life, and during every year of it, and you are right in saying that his character was without a blemish. . . .

"My best friend has gone from earth and I feel that I must now prepare to join him & look forward only to my own hour."

On Friday, November 17, the *Wabash* got under way in New York Harbor and steamed down the East River. From a tugboat Ellen and the children waved good-bye and watched until the frigate was lost from sight. As the *Wabash* passed Adm. S. C. Rowan's fleet near Sandy Hook, she saluted and then moved out to sea. Cump stood forward on the main deck, feeling the rise and fall of the prow, exulting as the ship increased the distance between him and Washington.

After reaching Gibraltar, Sherman and his companions said good-bye to Admiral Alden and journeyed on to Granada, Madrid, and Lyons. From Marseilles, Cump wrote Minnie: "The facilities of travel and comfort of living here are not so good as with us, and I pity Audenried, who is kept busy from morning till night with everlasting demands of servants and runners. I'd not take a party of ladies through Europe, and have all the bother of getting tickets, look after baggage and paying the everlasting fees, for all the pleasure of foreign travel. The cars also are not heated, and all that is attempted is a flat tub full of hot water, put in the cars to keep the feet warm."

In Naples Sherman and his friends went on an excursion and picnic to the ruins of Pompeii, during which the Italians made a special excavation for the general's benefit. "Large numbers of Americans participated in this picnic," remembered Audenried, "and in one of the ancient buildings toasts were drunk, songs sung, and the walls gave back Sherman's *March to the Sea*. The excavations did not bring forth any hidden treasures. With the exception of broken tiles, water-jugs, and . . . some copper coin . . . nothing was found.

"The party," Audenried continued, "made the ascent of Mt. Vesuvius, and wandered about the cone in a very dangerous proximity to the mouth. A few days after Vesuvius was emitting a stream of burning lava. Sherman was quite exhausted by this excursion, and I doubt if the marches of war so completely fatigued him."

In Egypt Sherman was greeted by Gen. Charles P. Stone, who had served in the United States Army and who was now adjutant general for the viceroy. After several days visiting museums, the pyramids, and paying official calls on Egyptian royalty, Sherman wrote Minnie, who loved horseback riding: "I have seen no place in Europe or Africa, so favorable as Washington for horseback exercise. In Rome, no one can ride on the smooth hard streets, and we have to send the saddle horses to the outskirts, and go out there in carriages. Here the dust is so suffocating, that there is no pleasure in riding, for the main roads are too dusty, and the cross roads are so narrow that one cannot proceed except at a walk."

On his last night in Cairo, collecting his thoughts on what he had seen and heard, Cump wrote to Tommy: "The time was and only ten or twenty years ago that a Jew or Christian dog was hunted and stoned through the streets of Cairo. Now however, the Christian dogs are tolerated universally as they are skilled mechanics and have brought steam engines to help the poor laborers in pumping water from the fields, railroads, that skim over deserts, and telegraphs that carry messages in minutes instead of at the expense of human toil and fatigue. The facilities of modern science are breaking down the religious prejudices .... and very soon at this rate all the barriers which have for hundreds of years separated the human family into warlike feuds will be leveled and all people can worship God in the manner that seems to them best.

"On looking over a field with its camels, asses, buffaloes, and cattle, all hard at work, old men and women, men, boys, and girls hoeing ... and watering their fields," he continued, one "... is carried back hundreds of years and can appreciate the advantages we enjoy in the United States. The villages are the most repulsive houses I have ever seen for people to live in, they are of mud and sunburnt brick and clustered so close that they look like wasp nests or an old abandoned brick Kiln. Indeed the fertile land is so small that the people seem to begrudge the people space enough to sleep on. . . . Our Negroes when slaves had better houses and better food & treatment than the Egyptian peoples, and the gap between the poor & rich was and is greater than between slave & his master."

Turning his attention to Tommy's schooling, Cump wrote: "I

repeat that if you keep a steady sure progress, always learning well what you do study, and not attempt to gloss over anything you will win in the end. . . . I am not satisfied that [the school in] Georgetown is a . . . [place] with Professors skilled in teaching modern sciences that . . . are remodeling the world, but your Mama thinks Religion is so important that everything else, must give place to it, and now that you are big enough to think for yourself, you must direct your mind to the acquisition of one class of knowledge or the other.

"Logic, Mathematics & the Natural exact Science," he added, embrace "knowledge of things and of laws as they actually exist—the languages and Moral studies contemplate men—& objects in the artificial situations arrived at by Experience or tradition, and I cannot but give the former a higher place among educational establishments, leaving the moral & religious training to the family, to the house.—Your religion is good enough and I would not shake your Faith in it so long as you leave to others a free choice according to their moral sense and their means of judgment."

From Egypt the party journeyed to Constantinople (Istanbul), and then to Sebastopol, Yalta, and Tiflis (Tbilisi) in the Caucasus, where "all speak Russian, certainly the most incomprehensible language possible. In all other languages, such as French, Spanish, Italian, I can make out at least what a servant wants to say, but in Russian I can make no head or tail; I cannot possibly remember the name of a person, town, river, or anything else for five minutes. . . . The Russian language is simply incomprehensible. It has thirty-six letters, and some of them, though like ours, differ in meaning."

Although he disliked the Russian language, Sherman was enthusiastic over Moscow: "Taken as a whole, it is more attractive than Rome or Constantinople. Its Asiatic character is represented in the architecture of its churches and in the appearance of its people, though the stores, hotels, palaces, and many private houses are of a European type." He liked the Russian's religious sincerity and zeal, and the combined Moslem and Catholic forms pleased him, as they reinforced his belief that true religious ideas were universal and that form and ceremony were unimportant.

From Saint Petersburg (Leningrad) Sherman wrote Tommy: "I've bought the girls what girls usually value most, jewelry, and for your Mama I have ordered a marble bust of myself, as well as a cameo. So that to finish the family I must get something for you and Cumpy. I thought for you a box of Mathematical instruments of the best quality, such as used by engineers and architects. I also thought at Geneva or London I'd buy for myself a new plain watch, and give you or Cumpy my present one which is really a first class gold watch. Now if there is anything special you prefer, not too costly, let me know, so that I can hear at Paris."

Sherman enjoyed Vienna, its people, its parks and gardens, its broad streets and avenues, and its fine business establishments. "In the company of our consul," Sherman recalled, "we put in . . . [an] evening by going to a garden called *Volksgarten*, where we heard Strauss's band, and saw Strauss, who looked like a wild musician, waving his arms to the music, and occasionally seizing his violin and torturing it for a few minutes. I saw the model of band-masters—one who grows and thrives in spite of fun and ridicule. The custom of the Germans of going to these cheap open air concerts must be, on the whole, healthful, socially and morally, for everybody bears testimony to utter absence of drunkenness and rowdyism. And yet the whole community seems, for pleasure and recreation, to rush for beer. Here and in all German cities, towns, etc., these gardens are institutions. . . ."

After sight-seeing in Geneva, the Sherman party inspected the battlefields of the recent Franco-Prussian War, and the general came away with a high regard for Prussian strategy and tactics. "I must admit," he noted, "that so far as my observation goes, the Prussian people are more intelligent and industrious than the French, and their troops very much superior in bearing, appearance, dress, and organization." Cump wrote Tommy that if his mother consented, he could join the group in Paris.

On July 6 Sherman arrived in Paris, and in the days that followed he and his friends marched on tirelessly to receptions, museums, churches, and government buildings. "A stranger seeing Paris full of carriages, horses, well-dressed people, stores crowded with goods, and every window displaying finery," Sherman wrote later, "could not realize that but a year and a half ago it was besieged and bombarded [by the Prussians], and later still was in the hands of an irresponsible mob."

After visiting the French countryside, Cump wrote Minnie: "I find no part of Europe more clean and healthy than New England, and the country near New York." Sherman's experiences did not cause him to reevaluate his belief in the superiority of the United States. Although he thoroughly enjoyed the wonders of Europe, Asia, and Africa, and the hospitality extended him, he never wavered in his conviction that his own heritage offered world leadership.

Sherman's son Tom arrived in Paris, and together they departed for England. During their stay in London, a small foreshadowing of a future conflict within the Sherman family was suggested by some of Cump's remarks. In one of her letters, Ellen made some comparisons between the Roman Catholic and Protestant religions, uncomplimentary to the latter. Cump made a small remonstrance: "I don't doubt your sincerity, but only fear that your zeal for your Cause absorbs all the better instincts of your nature and makes you see things through the colored lens you describe for me and others. I have afforded Tom every chance possible to conform to his Religion, and only want him whilst enjoying the widest privileges, not to question the sincerity of others."

On another point too he voiced a strong opinion. Ellen had reported the entrance of their niece Eleanor (daughter of Hugh Boyle Ewing) into a convent. This step, declared Cump, was natural for the girl, since all her education had tended in that direction. But, "I certainly do not wish [Ellie and Rachel] to follow their cousin into a Convent, but to grow up qualified to make good wives."

After a month and a half in England, the party boarded the steamer *Baltic* at Queenstown and made a speedy and comfortable passage to New York, arriving on September 16.

Saint Louis and Washington

By THE TIME Sherman arrived back in the United States, many people in the North were vigorously opposing the Radical programs on the tariff, railroad land grants, and other national issues. In the South testimony offered at a few trials of individuals indicted under the Ku Klux Act and evidence inadvertently publicized by a congressional committee's report disclosed that the severe political and social restrictions which the Radicals had fastened upon the South were retarding its recovery. Under mounting pressure, Congress passed a liberal amnesty act, which restored voting and officeholding privileges to most Southern whites. In addition, the Freedman's Bureau, the protector of Negro rights, was allowed to go out of existence.

Throughout September and October the nation was again engaged in a presidential campaign. General Grant was reelected for a second term by a majority of 763,000 votes and carried all but six states. His share of the popular vote, 55.6 percent, made his the most decisive victory since Andrew Jackson's in 1828.

The situation at the War Department was the same as when Sherman had left for Europe. Still disturbed over the loss of his power to Belknap, the general tersely wrote in his annual report: "No part of the Army is under my immediate control, and the existing Army regulations devolve on the Secretary of War the actual command of the military peace establishment, and all responsibility therefor, so that I forbear making any further recommendations or report."

A letter from General Sheridan in Chicago reported that there had been "no general hostilities of the Indians" during the summer of 1872, but that "the number of murders and depredations committed by small war parties... [was] greater than during the previous year." Sherman was disquieted over Indian affairs in general and conjectured that the red man's depredations would continue against the white settlements until major warfare broke out.

The army had not long to wait. During that winter and the spring of 1873, war with the Modoc Indians erupted along the Oregon-California border. The whites as well as the Indians massacred and scalped. In one instance the frontiersmen invited 46 red men to a peace conference and then systematically shot all but 3.

Captain Jack, the Modoc chief, and his warriors roamed the area around Tule Lake and resisted army units which sought to evict them. At midnight April 11/12 Sherman was awakened at home by General Townsend with the news that Gen. Edward R. S. Canby and another commissioner, who were sent to negotiate peace terms with the Modoc Indians, had been slain. At the White House Grant sanctioned "the most severe punishment," and Sherman wired Gen. Alvan C. Gillem to make an attack "so strong and persistent that their fate may be commensurate with their crime. You will be fully justified in their utter extermination."

Army detachments eventually rounded up Captain Jack and his braves, who had taken refuge in the rugged lava beds along the Oregon-California boundary. A military commission, after listening to testimony, found Captain Jack and three other Modoc guilty and sentenced them to death. They were hanged at Fort Klamath.

Later, during a House investigating committee hearing, a congressman asked Sherman: "In your judgment, if the War Department had charge of the Indians [instead of the Indian Bureau] would the Modoc war have occurred?"

Sherman replied: "My own opinion is that it would not have occurred.... It was brought on step by step, until finally it became a war, by our attempting to reconcile irreconcilabilities. I have no doubt that the Indians, in the aggregate and in detail, have suffered great wrong at our hands. But how are you going to settle this great continent from the Atlantic to the Pacific without doing some harm to the Indians who stand in the way? I do not know how you can do it. There has to be violence somewhere. If that violence be tempered with justice, you approach a just solution to the problem; but there must be violence or force used.

"The Government must use force," Sherman continued, "or individuals will do violence. For instance, we cannot allow the Indians to roam at large through Western Kansas and Western Nebraska, because if they do there will surely be collision and bloodshed. In order to prevent that, you must take these Indians and assign them a separate place where they *must* remain. . . . But they must be made to stay there. How the thing can be done without physical force I cannot comprehend. Moral force is not strong enough. Moral force is merely the impulse of the mind or conscience. The Indians hardly understand it."

In addition to his concerns over Indian problems Sherman was also worried by matters at the War Department and on Capitol Hill which were going badly for him. Before a House committee on military affairs, which was considering reducing the army from 30,000 men to 25,000, he said that the Regular Army was "a curious compound" of cavalry, infantry, and artillery and that Secretary of War Belknap was actually commanding the army.

During the committee hearings Sherman argued that reducing the army was dangerous to the national interests. "If reduction is forced upon the Army by the financial condition of the country (of which Congress must be the sole judge), I unhesitatingly say," Sherman declared, "that you had better cut off at the head than at the foot; that the most valuable part of our military establishment is in the inverse order of its general arrangement. I look upon two cavalry regiments or even infantry regiments as worth more than the whole general staff, *myself*, included. I would rather see Congress abolish me and my office, and turn me loose to get my own living . . . than to see it disband two such regiments."

Again he said: "The officers of the regular regiments naturally look to me as their representative here in Washington. Their interest in their profession has been very much shaken by the repeated reductions of the Army since the close of the war, every one of which reductions has fallen upon the line of the Army. This makes them feel insecure in their profession. They are fearful that at any moment they may be turned out to earn their living in the best way they can, and it shakes their faith in the perpetuity of their employment and profession.

"Even now," Sherman went on, "the best officers of the Army are applicants for paymasterships and staff positions, or for anything that looks like a harbor of refuge. I am sorry to see it, because I know it is injurious to our profession to have our most intelligent officers looking elsewhere for employment. . . . I think it to be the interest of the nation that the officers should have some assurance that the reduction of the Army is at an end."

For over a month Sherman and other high-ranking officers urged the House committee not to reduce the military establishment, but in the end they were defeated. Congress passed a bill cutting the army's size to 25,000 men.

As a result of this action, Sherman asked Grant to define more clearly his field of duty, but the president failed to do so. Belknap refused to answer the general's letters.

"Grant did not act generously, and friendly by me when president," Sherman wrote later, ". . . and when I personally appealed to him to protect me against the usurpations of Belknap he did not. . . . You know that during the whole time I never uttered a syllable of complaint and even now I don't want . . . my friends to intimate a word of complaint."

Sherman now had had enough of Washington and its politics. Therefore in the spring of 1874 he applied formally to the secretary of war for permission to move his headquarters in the fall from Washington to Saint Louis, citing the high expenses of living in the capital city. By going to Saint Louis, he emphasized, "I am centrally located, and should the occasion arise, I can personally proceed to any point on this continent where my services are needed." Both Belknap and Grant assented to Sherman's move.

Military men, however, disapproved. Who was going to represent them in Washington? Running off to Missouri, General Sheridan reiterated, would not solve any problems. "I assure you my dear General," he declared, "you shake the confidence of the people and the army in the stability and steadiness which they have always attached to your character. You bring a condition on the army which will ruin it forever by establishing a precedent in which its General in Chief [is] in retirement for all time to come. You endanger its very existence by putting its command absolutely in the hands of the Secretary of War . . . who can compromise our integrity by attempting to use us for personal or political purposes."

"Could I be of any service to the Army here," Sherman responded, "I would make any personal sacrifice, but without some recognition on the part of the President it is impossible."

One Republican newspaper in Washington alleged that Sherman was moving to Saint Louis because he was "not in harmony with the Administration" and therefore urged him to resign. "By my office I am above party, and am not bound in honor or fact to toady to anybody," Cump told John Sherman. "Therefore I shall never resign, and shall never court any other office, so they may reserve their advice to men who seek it."

Philemon Tecumseh Sherman, the general's youngest son, then only seven, recalled later: "I was too young at the time to comprehend it [leaving Washington], but later, through listening to table talk between my father and mother, I learned pretty much all about it.... The particular cause for the removal of my father's 'headquarters' was that the Secretary of War—General Belknap—was directing certain matters in the Army, over my father's head, leaving him ignorant of much that was done.... My father had felt hurt that General Grant had sustained Secretary Belknap in this matter. But that feeling quickly passed; and ... this incident ... [never] lessened my father's respect and admiration for General Grant's personal character or ability as a soldier."

In the early fall of 1874, before the Sherman family moved to Saint Louis, Tom Sherman left for his first year at Yale University, and Minnie became the wife of Lt. Thomas William Fitch, United States Navy, in one of the most lavish weddings ever witnessed in the capital. Ellen was determined to show Washington society what an impressive affair a Roman Catholic marriage could be. The Church of Saint Aloysius was crowded with celebrities—President Grant and members of his cabinet, congressmen, justices of the Supreme Court, generals and admirals, foreign diplomats, and prominent families, such as the Drexels of Philadelphia. The New York merchant Alexander T. Stewart sent the bride a $1,000 lace handkerchief, and from the khedive of Egypt came a diamond necklace insured for $80,000. The wedding was front page news. The *Washington Chronicle* headlines read, "Our Minnie: The

General's Daughter: The Sherman-Fitch Wedding: Grave Men and Handsome Women: A Gorgeous and Brilliant Display of Wedding Presents."

That fall the Sherman family moved back to their home on Garrison Avenue, in Saint Louis. Sherman's critics castigated him for fleeing Washington and relinquishing his duty, while some of his friends were perplexed over what looked to be a retreat from the life and politics of the army. Some viewed his action as short-sighted and petty; but perhaps Sherman, besides seeking a respite from Washington politics, wanted to be nearer the scene of the Indian troubles and to shake Grant and Belknap into the realiza-tion that the peaceful settlement of the West was basically the responsibility of the United States Army.

The most intimate picture of the Sherman family during those years in Saint Louis is best revealed in the unpublished "Recollec-tions of Early Days," written by the general's youngest son, Philemon Tecumseh, when he reached manhood.

Each evening at the dinner table, when the family was eating alone, Sherman always left the table before dessert, "bequeathing his share of it to me, unless warned in advance that it would con-sist of one of the few special things he liked, especially boiled apple dumplings, plum or fig pudding with hard sauce. . . . Although he ate sparingly and detested long dinners of many courses, my father was highly appreciative of good food. For him specially there were served at home dishes of hot red peppers, to be added to his soups, and hot sauces, a taste for which he acquired in the old days in California.

"On the side, my father regularly took two drinks of Bourbon whiskey and water a day, which he persisted in doing openly, instead of retiring to the woodshed—when on visits in the dry states of Iowa and Kansas."

After dinner the Shermans usually adjourned to the parlor, where Ellen played the piano or harp and Cump and the children sang, especially Irish and Scottish songs and Stephen Foster's "Negro melodies."

"My father was always . . . extremely fond of music—of a kind," Tecumseh said, "though he preferred it in short doses, not to exceed an hour. He was [especially] fond of all melodies; marches and national anthems, violin solos; and light operas including many of the higher class Italian operas. German opera, renditions on the piano of compositions by great masters, orchestral music generally and what was then known as 'chamber music' he couldn't stand."

As the months slipped by, Lizzie, now 23, took over the management of the house, to Ellen's relief, and gradually extended her control to include her father's wearing apparel, "by the simple process of removing his old hats, shoes, and clothes when she thought fit and ordering new ones to replace them. My father submitted cheerfully as to clothes, he liked neat suits and fresh linen, but he complained bitterly when his oldest, shabbiest and most comfortable hats and shoes disappeared."

During the afternoons when he was not at army headquarters, Sherman spent a good deal of time at home in his "office," or library, where ladies, except for momentary interruptions, were "taboo." The office had windows fronting Garrison Avenue, so that prospective callers could see in and ascertain whether the general was at home, "a great convenience to his cronies who dropped in for brief informal talks."

"In late afternoons," remembered Tecumseh, "there were streams of men coming in, many visitors of distinction, but in large part old soldiers seeking help or advice. Tradesmen and mendicants other than old soldiers were summarily dismissed.

"Union and Confederate veterans were treated alike; but they all had to have honorable discharges or equivalent papers. Many were in temporary distress only, dead broke for the time being and hungry but with work in prospect. Those my father fed (with ham, bread and butter, coffee, which the cook kept ready and which were eaten standing from the top of a high map case) and helped with a little money.

"To some he gave old clothes or an order on a special shop for clothes, shoes or a note to a railroad official requesting transportation. And to others he gave advice as to pensions or possibilities of employment. He never gave much money; but for his restricted clientele he carried on a charity bureau that in the aggregate cost a substantial proportion of his income."

When cornered by a "long winded talker," the general had "a defense in his ability to go to sleep anywhere and anytime, sitting up. Quite a number of times . . . I've noted looks of astonishment come over the faces of people who were boring him. He had gone to sleep!"

Sherman was particularly anxious that his children acquire correct reading habits. Instead of "dime novels," which the general abhorred, Tecumseh, by the time he was 11, was put to work reading military reports of the Indian campaigns and Washington Irving's *Adventures of Captain Bonneville*. "As time went on he led me through Shakespeare's tragedies and historical plays, nearly all of Scott's and Dickens' novels, some of Thackeray's, a number of Irving's, Marryatt's and Lever's works and many of Burns' and Scott's poems, besides later Bret Harte's and Mark Twain's stories and many histories and biographies as they were published.

"Lincoln's Gettysburg Address and Second Inaugural were marked by him for repeated study by me, as was a series of Wellington's Despatches, which he commended as models of lucidity and conciseness. . . . With much of my reading under my father's supervision he furnished me with appropriate maps, so that I knew on the map the . . . routes followed by Napoleon's, Wellington's, and Washington's armies. It added greatly to the interest and understanding of my readings."

For years after the war Sherman had been working off and on writing his memoirs. Finally, in his office in Saint Louis, he found time to finish them. "Sent off the manuscript of two volumes, mostly of the Civil War," he told Phil Ewing, "that may bring me some profit, but more controversy. I have carefully prepared it, and made it as little objectionable as possible, yet the statement of facts may revive old memories that it may be ought to remain in oblivion."

Sherman stated in the preface, which was written "to his comrades in arms, volunteers and regulars," that ten years had passed since the close of the Civil War and yet no satisfactory history of that conflict had been written. The *Memoirs*, he said, "is not designed as a history of the war, or even as a complete account of all the incidents in which the writer bore a part, but merely his recollection of events, corrected by a reference to his own memoranda, which may assist the future historian when he comes to describe the whole, and account for the motives and reasons which influenced some of the actors in the grand drama of war.

"I trust," he added, "a perusal of these pages will prove

interesting to the survivors, who have manifested so often their intense love of the 'cause' which moved a nation to vindicate its own authority; and, equally so, to the rising generation, who therefrom may learn that a country and government such as ours are worth fighting for, and dying for, if need be."

Direct, candid, often blunt, the memoirs are among the most articulate and engrossing ever written by an important general. Overnight they became a national best seller.

During the first years after their return to Saint Louis, Sherman was harassed by financial worries. The move to Missouri had been an expensive one, and the taxes on his property holdings were extremely high. He had been forced to sell his vacant house on I Street in Washington and borrow money—"A thing I hoped *never* to do!" His concern about the nation's economic condition increased his pessimism about his personal financial future. "Do study economy," he urged Tom at Yale, "for I see hard times ahead. Things are out of joint and you must observe that the whole country is effected [*sic*]."

From New Haven, Tom answered: "I am sorry I am unable to say: 'I will be economical,' for I am quite sensible of the fact that none of us boys know what economy is, as we never have had a chance to earn money, to feel its real value. I am living as you know with a dozen fellows who are pretty well off, dress well, and spend quite a good deal among themselves."

Then Tom added: "I try not to be extravagant, but between extravagance and economy it seems to me there is a long margin. College is a poor place at best to learn economy."

Sherman often stated to Tom that he was relying on him to help eventually in carrying some of the family's financial burdens. During these years the general's correspondence with Tom indicates that Cump was looking forward more and more to the time when he could place much of the family's financial management into his son's hands. "I want to give each of the children a good education," he wrote Tom, "and the equivalent of $10,000 on starting out on their own hook. This is the best I can promise and it will require economy and self denial on my part to do this! You are now old enough to help me and to understand the Mathematics of the situation."

Sherman wrote his son often, not only about financial affairs, but also about other matters. In one letter the general told Tom: "The chief advantage of your present college is to bring you into contact with the young men, who are likely to become the Leaders of the next Age. You will in the future constantly meet them and their acquaintance and friendship will be valuable always. Therefore without being too familiar keep on the best of terms with the fellow students."

In the fall of 1874 Grant dispatched Federal soldiers to New Orleans to sustain a minority Republican faction in power. Bitter rivalries between political factions had engulfed Louisiana for three years.

In Washington many congressmen were upset by Grant's reliance on force to prop up a minority group. Sherman shared this concern. However, he had watched passively as the attorney general and Secretary Belknap sent army units into Louisiana without consulting him. He had neither the inclination nor the authority to countermand orders from Washington. To the commander of the troops assigned to New Orleans, Sherman wrote: "The troops . . . were sent at the insistence of the Attorney Gen-[era]l . . . who doubtless supposed them necessary to prevent conflict and even bloodshed. He may have been right, but politically he has brought on a catastrophe which will cause infinite trouble. . . . Coercion by the military has been ever pregnant with danger, for the theory of our government, right or wrong, that the people of every State are competent to select their Governors and Rulers, is settled in this country, and I confess I looked upon the increased military display in New Orleans as wrong."

Popular indignation over the army's role in Louisiana politics reinforced Sherman's conviction that the military would lose public support if it became enmeshed in the South's affairs. "I have always thought it wrong to bolster up weak State Governments with our troops," he wrote John. "We should keep peace always, but not act as bailiffs, constables, & catch thieves. That should be beneath a soldier's vocation."

During the spring and summer of 1875 Sherman was again troubled over the tense Indian situation. Stories were current that gold seekers were ready to invade the Sioux lands in the Black Hills. The general announced that if the miners penetrated the reservation, they would be driven out by the army. Although rumors circulated that there would be an all-out Indian war that summer, the hot months passed without a major incident. The Sioux continued to make incursions into white man's territory, stealing cattle from the farms along the Union Pacific Railroad, but there was less damage to life and property in 1875 than in any previous year. Sherman predicted that as more and more immigrants settled on the plains, there would be fewer and fewer Indian raids, and eventually all the red men would be established on reservations. "But," he remarked, "until they acquire habits of industry in farming or in stock-raising, they will need food from the General Government."

The nation was beginning to think seriously about the presidential election of 1876. Who would replace General Grant? During his tenure Grant had proven to be a poor chief executive. One of his most serious weaknesses was his inability to cope with corruption in the government. He did not cause the corruption, nor did he participate in the rush to "fatten the public trough," but he did nothing to prevent the shocking scandals—the Crédit Mobilier, the "salary grab" act, the Whiskey Ring, election frauds, and others—that disgraced his administration.

Spending a few days with Orville Browning at his home in Quincy, Ill., Sherman spoke bluntly of how poor a president Grant had been. According to Browning's diary, the general remarked: "The President was very deficient in the qualities of a statesman—that he had no comprehension of the fundamental principles of civil governments, constitutions and laws—that he had been surrounded by a weak cabinet. . . ."

Further, he had failed to restore harmony among the various sections of the country. Sherman criticized Grant's mishandling of the South and his domination by the Radicals. The South was in a worse condition under Grant than at the close of the war. The preponderant share of leadership, influence, and power was exercised by the scalawags, native white Southerners who supported Radical Reconstruction, and by carpetbaggers, Northern Radicals who had moved into the South in numbers to demonstrate what "brains and sinew" could accomplish there.

The mere existence of the carpetbag governments within their borders seemed insulting and shameful to many Southerners. But carpetbag corruption made the affront even harder to bear. During the Grant Administration, the bonded debt of the 11 ex-Confederate states grew by over $100 million. To Sherman, all the animosities in the South, engendered by the Civil War, would long since have been allayed and all the damages repaired under a wise administration.

Turning to the upcoming presidential election, Browning asked Sherman if he would accept the candidacy if nominated.

"I do not wish to be President," Sherman said, "and I will not, under any circumstances, be a candidate."

Later that summer, while in Washington, Browning confided to John Sherman that he wished Cump would reconsider and become a candidate for the Republican nomination. John said his brother would never consent in advance, but if nominated by the Republican party, he thought Cump would not decline.

John, however, did not believe that his brother could ever be nominated, so he came out early in support of Gov. Rutherford B. Hayes of Ohio. This endorsement had Cump's wholehearted approval. As far back as 1871 he had been impressed with a speech Hayes had made at a soldier's reunion. "I agree with you," he wrote John, "that no one should be the President unless he was with us heart and soul in the Civil War; and Hayes fills the bill perfectly."

Early in 1876 scandal rocked the War Department when it was learned that Secretary Belknap had received bribes from a trader at Fort Sill, Indian Territory. Belknap resigned his office and was immediately impeached by the House of Representatives and tried by the Senate. A majority of the senators, but not the necessary two-thirds, voted for his conviction.

Upon learning of Belknap's resignation, Sherman wrote his son that "I am glad the thing has *come out*, for Belknap behaved shamefully to me. . . . Now Belknap has fallen so hard that his acts will never give me any more trouble." He added, however, that such developments would not alter his future conduct. "I will never remove to Washington. It is no place for us; we have reason to be thankful that we are out of the maelstrom of scandal & slander."

As a replacement, the president picked Alphonso Taft of

Cincinnati, a judge of more respectability than talent. No sooner had Taft taken office than he turned to Sherman for counsel, and without question, assigned to the general any prerogatives that he chose to assert, confining himself chiefly to matters of law and finance. Sherman now put aside his feelings about Washington and said he was willing to comply with the secretary's wish and return to the capital in the fall.

For Ellen the news of again living in Washington "hit like a regular bomb shell," as she hated the city and its social life. But she told Cump that if he wished to have the family with him, the question was settled. She did, however, refuse to ship her furniture east and pressured her husband not to buy any more Washington property. "I am unwilling to go into a new house of our own in Washington with the mean worn patched damaged dirty old furniture Mrs. Grant defrauded you into paying her enormously for . . . if we are to live temporarily in Washington let us rent or board in order to be unencumbered when we leave."

The Sherman clan was now well scattered. Minnie, who was the mother of a baby boy, lived in Pittsburgh. Her husband had resigned from the navy to become president of a company manufacturing wire cable. Tom was still at Yale; Rachel and Ellie were in a convent school near Cincinnati. Only Lizzie, still unmarried, and Tecumseh remained at home.

In his Saint Louis headquarters Sherman listened to his officers, who were predicting the outbreak of a massive Indian war on the plains. To General Sheridan he wrote that a showdown was near and that he was anxious to "finish this Sioux business, which is about the last of the Indians."

War broke out that spring. It was during this conflict that Col. George Armstrong Custer and his cavalry force made their famous "last stand" against Crazy Horse and Sitting Bull in the battle of the Little Big Horn on June 25, 1876. The Sioux annihilated Custer and his entire command.

News of the tragedy traveled slowly, and it was not until after the Fourth of July that word of the disaster reached the East. The whole nation was enraged, and westerners cried for "extermination" of the Indians.

Throughout the summer the Sioux eluded army units, but shortages of ammunition and food forced them to scatter. An ill-timed attack on a wagon train gave away the location of the largest group of hostiles, and their capture in October ended the war. Sitting Bull and others fled to Canada but, facing starvation, they returned several years later.

By the fall the Sherman family was again living in Washington, renting several suites at Ebbitt House. The financial worries which had plagued Cump for years were now increasing. Heavier taxes in Missouri were eating into his income from rents on which he depended to supplement his salary. Living expenses at Ebbitt House and the cost of official entertaining were exorbitant, while at the same time, Congress was threatening to slash the salaries of military officers and again reduce the size of the army.

Sherman was pleased when his son Tom, recently graduated from Yale, went to Saint Louis to manage his father's business interests and study law. With business acumen, he put the Shermans' financial affairs in order. He controlled all the rents and tax payments, paid all premiums on insurance policies (which the general often forgot to do), closely observed his father's banking operations, and with an eye on the market, advised on speculative ventures. Gradually, Sherman concentrated all of his financial affairs in Saint Louis.

Tom gave every indication that he fully intended to live and work in Saint Louis. He tried to hold on to the Garrison Avenue house by temporarily renting it. "My feeling in giving it up was this," he wrote, "that I was giving up a present enjoyment for the sake of future happiness, for, living in St. Louis, I shall always look forward to the time when some part of the family or the whole family will be gathered into the old house."

In the months that followed, the general came to depend upon Tom more and more. In many letters to his son, Cump used the phrase: "You may do what you please . . . always sure that I will approve of anything." It was Sherman's intention to move back to Saint Louis when he retired, settle down in peace with the family, and let Tom manage all his business interests.

With the approach of the 1876 presidential nominating conventions, dissension divided the Grand Old Party, as the Republicans had taken to calling themselves. Again General Sherman was urged to run. "I thought Every body knew my general opinions . . . ," he wrote a friend. "I cannot hesitate to answer you in such a way as to admit of no misconstruction. I never have been, am not now, and never will be a Candidate for the high office of President before any Convention, or the people. I shall always prefer to see that office filled by one of the millions who in the Civil War stood by the Union firmly and unequivocally; and of these I notice many names willing and capable, prominent that of General Hayes now Governor of Ohio, whom we know as a fine Officer, and a Gentleman in every sense. I do not however wish to be misconstrued as pressing my advise on anybody in his choice of the man."

When the Republican convention met in Cincinnati, the delegates, balking at the attempts to renominate Grant, threw their support to Hayes of Ohio. The Democrats had been out of office for 16 years. Eastern, Southern, and Western Democrats differed on important matters, such as money policy and the tariff, but hunger for the long-awaited spoils of office now united them temporarily. The Grant scandals, hard times, and the public outcry for reform all worked to their advantage. Responding to the national demand for virtue in public office, the Democrats nominated Samuel J. Tilden, a rich corporation lawyer, who had won a national reputation as a reform governor of New York.

On election night the first reports indicated that Tilden was winning. Later, in describing how the news was received at the White House, Commissioner of Education John Eaton wrote: "Sherman, with usual impetuosity, was pacing the room, lamenting with some profanity the fate of the Nation and especially of the army should the Democrats—otherwise the rebels—assume control, but Grant was perfectly calm and serene."

Despite the early returns the election ended in a deadlock. Amid threats of violence and insurrection, the question of the presidency was not settled until March, 1877, when a congressional committee decided in favor of Hayes. Already Sherman had ordered troops into Washington in case of violence and was prepared to shoot anyone who caused trouble in the streets. To a friend, he said: "If civil war breaks out, it will be a thousand times worse than the other war. It will be the fighting of neighbor against neighbor, friend against friend. . . . It is only a question of time until the politicians ruin us. Partisanship is a curse. These men are not howling for the country's good but for their own political advantage and the people are too big fools to see it. We are liable to smash into a thousand pieces every time we have an election."

Rutherford B. Hayes was inaugurated president of the United States without turmoil. He appointed John Sherman secretary of the treasury and thought of selecting Joseph E. Johnston as secretary of war. No single act within his grasp would so prove his goodwill toward the South as the presence in his official family of this ex-Confederate general. Sherman, however, although he had no personal objection, was convinced that Northerners, especially veterans, would resent the appointment. John Sherman wrote Hayes: "I have conversed with General Sherman. He gives an excellent account of Joe Johnston, his habits, character, and associations, and he thinks his personal merits may surely be recognized by appointment as Marshal of Virginia or some other similar position; but he is of the opinion that his designation to a Cabinet office would not be wise." President Hayes finally selected George Washington McCrary, an Iowa lawyer and judge, who was little inclined to challenge General Sherman or his actions.

Soon after his inauguration President Hayes withdrew Federal troops from the South, completing the evacuation in late April, 1877. This act marked the end of Radical Reconstruction, and the machinery of politics and government in the Southern states passed under the control of Democratic white "home rule." Twelve years after it began, the Radical program was abandoned. To Hayes, peaceful self-government in the South was an "imperative necessity." Radical Reconstruction had collapsed because of the determined opposition by Southern whites to the Reconstruction state governments and because of a lack of interest in the North over Reconstruction issues. Northerners came to view the questions of racial adjustment and Negro rights as of regional rather than of national concern.

Sherman was impressed with Hayes's policies. The president's decision to terminate the use of troops in the Southern states won his special praise. Possibly, Sherman thought, this might be the first step in a relaxation of party tensions and alignments throughout the nation. "I hope that time will build up parties less compromised by old issues than heretofore," he wrote John. "If all men aim at the general safety & prosperity it seems that the past might well be forgotten."

During the summer of 1877 Sherman decided to tour the West and took Tom along for company. With an escort of cavalry they journeyed into the wilds of Montana. The roads were atrocious, and the troopers had difficulty clearing away the trees and rocks and cutting down the steep banks of the creeks.

From Missoula Sherman wrote his youngest son, Tecumseh: "Tommy enjoys this life very much. We ride nearly all day getting breakfast at 5 AM and dinner after we reach camp, when its sometimes near dark. We have soldiers fare and sleep on the ground.... We have but one tent and sleep with our clothes on. ... We all have muskets and are ready for the Indians if they come, but we are not hunting Indians. Since we were at the National Park the Indians have been there and killed some visitors, but we are safe.... We will pass among the tribes on our way to Walla Walla, but they are known to be friendly, besides we now have a good escort.... The rivers and creeks of this region are cold and clear and have plenty of trout. There were so many trout in the Yellowstone that we are all tired of them."

On this trip Sherman made detailed notes on the agricultural and mining possibilities of the country, as well as on the terrain and its tactical problems. He spoke of the magnificent farming country, of the thousands of productive acres which would soon be open to settlers.

By mid-October Sherman was again in the capital. President and Mrs. Hayes were extremely popular in Washington social circles. Sunday evenings at the White House had a character all their own. Intimate friends, including the Shermans, were often invited to a family dinner, and others would join the group later for an hour of conversation and music in the Red Room. Hymn books were distributed, and with someone at the piano, one favorite hymn after another would be sung.

Sherman saw a good deal of the president and his wife. He and Lizzie often accompanied Mrs. Hayes to concerts, the opera, and other social events when the president was engaged with the duties of his office. While Ellen was in Saint Louis visiting Tom, Cump and Lizzie were busy almost every night, attending parties and receptions and the Marine Corps balls at the Army and Navy Club.

"My father habitually made engagements for four evenings a week," Tecumseh wrote later, "striving to keep the remaining evenings free. On his free evenings he often took me to the old National Theatre . . . where he spent much of his time behind the scenes, hobnobbing with the players off stage, I tagging along."

It was in Washington where Tecumseh "met with the one and only instance of physical discipline by my father. I was suffering excruciatingly from earache, lying on a bed and howling as loudly as I could give expression to my feelings. My father burst into the room, leaned over me, clasped his fingers over my nose to shut off my wind and sharply told me to 'stop it.' And then, gently, he explained that no matter how much I might be suffering I must not be a cry-baby or act so as to annoy others—that the most permissible was to moan quietly—that whenever I was suffering I could tell him and he would always sympathize and do all he could to relieve me; but that if I yelled and cried he would have nothing more to do with me.

"Thereafter," Tecumseh added, "his only method of discipline was sarcasm—acute, bitter, and that hurt but was always just and carried no aftermath. And from that time on whenever he told me to do a thing I did it quick. . . . He treated me so that it was always desirable and pleasant to be with him."

On Capitol Hill, Congress was still antagonistic toward the Regular Army. The Custer massacre had created a flurry of concern, but this quickly subsided. Congressional military appropriations declined, and in 1877, Congress failed to allot any money for the support of the army until November 30. "In all Republics where war exists the country is extravagant, but as soon as peace returns it falls into other extremes," Cump wrote to Minnie. "This has been especially the case with us. In 1865 nothing was too good for us, but gradually Congress has got meaner and meaner, bearing down on the Regular Army. The old Volunteers like Logan . . . in Congress say they were turned out at the end of the war to earn their own living, and they don't see any reason why the Regulars should be excepted. Now we find ourselves simply left out in the cold without a dollar, and many contend that the army expires July 1st, next, and that the country can get along without it and save $30,000,000 a year to the tax payers. Nevertheless we must go on without pay till Congress chooses to appropriate, still it is far from being certain.

"If I could see something reasonably certain," he went on, "I would not hesitate to try it, but I do not see anything now, and will calmly await the action of Congress. The Navy has been treated quite as bad as the Army, and many of the officers have been found to seek civil employment for a living."

Although Sherman constantly faced difficulties with Congress, he himself did little to aid the army's cause. He never displayed an ability to work effectively with politicians, and often he remained silent rather than risk being drawn into heated arguments. Many times he presented reform measures to congressional committees, but he inevitably stood aside as Congress passed over his proposals in favor of stopgap measures. Sherman insisted that the military was above politics and argued that legislation should be debated solely on the strengths and weaknesses of each program. But in a democracy, few popular issues are ever settled on such a lofty plane. Ultimately, Sherman failed in his efforts to persuade the legislature of the need for army reform, because he was never able to convince the politicians that by ignoring his arguments, the nation faced military disaster.

Besides the ongoing fight with Congress over appropriations, Sherman was daily engaged at the War Department answering piles of correspondence. "Its amusing to me to have such a medley of letters," he wrote Major Turner, "each representing some class with which at one time or other of my chequered career I've been associated. The old Regulars write for favors on the theory that they alone have a claim on my time and charity. Californians appeal to me as I was once one of them. Ohio people because I happened to be born there, Southerners because a critical period of life was spent there...."

One letter especially interested Sherman. A young schoolgirl, aged 16, who had corresponded with an army officer she had never seen, wrote a lengthy letter to the general. It had been merely a friendly correspondence with the lieutenant, but sufficiently intimate to make the girl's father put a stop to it. She addressed a letter of inquiry to the General of the Army, William Tecumseh Sherman, asking the whereabouts of the officer. She signed it with her initials, hoping the general might mistake her for a man and accord her an immediate answer. He was not deceived, but his reply was prompt.

Writing to "My darling young lady," he said that there were two officers of the same name, one a captain serving on the Upper Missouri and one a lieutenant garrisoned in California. "If you tell me *honestly* why you want to know all about him, what is your interest in the officer," Sherman said, "I can always find out about him."

Availing herself of this cordial invitation, she wrote again to say that the lieutenant was the officer in whom she was interested. She thanked the general profusely and asked, "How did you know I was a school girl? I flattered myself," she continued, "you would think me a man or at least an old aunt; but I am a girl, an unsophisticated little country girl, if you will; but an American girl, with a warm and true interest of the whole United States Army." She emphasized that the lieutenant was not her lover—"my interest in him is purely friendly."

The general and the girl continued their correspondence for several months. Sensing that she was in love, he checked up on the lieutenant and discovered that he was about to marry.

"The Lieutenant," Sherman wrote, "will soon marry a lady of long acquaintance and more suitable in years to his somewhat advanced age. Therefore think of him as an old friend who watched with interest the most captivating object possible, a young schoolgirl just budding into womanhood, probably not dreaming that that girl had her own secret thoughts. . . . You will marry sometime yourself, then laugh at me, the old fool who thought he might bring together two happy souls. I don't regret the effort." Sherman was to hear no more from this girl until her marriage. He then sent her a letter that was full of good wishes and bright hopes. As if in a footnote he added: "I am retiring from active life just as you are entering it. It is morning with you, evening with me; my footsteps are nearing the last slope, where the sun of life goes down, yours are bouyantly bounding up towards the first hilltops, with the dawn of a glorious morning for your background. May the sun shine on your young head through a long, bright life."

During the month of May, 1878, while Ellen was still visiting in Saint Louis, Cump received a letter from Tom. "I have long had something in my mind," Tom said, "that I have wanted to tell you and that I have often had on my tongue to say, but which I have postponed mentioning from time to time. I have never intended to devote my life to the practice of law.... The real reason and the only reason why I have chosen not to be a lawyer,—and that is what I so much fear will disappoint you—is that I have chosen another profession, in one word I desire to become a priest—a Catholic priest."

Duke of Louisiana

CUMP'S IMMEDIATE REACTION to Tom's letter was stark disbelief, which was rapidly transformed into anger. He regarded Tom's entry into the priesthood as a family catastrophe. In letters to Tom and Ellen he threatened "extreme measures," and to his old friend, Major Turner, he wrote: "I cannot help regarding him as a deserter.

"God—my idea of God is that He has given man reason," Sherman told Turner, "and Tom has no right to disregard it. Tom could SERVE his God and church better in St. Louis than shut up in a cloister.... I think he owes me some return for the time, money & affection I have bestowed upon him and to have deferred action until I could have reconciled my feelings & plans of life. Therefore I fear Tom has committed a sin so great in the eyes of God that no amount of penance can possibly wipe it away. By acts of positive goodness, action—and not penalty—he may make amends."

In another letter to Turner, Sherman declared: "I have never thrown obstacles in his way to practice the religion of his mother and do not now question his right as to himself of being as ardent a Catholic as his conscience appears, but I do oppose most vehemently his purpose to abandon to desert me now.... I have four daughters all dependent in a contingency not unlikely of my death upon him my oldest son. This duty he has no right to throw off. Even to save his own soul or the soul of others. His own peace of mind must be secondary to his duty to others .... death, suicide on his part could have been borne but deliberately to abandon us all and shut himself up in a Catholic church ... will be [the] end.

370

... Worse than this even I will be haunted with the dread of the same fate being prepared for my other boy.

"I was preparing him to be a lawyer in St. Louis where I hoped in three or four years more I would retire from the Army and settle down with my family," Sherman continued. "Now if I had had the slightest hint of his thoughts pointed in another direction I could have provided accordingly, but I had no such hint but quite the contrary, a seeming willing acquiescence in my plans until the very last minute when concealment was no longer possible when I was advised. This was not right. I must have some feeling. I would not be a man otherwise. ...

"He was the keystone of my Arch," Cump said, "and his going away lets down the whole structure with a crash."

From Saint Louis Tom replied to his father's angry letter. "I received ... your letter ... which I have read many, many times, and the burning words of which have sunk deep into my mind and heart," he said. "During the time that I have contemplated the grave step ... I have been suffering in anticipation the pain of your disappointment, and the grief of having wounded you; but I feel that grief and pain a hundred-fold more sharply now that I hear from your own lips as it were, how much you are hurt and chagrined, and how highly you disapprove of my choice of a profession. However I am still confirmed in my resolution.

"It is a terrible thing for us both," Tom went on, "and therefore the sooner it is over the better. We stand on two sides of the shield and neither of us can see fully the other's side—starting with different premises we reach different conclusions, and each of us feels that argument is vain and useless."

Ellen, who was still in Saint Louis, denied any responsibility for Tom's decision and appealed to her husband's sense of principle, which "will eventually cause you to feel that he must act according to his own convictions. No disgrace or 'ruin' can befall you except by your own act."

Sherman's nephew Thomas Ewing III, then a lad of 15, visited his uncle in Washington that May. He remembered: "He did not know that I knew about it and when I went to his office to get a map which he was having made for me, he turned on me suddenly and told me what was going to happen. I had never seen on any person's face an expression of quite so intense feeling; it was so intense that it frightened me so I could make no response. . . . When he saw that I would say nothing he turned with a sharp gesture and sat down at his desk and I left the room."

When Cump finally realized that his son was in earnest, he was baffled and grief-stricken. There was a last-ditch appeal by Sherman to a friend, John Cardinal McCloskey of New York City. When the cardinal supported Tom, the general dropped all protests and directed his anger against the Roman Catholic church.

Sherman confided to Turner that the church was "a public enemy," whose policies would eventually lead to violence. This selfish institution had committed a crime in removing his son "from the legitimate work cut out for him." Claiming the right to educate their children at their parents' expense, the church then "under inspiration called 'vocation' stole the children for its own sake."

To Minnie, Cump wrote: "Tom's . . . course has embittered me more than I ought to write. I try to check my feelings against him personally but cannot against the cause of his action, the Catholic Church. I realize that all I held most dear and whom I have tried to provide for liberally are not mine, but belong to a power that heeds no claim but its own; who takes unfeelingly . . . my son whom I had trained to assist me in the care of a large and expanding family."

In early June, ordered to make his novitiate in England, Tom bid farewell to his mother, sisters, and brother in Saint Louis. Instead of journeying directly to New York City, he decided to go to Washington to say good-bye to his father. There is no record of that scene between father and son, but on June 4 Cump wrote his daughter Ellie: "If Tom sails tomorrow he leaves us forever and casts his lot among those [with] whom I can have no intercourse." On June 5, 1878, Tom left for England.

Cump could not adjust to Tom's disregard of his ambitious hopes for him, nor could he rid himself of anger and bitterness. He commanded his son never to write him again, and in early July, made out a new will which cut Tom off completely. Ellen wrote Cump: "It is a pity you injure yourself in this way because Tom, dear fellow, would give his share to his sisters & he will never need it. . . . You can only wound the heart of the son who loves you above everything on this earth. I hope you will feel more kindly for you will be unhappy until you do."

That September, hoping to forget his troubles, Sherman headed west on an extensive inspection tour. When he returned to Washington, he was a bit more sympathetic toward the red man. "Our people are permeating a whole continent," Sherman told Turner, "leaving no room for the poor Indian. Game is fast disappearing in the very recesses of our mountains and plains. So that the Indian must steal for food or work. The latter is so abnormal to their habits and customs that it cannot be expected.

"Congress will not appropriate enough money for their entire subsistence," Sherman continued, and "the consequence is war. The problem is simply insoluble. We cannot stop emigration and probably ought not if we could.... [The Indians] *wont* work and *must* steal the cattle of the Ranchmen or starve. Now you & I know that our Ranchmen wont stand by and see a Camp of lazy Indians deliberately living off their herd—a row follows—somebody is killed & the explosion is certain."

To the secretary of war, Sherman wrote that the vast plains region had "already passed into the condition of a farming or pastoral country traversed by many railroads. The game is nearly all gone, the Indian has been forced on to small reservations....

"It is not expected that these pasture-fields can be used by the two races in common without everlasting conflict; but the reservations already set apart for the Indians are large enough, and should suffice for them ultimately to raise all the meat and grain necessary for their subsistence; but mean time they must have more food, else they will steal and fight. To convert the Indians into a pastoral race is the first step in their upward progress toward civilization; that of agriculturist must be the next stage, though slower of realization; but in this direction is the sole hope of rescuing any part of the 'nomade' Indians from utter annihilation.... Congress alone can provide a remedy, and, if prevention be wiser than cure, money and discretion must be lodged somewhere in time to prevent starvation."

Tom's departure for England had built a barrier between Ellen and Cump. Instead of moving to Washington to be with her husband that fall, Ellen rented a place in Baltimore and moved there with the younger children, Rachel and Tecumseh. She justified a separate residence by reasoning that the fatigue of official receptions and the glare and excitement of Ebbitt House would undermine her health. For years Ellen had disliked the official entertaining forced upon her by her husband's position as General of the Army, and more and more, she had relinquished her duties as hostess to her daughters. The Washington social swirl bored Ellen, yet in the past, she had dutifully followed her husband to the capital. But now Ellen used Cump's bitterness toward Tom as an excuse to stay away from the rigors of Washington and from her husband, who of necessity felt obligated to attend all public and social functions in the capital.

"It is true you feel as you have often told me," she wrote Cump from Baltimore, "that I did very little & did that very poorly, but I have done my best and I might almost say my last. No duties of public office devolve upon me; I am a poor plain old woman; I have sought to do my duty in the past . . . and I shall work to do it still & unto the end but I owe the public nothing & I am nothing to the public."

During the fall of 1878 Cump and his daughters Ellie and Lizzie, who then were acting as his Washington hostesses, made visits to Baltimore, but the family correspondence indicates increasing estrangement between Cump and Ellen.

At Christmas Cump stayed in Washington, pleading that the military situation kept him at his desk. Ellen, however, joined him for the New Year's reception. That this gesture was a sop to the public and did not indicate a genuine reconciliation is indicated by the note she jotted to Cump: "I concluded it to be almost necessary to the maintenance of my true position in the eyes of the world, which for the peace of mind of my daughters I must somewhat regard, that I should use the occasion of the New Year's Day to receive guests where you are living." Probably determined to maintain her position as wife and to counter any gossip, Ellen returned to Washington permanently soon after the first of the year.

The general was one of the most popular personalities in Washington. Frequently escorting one of his daughters, Cump enjoyed the theater, balls, and state dinners, both because his pleasure in social amusements increased with age and because, as he said later, "I was always fond of seeing young people happy." He achieved a reputation as an excellent dancing partner and attracted women young and old. One friend, who saw much of the general during these years, related that "I never saw a man so run after by womankind in my life." He was as ready to give his arm to an old lady as to kiss a young lass. The social correspondent for the *Independent* reported that there was no more delightful entertainer in all of Washington than General Sherman. One gentleman confessed that it was impossible not to enjoy himself with Sherman, as the general was so witty he took the ladies "by storm in every parlor that he visited."

Ellen often resented that her husband was in the limelight so much of the time, occupied by social engagements and public commitments. "I'd be glad," she had once written him from Baltimore, "if ever I could see you alone in your room or be sure that a stranger were not in the seat at your elbow at the table and waited upon to the exclusion of myself as is likely to be the case."

In February, 1879, Cump decided upon a trip through the South to inspect military installations and to gain some opinion of Southern feeling. "If I was the devil incarnate as many thought me in 1865," he wrote Turner, "I surely exposed myself to revenge or insult." He went to Chattanooga, Dalton, Rome, Atlanta, and Savannah, cities which Sherman's army had "swept as a hurricane." Crowds of whites and blacks thronged to the railroad depots to see the general. To his surprise and delight they were respectful, and he did not hear a single rude word or witness an offensive act. At every hotel his party was shown to the best rooms and tables, and all classes of citizens, rich and poor, flocked about him as he walked the streets. Southern bitterness and hatred toward him seemed to have dissipated.

Answering a letter from an Atlantan, E. P. Howell, Sherman extolled the opportunities and resources to be found in Georgia but remarked that the South had not kept pace with such states as California, Iowa, Wisconsin, or Kansas within the past generation, because "emigration would not go where slavery existed. Now that this cause is removed there is no longer any reason why Georgia, especially the northern part, should not rapidly regain her prominence among the great States of our Union. . . . I am satisfied from my recent visit that Northern professional men, manufacturers, mechanics, and farmers may come to Atlanta, Rome, and Chattanooga with a certainty of fair dealing and fair encouragement. Though I was personally regarded the bete noir of the late war in your section, the author of all your woes, yet I admit that I have just passed over the ground desolated by the civil war, and have received everywhere nothing but kind and courteous treatment from the highest to the lowest, and I heard of no violence for opinion's sake. Some Union men spoke of social ostracism, but I saw nothing of it, and even if it exists it must disappear with the present generation."

This letter was reprinted in full in the *New Orleans Picayune* under the headline, " 'Go South' The Beauty and Fertility of Georgia—the Flattering Opinion Gen. Sherman has of the Southern States."

In New Orleans at Mardi Gras time, Sherman enjoyed a royal welcome. Landing at the Canal Street steamboat dock, he was escorted by several regiments of infantry through the streets and the ever-increasing crowds. Ex-Confederate General Hood, on horseback, stopped the procession, and Rex, the king of the Carnival, thanked Sherman for coming.

That night at Exposition Hall he watched as Rex crowned the queen of the Mardi Gras, and later in the royal banquet room of the St. Charles Hotel, "My health was drunk standing and with evident heartiness," recalled Sherman. "Rex then made to me a fine speech, referring to past events fairly and well and declared me a Duke of Louisiana, putting on my breast a decoration. I replied in the same vein, then ... [my aides] were similarly toasted and complimented and friendly General Hood ... referred to our former relations as opposing generals, but with compliments more than I expected."

The following day, Carnival Day, Sherman and Rex stood together before a crowd of 10,000 people near the New Orleans Club and drank each other's health. Escorting the general to his throne, Rex presented him to the queen and "again thanked me positively for contributing to the honor and pleasure of his annual visit."

The editor of the *Picayune*, in listing the advantages to be gained from the Mardi Gras, mentioned that the festivities helped businessmen, demonstrated to strangers the wonders of New Orleans and its mild winter climate, and indicated to visitors "the utter falsity of the stories which attribute to our people a churlish disposition toward Northern citizens, and an unwillingness to mingle with them on terms of friendship and social intimacy. ... [Northerners] will learn how unfounded, how malicious, in fact, are the accusations that the thing called 'social ostracism' is practiced or is encouraged by the people of this city. The testimony of their own experience will confirm Gen. Sherman's generous admissions that the stories of 'ostracism' whispered to him by so-called Union men and 'loyalists' had no substantial foundation. ... If there is prejudice against Northern men, it is a prejudice directed only against those who have identified themselves with a career of plunder and oppression which aroused the resentment of honest Republicans as well as of honest Democrats."

From New Orleans Sherman journeyed to Baton Rouge, Vicksburg, and Jackson. On the train heading northward from Jackson, Sherman was sitting in the rear car when a former Confederate colonel, whom he knew, approached him and said that Jefferson Davis, the ex-president of the Confederacy, was in the next car. He urged Sherman to see him. "I said to him frankly," Sherman recalled, "that I was never personally acquainted with him, that I had not a shadow of hard feelings toward the officers and soldiers of the Confederate armies, nor would I harbor malice against their politicians, but I did not feel like going out of my way to see him, Davis. ... [The colonel] said that I was right, that Davis clung too long to his prejudices. ..."

When Sherman returned to Washington, he wrote a lengthy letter to Turner about his travels in the South. "My trip," he said, "was in its whole extent most enjoyable, that the people high and low received me with absolute cordiality and friendship, and that I discussed all matters which arose as free from apprehension or prejudice as I would in Missouri or Ohio.

"Now my conclusion is," he continued, "that with exceptions it is admitted that the war was a necessity—that we prosecuted it with vigor, success and not with more vindictive feeling than are common in civil wars; that the combatants showed no malice, but in reconstruction the repression of whites was carried too far, and too much support given the Negro; that the freedom of the Negro is sure, but he can only have that measure of political influence which he can enforce or influence by the acquisition of knowledge & property."

Definite signs of industrial activity and progress were evident in eastern Tennessee, northern Georgia, parts of Florida, and the city of New Orleans, but Alabama, Mississippi, and the "prime parts" of Georgia showed little or no advancement since the war. Although somewhat encouraged by what he had seen of conditions on his trip, Sherman maintained that the South could never compare with the Old Northwest and his native Ohio. "The truth is the Northwest is *our* country," he assured Turner. "It has more life, more substance, more real wealth than all the rest. The south is dead poor because they exclude new men, new immigrants."

As General of the Army, Sherman was kept busy with "routine matters of no earthly interest save to the officers and soldiers concerned." "But," he wrote, "these things have to be done, transfers, movements of troops, leaves of absence, Reports, Returns, etc. An army like a family has an infinite variety of wants which can only be reconciled by minute attention to detail."

During the year a situation arose at West Point which caused reverberations within the high command of the army. In 1879 the only Negro cadet at the military academy, Johnson C. Whittaker, had been declared deficient by the academic board. The superintendent, Gen. John M. Schofield, suggested that he be dropped back a class but not dismissed. The cadet had managed to struggle along, never doing well, but not flunking out. Then, on the morning of April 6, 1880, an officer discovered Whittaker tied to his cot, seriously injured about the head and face. Three masked men, Whittaker reported, had attacked him during the night. The news quickly reached New York City, where newspapers turned the Whittaker case into a national sensation.

Sherman called for a complete investigation which disclosed that Whittaker's injuries were self-inflicted, prompted, it was believed, by fear of an upcoming examination. Whittaker, however, refused to admit his guilt. General Schofield tried to expel him on disciplinary grounds, but President Hayes would permit him to be discharged only if it were found that he had failed in his studies. Sherman refused to be "humbugged by a boy, be he white or black." To Major Turner he wrote: "Slavery is forever gone as a part of our system. I suppose also we are bound by the dogma of universal suffrage. . . . But social equality is a question of fashion, of individual preference, or prejudice, beyond the reach of a statute. . . . You can lead a horse to water, but cannot force him to drink. You can bring white and black into the ranks, side by side, equal in the eyes of the law, but not in social life." The politicians would learn that their power was limited, that "they may declare a pound of lead equal to a pound of silver, but they cannot make you accept a pound of lead as a pound of silver in payment of a debt."

In his annual report, Sherman declared that every cadet at West Point was an appointee of a member of Congress, and therefore the corps was a youthful counterpart of Congress. "The same laws, the same Regulations, the same instruction, books, clothing, and food are common to all," Sherman wrote, "and a more democratic body never existed on earth than is the Corps of Cadets. Prejudice is alleged against colored cadets. Prejudice of race is the most difficult thing to contend against of any in this world. There is no more of such prejudice at West Point than in the community at large and the practice of social equality at West Point is in advance of the rest of the country."

As the months and years passed, Sherman, more than any other American, personified to millions the Civil War years of 1861–65. He himself loved best to gather with his "boys," and to hear them shout for "Uncle Billy," as they still did whenever the Grand Army of the Republic held its encampments.

By 1880 he had spoken to at least 1,000 veterans' reunions. Always he talked directly to the men. "No, my friends," he told the members of the Society of the Army of the Tennessee, "there is nothing in life more beautiful than the soldier. A knight errant with steel casque, lance in hand, has always commanded the admiration of men and women. The modern soldier is his legitimate successor and you, my comrades, were not hirelings; you never were, but knight errants transformed into modern soldiers, as good as they were and better. Now the truth is we fought the holiest fight ever fought on God's earth."

On August 11, 1880, in Columbus, Ohio, 5,000 GAR veterans

along with masses of civilians had gathered at the state fair in the pouring rain. President Hayes was the last scheduled speaker. When he finished, the program was over, and the notables began descending from the stand. The veterans began demanding "Sherman! Speech! Uncle Billy!" Sherman stepped forward in the rain.

"Fellow soldiers," he declared, "my speech is not written, nor has been even thought of by me. It delights my soul to look on you and see so many of the good boys left yet. They are not afraid of the rain; we have stood it many a time."

He went on: "I came as part of the escort for the President, and not for the purpose of speaking to you, but simply to look on and let the boys look at Old Billy again. We are to each other all in all as man and wife, and every soldier here today knows that Uncle Billy loves him as his own flesh and blood.

"The war is now away back in the past and you can tell what books cannot. When you talk you come down to the practical realities just as they happened. You all know that this is not soldiering here.

"There is many a boy here today who looks on war as all glory, but, boys, it is all hell. You can bear this warning voice to generations yet to come. I look upon war with horror." He smiled, and added, "But if it has to come I am here."

At the conclusion of his impromptu speech, the vast roar of applause lasted for ten minutes or more. Sherman was flushed with elation at such an ovation. For more than an hour he stood in the rain, receiving plaudits from the veterans who crowded forward to shake his hand. Long before he finished greeting his well-wishers, President Hayes and his immediate party, almost unnoticed, had left the scene.

When Sherman returned to the capital, the family moved out of Ebbitt House and into a rented house on 15th Street, Southeast, not far from the John Shermans. "While we were in Washington," recalled Tecumseh, "my mother never went out socially, one or another of my sisters always replaced her. But she enjoyed receiving visitors at home, of whom there was always an endless stream.

"My father, on the other hand, went out in the evenings continually, more than he wanted to; but even when he went out in the evenings he first dined lightly at home and he drew the line rigorously at teas and other afternoon functions, preferring to hold late afternoon receptions of his own in his office at which everybody had a comfortable drink."

Tecumseh noted too how his father's appearance was changing. "The red finally passed out of my father's hair and beard," he wrote. "Within my memory his hair had changed from dark red to dark brown, which color it remained without a trace of grey, until his death. His beard, however, which he kept closely trimmed, changed from light red to white. In common with nearly all the men of his family, he wore a beard for the specific reason that his skin was so thin that shaving caused prolonged bleeding and excessive soreness. . . . Likewise at this time he took to wearing glasses for reading . . . . large tortoise shell spectacles which lasted him and which he used exclusively for the rest of his life."

That spring Ellie, the gayest of the Sherman daughters, married Lt. Alexander Thackera, United States Navy. "It was," said Tecumseh, "a small house wedding but resplendent with Army and Navy uniforms. Among the guests were President and Mrs. Hayes, Admiral Porter, John Sherman . . . and many others."

Tecumseh Sherman often visited his uncle's house and remembered John Sherman as "an animated conversationalist, interesting and interested in others.

"He was fond of jokes and was a persistent tease," he continued, "but generally there was a time limit on his sociability after which he retired to his sanctum or plainly wanted to. . . . He had the best of food and liked it, but ate sparingly. He had no tabus about drinking; but habitually drank only sherry and beer in small quantities and often abstained without reluctance in deference to the 'blue ribbon' sentiments of others.

"He took far too little exercise. To the end, he was spare (much underweight), light on his feet and a good walker. . . . He adhered to a black frock suit, with silk hat and white linen— though in hot weather he resorted to a black Alpaca jacket, and when traveling or driving in the dust he sometimes wore linen dusters. . . . He had lots of visitors, and was accessible and cordial to visits from friends. But he had few old cronies welcome to stop in on him just for a drink."

As secretary of the treasury, John Sherman occupied a place where his native skill at the management of economic affairs would

be most effective. Hayes had strongly backed the Specie Re-
sumption Act of 1875, which called for the government to redeem
with gold the soft-money greenbacks that had helped finance the
war, thus reducing the amount of greenbacks in circulation. The
measure became effective in January, 1879. On this subject John
Sherman had a thorough knowledge and vast experience acquired
in 16 years of membership on congressional finance committees.
Closely involved in the wartime establishment of the greenback
currency, he was now in a position to protect the nation's credit
by making the greenbacks redeemable in gold, despite the opposition of the inflationists.

Also in Washington in 1880, was Tom Ewing, then a member
of the House of Representatives. He had returned to Lancaster
soon after the war and had been a conspicuous leader in the greenback wing of the Democratic party. From 1877 to 1881, he represented the Lancaster district in Congress, and as a member of that
body, was the leader in the movement for the preservation of the
greenback currency, much to John Sherman's chagrin. Tom
Ewing's candidacy for the governorship of Ohio in 1879, on the
Democratic ticket, had been the last gasp of the greenback movement in Ohio, and although he was defeated, his brilliant campaign
had attracted nationwide attention. He was to retire from politics
in 1881 and move to New York City to practice law.

Cump Sherman was already brooding on retirement. Old men
should step aside, he said, to make way for younger officers. His
retirement on full pay and allowances would give his friend
General Sheridan a chance for overall command and would permit
some worthy colonel to assume Sheridan's duties. Sherman was
nearing 62 and already had commanded the army 16 years, longer
than either Gens. Winfield Scott or Ulysses S. Grant. "I look on
my life's work as done, by no means perfect, yet a part of the
whole—a fair share," he wrote Turner. If his son Tom had been
settled as a lawyer in Saint Louis, handling the family's business
affairs, he would not have hesitated to retire.

Cump's attitude toward Tom was beginning to change, and he
wrote him several letters. "I was much pleased at the receipt of
your last letter," Tom replied, "as it showed me that I had mis-
understood or exagerrated what you had said in previous letters,

and that I need not have been so timid about writing again."
Having completed his studies in England, Tom returned to the
United States, and with Rachel, who had met the ship in New York,
"went directly to see his father, who was alone in Washington
while Ellen and the Children were vacationing in Pennsylvania."

"When Tom reached Washington with me," remembered
Rachel, "we were horribly agitated not knowing how my father
would receive him. He was not at the depot and we were met by
his orderly, Pat, and the carriage. At the house our old nurse
Emily opened the door and motioned to the parlor door which
was slightly open. Tom went in and with a cry my father threw
his arms about him and I left them standing, clasped in each others
arms, I closed the door and went to my room.

"We later dined together at the Riggs home," she continued,
"and he introduced my brother to all the senators and representatives who I must say looked half frightened and then so relieved!
Every one knew of his distress and sorrow on his [Tom's] leaving.
But he had the tenderest heart and loved us devotedly and he
could never bear malice toward any one."

After several days Tom went on to Pennsylvania to see the rest
of the family. He lost no time in writing his father, thanking him
for the pleasant visit and his kind reception, "which I had no right
to expect. I could not help seeing that it cost an effort on your
part to overcome the repugnance my strange dress naturally excited, and I can't tell you how gratified I was to find that your
generous affection had the upper hand so entirely."

On September 1, 1880, after attending a reunion of the
Twenty-third Regiment at Canton, Ohio, President Hayes and his
official party of 16, including General Sherman and his daughter
Rachel, began a two-month trip to California and the Pacific
Northwest. It was the first time a president of the United States
had visited the West Coast while in office. Most of the way they
traveled by rail, but occasionally, where the lines were not completed, they were forced to board stagecoaches and steamboats.

Sherman's annual report that year was filled with talk of the
western railroads, which "have completely revolutionized our
country in the past few years, and impose on the military an entire
change of policy.

"Hitherto we have been compelled to maintain small posts

along wagon and stage routes of travel," Sherman continued. "These are no longer needed, because no longer used, and the settlements which grow up speedily along the new railroads afford all the security necessary, and the regular stations built for storage at convenient distances afford the necessary shelter for stores and for the men when operating in the neighborhood. . . .

"The progress of settlement west of the Mississippi in the past fifteen years," he added, "has been prodigious. Hardly a mountain but has been 'prospected' for gold and silver, and now prosperous farms and cattle ranches exist where ten years ago no man could venture. This is largely due to the soldier, but in an equal, if not greater measure, to the adventurous pioneers themselves, and to that new and greatest of civilizers, the railroad."

President Hayes's transcontinental trek ended in Fremont, Ohio, on the day before the presidential election. Hayes had announced long ago that he would serve only one term as president. After a drab campaign in the fall of 1880, while Hayes and Sherman were in the West, James A. Garfield, a Republican, defeated the Democratic candidate, Winfield Scott Hancock, by only a slim plurality. Garfield had reached the presidency after a brilliant Civil War career and an arduous apprenticeship in Congress. John Sherman was chosen to fill Garfield's unexpired term in the United States Senate.

Early the following year, before Garfield was inaugurated, Sherman became exceedingly irritated with President Hayes, who had made promotions of which Sherman did not approve and had recommended the new rank of captain general for ex-president Grant.

When he left the presidency, Grant had had no further political ambitions and had departed for a trip around the world. Sherman had been devoted to President Hayes and his wife for four years and had constantly worked to make the Hayes Administration successful. It had been a rank injustice, Sherman thought, for Hayes now to slap him down publicly by returning Grant to the army as captain general over him. The law stated specifically that no retired army officer could be "assigned to duty of any kind or be entitled to receive more than the pay provided by law for retired officers of his grade."

"I . . . [shall] resent any attempt to supersede me in command or rank by anybody," Sherman told Turner. "I will be most happy to have Grant's name enrolled there [as Captain General]," he wrote John Sherman, "but my judgment is that all should be treated alike."

Hayes replaced General Schofield, who was involved in the Whittaker case, with Gen. Oliver O. Howard, for whom the Negroes of the nation had a high regard, as superintendent at West Point. "I was not consulted," Sherman remarked bitterly, "and wash my hands of the whole thing." To Turner he wrote that the president's actions indicated "he must be very weak, thus to be used by intriguing aspirants ... but I don't intend to have any trouble with him at this final period of administration."

The president realized that General Sherman was deeply disturbed, and in mid-February, just a month before he left office, he went to the general and apologized for his seeming slight in the matter of Grant and his treatment of Schofield. The matter was patched up. "The Entente Cordiale is completely restored," Sherman told Turner. "I simply stood off until he came of his own volition."

In May Rachel Sherman traveled abroad for "self-improvement," and Ellie's husband, Alex Thackera, resigned from the navy to take a job in his father's business in Philadelphia. "Anything is better than a Navy officer with a wife & baby," Sherman wrote Turner, "but I always feel afraid to advise an officer to change his profession." Cump was sure now that the Thackera family was well on its way, and Minnie Fitch was fairly well established. There were only Lizzie, Rachel, and Tecumseh to worry about. Cump was now free of debt, and in addition to his yearly income of $15,000, he had money in the bank and owned property worth almost $100,000.

That spring Jefferson Davis published *The Rise and Fall of the Confederate Government*, which infuriated Sherman when he read it. His own *Memoirs* had disparaged the ex-Confederate president, especially in Davis's differences with Gen. Joseph E. Johnston.

In his book Davis assailed both Johnston and Sherman and branded Sherman's depopulation order as the most inhuman act "since Alva's atrocious cruelties in the Netherlands." General Beauregard also attacked Sherman in print for compelling prisoners of war to unearth Confederate mines.

Outraged, Sherman fought back. "I pitched into Jeff Davis not for my own reputation but for his blind disregard for the truth," he wrote. At every pause in the war, "I tried to help the South." Sherman resented the charge that he had been responsible for burning Columbia, S.C. "I saw with my own eyes all the bridges burned ahead of us by Hampton's Cavalry," he wrote Turner. "In the next war, all of that breed must be punished before the tide of civilization. I was in hopes that Jeff Davis had learned something, but I am convinced that he is the type of a class that must be wiped off the face of the earth and unless I was convinced that his book will accomplish this end I would favor starting in again and not stopping till the thing was complete."

The Sherman-Davis controversy extended to the floor of the United States Senate. Backing up his brother, John Sherman termed Davis and his associates "conspirators and traitors" and closed his remarks by saying: "I am sorry this debate has sprung up.... But, sir, whenever in my presence, in a public assemblage, Jefferson Davis shall be treated as a patriot, I must enter my solemn protest."

General Sherman was assaulted in other quarters. The Washington correspondent for the *Cincinnati Gazette*, H. V. Boynton, who had served in the Army of the Cumberland under Generals Buell and Thomas, published a volume, *Sherman's Historical Raid; the Memoirs in Light of the Record*. Boynton attacked Sherman by citing the general's failure to credit Buell with rescuing himself and Grant at Shiloh, his neglect in not indicating that it was Grant's idea to march to the sea, and many other matters.

Investigating Boynton's motives, Sherman concluded that they were inspired by his old enemies, the bureaucrats of the War Department, among whom was Col. Orville E. Babcock, who had once served on Grant's presidential staff, and later, was deeply involved in the Whiskey Ring scandal. To John Sherman, Cump wrote: "I know he [Boynton] was paid $600 Government money and supplied with hired clerks to copy the extracts of official reports.... Babcock was the main spirit and his motive was to prevent my influence in cutting the wings of the Staff Corps in Washington who are inimical to the Real Army which does the work." Sherman told a reporter that Boynton would "do anything for Money" and would "slander his own mother for a thousand dollars."

Sherman later learned that Boynton had prepared charges and specifications against him, which had been recorded and had been seriously considered by the War Department. To friends, Sherman confided that he would demand a trial to expose the "damnable conspiracy" against him which Belknap and others had hatched during the Grant Administration. "Self respect," he told Hayes, "forced me to remove my headquarters to St. Louis. In this Boynton was the tool and I want his testimony under oath."

The trial, however, was never held, as in July, 1881, the nation was stunned at the news that Charles Guiteau, a disgruntled office seeker, had shot President Garfield in the Washington railroad station. Sustaining a severe wound, Garfield was carried back to the White House. Police quickly apprehended Guiteau and held him in the district jail. To prevent a mob lynching and to protect Garfield if an assassination plot were afoot, Sherman ordered Regular troops to surround the White House and jail and to patrol the streets.

Garfield improved, and in mid-July Sherman left Washington for Ohio and a much-awaited reunion with his brother in Mansfield. During the evening of July 21, a large procession of veterans and civilians, headed by a brass band, marched onto the Sherman grounds, and Cump and John came out on the portico to meet them. A former colonel stepped forward and made a brief speech:

General Sherman: —We, the soldiers of the war for the Union, of Richland County and its surroundings, together with our citizens, have come . . . to pay our respects to you. We come, with feelings of profound regard, to see and welcome you, our great strategic war chief, and the hero of the glorious "March to the sea."

Cump responded by thanking the crowd for the cordial reception, and said: "I cannot distinguish to-night who are and who are not soldiers, but let me say to you, soldiers, I am very glad to meet you again, after so many years, in this time of peace, when yet the recollection of hardships of war is a bond of comradeship among us. We fought, not for ourselves alone, but for those who are come after us. . . . But this is not the time nor place to recount the past."

He hesitated a moment, looking out at the throng, then continued: "I want to say to you, teach your children to honor the flag, to respect the laws, and love and understand our institutions, and our glorious country will be safe for them.

"My friends, I heartily appreciate this splendid tribute of your friendship and respect. I thank you. Good-night."

Cump was cheered lustily. After a short address by John Sherman, the crowd was asked into the dining room for refreshments.

In August President Garfield took a turn for the worse. The cabinet, doctors, and the Garfield family gave up hope, but then he seemed to rally.

Back in the capital, Sherman went to the White House, and to the cabinet, detailed his plans for the public safety should the president die. If the force of Regulars then on hand were not enough to guard Guiteau and the jail from a mob, he could draw additional men from surrounding places.

Garfield died on September 19, and Chester A. Arthur was sworn in as president. Fortunately, there was no violence in the streets. For two days Garfield's body lay in state in the Capitol Rotunda and was then taken to Ohio for burial. Guiteau was tried and executed.

In late September, after the Garfield funeral, Ellen returned from a long sojourn with Minnie. She brought young Willie Fitch with her. Cump was delighted to see his grandson. He had bought a horse for Tecumseh, and every day one of the general's aides took Willie to the Smithsonian grounds for a ride. "If you entrust me with his education," he wrote Minnie, "I will insist on riding and swimming among his first acquirements. With a good appetite and plenty of outdoor exercise, he will be able to hold more head knowledge than if trained in ordinary schools. He has a good head and a good constitution and if allowed to scuffle with boys at school, will be the better able to grapple with men physically and mentally when he reaches manhood."

"...I have reason to be content."

ONCE AGAIN the general began preparing for a trip to Georgia. Six months earlier the two senators from that state had invited him to Atlanta for a trade fair, at which local products would be exhibited. Sherman was extremely interested in the development of the region where during the war he had been forced into harsh acts.

With two aides he arrived in Atlanta on the evening of November 14 and registered at the Kimball House. Outside the hotel the general told a newsman: "I am glad to be here, away from all forms and ceremonies, and with an opportunity to see and enjoy what I have learned is a splendid exhibition...." Sherman was also reported to have said that he had come to Atlanta in the capacity of a private citizen and had requested city officials not to make his visit one of "particular moment." "While he will be pleased to meet his friends and acquaintances personally," the reporter remarked, "he has declined all proffers to do [so] in a formal and official manner."

On the morning of the 15th, Sherman, his aides, and the president of the exposition rode out to the fairgrounds and spent the entire day there. The attendance was 10,000, some 2,000 more than on any previous day, and Cump was sure that the crowd had turned out to stare at "Sherman, the Vandal."

In the afternoon, he was invited to attend a meeting of Mexican War veterans in the main hall of the fairgrounds. He was asked to sit on the platform, but he declined and took a seat in the front benches with the veterans.

Once the main oration was over, Cump made a move to leave, but the veterans began to chant: "We want Sherman!" "I had not

389

the remotest intention to take part," he said later, "but a Mexican War veteran came to me asking me as a . . . veteran to say a few words to my old comrades. This was a call no man could resist."

Sherman mounted the speakers' platform and to the assemblage, he said: "I have told many to-day in Atlanta that my purpose was not to speak one word on this occasion. . . . But being here and being urged to speak a few words as an old Mexican veteran, I feel that I can refuse nothing to the soldiers, however averse I may feel toward doing so. I regard soldiery as being something so pure and ennobling that whoever has felt the spurt once can never forget it, and whenever I am called upon, whether it be by the soldiers of the Florida war or any other war, my heart responds as by inspiration."

The general spoke of his connection with the Mexican War and then continued: "Now, gentlemen. . . . I see no reason why we may not now declare with Webster, 'thank God, I am an American citizen.' We are American citizens. I thank God that I am one, and I tell you that I can go to any spot from Maine to Texas, and stop where I please, so long as I behave myself and obey the laws of the place, and that is the spirit of the government. That is what made us the United States of America, and the foundation stone upon which governments are built for this continent.

"We fought our mother and acquired our independence, and to-day we are the same nation, the same soldiers, the same government, the same flag, and, so far as I am concerned, I am just as friendly to Georgia as I am to my own native state of Ohio. [Immense applause]. . . . Our government is worth fighting for.

"I have come to-day," he added, "to look upon these buildings where once we had battle-fields, and I delight more to look upon them than to look upon the scene which was here enacted sixteen years ago, and I say that every noble man and every kindly woman over this broad land takes as much interest in your prosperity and in this exposition as do those who are sitting in this presence today. . . ."

"The Mexican War veterans," reported the *Atlanta Constitution,* "called on General Sherman during the day and many of them who knew him personally during the war went over with him the desperate scenes they had passed together."

That night Sherman and his staff were invited to a banquet given by the cotton men of Atlanta for their counterparts in South Carolina, but he was forced to decline as he had already accepted an invitation to occupy a private box at the opera house.

After Sherman and his party left the city, the *Constitution* reprinted, under the headline "Destruction of Atlanta—Sherman's Inhuman and Ferocious Conduct," two accounts detailing the burning of Atlanta, one from the *Annual Cyclopedia* and the other from Jefferson Davis's book. On the following day, however, an editorial, devoted to Sherman's visit, appeared in the *Constitution.*

"There are two or three newspapers that have tried to work up prejudice against Atlanta and the cotton exposition by allusions to 'Sherman's Day' and General Sherman's visit to this city," it said. "To begin with, there has been no 'Sherman day' at the exposition, and no thought of having one. General Sherman did visit the exposition, as he had every right to do. He came as a private citizen and was met politely—just as any other private citizen would have been. With admirable good sense and taste, he asked that he be allowed to study the great exposition, simply as any other citizen. There are special reasons why General Sherman would not expect the people of Atlanta to meet him with any great demonstrations of joy. On the other hand there is every reason of good breeding why they should treat him civilly and politely. Nothing was done that could have offended the most sensitive critic on either side. . . .

"General Sherman went through the buildings quietly and decorously, meeting here and there an acquaintance or an old comrade," it continued. "He showed genuine interest in what he saw, and no interest whatever in outside matters. . . . General Sherman left Atlanta delighted with his visit. He doubtless appreciated the manly and frank manner of his reception, and respects our people more than if the most elaborate formalities had been tendered him. It is but just to say that he won the respect of many of our people by the unaffected and straightforward way in which he took things, and his sensible understanding of the situation. . . ."

After he returned to Washington, Congress passed a bill fixing 64 years as the age limit of retirement. An offer to exempt General

Sherman was extended, but he refused, stating that "no man could know or realize when his own mental and physical powers began to decline."

His 64th birthday was not until February 8, 1884, but he anticipated retiring earlier, saying: "It is better that the change should occur with the new Congress. The country is now prosperous, and the army is in reasonably good condition, considering the fact that peace and politics are always more damaging than war."

To Minnie he confided: "I'm in the best possible condition to retire *now* and feel disposed to act of myself, without waiting to be passed out, as too many have been.

"I have seen so many good men cling to places too long," he added, "and when age and infirmity comes are less prepared than if they had taken the step in time. I think it best to have our own house where we can assemble our scattered furniture, books, pictures, etc. It is generally admitted that I have done a reasonable share of work in this life, and that I am entitled to take it easy the remainder of my days. The social life in Washington never has been agreeable to your Mama, but is incident to my office, therefore I agree with her, that although Washington is a most beautiful city, we will be more at ease in some other place, and though St. Louis might not be a first choice, it is good enough."

Before retiring, he took a final tour of the West, which he loved so well, traveling by train, ambulance, horseback, and steamer. He enjoyed most roughing it with his companions in the woods of Montana and Idaho, away from telegraphs and mail. "I think everybody should go into camp once a year to learn how superfluous are most of what are deemed necessaries of life, the cost of which weighs down men of families," he reported to Minnie.

All along the route, in army posts and in the cities, old comrades protested Sherman's surrendering of his command while still so vigorous in mind and body. But Sherman was sure he had made the right decision.

From Santa Fe, N. Mex., in September, 1883, he wrote Ellen: "The whole Western world recognizes the truth that since the close of the Civil War I have so used my power and office as to encourage the growth and development of the great West, giving me a hold on their respect and affections worth more than gold. I have been traveling, in three months, in beautiful cars ... over an extent of more than ten thousand miles of country, every mile of which is free from danger of savage and is being occupied by industrious families. Of course the Army has not done this, but the Army has gone ahead and prepared the way, and year by year I have followed up with words of encouragement. . . . I honestly believe in this way I have done more good for our country and for the human race than I did in the Civil War." A month and a half later, he wrote out his brief order relinquishing his command, rose from his desk at the War Department, gave General Sheridan his chair, shook hands, and departed as casually as on any afternoon.

In a letter to Sheridan two weeks later, Sherman wrote a lengthy evaluation of his career as General of the Army. He admitted that he had failed in the matter of the army's relationship with Congress, an area which always remained a mystery to him. He explained that he had never found the right arguments to persuade politicians of the army's importance to the nation. Perhaps, he added, no logical presentation could have prevented congressmen from attacking the military, for during periods of peace the army appeared to many to be an extravagance. Finally, Sherman said that he had no recommendations as to the course his friend should pursue. "The command of the Army at Washington," he said, "never sat easy on my conscience, because it was not command, but simple acquiescence in the system which has grown up in Washington, where the President commands, the Secretary of War commands, each Head of Bureau commands, and the real General is a mere figurehead. If you change this you will be more successful than I was." Mistrustful of politicians, Sherman never developed a technique for working with them, and he refused to concede that military policy was as much a matter for congressional debate as were those concerning tariffs and monetary affairs.

Sherman wasted little time packing his belongings and heading for Saint Louis. Ellen and the family had already moved into the house at 912 Garrison Avenue. The furniture was all in place, the paintings and mirrors hung. "We all feel deeply interested in the home," Ellen wrote, and "believe there will be perfect content on the part of all—more than content."

There was a huge family reunion the following April, with the children and grandchildren—the Thackeras and the Fitches—converging on the old home. In honor of the occasion of his father's retirement, Tom Sherman wrote:

To Papa

What crown shall deck his brow?
Wears he the laurel now?
Weave we the holly bough,
With myrtle entwine him.

Spray of the stanch old yew
Sprigs of the oak so true
Broad beech and buck-eye too
Bud to enshrine him.

Gone are his days of war,
Danger and strife are o'er
Comes now the autumn hoar,
Sweet peace enfolds him.

Garlands must hide his sword,
Heap high the genial board,
By loving hearts adored
Home ties shall hold him.

                                    T.E.S.

"My happiest recollections of our life then," Tecumseh wrote later, "are of our family dinners, when my father and mother were both present, without strangers to restrain their intimacy, which occurred more frequently during our stay in St. Louis in the 1880s than at any other time during my memory.

"My father," he went on, "had a keen wit, a fund [of] reminiscences and much vividness in expression, whereas my mother was a fountain of good humor and knew how to draw my father out and to direct the conversation in most interesting channels. They differed in opinions enough to occasion some lively arguments with sharp repartees. It is clear that mother and father both superlatively enjoyed their conversations, with freedom from all restraints."

As the time for the presidential nominating conventions ap-

Portrait of General William T. Sherman by L. Hart Darragh. Date of the
rendition thought to be 1889

One of the Sherman homes after the Civil War, at 912 North Garrison
Avenue, in Saint Louis

An 1890 picture of the survivors of Sherman's regiment (1st battalion, 13th U.S. Infantry). Sherman is in first row, center

The Sherman family at Senator John Sherman's home in Mansfield, Ohio, c. 1886. Senator Sherman stands sixth from left; General Sherman, eighth; and his wife, eleventh; Philemon Sherman sits second from left

proached in the summer of 1884, all of Sherman's disclaimers about his candidacy failed to convince his friends, who hoped he could be persuaded to run. But the general was adamant; under no circumstances would he be a presidential candidate.

Already he had written Minnie: "I am not going to commit the folly of giving up the peace and quietude of the remainder of my life for such empty honor. The office has no temptation for me, on the contrary quite the reverse."

"I'm truly rejoiced that you are so positive in rejecting all advances of politicians to secure you for the Presidency," Ellen wrote Cump when he was out of the city. "Were you to be a candidate I should consider it the ruin of your family, so I am thankful that you do not contemplate it."

Just before the convention Sherman explained to a friend: "In as much as John Sherman is and of right may be a candidate, I wish not to damage *his* chances, and therefore [have] advised my name be not even mentioned."

A cousin of Ellen's and a long-time Republican politician, James G. Blaine of Maine, was the leading candidate for the Republican nomination. But letters kept pouring into Saint Louis, urging Sherman to reconsider and to accept if chosen. Despairing of victory as strength began to develop behind President Arthur and Sen. John Logan, Blaine wrote Sherman nine days before the convention.

"It is more than possible," he said, "that you may be nominated for the Presidency. If so you must stand your hand, accept the responsibility, and assume the duties of the place to which you will surely be chosen if a candidate. You must not look upon it as the work of the politicians. If it comes to you, it will come as the groundswell of popular demand—and you can no more refuse than you could have refused to obey an order when you were a lieutenant in the Army. If it comes to you at all it will come as a call of patriotism. It would, in such an event, injure your great fame as much to decline as it would for you to seek it."

Sherman replied: "I have had a great many letters from all points of the compass to a similar effect, one or two of which I have answered frankly; but the great mass are unanswered. I ought not to subject myself to the cheap ridicule of declining what is not offered, but it is only fair to the many really able men who rightfully aspire to the high honor of being President of the United States to let them know that I am not and must not be construed as a rival.

"In every man's life there occurs an epoch when he must choose his own career, and when he may not throw the responsibility, or tamely place his destiny in the hands of friends. Mine occurred in Louisiana when, in 1861, alone in the midst of a people blinded by supposed wrongs, I resolved to stand by the Union as long as a fragment of it survived to which to cling. Since then, through faction, tempest, war and peace, my career has been all my family and friends could ask. . . .

"I will not in any event," Sherman went on, "entertain or accept a nomination as a candidate for President . . . for reasons personal to myself. I claim that the Civil War, in which I simply did a man's fair share of work, so perfectly accomplished peace, that military men have an absolute right to rest, and to demand that the men who have been schooled in the arts and practice of peace shall now do their work equally well. Any senator can step from his chair at the capitol into the White House, and fulfill the office of the President with more skill and success than a Grant, Sherman, or Sheridan, who were soldiers by education and nature, who filled well their office when the country was in danger, but were not schooled in the practices by which civil communities are, and should be, governed. . . .

"I have my personal affairs in a state of absolute safety and comfort . . . and would account myself a fool, a madman, an ass, to embark anew, at sixty five years of age, in a career that may, at any moment, become tempest-tossed by the perfidy, the defalcation, the dishonesty, or neglect of any one of a hundred thousand subordinates utterly unknown to the President of the United States, not to say the eternal worriment by a vast host of impecunious friends and old military subordinates. Even as it is, I am tortured by the charitable appeals of poor distressed pensioners, but as President, these would be multiplied beyond human endurance.

"I remember well the experience of Generals Jackson, Harrison, Taylor, Grant, Hayes, and Garfield, all elected because of their military services, and am warned, not encouraged, by their sad experiences. No,—count me out. The civilians of the U. S.

should, and must, buffet with this thankless office, and leave us old soldiers to enjoy the peace we fought for, and think we earned."

When the Republican convention opened in Chicago, one of the delegates, J. B. Henderson, wired the general. The gist of the message was that mounting sentiment for General Sherman could not be checked. To this Sherman replied: "Please decline any nomination for me in language strong but courteous." His backers at the convention, however, continued working and hoping. Two days later Henderson shot off another telegram.

Tom Sherman was visiting his parents that summer and was in the library when the wire came. Cump tore it open and read: "Your name is the only one we can agree upon, you will have to put aside your prejudices and accept the Presidency." Tom watched closely as his father, without taking his cigar from his mouth and without changing his expression, scribbled off his answer: "I will not accept if nominated and will not serve if elected."

He tossed it over to Tom to be handed to the messenger and then went on with the conversation. At that moment, remembered Tom, "I thought my father a great man."

The convention finally nominated James G. Blaine; the Democrats, Grover Cleveland of New York.

In November, after a lusty campaign, Cleveland won the presidency, but his popular plurality was only 23,000 votes out of the 10 million-odd cast.

The following July the general and his son Tecumseh were on a trip to Fort Snelling, Minn., when they received the news that Grant was dead from cancer. For some years Sherman had been troubled over the general's health and his financial plight. Grant had lost all his liquid assets, $100,000, in a speculative banking scheme.

When the nation learned of Grant's death, sad tributes came from Ohio, California, Missouri, and Illinois, from Vicksburg, Chattanooga, and Richmond, from Philadelphia, Washington, and New York. The mistakes of Grant, the politician, were forgotten as the nation honored Grant, the soldier.

On August 8 hundreds of prominent Americans and other people by the thousands arrived in New York City to pay their last respects to General Grant. The funeral procession down

Broadway was led by General Hancock. Generals Sherman, Joseph E. Johnston, Philip Sheridan, John Logan, Simon B. Buckner, Admiral David Dixon Porter, ex-Secretary of the Treasury George Boutwell, George Childs and George Jones, the pallbearers, rode in carriages just ahead of the marching veterans.

Bishop William Harris of the Methodist Episcopal church at "Riverside" read the funeral service. After he finished, the pallbearers carried Grant's coffin to the vault. A bugler stepped forward from the ranks and sounded "Taps." As the last note died away, the men of the Seventh Regiment fired three volleys, followed by three more from the Twenty-second Regiment.

"During the war," Sherman wrote a friend later, "Grant confided in me as in an elder brother. His flatterers convinced him more than ever that he was as transcendant in politics and finance as in war, and in his own military success was even to himself a mystery. . . ."

To another friend, who had remarked about the scandals of the Grant Administration, he said: "It is not my office to defend Grant for time has stamped his fame as real not accidental. Grant's whole character was . . . a combination of strength and weakness not paralleled by any whom I have read in ancient or modern history. The good he did lives after him—let his small weaknesses be buried with his bones."

In Saint Louis Sherman spent much of his time answering, in his own hand, a flood of mail which never slackened. After finishing up his day's correspondence, he would usually sit back with a cigar and book. A walk or ride in the afternoons filled in the time until evening, when he was always socially engaged at the theater, the opera, dinners, and card parties. Rarely was there a free evening.

During the fall of 1885 the Sherman family's expenses began to mount again. Minnie's husband had fallen into severe financial straits. In a year's time Tecumseh would be ready for Yale, and this too would drain the Shermans' savings. Household expenses multiplied and Cump confessed to Ellie: "It costs me more than if we were living at the Grand Hotel in Paris." With his family scattered, he thought it absurd to keep up the big house on Garrison Avenue with its six servants, five horses, seven carriages, and the heavy taxes and assessments. Ellen suggested moving east, as she wanted to be near Tecumseh when he was at Yale. Cump decided to move the family into a hotel in New York City and to transfer his office, books, and papers to the downtown government building.

The Shermans rented their house in the summer of 1886, and Ellen, Rachel, and Tecumseh went to Marietta, Pa., to visit the Thackera family while Lizzie and Cump traveled to the West Coast.

From San Francisco Sherman sent his son a check for $500 to help get him started at Yale. "I will provide for you liberally, but not extravagantly, until you can provide for yourself," he wrote Tecumseh. "The first duty of a son is to become self-supporting, and independent, next to assist or provide for those dependent upon him, and last to provide for the future." He reiterated that Tom had reversed these natural laws and had imposed on his father burdens which he himself ought to have borne. The general was still unable to accept Tom's vocation and at times feared that the church might also take Tecumseh. "The Catholic Church," Sherman wrote a friend, "is ... a very monster. It took from me my son Tom on whom I had a right to depend in my old age, and it renders me suspicious of this my last chance in 'Cump.' He seems to be self possessed, and promises to devote himself to worldly instead of Heavenly matters. Still the insidious plans of those who rule the Church cannot be detected till the mischief is done, as in Tom's case. ... If the same result is to happen to Cump of course I will simply give up, and confess that the Catholic Church is more powerful than the Gov't and should support the family."

The Sherman family, now numbering four—Lizzie, Rachel, Ellen, and Cump—moved into a five-room suite in the Fifth Avenue Hotel, New York City, and Cump set up his office on the ground floor of the army building, at the corner of Green and Houston. Each Saturday he drove to lower Manhattan to see his friend Grenville M. Dodge, who had directed the building of the Union Pacific Railroad. The two generals would spend all afternoon "looking at the Bay," planning lengthy railroad excursions or refighting the Civil War.

Quickly Sherman discovered that living in New York City was not inexpensive, and he pledged his family to rigid economy. This was difficult, as Rachel was endless in her wants. "Were it not for the demands of society, of gay society, we certainly have comfort and peace but in that there is no limit and Rachel thinks that is New York," wrote Ellen.

"My father," remembered Tecumseh, "continually and bitterly complained of ... [the family's] extravagance. That, however, meant less than may seem. My father's entire income was supposed to belong to the family. It was allocated to the members and to special purposes, from time to time, by my father and mother in private conferences, without any apparent friction. It is true that my father occasionally complained that the family was living above its income and that we were 'headed for the poorhouse' but though my mother commonly pooh-poohed the latter prediction she cooperated duly in restrictions on expenditures.

"My mother seldom went out, except to church and an occasional matinee," Tecumseh added, "but she ... had many visitors in the afternoons. ... My father, on the other hand, continued active. He attended all the good plays at the theaters, besides the minstrels, circus and Buffalo Bill's Wild West whenever they came to town, and went to dinners, banquets and G.A.R. and other military association meetings, so frequently as to be seldom at home in evenings."

On a trip to Washington Sherman met Mrs. Grover Cleveland, the president's wife, at a cabinet dinner. In an interview with a reporter from the *Hartford Courant*, he remarked: "She is a very remarkable girl, perfectly quiet and self-possessed, and absolutely without affectation, accepting the dignity of her position with almost a queenly graciousness. I thought her very like the Princess of Wales, and I told her so, and she was very pleased."

While in Detroit visiting Tom, who was teaching there, Ellen noticed the interview in the newspaper and hastily wrote Cump: "Please let me know how much authority there is for the story as I will have it brought to my notice everywhere I go."

On February 8, 1888, Cump celebrated his 68th birthday in his rooms at the Fifth Avenue Hotel. Cards and presents flooded in from all parts of the country, but he wrote Minnie, "nothing gives me the consolation so much as to feel that I possess the love of my children and general confidence of the best men in the United States. ... On the whole after sixty eight years I have reason to be content."

In June, with Ellen feeling unwell, only Lizzie and Cump went up to New Haven to see Tecumseh graduate from Yale. Immediately after the ceremonies, the young man left for a summer vacation. By letter his father lectured him on economy. "I am accustomed to command and be obeyed. Therefore I may be seemingly harsh, but I want to provide for you all as liberally as possible. I want you to think for yourself and to know that money represents human labor. Every dollar I spend costs somebody a hard day's work. If Tom had helped us as he should ten years ago, I feel that I should not now be in this straight [*sic*]. I now depend on you. Thus I want you as soon as possible to secure a good room near us and work hard to take my place."

Lizzie, Rachel, and Cump searched the city for economical hotels and flats. Nothing seemed suitable, until at last they found a new, four-story house at 75 West 71st Street. The owner would not rent. It was to be sold immediately. Cump decided to incur the risk and borrow the necessary capital, even though he had never lost his horror of debt. Ellen was overjoyed. From Woodstock, Md., where she was visiting Tom, she wrote: "My heart feels very much at rest since I can go in fancy any hour of the day or night to *our own home.*"

After moving into their new house in September, Ellen's health failed. For years she had been troubled with a bad heart. Cump refused to admit that she was ill, although in late October, she was confined to bed with around-the-clock nursing.

On November 28 the general was seated in his office when the nurse came to the head of the stairs and called to him that Mrs. Sherman was dying. Distraught, he sped up the stairs, calling: "Wait for me Ellen, no one ever loved you as I love you." If she was alive when he reached her bedside, it was only for a moment.

In the days after he buried his wife, Cump hardly spoke to a soul. The Sherman home was filled with grief-stricken relatives and friends, but the general refused all well-meant offers of sympathy. He sat alone in his bedroom for long hours in black melancholy. His children hardly dared to disturb him. The servants who brought him food came silently, almost furtively.

Unremitting grief preyed upon him. His gauntness became pronounced, and his face wore the strange look of one who had been through a long illness. Ellen was gone and he had only his memories, sad and sweet, going back to youth and their first days together as youngsters.

Such was the intensity of his mourning that the family was deeply concerned and fearful that he might give up everything and become a recluse. Tom wrote his father: "Your life is of such great value to many, to your family, to your relatives, and to friends whose names are legion, to the old soldiers, to the Union, that I trust that you will not tire of it. You are still a power in the land."

Sadly, painstakingly, Cump turned to the mountain of mail which had inundated the house at Ellen's death. To his friend ex-President Hayes, he wrote: "If Charity of Act—not of opinion —if fidelity to the Catholic Church be a Key to Heaven surely she is there; but in her later days, & nights—when dreams told of her inmost thoughts, they went to her first born children, and asked to rest near our William, buried at Calvary Cemetary [in] St. Louis—that is done."

By February he seemed to have recovered from his melancholy and once again was taking part in the social life of New York. Lizzie took over the household chores. Ellie and Minnie and their children often visited their father. Tecumseh was busy at the New York law offices of Evarts and Choate.

On February 8, his birthday, Cump gave a small dinner party for special friends, among whom were Gens. Oliver O. Howard and Henry W. Slocum. With these two officers he had begun that famous march from Atlanta to the sea in November, 1864, and they were among the few leaders of the armies of the Republic who still survived. "Our family circle is diminishing," Cump wrote Minnie that night. "Old Army associates are dropping faster, not a mail but announces the death of some one or more, comparatively young as myself—the wear and tear of war diminishing their lease of life. I go right along the same, and am sure that moderate recreations are as good medicine as any doctor can administer."

"My father went out to dinners and banquets often, though less than before, and made fewer speeches," wrote Tecumseh. "But his principal relaxation away from home continued to be the theater. He had charge accounts at the principal theaters, writing ahead to have two, three or four of the best seats available reserved for him; but he often dropped in alone, to sit for a while in the manager's box or any spare seat. He seldom sat through a play but saw the first half one night and the second half the next night, visiting back stage or going around to the Club during the unseen half."

During those years Sherman went to West Point nearly every June to attend graduation exercises and to hand out diplomas to his beloved cadets. On one visit he led a group of foreign dignitaries and an official West Point escort to his old room in the barracks. When he entered, two cadets leaped to their feet, saluted, and stood rigidly at attention. Looking around, Sherman's gaze rested on the fireplace.

"In my day we always kept edibles in that chimney, although forbidden," he said. "I wonder if there are any there now?"

Borrowing a cane from one of the party, he poked up a corner of the chimney, loosened a board, and a whole shelf of delicatessen goods tumbled down.

"The poor cadets," recalled Tecumseh, "were thunderstruck. But my father directed them to put back their hidden store, and consoled them by remarking that the several officers in his party were not on duty and thus had 'seen nothing.'"

General Sherman refused to attend Tom's ordination as a priest, declaring that he wanted to be as far away as possible "when such a sacrifice is made." He made an all-expense-paid trip to Denver to assist in the city's Fourth of July celebration.

Throughout the rest of the year, he kept busy with official duties. He headed a New York City committee to aid the Johnstown, Pa., flood victims and attended the centennial celebration of George Washington's inauguration.

A storm of telegrams and letters poured in upon the Sherman residence when Cump observed his 70th birthday. It took three birthday dinners to accommodate all his friends. The guest lists were long, including John Sherman, who came up from Washington, Generals Howard and Slocum, and a host of prominent New Yorkers.

A month or two later ex-President Hayes and a friend paid a social call on the general. As they neared the Sherman home they observed workmen fixing flags at the doorstep. A passerby explained that 500 schoolchildren were to march in review before General Sherman.

Hayes found the general with Ellie Thackera and her two children in the parlor. Cump invited Hayes to stand with him, and together they watched the boys pass down 71st Street in military array. On the following evening Cump met Hayes at his hotel, and they went to Delmonico's, where, after dinner with friends, they listened to a reading of a historical paper on the attempts to reinforce Fort Sumter in 1861.

That same month Cump went with Rachel to Washington for John Sherman's birthday celebration and to attend a wedding. He dined with President Benjamin Harrison at the White House. "I could have dined three times a day during our stay in Washington," Cump wrote, "but reserved the time for numerous visits with friends." In August he was in Boston at the encampment of the Grand Army of the Republic and in September in Chicago for the reunion of the Army of the Tennessee. That fall, however, he slowed down, unable to keep up the social pace. "Indeed I am trying to adjust my habits to my years," he told a friend, "and not to tax my strength beyond reason. As it is by force of circumstances I find myself more and more in demand as a social lion."

Christmas was spent with Ellie and her family in Rosemont, Pa. Soon afterward Cump was again in Washington, visiting with the president, vice-president, and members of the cabinet. On February 1, 1891, he wrote Minnie that he would soon be 71 and "I feel no different in strength than twenty years ago." This was Cump's last letter to his beloved Minnie.

A few days later, going out to the theater on a bleak night, he caught a chill, which turned to erysipelas of the face and throat, then to pneumonia. His power of speech failed before he lost consciousness.

On February 12 Rutherford B. Hayes noted in his diary: "No hope for Sherman. . . . He was my best friend. Long before any other prominent man, he said, 'Our President should be one of the volunteers, a man of character, a soldier of approved record, a man like Governor Hayes of Ohio.'"

On that same day, Lizzie recorded in her diary: "There seemed to be no hope—sent for another nurse, who watched through the night." With love but without understanding, the Sherman children summoned Father Byrnes, a Roman Catholic priest, who administered extreme unction.

In his room where a blessed candle was burning, Cump's children and John were at his side when he died quietly on February 14.

Generals Oliver O. Howard, Henry Slocum, and Grenville Dodge directed the funeral arrangements in New York. After a brief service at the house on February 19, with Father Tom Sherman officiating, the funeral procession began through the streets of the city, the cortege consisting of detachments of the Regular Army, West Point cadets, and delegations from patriotic societies.

"I vividly recall the impressive scene in the city of New York when his body was started on his long journey," wrote John Sherman. "The people of the city, in silence and sadness, filled the sidewalks from 71st to Courtland Street, and watched the funeral train, and a countless multitude in every city, town and hamlet on the long road to St. Louis expressed their sorrow and sympathy."

When the train reached Saint Louis on February 21, the funeral procession started from the depot for Calvary Cemetery, with Gen. Wesley Merritt acting as grand marshal. Arriving at the grave next to Ellen's, Father Sherman read the Roman Catholic funeral service, and a battalion of the Thirteenth Regular Infantry, Cump's old regiment, fired the final salute.

From the Kentucky Military Institute, Professor Boyd, Sherman's friend from seminary days, who had served in the Southern armies, wrote Tecumseh: "I did know your father personally and well. . . . Of all the leading northern or Union men, generals and statesmen, I think he knew the South and its people the best. . . . and no man of us was more highly esteemed and beloved and had his sense of duty permitted him to stay with us [in 1861], he would today be a southern idol along with Lee, Jackson and the Johnstons. And God only knows how different *might* have been the result, had his great abilities been thrown on our side!

"I think it was just then, in the Pine Woods of La., from 1859 to 1861," Boyd continued, "that yr. Father's character loomed up *grandest*. [He left] . . . his best and truest friends, because *he thought we were wrong!* Still his great loving heart never ceased to beat warmly for us of the South, and all thro' that terrible struggle, Genl Sherman had more warm, devoted friends in the *Southern* Army than any *Southern* general had!"

President Harrison, who had in 1864 participated in the Atlanta campaign, announced General Sherman's death to both Houses of Congress, and added: "The death of William Tecumseh Sherman . . . is an event that will bring sorrow to the heart of every patriotic citizen. No living American was so loved and venerated as he. To look upon his face, to hear his name, was to have one's love of country intensified. He served his country, not for fame, not out of a sense of professional duty, but for love of the flag and of the beneficent civil institutions of which it was the emblem. He was an ideal soldier, and shared to the fullest the *espirit de corps* of the army; but he cherished the civil institutions organized under the constitution, and was a soldier only that these might be perpetuated in undiminished usefulness and honor. . . ."

Bibliographical Note

Besides relying heavily upon the Sherman and Ewing family manuscripts and edited letters and diaries, I have leaned upon significant secondary materials on which to base certain chapters or themes: `the presidency of the Louisiana Military Academy, Walter L. Fleming's "William Tecumseh Sherman as College President," *South Atlantic Quarterly*; total war concept, John B. Walters's "General William T. Sherman and Total War," *Journal of Southern History*; relationships with Gen. Henry W. Halleck, Stephen E. Ambrose's *Halleck, Lincoln's Chief of Staff*; use of railroads, Jesse C. Burt's "Sherman, Railroad General" and Armin Mruck's "The Role of Railroads in the Atlanta Campaign," both in *Civil War History*; battlefield terrain, Bruce Catton's works; occupation of Milledgeville, Ga., James C. Bonner's "Sherman at Milledgeville in 1864," *Journal of Southern History*; occupation of Savannah, Ga., John P. Dyer's "Northern Relief for Savannah During Sherman's Occupation [1864-65]," *Journal of Southern History*, and Josef C. James's "Sherman at Savannah," *Journal of Negro History*; march through the Carolinas, John G. Barrett's "Sherman and Total War in the Carolinas," *North Carolina Historical Review*; relationships with Secretary of War Stanton, Benjamin P. Thomas and Harold M. Hyman's *Stanton, The Life and Times of Lincoln's Secretary of War*; reconstruction, Eric L. McKitrick's *Andrew Johnson and Reconstruction*; relationships with Ulysses S. Grant after the war, William B. Hesseltine's *Ulysses S. Grant, Politician*; relationships with Thomas Sherman, Joseph T. Durkin's *General Sherman's Son*; the West after the war, Robert G. Athearn's *William Tecumseh Sherman and the Settlement of the West*, and William H. Leckie's *The Military

411

Conquest of the Southern Plains; attitudes toward the Negro, Robert K. Murray's "General Sherman, The Negro, and Slavery: The Story of An Unrecognized Rebel," *Negro History Bulletin;* attitudes toward religion, Jack J. Detzler's "The Religion of William Tecumseh Sherman," *Ohio History.*

Unlike previous biographers of Sherman, I have purposely refrained, except on rare occasions, from utilizing regimental histories, memoirs, or the time-honored *Battles and Leaders of the Civil War.* Although some of this material is first-rate literature, much of it was written well after the events described and inaccuracies have occurred. Rachel Sherman Thorndike's *The Sherman Letters,* and M. A. DeWolfe Howe's *Home Letters of General Sherman* should also be used with caution, as their texts differ, sometimes drastically, with the manuscript copies.

Helping to make this bibliography possible were the staffs of the Iowa State Department of History and Archives; Illinois State Historical Library; Ohio Historical Society; Notre Dame University Archives; Rutherford B. Hayes Library, especially its director, Watt P. Marchman; United States Military Academy Library and Museum; Library of Congress, Manuscript Division, especially John Knowlton, William H. Mobley, and Carolyn H. Sung. I also thank Lynn Pancoast, Janet Morris, and Carol Ann Tylecki, University of Delaware students.

Bibliography

MANUSCRIPTS

Nathaniel Banks Papers: Illinois State Historical Library; University of Texas (microfilm).

Grenville M. Dodge Papers: Iowa State Department of History and Archives.

Hugh Boyle Ewing Papers: Ohio Historical Society.

Philemon Beecher Ewing Papers: Ohio Historical Society.

Thomas Ewing Papers: Kansas State Historical Society (microfilm); Ohio Historical Society.

Thomas Ewing Family Papers: Library of Congress, Manuscript Division; Notre Dame University Archives.

Andrew Hull Foote Papers: Library of Congress, Manuscript Division.

Benjamin H. Grierson Papers: Illinois State Historical Library.

Rutherford B. Hayes Papers: Rutherford B. Hayes Library, Fremont, Ohio.

Andrew Johnson Papers: Library of Congress, Manuscript Division (microfilm).

Abraham Lincoln Papers: Illinois State Historical Library.

John A. McClernand Papers: Illinois State Historical Library.

David Dixon Porter Papers: Library of Congress, Manuscript Division.

John Sherman Papers: Library of Congress, Manuscript Division.

William T. Sherman Papers: Library of Congress, Manuscript Division; Notre Dame University Archives; Ohio Historical Society; United States Military Academy.

UNITED STATES GOVERNMENT DOCUMENTS

Annual Report of the Secretary of War. Army-Staff Organization, 42d Cong., 3d sess., H. Rept. 74.

Diplomatic Correspondence with Mexico, 1866–1868, 39th Cong., 2d sess., *House Ex. Doc.,* No. 1, pt. 3; 40th Cong., 2d sess., *House Ex. Doc.,* No. 1, pt. 2.

Letter from the Secretary of the Interior, Communicating . . . information in relation to the late massacre of the United States troops by Indians at or near Fort Phil. Kearney, in Dakota Territory, 39th Cong., 2d sess., *Sen. Ex. Doc.,* No. 16.

Letter of the Secretary of War, Communicating . . . the official reports, papers, and other facts in relation to the causes and extent of the late massacre of United States troops by Indians at Fort Phil. Kearney, 39th Cong., 2d sess., *Sen. Ex. Doc.,* No. 15.

Letter from the Secretary of War . . . relative to the issue of a large number of arms to the Kiowas and other Indians, 39th Cong., 2d sess., *House Misc. Doc.,* No. 41.

Letter of the Secretary of War, Communicating . . . further information respecting armed expeditions against the western Indians, 40th Cong., 1st sess., *Sen. Ex. Doc.,* No. 7.

Letter of the Secretary of War, Communicating . . . information in relation to an order issued by Lieutenant General Sherman in regard to the protection of trains on the overland route, 40th Cong., 1st sess., *Sen. Ex. Doc.,* No. 2.

Letter from the Secretary of War . . . in relation to the late expedition against the . . . Indians, in the Territory of Montana, 41st Cong., 2d sess., *House Ex. Doc.,* No. 269.

Letter from the Secretary of War . . . transmitting a communication from General Grant on Indian Affairs, 39th Cong., 2d sess., *House Misc. Doc.,* No. 40.

Letter from the Secretary of War . . . transmitting information respecting the protection of the routes across the continent to the Pacific from molestation by hostile Indians, 39th Cong., 2d sess., *House Ex. Doc.,* No. 23.

Letter from the Secretary of War, transmitting A communication from Lieutenant Sherman, relative to the subsistence of certain Indian tribes by the War Department, &c., 40th Cong., 2d sess., *House Ex. Doc.,* No. 239.

Message from the President of the United States, Communicating, Information . . . in relation to California and New Mexico, 31st Cong., 1st sess., *Sen. Ex. Doc.,* No. 18.

Message of the President of the United States . . . calling for information respecting any correspondence or proceedings in relation to the self-styled Vigilance Committee in California, 34th Cong., 1st sess., *Sen. Ex. Doc.,* No. 101.

Message from the President of the United States, Transmitting . . . copy of a letter to the Secretary of War, by General W. T. Sherman, 48th Cong., 2d sess., *Sen. Ex. Doc.,* No. 36.

Message from the President of the United States, transmitting Copies of the correspondence and papers relative to the war with the Modoc Indians in Southern Oregon and Northern California, during the years 1872 and 1873, 43d Cong., 1st sess., *House Ex. Doc.,* No. 122.

Official Records of the Union and Confederate Navies in the War of the Rebellion, 26 vols.

Papers Relating to Foreign Affairs, 1866, pt. 3.

Report of the Committee on Military Affairs of the House of Representatives upon the Reduction of the Military Establishment and in Relation to the Fortifications and Works of Defense, 43d Cong., 1st sess., H. Rept. 384.

Report of the Joint Committee on the Conduct of the War, 37th Cong., 3d sess., Sen. Rept. 108; 38th Cong., 2d sess., Sen. Rept. 142.

Report of the Secretary of War, Communicating . . . correspondence in relation to the proceedings of the Vigilance Committee in San Francisco, California, 34th Cong., 3d sess., *Sen. Ex. Doc.,* No. 43.

Report on Army Organization, 40th Cong., 3d sess., H. Rept. 33.

Reports of Inspection Made in the Summer of 1877 by Generals P. H. Sheridan and W. T. Sherman of Country North of the Union Pacific R. R.

Testimony in Relation to Indian War-Claims of the Territory of Montana, 42d Cong., 2d sess., *House Misc. Doc.,* No. 215.

Testimony Taken by the Committee on Military Affairs in Relation to the Texas Border Troubles, 46th Cong., 2d sess., *House Misc. Doc.,* No. 64.

Transfer of the Bureau of Indian Affairs to the War Department, 46th Cong., 2d sess., H. Rept. 1393.

The War of the Rebellion: A Compilation of the Official Records of the Union and Confederate Armies, 128 vols.

NEWSPAPERS

Atlanta Constitution, Harper's Weekly, London Times, New Orleans Picayune, The New York Independent, New York Times, New York Tribune.

DIARIES, LETTERS, MEMOIRS,
AND REMINISCENCES

Abernethy, Byron R., ed. *Private Elisha Stockwell, Jr. Sees the Civil War.* 1958.

Andrews, Eliza F. *The War-Time Journal of a Georgia Girl, 1864–1865.* 1908.

Arbuckle, John C. *Civil War Experiences of a Foot-Soldier Who Marched with Sherman.* 1930.

Ashcraft, Allan C., ed. "Mrs. Russell and the Battle of Raymond, Mississippi," *Journal of Mississippi History* 25 (1963):38–40.

Athearn, Robert G., ed. "An Indiana Doctor Marches with Sherman: the Diary of James Comfort Patten," *Indiana Magazine of History* 49 (1953):405–22.

Audenried, J. C. "General Sherman in Europe and the East," *Harper's* 47 (1873):225–42, 481–95, 652–71.

Beale, Howard K., ed. "Diary of Edward Bates, 1859–1866," *Annual Report of the American Historical Association* (1933).

Beale, Howard K., and Brownsword, Alan, eds. *Diary of Gideon Welles, Secretary of the Navy Under Lincoln and Johnson,* 3 vols. 1960.

Beatty, John. *The Citizen-Soldier; or Memoirs of a Volunteer.* 1879.

Berger, Homer H., ed. "Sherman's Occupation of Savannah: Two Letters," *Georgia Historical Quarterly* 50 (1966):109–15.

Black, Wilfred W., ed. "Civil War Letters of George M. Wise," *Ohio Historical Quarterly* 65 (1956):53–81.

―――――. "Marching through South Carolina: Another Letter of Lieutenant George M. Wise," *Ohio Historical Quarterly* 66 (1957):187–95.

―――――. "Marching with Sherman through Georgia and the Carolinas: Civil War Diary of Jesse L. Dozer," *Georgia Historical Quarterly* 52 (1968):308–30, 451–73.

Bok, Edward W. *The Americanization of Edward Bok.* 1920.

Bradley, G. S. *The Star Corps; or, Notes of an Army Chaplain, during Sherman's Famous 'March to the Sea.'* 1865.

Bratton, J. R. "Letter of a Confederate Surgeon on Sherman's Occupation of Milledgeville," *Georgia Historical Quarterly* 32 (1948): 231–32.

Browning, Orville Hickman. *The Diary of Orville Hickman Browning,* 2 vols. Edited by James G. Randall and Theodore C. Pease. 1925, 1933.

Bryan, T. Conn, ed. "A Georgia Woman's Civil War Diary: The Journal of Minerva Leah Rowles McClatchey," *Georgia Historical Quarterly* 51 (1967):197–216.

Buell, Don C. "Shiloh Reviewed," *Century* 9 (1886):749–81.

Burge, Dolly S. L. *A Woman's Wartime Journal . . . With an Introduction and Notes by Julian Street.* 1918.

Byers, Samuel H. M. "The Burning of Columbia," *Lippincott's* 29 (1882):255–61.

Cadman, George H. "A Billy Yank's Impressions of the South," edited by Carrol Hunter Quenzel, *Tennessee Historical Quarterly* 12 (1953):99–105.

Cadwallader, Sylvanus. *Three Years with Grant.* Edited by Benjamin P. Thomas. 1956.

Cain, J. Isaiah. "The Battle of Atlanta as Described by a Confederate Soldier," contributed by Andrew F. Muir, *Georgia Historical Quarterly* 42 (1958):109–11.

Chase, Salmon P. "Diary and Correspondence of Salmon P. Chase," *Annual Report of The American Historical Association* (1903).

————. *Inside Lincoln's Cabinet: The Civil War Diaries of Salmon P. Chase.* Edited by David Donald. 1954.

Chesnut, Mary Boykin Miller. *A Diary from Dixie.* Edited by Ben Ames Williams. 1949.

Clarke, John T. "With Sherman in Georgia," Missouri Historical Society, *Bulletin* 8 (1952):356–70.

Cohen, Fanny. "Fanny Cohen's Journal of Sherman's Occupation of Savannah," edited by Spencer B. King, Jr., *Georgia Historical Quarterly* 41 (1957):407–16.

Colby, Carlos W. "Bullets, Hardtack and Mud: A Soldier's View of the Vicksburg Campaign," edited by John S. Painter, *Journal of the West* 4 (1965):129–68.

Commager, Henry Steele, ed. *The Blue and the Gray: The Story of the Civil War as Told by Participants*, 2 vols. 1950.

Connolly, James A. "[Diary and Letters of] Major James Austin Connolly," Illinois State Historical Society, *Transactions* (1928):215–438.

Cook, Charles N., and Ball, Lafayette. "Letters of Privates Cook and Ball," *Indiana Magazine of History* 27 (1931):243–68.

Crosley, George W. "Lieutenant Crosley Tells of 3rd Iowa at Shiloh," *Civil War History* 2 (1956):139–44.

Dana, Charles A. *Recollections of the Civil War*. 1898.

Davis, Theo. R. "With Sherman in his Army Home," *Cosmopolitan* 12 (1891):195–205.

Disbrow, Donald W., ed. "Vett Noble of Ypsilanti: A Clerk for General Sherman," *Civil War History* 14 (1968):15–39.

Dodge, Grenville M. *Personal Recollections of President Abraham Lincoln, General Ulysses S. Grant and General William T. Sherman.* 1914.

Eaton, Clement, ed. "Diary of an Officer in Sherman's Army Marching through the Carolinas [Dexter Horton]," *Journal of Southern History* 9 (1943):238–54.

Erickson, Edgar L., ed. "With Grant at Vicksburg—From the Civil War Diary of Captain Charles E. Wilcox," Illinois State Historical Society, *Journal* 30 (1938):441–503.

Ewing, Charles. "Sherman's March Through Georgia: Letters from Charles Ewing to His Father Thomas Ewing," edited by George C. Osborn, *Georgia Historical Quarterly* 42 (1958):323–27.

Ewing, Thomas. "Diary of Thomas Ewing, August and September, 1841," *American Historical Review* 18 (1912):97–112.

Fauntleroy, James H. "Elk Horn to Vicksburg," edited by Homer L. Calkin, *Civil War History* 2 (1956):7–43.

Grant, Ulysses S. "The Battle of Shiloh," *Century* 29 (1885):593–613.

———. "Letter [of Grant] to his father, on the Capture of Vicksburg," *American Historical Review* 12 (1906):109.

Hanger, George W. "With Sherman in Georgia—a Letter from the Coast," contributed by F. B. Joyner, *Georgia Historical Quarterly* 42 (1958):440–41.

Hannahs, Harrison. "General Thomas Ewing, Jr.," Kansas State Historical Society, *Collections* 12 (1911–12):276–82.

Harwell, Richard B., ed. "The Campaign from Chattanooga to Atlanta as Seen by a Federal Soldier [Ira B. Read]," *Georgia Historical Quarterly* 25 (1941):262–78.

Hass, Paul H., ed. "The Vicksburg Diary of Henry Clay Warmoth (April 3, 1863–May 26, 1863)," *Journal of Mississippi History* 31 (1969):334–47; 32 (1970):60–74.

Hay, John. *Lincoln and the Civil War in the Diaries and Letters of John Hay.* 1939.

Hayes, Rutherford Birchard. *Diary and Letters of Rutherford Birchard Hayes, Nineteenth President of the United States,* 5 vols. Edited by Charles R. Williams. 1922–26.

Hesseltine, William B., and Gara, Larry, eds. "Sherman Burns the Libraries," *South Carolina Historical Magazine* 55 (1954):137–43.

Hinkley, Julian W. *A Narrative of Service with the Third Wisconsin Infantry.* 1912.

Hitchcock, Henry. *Marching with Sherman.* Edited by M. A. DeWolfe Howe. 1927.

Hood, John B. *Advance and Retreat: Personal Experiences in the United States and Confederate States Armies.* 1880.

Howard, Oliver Otis. *Autobiography,* 2 vols. 1908.

Howe, M. A. DeWolfe, ed. *Home Letters of General Sherman.* 1909.

Jackson, Oscar L. *The Colonel's Diary: Journals Kept Before and During the Civil War by the Late Colonel Oscar L. Jackson of New Castle, Pennsylvania, Sometime Commander of the Sixty-Third Regiment Ohio Volunteer Infantry.* 1922.

Johnson, Robert U., and Buel, Clarence C., eds. *Battles and Leaders of the Civil War,* 4 vols. 1884–88.

Johnston, Joseph E. *Narrative of Military Operations.* 1874.

Jones, Jenkin L. *An Artilleryman's Diary.* 1914.

Jones, Katharine M., ed. *When Sherman Came: Southern Women and the 'Great March.'* 1964.

Keller, Dean H., ed. "A Civil War Diary of Albion W. Tourgee," *Ohio History* 74 (1965):99–131.

Kellogg, Mary F., comp. *Army Life of an Illinois Soldier, Including a Day by Day Record of Sherman's March to the Sea; Letters and Diary of Charles W. Wills.* 1906.

Lay, Henry C. "Sherman in Georgia," *Atlantic* 149 (1932):166–72.

LeConte, Joseph. *'Ware Sherman: a Journal of Three Months' Personal Experience in the Last Days of the Confederacy.* 1937.

Lewis, Donald W., ed. "A Confederate Officer's [Capt. Samuel McKittrick] Letters on Sherman's March to Atlanta," *Georgia Historical Quarterly* 51 (1967):491–94.

Lincoln, Abraham. *Collected Works*. Edited by Roy P. Basler et al. 8 vols. 1953.

Lord, W. W., Jr. "In the Path of Sherman," *Harper's* 120 (1910): 438–46.

Lusk, William T. *War Letters of William Thompson Lusk, Captain, Assistant Adjutant General United States Volunteers, 1861–1863*. 1911.

Lyman, Theodore. *Meade's Headquarters, 1863–1865*. Edited by George Russell Agassiz. 1922.

McCarter, James. "The Burning of Columbia Again," *Harper's* 33 (1866):642–45.

McClellan, George B. *McClellan's Own Story*. 1887.

McClure, A. K. *Abraham Lincoln and Men of War-Times*. 1892.

McClurg, Alexander C. "The Last Chance of the Confederacy," *Atlantic* 50 (1882):389–400.

Macy, William M. "The Civil War Diary of William M. Macy," *Indiana Magazine of History* 30 (1934):181–97.

Martzolff, Clement L., ed. "Address [by Thomas Ewing] at Marietta, Ohio, 1858," *Ohio Archaeological and Historical Quarterly* 28 (1919):186–207.

———. "The Autobiography of Thomas Ewing," *Ohio Archaeological and Historical Quarterly* 22 (1913):126–204.

Matthews, James Louis. "Civil War Diary of Sergeant James Louis Matthews," edited by Roger C. Hackett, *Indiana Magazine of History* 24 (1928):306–16.

Maynard, Douglas, ed. "Vicksburg Diary: The Journal of Gabriel M. Killgore," *Civil War History* 10 (1964):33–53.

Mead, Rufus, Jr. "With Sherman Through Georgia and the Carolinas: Letters of a Federal Soldier," edited by James A. Padgett, *Georgia Historical Quarterly* 33 (1949):49–81.

Merrill, Samuel. "Letters from a Civil War Officer," edited by A. T. Volwiler, *Mississippi Valley Historical Review* 14 (1928):508–29.

Miers, Earl Schenck, ed. *When the World Ended. The Diary of Emma LeConte*. 1957.

Newcomer, Lee N., ed. " 'Think Kindly of us of the South:' a Letter [by Harvey W. Walter] to William Tecumseh Sherman," *Ohio History* 71 (1962):148–50.

Nichols, George W. *The Story of the Great March.* 1865.

Nichols, Roy F., ed. "William Tecumseh Sherman in 1850," *Pennsylvania Magazine of History and Biography* 75 (1951):424–35.

Norton, Eliot. "Tales at First Hand," *Blackwood's* 233 (1933):33–42.

Norton, Oliver W. *Army Letters, 1861–1865.* 1903.

Orme, William W. "Civil War Letters of Brigadier-General William Ward Orme, 1862–1866," Illinois State Historical Society, *Journal* 23 (1930):246–315.

Partin, Robert L., ed. "A Confederate Sergeant's Report [Hiram T. Holt] to His Wife During the Campaign from Tullahoma to Dalton," *Tennessee Historical Quarterly* 12 (1953):291–308.

Patrick, Robert. *Reluctant Rebel [His] Secret Diary, 1861–1865.* Edited by F. Jay Taylor. 1959.

Pierson, Stephen. "From Chattanooga to Atlanta in 1864—A Personal Reminiscence," New Jersey Historical Society, *Proceedings* 16 (1931):324–56.

Plummer, Leonard B., ed. "Excerpts from the [Christian W.] Hander Diary," *Journal of Mississippi History* 26 (1964):141–49.

Porter, David D. *Incidents and Anecdotes of the Civil War.* 1885.

Quaife, Milo M., ed. *From the Cannon's Mouth: The Civil War Letters of General Alpheus S. Williams.* 1959.

Quillin, Martha. "A Letter on Sherman's March Through Georgia," edited by George W. Clower, *Georgia Historical Quarterly* 37 (1953):160–62.

Reynolds, Donald E., and Kele, Max H., eds. "A Yank in the Carolinas Campaign: The Diary of James W. Chapin, Eighth Indiana Cavalry," *North Carolina Historical Review* 46 (1969):42–57.

Rziha, John. "With Sherman Through Georgia: A Journal," edited by David J. DeLaubenfels, *Georgia Historical Quarterly* 41 (1957): 288–300.

Schofield, John M. *Forty-Six Years in the Army.* 1897.

Shanks, William G. F. "Recollections of General Sherman," *Harper's* 30 (1865):640–46.

Sheridan, Philip H. *Personal Memoirs,* 2 vols. 1888.

Sherman, John. *Recollections of Forty Years in the House, Senate and Cabinet: An Autobiography,* 2 vols. 1895.

Sherman, Minnie Ewing. "My Father's Letters," *Cosmopolitan* 12 (1891):64–69, 187–94.

Sherman, William T. "A Sheaf of Sherman Letters, 1863–81," edited by James Grant Wilson, *The Independent* 54 (1902):213–15.

————. "Camp-Fires of the G. A. R.," *North American Review* 147 (1888):497–502.

————. "General Sherman on his Own Record," edited by J. W. Young, *Atlantic* 108 (1911):289–300.

————. "General Sherman's Tour. Extracts from the Diary of General W. T. Sherman," *Century* 57 (1899):729–40, 866–75; 58 (1899): 278–87.

————. "Graduation Address, USMA, 1869," *Army* 16 (1966):61–65.

————. *Memoirs of General William T. Sherman*, 2 vols. 1893.

————. "Sherman and the San Francisco Vigilantes," *Century* 43 (1891):296–309.

————. "Sherman's Estimate of Grant," *Century* 70 (1905):316–18.

————. "Unpublished Letters of General Sherman," *North American Review* 152 (1891):371–75.

Sherman, William T., and Sherman, John. "Letters of Two Brothers," edited by J. D. Cox, *Century* 45 (1892–93):88–101, 425–40, 689–99, 892–903.

Simms, L. Moody, Jr., ed. "A Louisiana Engineer at the Siege of Vicksburg: Letters of Henry Ginder," *Louisiana History* 8 (1967):371–78.

Snure, Samuel E. "The Vicksburg Campaign as Viewed by an Indiana Soldier," *Journal of Mississippi History* 19 (1957):263–69.

Sosnowski, Sophie. "The Burning of Columbia," edited by Lester Hargrett, *Georgia Historical Quarterly* 8 (1924):195–214.

Thorndike, Rachel Sherman, ed. *The Sherman Letters, Correspondence Between General and Senator Sherman from 1837 to 1891.* 1894.

Upson, Theodore F. *With Sherman to the Sea. The Civil War Diaries, Letters and Reminiscences of Theodore F. Upson.* Edited by Oscar O. Winther. 1943.

Weaver, Henry C. "Georgia Through Kentucky Eyes: Letters Written on Sherman's March to Atlanta," edited by James M. Merrill and James F. Marshall, *Filson Club History Quarterly* 30 (1956):324–39.

Weller, Ella F., ed. "Stranger than Fiction. A True Story Told Mainly in a Series of Unpublished Letters by General Sherman," *McClure's* 8 (1897):546–50.

Wilson, James Harrison. *Under the Old Flag*, 2 vols. 1912.

Zearing, James R. "Letters Written by Dr. James R. Zearing to his Wife Lucinda Helmer Zearing during the Civil War, 1861–1865," Illinois State Historical Society, *Transactions* (1921):150–202.

ARTICLES

Ambrose, Stephen. "The Union Command System and the Donelson Campaign," *Military Affairs* 24 (1960):78–86.

————. "William T. Sherman," *American History Illustrated* 1 (1967):5–12, 54–57.

Anders, Leslie. "Missourians Who 'Marched through Georgia,' " *Missouri Historical Review* 59 (1965):192–209.

Athearn, Robert G. "General Sherman and the Western Railroads," *Pacific Historical Review* 24 (1955):39–48.

Barrett, John G. "Sherman and Total War in the Carolinas," *North Carolina Historical Review* 37 (1960):367–81.

Bearss, Edwin C. "General William Nelson Saves the Day at Shiloh," Kentucky State Historical Society, *Register* 63 (1965):39–69.

————. "Sherman's Demonstration Against Snyder's Bluff," *Journal of Mississippi History* 27 (1965):168–86.

Bonner, James C. "Sherman at Milledgeville in 1864," *Journal of Southern History* 22 (1956):273–91.

Boylan, Bernard L. "The Forty-Fifth Congress and Army Reform," *Mid-America* 42 (1959):173–86.

Burt, Jesse C., Jr. "Sherman, Railroad General," *Civil War History* 2 (1956):45–54.

————. "Sherman's Logistics and Andrew Johnson," *Tennessee Historical Quarterly* 15 (1956):195–215.

Catton, Bruce. "Hayfoot, Strawfoot!" *American Heritage* 8 (1957): 30–37.

Chaddock, Robert E. "Ohio before 1850," *Columbia University Studies in History, Economics and Public Law* 31 (1908).

Clauss, Errol M. "Sherman's Rail Support in the Atlanta Campaign," *Georgia Historical Quarterly* 50 (1966):413–20.

Coffman, Edward M. "Army Life on the Frontier, 1865–1898," *Military Affairs* 20 (1956):193–201.

Cooling, Benjamin F. "Alabamians in the Forts Henry and Donelson Campaign," *Alabama Historical Review* 26 (1964):217–34.

————. "The First Nebraska Infantry Regiment and the Battle of Fort Donelson," *Nebraska History* 23 (1964):131–45.

Coulter, E. Merton. "Sherman and the South," *North Carolina Historical Review* 8 (1931):41–54.

Cox, Jacob D. "The Sherman-Johnston Convention," *Scribner's* 28 (1900):489–505.

DeLaubenfels, D. J. "Where Sherman Passed By," *Geographical Review* 47 (1957):381–95.

Detzler, Jack J. "The Religion of William Tecumseh Sherman," *Ohio History* 75 (1966):26–34, 68–70.

Downer, Edward T. "Ohio Troops in the Field [1861–65]," *Civil War History* 3 (1957):253–84.

Dyer, John P. "Northern Relief for Savannah During Sherman's Occupation [1864–65]," *Journal of Southern History* 19 (1953):457–72.

Eastwood, Bruce S. "Confederate Medical Problems in the Atlanta Campaign," *Georgia Historical Quarterly* 47 (1963):276–92.

Eisenschiml, Otto. "The 55th Illinois at Shiloh," Illinois State Historical Society, *Journal* 56 (1963):193–211.

Engerud, H. "General Grant, Fort Donelson and 'Old Brains,' " *Filson Club History Quarterly* 39 (1965):201–15.

Fleming, Walter L. "General William T. Sherman as a History Teacher," *The Educational Review* 40 (1911):235–38.

————. "William Tecumseh Sherman as College President," *South Atlantic Quarterly* 11 (1912):33–54.

Fornell, Earl W. "The Civil War Comes to Savannah," *Georgia Historical Quarterly* 43 (1959):248–60.

Futrell, Robert J. "Federal Military Government in the South, 1861–1865," *Military Affairs* 15 (1951):181–91.

Garfield, Marvin H. "Defense of the Kansas Frontier, 1866–1869," *Kansas Historical Quarterly* 1 (1932):326–44, 451–73.

Gray, Tom S., Jr. "The March to the Sea," *Georgia Historical Quarterly* 14 (1930):111–38.

Harn, George U. "John Sherman," *Ohio Archaeological and Historical Publications* 17 (1908):309–36.

Hartje, Robert. "Van Dorn Conducts a Raid on Holly Springs and Enters Tennessee," *Tennessee Historical Quarterly* 18 (1959):120–33.

Hay, Thomas R. "Confederate Leadership at Vicksburg," *Mississippi Valley Historical Review* 11 (1925):543–60.

Hill, James D. "The Burning of Columbia Reconsidered," *South Atlantic Quarterly* 25 (1926):269–82.

Hughes, N. C., Jr. "Hardee's Defense of Savannah," *Georgia Historical Quarterly* 47 (1963):43–67.

Huling, Polly. "Missourians at Vicksburg," *Missouri Historical Review* 50 (1955):1–15.

James, Josef C. "Sherman at Savannah," *Journal of Negro History* 39 (1954):127–37.

Johnston, Frank. "The Vicksburg Campaign," Mississippi Historical Society, *Publications* 10 (1909):63–90.

Jones, Archer. "Confederate Strategy from Shiloh to Vicksburg," *Journal of Mississippi History* 24 (1962):158–67.

———. "The Vicksburg Campaign," *Journal of Mississippi History* 29 (1967):12–27.

Jones, James P. "The Battle of Atlanta and McPherson's Successor," *Civil War History* 7 (1961):393–405.

———. "General Jeff C. Davis, U.S.A., and Sherman's Georgia Campaign," *Georgia Historical Quarterly* 47 (1963):231–48.

Kite, Elizabeth S. "Genius of the Civil War," *Commonweal* 27 (1938): 541–43.

Lee, Stephen D. "The War in Mississippi after the Fall of Vicksburg, July 4, 1863," Mississippi Historical Society, *Publications* 10 (1909): 47–62.

Liddell Hart, B. H. "Sherman—Modern Warrior," *American Heritage* 13 (1962):21–23, 102–106.

Livermore, W. R. "Campaign around Vicksburg, 1862," Massachusetts Historical Society, *Proceedings* 43 (1910):233–36.

Lobdell, Jared. "A Civil War Tank at Vicksburg," *Journal of Mississippi History* 25 (1963):279–83.

Luvaas, Jay. "Johnston's Last Stand—Bentonville," *North Carolina Historical Review* 33 (1956):332–56.

McWhiney, Grady. "Braxton Bragg at Shiloh," *Tennessee Historical Quarterly* 21 (1962):19–30.

Mardock, Robert W. "The Plains Frontier and the Indian Peace Policy, 1865–1880," *Nebraska History* 49 (1968):187–201.

Massey, Mary E. "Southern Refugee Life during the Civil War," *North Carolina Historical Review* 20 (1943):1–21, 132–56.

Moore, Ross H. "The Vicksburg Campaign of 1863," *Journal of Mississippi History* 1 (1939):151–68.

Mruck, Armin. "The Role of Railroads in the Atlanta Campaign," *Civil War History* 7 (1961):264–71.

Murray, Robert K. "General Sherman, The Negro, and Slavery: The

Story of An Unrecognized Rebel," *Negro History Bulletin* 22 (1959):125–30.

Naroll, Raoul S. "Lincoln and the Sherman Peace Fiasco—Another Fable?" *Journal of Southern History* 20 (1954):459–83.

Nichols, Jeanette P. "John Sherman: A Study in Inflation," *Mississippi Valley Historical Review* 21 (1934):181–94.

————. "Rutherford B. Hayes and John Sherman," *Ohio History* 77 (1968):125–38.

O'Connor, Richard. "Sherman: Imaginative Soldier," *American Mercury* 67 (1948):555–64.

Owsley, Frank L. "Defeatism in the Confederacy," *North Carolina Historical Review* 3 (1926):446–56.

Pfanz, Harry W. "The Surrender Negotiations between General [Joseph E.] Johnston and General Sherman, April 1865," *Military Affairs* 16 (1952):61–70.

Prickett, Robert C. "The Malfeasance of William Worth Belknap, Secretary of War, October 13, 1869 to March 2, 1876," *North Dakota History* 17 (1950):6–51, 97–130.

Randall, James G. "John Sherman and Reconstruction," *Mississippi Valley Historical Review* 19 (1932):382–93.

————. "The Newspaper Problem In Its Bearing Upon Military Secrecy during the Civil War," *American Historical Review* 23 (1918):303–23.

Rhodes, James Ford. "Sherman's March to the Sea," *American Historical Review* 6 (1901):466–74.

————. "Who Burned Columbia?" Massachusetts Historical Society, *Proceedings* 15, ser. II (1901):264–74.

Roland, Charles P. "Albert Sidney Johnston and the Loss of Forts Henry and Donelson," *Journal of Southern History* 23 (1957):45–69.

Root, George A., and Hickman, Russell K "Pike's Peak Express Companies," *Kansas Historical Quarterly* 13 (1944):163–94, 211–42, 485–526.

Smalley, E. V. "General Sherman," *Century* 5 (1884):450–62.

"Thomas Ewing," *New-England Magazine* 8 (1835):382–92.

Walters, John B. "General William T. Sherman and Total War," *Journal of Southern History* 14 (1948):447–80.

Weatherford, John. "Ohio and the Civil War in Manuscripts," *Civil War History* 3 (1957):307–13.

Whitesell, Robert D. "Military and Naval Activity Between Cairo and

Columbus," Kentucky State Historical Society, *Register* 61 (1963): 107–21.

Wiley, Bell Irvin. "Billy Yank and the Black Folk," *Journal of Negro History* 36 (1951):35–52.

_____. "Billy Yank Down South," *Virginia Quarterly Review* 26 (1950):559–75.

Wilson, Edmund. "Uncle Billy," *New Yorker* 34 (1958):114–44.

Woody, Robert H. "Some Aspects of the Economic Condition of South Carolina After the Civil War," *North Carolina Historical Review* 7 (1930):346–64.

Yates, Richard E. "Governor Vance and the End of the War in North Carolina," *North Carolina Historical Review* 18 (1941):315–38.

BOOKS

Ambrose, Stephen E. *Duty, Honor, Country: A History of West Point.* 1966.

_____. *Halleck, Lincoln's Chief of Staff.* 1962.

Andrews, J. Cutler. *The North Reports the Civil War.* 1953.

Athearn, Robert G. *William Tecumseh Sherman and the Settlement of the West.* 1956.

Badeau, Adam. *Grant in Peace.* 1888.

Baldwin, Leland D., and Kelley, Robert. *The Stream of American History.* 1965.

Barnard, Harry. *Rutherford B. Hayes and His America.* 1954.

Barrett, John G. *Sherman's March Through the Carolinas.* 1956.

Baxter, Maurice G. *Orville H. Browning, Lincoln's Friend and Critic.* 1957.

Bemrose, John. *Reminiscences of the Second Seminole War.* Edited by John K. Mahon. 1967.

Billington, Ray Allen, and Hedges, J. B. *Westward Expansion: A History of the American Frontier.* 1960.

Boyd, James P. *The Life of General William T. Sherman.* 1892.

Bradley, Erwin S. *Simon Cameron, Lincoln's Secretary of War: A Political Biography.* 1966.

Bryant, Edwin E. *History of the Third Regiment of Wisconsin Volunteer Infantry.* 1891.

Burton, Katherine K. *Three Generations: Maria Boyle Ewing (1801–*

1864); Ellen Ewing Sherman (1824–1888); Minnie Sherman Fitch (1851–1913). 1947.

Caldwell, Robert G. *James A. Garfield, Party Chieftain.* 1931.

Capers, Gerald M., Jr. *The Biography of a River Town: Memphis—Its Heroic Age.* 1939.

Carman, Harry J. et al. *A History of the American People,* vol. 1. 1967.

Carpenter, John A. *Sword and Olive Branch: Oliver Otis Howard.* 1964.

Catton, Bruce. *The Coming Fury.* 1961.

————. *Never Call Retreat.* 1965.

————. *Terrible Swift Sword.* 1963.

————. *This Hallowed Ground: The Story of the Union Side of the Civil War.* 1956.

Cleland, Robert Glass. *A History of California: The American Period.* 1939.

Cox, Jacob D. *Atlanta.* 1882.

————. *The March to the Sea, Franklin and Nashville.* 1913.

Crozier, Emmet. *Yankee Reporters, 1861–65.* 1956.

Current, Richard N. et al. *American History: A Survey.* 1966.

Dewitt, David M. *The Impeachment and Trial of Andrew Johnson.* 1903.

Dick, Everett N. *The Sod-House Frontier, 1854–1890.* 1938.

Dodge, Mary Abigail [Gail Hamilton]. *Biography of James G. Blaine.* 1895.

Donald, David, ed. *Why the North Won the Civil War.* 1960.

Durkin, Joseph T. *General Sherman's Son.* 1959.

Dyer, John P. *The Gallant Hood.* 1950.

Force, Manning F. *General Sherman.* 1899.

Gaeddert, Gustave R. *The Birth of Kansas.* University of Kansas, Social Science Studies. 1940.

Garraty, John A. *The American Nation: A History of the U.S.* 1966.

Gosnell, H. Allen. *Guns on the Western Waters: The Story of River Gunboats in the Civil War.* 1949.

Harrington, Fred Harvey. *Fighting Politician, Major General N. P. Banks.* 1948.

Hesseltine, William B. *Lincoln's Plan of Reconstruction.* 1963.

————. *Ulysses S. Grant, Politician.* 1935.

Hesseltine, William B., and Wolf, Hazel C. *The Blue and the Gray on the Nile.* 1961.

Hirshson, Stanley P. *Grenville M. Dodge, Soldier, Politician, Railroad Pioneer.* 1967.

Hofstadter, Richard et al. *The American Republic,* 2 vols. 1959.

Hughes, Nathaniel C. *General William J. Hardee, Old Reliable.* 1965.

Johnson, W. Fletcher. *Life of William Tecumseh Sherman.* 1891.

Leckie, William H. *The Military Conquest of the Southern Plains.* 1963.

Lewis, Lloyd. *Sherman, Fighting Prophet.* 1932.

Liddell Hart, B. H. *Sherman, Soldier, Realist, American.* 1929.

McAllister, Anna. *Ellen Ewing, Wife of General Sherman.* 1936.

McKinney, Francis F. *Education in Violence: The Life of George H. Thomas and the History of the Army of the Cumberland.* 1961.

McKitrick, Eric L. *Andrew Johnson and Reconstruction.* 1960.

Mahon, John K. *History of the Second Seminole War, 1835–1842.* 1967.

Malone, Dumas, and Rauch, Basil. *Crisis of the Union, 1841–1877.* Empire for Liberty, vol. 3. 1960.

————. *The Republic Comes of Age, 1789–1841.* Empire for Liberty, vol. 2. 1960.

Merrill, James M. *Battle Flags South: The Story of the Civil War Navies on Western Waters.* 1970.

————. *Spurs to Glory: The Story of the United States Cavalry.* 1966.

Miers, Earl Schenck. *The General Who Marched to Hell.* 1951.

————. *The Web of Victory: Grant at Vicksburg.* 1955.

Milligan, John D. *Gunboats Down the Mississippi.* 1965.

Milton, George Fort. *Age of Hate: Andrew Johnson and the Radicals.* 1930.

Morison, Samuel Eliot, and Commager, Henry Steele. *The Growth of the American Republic,* 2 vols. 1957.

Muzzey, David S. *James G. Blaine, A Political Idol of Other Days.* 1934.

Nevins, Allan. *Ordeal of the Union,* 2 vols. 1947.

Parks, Joseph H. *General Leonidas Polk, C. S. A.: The Fighting Bishop.* 1962.

Patrick, Rembert W. *The Reconstruction of the Nation.* 1967.

Pemberton, John C. *Pemberton, Defender of Vicksburg.* 1942.

Porter, George H. *Ohio Politics During the Civil War Period.* Columbia University Studies, XL, no. 2, whole no. 105. 1911.

Randall, James G. *The Civil War and Reconstruction*. 1937.

Robins, Edward. *William T. Sherman*. 1905.

Roland, Charles P. *Albert Sidney Johnston, Soldier of Three Republics*. 1964.

Roseboom, Eugene H. *The Civil War Era, 1850–1873*. The History of the State of Ohio, vol. 4. 1944.

Sefton, James E. *The United States Army and Reconstruction, 1865–1877*. 1967.

Seitz, Don C. *Braxton Bragg, General of the Confederacy*. 1924.

Smith, William E. *The Francis Preston Blair Family in Politics*, 2 vols. 1933.

Starr, Louis M. *Bohemian Brigade: Civil War Newsmen in Action*. 1954.

Thomas, Benjamin P., and Hyman, Harold M. *Stanton, The Life and Times of Lincoln's Secretary of War*. 1962.

Walker, Peter F. *Vicksburg: A People at War, 1860–1865*. 1960.

Weigley, Russell F. *History of the United States Army*. 1967.

Weisberger, Bernard A. *Reporters for the Union*. 1953.

Weisenburger, Francis P. *The Passing of the Frontier, 1825–1850*. The History of the State of Ohio, vol. 3. 1941.

West, Richard S., Jr. *The Second Admiral: A Life of David Dixon Porter, 1813–1891*. 1937.

Williams, Charles R. *The Life of Rutherford Birchard Hayes*, 2 vols. 1914.

Williams, T. Harry. *P. G. T. Beauregard: Napoleon in Gray*. 1955.

———. *McClellan, Sherman and Grant*. 1962.

Wilson, James H. *The Life of John A. Rawlins*. 1916.

Wyllie, Irvin G. *The Self-Made Man in America: The Myth of Rags to Riches*. 1954.

DOCTORAL DISSERTATIONS

Andrews, Richard A. "Years of Frustration: William T. Sherman, The Army, and Reform, 1869–1883." Ph.D. dissertation, Northwestern University, 1968.

Hendricks, George L. "Union Army Occupation of the Southern Seaboard, 1861–1865." Ph.D. dissertation, Columbia University, 1954.

Lucas, Marion B. "The Burning of Columbia." Ph.D. dissertation, University of South Carolina, 1965.

Marszalek, John F., Jr. "W. T. Sherman and the Press, 1861–1865." Ph.D. dissertation, Notre Dame University, 1968.

Miller, Paul I. "Thomas Ewing, Last of the Whigs." Ph.D. dissertation, Ohio State University, 1933.

Ulrich, William J. "The Northern Military Mind in Regard to Reconstruction, 1865–1872: The Attitudes of Ten Leading Union Generals." Ph.D. dissertation, Ohio State University, 1959.

MASTER OF ARTS THESIS

Bridges, Roger D. "The Impeachment and Trial of William Worth Belknap, Secretary of War." State College of Iowa, 1963.

Index

PRINTED IN U.S.A.